SOLVING THE POWERPOINT PREDICAMENT

INCLUDES CD

USING DIGITAL MEDIA FOR EFFECTIVE COMMUNICATION

W9-DDD-781

SOLVING THE POWERPOINT PREDICAMENT

USING DIGITAL MEDIA FOR EFFECTIVE COMMUNICATION

Tom Bunzel

800 East 96th Street
Indianapolis, Indiana 46240

10-07

Many of the designations used by manufacturers and sellers to distinguish their products are claimed as trademarks. Where those designations appear in this book, and the publisher was aware of a trademark claim, the designations have been printed with initial capital letters or in all capitals.

The author and publisher have taken care in the preparation of this book, but make no expressed or implied warranty of any kind and assume no responsibility for errors or omissions. No liability is assumed for incidental or consequential damages in connection with or arising out of the use of the information or programs contained herein.

The publisher offers excellent discounts on this book when ordered in quantity for bulk purchases or special sales, which may include electronic versions and/or custom covers and content particular to your business, training goals, marketing focus, and branding interests. For more information, please contact:

> U. S. Corporate and Government Sales
> (800) 382-3419
> corpsales@pearsontechgroup.com

For sales outside the U. S., please contact:

> International Sales
> international@pearsoned.com

This Book Is Safari Enabled

 The Safari® Enabled icon on the cover of your favorite technology book means the book is available through Safari Bookshelf. When you buy this book, you get free access to the online edition for 45 days.

Safari Bookshelf is an electronic reference library that lets you easily search thousands of technical books, find code samples, download chapters, and access technical information whenever and wherever you need it.

To gain 45-day Safari Enabled access to this book:

- Go to http://www.quepublishing.com/safarienabled
- Complete the brief registration form
- Enter the coupon code QIH2-GF4I-8X1E-EQIQ-XN2A

If you have difficulty registering on Safari Bookshelf or accessing the online edition, please e-mail customer-service@safaribooksonline.com.

Visit us on the Web: www.quepublishing.com

Library of Congress Cataloging-in-Publication Data:

Bunzel, Tom.
  Solving the powerpoint predicament : using digital media for effective communication / Tom Bunzel.
    p. cm.
  Includes index.
  ISBN 0-321-42344-5 (pbk. : alk. paper)
1. Microsoft PowerPoint (Computer file) 2. Presentation graphics software. 3. Lectures and lecturing—Data processing. I. Title.
  PN4193.L4B788 2007
  005.5'8—dc22
                            2006019903

ISBN: 0321423445
Text printed in the United States on recycled paper at R.R. Donnelley in Crawfordsville, IN.
Second printing, November 2006

This book is dedicated to my mother, father, and Alan Shapero.

CONTENTS

ACKNOWLEDGMENTS

This book would not have been possible had I not benefited from the wisdom of and exposure to many other people, particularly experts in the technology, presentation, communication, and related fields.

Many of these people are mentioned within these pages with referral information, but I also owe them a special debt for helping to shape the ideas in this manuscript.

In no particular order, I need to thank:

My agent, Lynn Haller

My editors, Elizabeth Hurley Peterson, Sheri Cain and Ben Lawson as well as Andy Beaster and Dan Scherf

My colleagues, Terrence Gargiulo and James Gonzalez, fellow instructors from Learning Tree, with whom I have had hours of discussion and collaboration

Doug Blattner

Jim Bass

Gregg Ketter, with whom I've had a few skirmishes but from whom I have learned a lot

Gene Zelazny

Dr. Leslie Lundt, Bruce Friedman, and Eric Bailey, CTS

Mario Simonaitis, Billy Poncher, Richard Saunders, Jay Friedman, Geoffrey Montagu, Ted Tesser, Fred Title, Darko Juric, and Michael Miller

Dr. Todd Yamada

Dr. Steven Stahl, Richard Davis, Nancy Muntner, Darius Shayegan, and Cristina Damatarca of the Neuroscience Education Institute

Lou Achille

Dr. Alan Yellin, Dr. Howard Moss, and Dr. Nancy Rossen

For the past several years, I've been part of an amazing networking group of presentation professionals—the Presentations Council of InfoComm International (http://snipurl.com/m665). I've worked closely with three awesome chairmen—Bob Befus, Ray Guyot, and Todd Dunn—and I would recommend this organization to anyone wishing to broaden their educational and professional horizons in this field.

My colleague Rick Altman produces one of the most intimate yet powerful programs for presentation professionals each year, PowerPoint LIVE (http://www.altman.com). Through my participation, I've been privileged to meet some of the most accomplished people in the industry and learn from them, including the following:

Troy Chollar and Glen Millar, the masters of animation

Kathy and Bruce Jacobs

Steve Rindsberg

Julie Marie Irvin, Mary Waldera, and Korie Pelka

Nancy Duarte

Julie Terberg

Cliff Atkinson

Brian Peterson of Waggener Edstrom and Ric Bretschneider and Pete Card of Microsoft

Jim Endicott

Rob Lindstrom

Michelle Gallina

Betsy Weber

Don Brittain and Mike Wilson

Tony DeAscentis at Turning Technologies

About the Author

Tom Bunzel specializes in knowing what presenters need and how to make technology work. He has appeared on Tech TV's *Call for Help* and has been a featured speaker at InfoComm and PowerPoint LIVE, as well as working as a "technology coach" for companies including Iomega, Community Vision, and the Neuroscience Education Institute.

Tom Bunzel has written a number of books, the latest being *Teach Yourself PowerPoint 2003 in 24 Hours* and *Easy Digital Music* for Que Publishing. Tom Bunzel's other books are *Easy Creating CDs and DVDs*, *How to Use Ulead DVD Workshop*, *Digital Video on the PC*, and the update to Peachpit Press' *Visual QuickStart Guide to PowerPoint 2002/2001*. He was a contributing editor to Presentations Magazine and writes a weekly column as the Office Reference Guide for InformIT.com.

As an instructor for Learning Tree International, Bunzel has taught several courses: "Integrating Microsoft Office" and "Creating Interactive Websites—Hands On." He has worked with many speakers, including helping Gregg Ketter of KTTV-TV with his motivational, customer service, and sales speeches, and he trained the principals of MTA Films and Todd Yamada, D.D.S., in PowerPoint and multimedia production. Bunzel has also lectured at the Los Angeles Athletic Club, Communicate (a multimedia facility), and at the San Diego Computer Expo.

Tom can be reached through his website (www.professorppt.com).

PREFACE

What Is the PowerPoint Predicament?

Several years ago, I attended a networking breakfast where several entrepreneurs were pitching their start-up companies to a panel of venture capitalists. It was set up as a competition, and one of the entrants didn't show up, so the moderator asked if anyone in the audience had a concept they wanted to present.

At the time I was on the "board" of an Internet start-up (like everyone else I knew in the technology arena) hoping to get funded. I volunteered, and without any notes or preparation, I spoke for five minutes and ended up winning the competition.

Afterward, several colleagues congratulated me (I won a T-shirt—no funding), and several said, more or less, you were great, but imagine if you'd been able to prepare with PowerPoint (they knew my specialty)—you would have been even better.

As I reflected at the time, I suggested that the opposite was the case. I realized that my adrenaline rush at putting myself in that position, and my realization of the need to focus and really communicate my message along with my passion for the project, resulted in a connection to the audience I may not have achieved if I'd merely presented a slide show.

Now, several years later, having been exposed to many more polished and exemplary speakers who use electronic presentations effectively—and many others who don't—I realize that at the time I also might have been tempted to simply throw up some slides and depend upon them to tell a story.

From that point on, I decided that I would always examine the subject matter through the eyes of a seasoned presenter, structure my talk accordingly, and only use PowerPoint to dramatize the most compelling aspects of my project.

I would have a reason for every slide I put up, and I would use the technology for good rather than for evil.

At all costs, I would do whatever I could to avoid "death by PowerPoint" because using this ubiquitous program can have the opposite effect of what you intend—instead of galvanizing an audience and helping to convey a message, a series of dull slides can put your attendees into a trance.

When I appeared on Tech TV, I was asked if that's PowerPoint's fault. Obviously, it isn't—it's mainly the fault of those who use PowerPoint badly.

If PowerPoint has a fatal flaw, it's that it's just too seductive and easy. I often get asked what the heck there is to actually teach in terms of using PowerPoint. Can't anybody click in the placeholders and fill up slides with titles and bullets?

The answer is in this book. The secret to using PowerPoint effectively is twofold:

- You must realize that creating a PowerPoint slide show is not the same as creating a *presentation*. Creating a PowerPoint file is deceptively easy—it's just a matter of clicking in the right places and creating a set of slides that may even look fairly nice.

    But we all know the results of presenting a disorganized, poorly conceived slide show—it can have serious consequences.

    We could lose a sale or account, fail to inform or inspire, and perhaps even lose our credibility before our colleagues and associates.

    Even if the show is self-running (for a kiosk, video, or commercial break—an animation technique we'll cover in Chapter 4), it had better be more than just a bunch of slides. It must tell a story, deliver a message, and serve a purpose.

- In using technology to communicate more effectively, every instance must have with a *raison d'etre*—the French term for "a reason for being."

    Polished speakers know this. It may be why "soft skills" presentation books are practical: they tell you how to prepare, where to stand, which jokes to tell, and other very specific details about how to be successful as a speaker.

But inevitably computer books *only* teach you how to run a program. That's where we will take a different track.

Everything we cover in the technology parts of this book will proceed from a *reason for its use* to accomplish a specific goal—to communicate more effectively.

Poor PowerPoint users shoot themselves in the foot by thinking that if it's in the program, it's got to go into the presentation. They fill their slides with animation, transitions, and page after page of unreadable text and then wonder why their presentation did not yield the desired results.

So let's start with this premise: *nothing goes into the slide show unless we know why it's there*.

A Word about Versions

Although some readers of this book might already have PowerPoint 2007, many others will still have version 2003, 2002/XP, or even 2000 when this book is published.

As we get into add-ins and more sophisticated features that may require the later versions or cover the latest aspects of the program that came out in Office 12, this will be mentioned and relevant screenshots included.

But for most of the conceptual material, screenshots from PowerPoint 2003 will be used. Where appropriate, I will also mention how these same features can be accessed in prior versions.

For some tasks, I will refer to other third-party programs; inevitably these also evolve faster than a publisher or writer can produce a manuscript, so I will concentrate on the major features of these programs and show the essential concepts that enable you to get things done: capture screens or video, create diagrams, or author a DVD.

Obviously, this book is not intended to be a manual for any of these programs. It should serve to point the way for when and how to use PowerPoint (and its cousins) to tell your story, and it is my intention to clearly establish the *why* along with the essential *how to* for the programs and versions we cover.

This Book's Target Audience

Anyone who needs to make a presentation that has something at stake and who believes that his or her message can be enhanced by a program like PowerPoint or the use of digital media will benefit from the concepts in this book. Such users will include

- Executives and managers who need to present and can't rely on a support staff
- Small business users and professionals (doctors, dentists, attorneys) who need the competitive advantage of high-impact presentations
- Technical professionals who need to convey detailed financial or strategic messages to large and small groups
- Educators and students who want to use digital media to more effectively communicate in the classroom
- Religious leaders who want to combine video, imagery, and audio to inspire their congregations
- Individuals with personal messages to deliver in person, online, or using the latest digital media (DVD, HDTV, etc.)

These presenters generally have a product, service, or concept to sell or promote—they have a lot to lose if their ideas are not well received, and they generally understand that creating powerful visuals and communicating with maximum effectiveness is a matter of survival. Digital tools like PowerPoint and its complementary programs and features can help anyone tell a story, convince or inspire an audience, or teach a difficult subject more effectively.

Getting Started

This book includes eight chapters that discuss the various features of PowerPoint:

- Chapter 1, "Planning an Effective Presentation," discusses planning a presentation as a key to success.
- Chapter 2, "Implementing Professional Design Principles," discusses using proven design principles to craft the message.
- Chapter 3, "Creating Dynamic Visuals," discusses creating visuals that tell a story or prove a point.
- Chapter 4, "Secrets of Animation and Navigation," discusses why, when, and how to use navigation and animation to maximize communication effectiveness.
- Chapter 5, "Using Video and Audio Effectively," discusses using multimedia and mastering its file formats and features.
- Chapter 6, "Powerful Presentation Tools," discusses understanding complementary programs that expand PowerPoint's sphere of influence.
- Chapter 7, "The Latest Technologies: Beyond PowerPoint to the Future," discusses taking advantage of the latest technologies including web presentations and DVD formats.
- Chapter 8, "Delivering a Killer Presentation," discusses the ultimate goal: delivering a successful presentation using all of the tools at your disposal.
- The book companion CD-ROM contains numerous PowerPoint presentations and other examples from the book, two sample chapters from Cliff Atkinson's *Beyond Bullet Points: Using Microsoft PowerPoint to Create Presentations That Inform, Motivate, and Inspire*, and trial software from Instant Effects (OfficeFX), Serious Magic (Ovation and Vlog It!), and TechSmith (Camtasia and Snag It).

When we understand the program and have recognized the pitfalls of PowerPoint—such as the propensity to use only titles and bullets—we can begin to explore its vast potential to enhance communication, mainly by creating effective visuals and other support material.

Again, it's important to remember that visuals alone will not make up for the lack of a message, a talented and passionate speaker, or a coherent communications strategy. They are all part of the package.

But most people will acknowledge that when properly used, electronic tools can be invaluable in communicating effectively.

What we'll do in this book is to examine the basic principles of effective communication and presentation, many of them time honored and propounded by experts in the field, and then see how to apply them using the latest technology.

On that point, let's think of PowerPoint simply as the main example of electronic presenting. In Chapter 5, we'll cover other communication resources in depth, but throughout the book, the examples and concepts are intended to work with a range of presentation programs, some of which may be better suited to the task at hand than others. (You may have other tools with which you are familiar that will enable similar results.)

For example, there are plenty of programs that do flowcharts—if you have such a need. We will show you the circumstances in which to use a flowchart and how to do it *sequentially with animation*. When we mention other programs (like Visio), it's because they can help you to quickly create specific types of charts—like timelines.

PowerPoint and Excel also have graphs. Boy, do they ever. But until you need to show a specific type of chart to convey a certain concept or message, will you have the incentive to really learn how to create it? We doubt it, so we'll begin with some key concepts and then show you how to create the relevant graphs.

In Chapter 3, we will provide quick and easy methods for creating many different types of charts, but we will start with the essential *why*. As we do throughout this book, we will begin by framing the message or concept we want to deliver, and then having determined the goal, we will be motivated and inspired to more easily create the type of visual or other element we need.

Proceeding in this fashion, we will see that PowerPoint on its own is just the beginning.

First, it can help you shape and define a clear message or hopelessly obscure it.

Then, as it interacts with the other Microsoft Office programs to project their content and uses these programs to create supplemental materials like handouts or reports, it broadens its reach as a communications tool.

As a mature program, PowerPoint has also attracted a host of add-ins and other visiting programs that make it even more effective, again in specific scenarios to accomplish specific goals.

There are add-ins that empower video creation, DVD production, rehearsal, web distribution, 3D backgrounds, and a wide spectrum of other enhancements that can make business and other communications much more dramatic and effective.

As we go along, we'll use examples and case studies to stimulate your thought processes as to which features to use, when to use them, and how to make them as bulletproof (pun intended) as possible.

So let's get started.

CHAPTER 1

Planning an Effective Presentation

If you're going to give a presentation, have something to say. For most presenters, the blank page (or slide) is the first major hurdle.

I still remember playing chess at summer camp—I was an average player with the ambition to excel. Then one winter I read an elementary book on chess openings that covered just the first few opening moves. The following summer I became one of the better players just by applying some basic strategy—and setting up my pieces in a strategic and organized fashion before I dove into the match.

If writing were that easy, I'd be out of a job. But there are also certain tried and true principles for formulating our presentations, many of which we can learn from experts in the field and eventually apply in PowerPoint. What we will do in this chapter is provide and compare some potential tools and frameworks for planning what you want to say—not just to get through your presentation or a set of slides—but to enthusiastically look forward to the event and achieve the results you want.

In any business library there is a wealth of material on the "soft skills" aspect of creating presentations and on how to structure and deliver a presentation without using any technology. In this chapter, we'll begin by reviewing what some very accomplished consultants, practitioners, and authors suggest for planning and structuring your presentation, and then we'll combine that with using PowerPoint and other practical techniques that will help you to craft an effective message.

After developing a strategy, we'll move to structure, organization, and some techniques for elementary storyboarding—while developing our own personal style. At each point we'll move from theory to practice and use PowerPoint to achieve concrete results. But we'll only use detailed step-by-step sequences for planning our presentation—never just to learn the program.

Finally, we will also consider various concepts, structures, and techniques that go beyond an ordinary linear presentation and conclude with a fictional case study so that every aspect of our work will be based upon real-world scenarios.

Of necessity in this book format, we'll have to proceed in a straight path, but because much of what we hope to achieve is visual, you can get an idea of where we're headed in Diagram 1 and perhaps go directly to the topics that interest you.

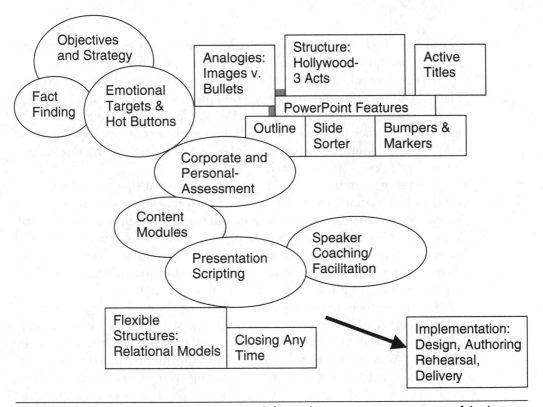

DIAGRAM 1   Planning a presentation is a multifaceted process. Here are some of the key elements we cover in this chapter.

Hopefully, at the end of this chapter, you will have a fresh perspective on how you can craft future presentations along with concrete techniques for putting forth your own ideas to connect on a deeper level with your audience.

Using AutoContent Wizard to Get Started

Let's see what PowerPoint itself has to offer in terms of starting from scratch.

Since its inception PowerPoint has featured an "AutoContent Wizard," which is essentially a cookie-cutter step-by-step beginning for *non-writers* to begin to decide what their presentation should say. Many users still don't even know it's there—while others seem to find it adequate for charting their presentation course and getting started. So let's examine the Auto-Content Wizard before going on to some more sophisticated tools for presentation planning and structure:

1. If you choose File > New in PowerPoint, the New Presentation Task Pane will open. One of the choices will be to create a new presentation From AutoContent Wizard.
2. Click Next to choose a Presentation Type, and click All to reveal the full range of possible boilerplate presentations to begin with, as shown in Figure 1-1.

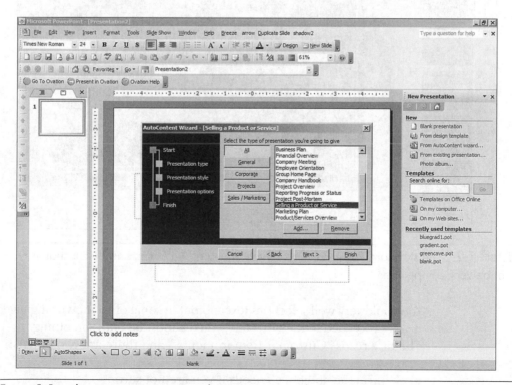

FIGURE 1-1   The AutoContent Wizard gives you a roadmap to begin a new presentation.

3. If we select Selling a Product or Service and click Finish, we can see an entirely constructed sample presentation. With the Slides tab selected, we can scroll through the presentation and see that there are a few slides with potential diagrams for visuals, but for the most part, the sample presentation is asking us to fill in lots of titles and bullets.

The very first slide is typical, as shown in Figure 1-2. You are asked to fill in some "Objectives," and you may well be tempted to put in something like, "We really want to sell you lots of new stuff (that's probably no better than our old stuff)."

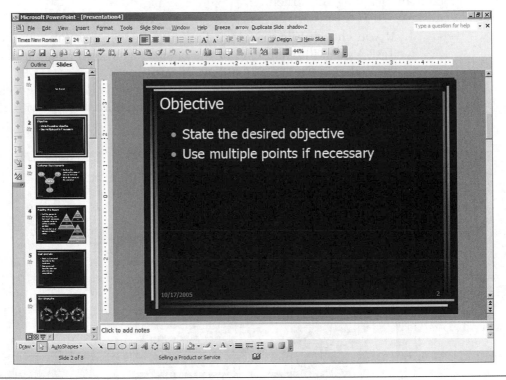

FIGURE 1-2 The standard PowerPoint presentation begins with titles and bullets that may not be very compelling.

You could very well select this text and put in some of your own language, and if you proceeded to the next slide, you'd almost be onto something.

The title reads "Customer Requirements," and there are two bullets:

■ Confirm the audience's needs if you are not sure
■ State the needs of the audience

WRITING BETTER BULLETS   There's a good reason why the items in Power-Point slides are called bullets, and it's not because they are supposed to cause Death by PowerPoint.

Bullets are meant to express key concepts succinctly, and you (or the speaker) are meant to amplify these points and say interesting, profound, and meaningful things about the topic.

The key element of bullets is breaking up unreadable material into manageable "thought-chunks."

There are many theories about how many bullets are appropriate for a slide, but the key thing to remember is that each slide should really be about only one topic, and the number of bullets shouldn't exceed one-third of the square root of your total number of slides.

Taking into account that this is already the third slide—at least we're finally going to focus on the audience. We've also got a visual (the diagram in the slide) that we could conceivably use to illustrate some kind of needs structure or relationship.

The question becomes: Is this the best way to plan a presentation?

If you had limited time and resources, or if you were extremely confident that you had a surefire solution to whatever you perceived the audience's issue to be, you could fill in the rest of the wizard-created presentation, and you would have a *slide show*.

But would it meet the audience's objectives, much less your own?

Let's explore some alternatives.

Planning a Strategy

One of the ways I have been blessed since I entered this field has been as a participant in at least two groups that network and share information in the presentations industry: the PowerPoint LIVE conference and InfoComm International. The latter runs a trade show primarily for the audiovisual industry, and I am a member of the more content-oriented Presentations Council, which hosts a number of educational events, including "Super-Tuesday" prior to the InfoComm Show. (See the section, "Resources," for web locations.)

Jim Endicott of Distinction Services has spoken at both of these events, and I can think of no more eloquent proponent of strategic planning in the presentation field.

Jim begins with two main questions, which he asks himself before working with a client on an important presentation:

- What's at stake?
- Can you identify the pain?

Think about the bland presentation that we began to create using the AutoContent Wizard. Imagine if we were addressing a group of executives, and the outcome of the presentation would determine whether we were going to receive a multimillion-dollar contract or it would go to our competitor.

Would we feel comfortable with such an average-looking presentation that did not convince our audience that we truly understood their concerns and were equipped to meet them?

Obviously we could change the design of the AutoContent Wizard presentation, and perhaps our graphics team could put some more exciting visuals or some demonstrative video into the slide show. We will cover many of these specific techniques in the coming chapters.

But how many times will a top executive or sales professional face this kind of presentation challenge on his or her way to a meeting, with only limited resources to implement changes in the slide show or his or her delivery? And what if the final outcome could *make or break the company*?

Putting In the Time

Korie Pelka, corporate communications manager for a public company, tells the story of imploring her boss to spend more time with her prior to taking off with one of her PowerPoint slide shows.

"Do you know what airplanes are for?" the executive asked her. She shook her head. "Plane flights are there for creating presentations."

Let's go back to Jim's first question: What's at stake?

Not every presentation has a multimillion-dollar contract or sale in the balance. But if you are reading this book, then certainly some aspect of your professional or personal life depends upon the outcome of a presentation you are contemplating.

Maybe it's whether your colleagues learn a new skill, are motivated in their endeavors, or are inspired as a result of a Saturday or Sunday sermon. Obviously these issues matter to you as much as the outcome of the sales presentation in the previous example. In all of these instances, you obviously owe it to yourself and to your audience to use the full resources at your disposal to make your presentation as effective as possible.

Along these lines, Jim makes another excellent point: it's really not so much about you giving a presentation as it is about the audience *getting it*.

Look at the final slide in the generic AutoContent Sales Presentation—it is a call to action. Particularly in the competitive sales situation, you have a very specific outcome in mind—you want a commitment from your audience.

Key to the success of any presentation is your connection with the audience in terms of credibility and their continuing interest in paying attention to you.

How is this achieved? I submit that Jim's second question may be the quickest way I have ever heard to enable such a connection.

Have you heard the expression "I feel your pain"? As much of a cliché as it may be, if an audience senses that you truly understand what matters to them, then they will be acutely attentive and receptive to your proposed solution.

The alternative is what many presenters still do—which is to talk about their own qualifications and personal history before addressing the needs of the audience. This sort of self-centered approach can have the most beautifully crafted slides, but it is doomed to failure.

So in terms of planning the presentation, Jim speaks about identifying the pain.

Fortunately, in a highly competitive sales situation, this is generally doable—because if your product or service does not address a customer need, you're not going to be in business very long.

Adding Some Drama

In your planning, what's important is not just identifying the need of the audience, but *dramatizing it*.

This is where the electronic media is so powerful.

Let's reconsider the awful "Objective" slide (refer to Figure 1-2). What if we changed this:

Customer Requirements

- Confirm the audience's needs if you are not sure
- State the needs of the audience

To this:

Our Roadside Solution

- Offer instant communication between the customer and a central switchboard
- Bring assistance no matter where you are or what happened
- No cell phone necessary

It's a lot more compelling in terms of language, but it's still just a bunch of bullets or words. You could have the most magnetic speaker in the world pointing to this slide, and it still wouldn't measure up to what Jim Endicott describes in one of his case studies.

Instead of this slide showing "Objectives," Jim showed no slide at all. He played an actual audio recoding of a motorist in a real-life emergency situation and the immediate response in the same recording of the representative of his client, OnStar.

Many of you have since heard radio commercials with some of the same scenarios.

Imagine the impact upon the imagination when such a recording is played, compared to when the three foregoing bullets are projected and expounded upon.

In Chapter 5, "Using Video and Audio Effectively," we will cover the technical issues of how to create and play back an audio file like this during a presentation. If you're already convinced and want to leap forward to this section, obviously you can do so at any time.

But in terms of planning a presentation that takes advantage of the electronic media (and PowerPoint as a platform for its delivery), this was one of the most effective examples I've seen (or rather heard).

Jim's point, in terms of the audience *getting it*, is that using all of the senses and appealing to the experience and emotion of the audience is the most powerful way to set the stage for your presentation. There may be no better way to identify the pain and establish credibility with your audience.

One of my clients that worked with pharmaceutical companies helped produce thousands of slides in PowerPoint presentations that would convince caregivers to use specific drugs and regimens to treat primarily neurological issues, like Alzheimer's disease.

As you can imagine, there were hundreds of slides with effective diagrams, some of them animated (which we will also cover in due course), and charts attesting to the efficacy of various treatment modalities. But almost every speaker with whom I consulted and who wanted to use the slides was concerned with one issue—how to get the "before and after" case study video to play properly—because they knew that in their desire to propound a treatment nothing would identify the pain (and the potential solution) as dramatically as a video clip of actual patients.

NOTE The participating physicians also benefited from three days of speaker coaching (see the following), and by the third day, all of them opened their practice oral presentations with personal stories about their own experiences with treatment and patients, which served to dramatize the subject matter in a way that led directly into the slides—with the audience much more attentive.

Finding the Message

The generic presentations in the AutoContent Wizard and the bullet-laden creations crafted on airplanes are primarily intellectual exercises. Although there is certainly a time and a place for appealing to logic in almost every presentation, I would submit that it is probably best left aside in the initial planning stage, where *identifying the emotional dimension of your message* is of paramount importance.

What are the processes you can employ to help you identify the emotional hot buttons of your audience?

One of my friends is a photographer who recently moved back to New Jersey and got a small job shooting digital photos for a website of a new client. He called me during the gig to ask me whether I thought he should deliver raw uncompressed versions of the photos or whether I thought the client expected to get processed (cropped and compressed) images that they could pop directly into their website.

I'm sure you're ahead of me on this one, but the obvious solution (that many presenters are afraid to do for fear of imposing or looking dumb) is to *ask the client prior to the presentation exactly what they hope to achieve.* Guessing or asking a third party is a poor substitute.

Let's consider a training event as an example.

In this situation, a presenter can truly shine by dazzling an audience with incredible demos of technology or win them over with personal charm. But in most cases, the takeaway is *knowledge*—the presenter who convinces the client that he or she will follow up and measure the results of the training, perhaps a month or more later, will probably win the job.

To accomplish this, the presenter would be well advised to consult in detail with the client and submit a concrete proposal as to the scope of the training and the anticipated results.

Unfortunately, in a sales situation, the metric is more cut and dried. Either you get the account, contract, or sale, or you don't.

For this reason, many presentation consultants like Jim Endicott use a planning document or worksheet to scope out the parameters of the project and go to great lengths to establish within this form not just the logistical aspects of the presentation (size of audience, venue, projection needs) but more importantly the emotional expectations of the prospective client.

In the OnStar example, presumably such an entry would read along the lines of "to demonstrate compelling value to a car manufacturer in order to invest substantially in implementing our product."

This clear value proposition would lead a creative presenter to look for and hopefully find the audio example previously described.

Establishing Clarity in the Message

In another example, Jim Endicott of Distinction Services shows an actual slide show, and slide after slide, he asks the audience to call out what product or service is being offered in the presentation. Finally, in a slide late in the presentation, it becomes clear that the target is law firms and that the value proposition is full-scale document scanning and indexing for real-time courtroom access to information.

In Jim's reworked presentation, the pain is identified at the outset—litigators can't always get information as quickly as they need it because it is in a variety of different formats, many of them nondigital (legal pads, phone messages, printed documents, and so on).

With this need clearly established, the presentation can go on to show the features of the product or service and convince the audience of its wonderfulness.

NOTE On this book's CD in the folder Samples, you can find the before/after presentations for his client (Omnidox) created by Jim Endicott for Distinction Services.

On the other hand, without this value being laid out clearly at the beginning of the presentation (perhaps with an attorney fumbling through an accordion file for a lost document—either on video or in a picture), why would the audience even care about how great the vendor's scanning and processing capabilities are or how many documents they can process per hour or day?

Visual or auditory analogies are miniature stories that plant the seeds of your objectives in your audience's minds. To forge this sort of connection, remember that *features don't matter much to someone who has not seen or heard any benefits*.

A planning document is probably the best way to establish expectations and get a sense of the emotional stakes involved in your presentation. If you are a consultant, it can also be invaluable in settling any disputes as to the scope of the project in terms of whether video is included, whether handouts are expected and in what format, and what sort of backup is contemplated and capable of being used in an emergency by the presenter, for example.

NOTE Examples of planning documents are included on this book's CD in the folder for this chapter.

Other Research Techniques

In the absence of a planning document (presentation clients are notoriously as inaccessible as busy presenting executives), research is the obvious next step.

You should definitely visit the website of the prospective client or audience members to familiarize yourself thoroughly with their concerns. In the OnStar example, it would be helpful to know what kind of roadside services are currently being offered and their limitations.

In the medical field, there are side effects that can be almost as harmful, if not more harmful, than the condition being treated. This is an obvious part of identifying the pain.

If you were creating a presentation for a condo development, you would research the concerns of the potential buyers. Eventually, you might choose one or more important value propositions that address these issues, including

- Location/availability
- Financing/affordability
- Resale value/appreciation

Depending upon which of these were perceived as most significant, you might create picture or diagram slides as follows:

- Include a map of the desirable location showing the decreasing availability of units—using scarcity and fear of losing out to motivate the audience/potential buyers.

- You might be tempted to use charts to show financing or affordability, but images of middle-class or lower-middle-class homeowners or video testimonials by "people like us" might be even more advantageous from a sales perspective.
- Pictures of nearby upscale communities may enhance the case for resale value, or you might consider using interactive "dashboards" based on spreadsheets that project values according to various scenarios. (Interactive charts using Crystal Xcelsius are covered in Chapter 6, "Powerful Presentation Tools"). Even tables showing the relative increase in value of similarly located and priced communities would be preferable to a verbose or boring bullet slide.

One district attorney in a training session told me that besides showing actual transcripts of testimony in his trial, he uses PowerPoint tables to simply show what he intends to prove, what the evidence is, and then a large check mark to tell the jury (or judge) that it is an established fact.

NOTE We provide a quick intro to tables in the section, "Using Markers or Bumpers as a Section Roadmap."

In most cases, your research will take you online and to the collateral material of your client or prospective audience (scanned photos, brochures, and so on that may be available in the waiting area while you are nervously anticipating your meeting).

Acquiring and Using Web Images

Images on the web are easy to acquire. Right-click on the picture, and in most cases (using Internet Explorer), you can save the target as a file (GIF, PNG, or JPG) to a folder on your hard drive. To bring it into your Power-Point slide, click Insert > Picture from File.

NOTE We cover the techniques involved in using images extensively in Chapter 3, "Creating Dynamic Visuals."

If the image is protected, you might not want to use it, but it is still available with a simple screen capture. Press the PrtScr(n) button on your keyboard to put the entire monitor screen into memory. (Various keyboards may name this button slightly differently.) Then crop the image after pasting it into an image editor, or use the Picture Toolbar in Power-Point to crop the appropriate area of the image, as shown in Figure 1-3.

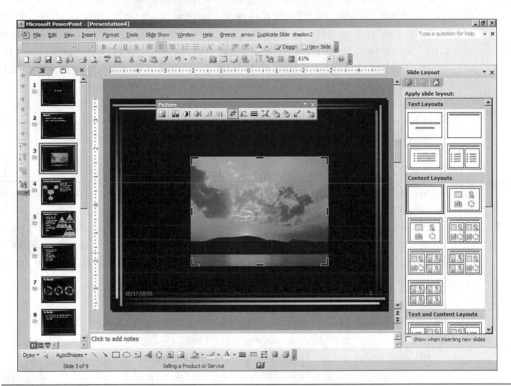

FIGURE 1-3   The Picture Toolbar lets you crop an image directly in PowerPoint.

Video and Shockwave files online may be downloaded if available; otherwise, a look inside your Temporary Internet Files folder may yield valuable goodies that you can move to other folders and potentially reuse in PowerPoint presentations.

TARGETING THE PRESENTATION   Even a tiny logo taken from a client's website and inserted in the Master Slide so that it appears on every slide in your presentation strategically suggests to the audience that you have created this presentation specifically for this occasion. Of course, whether you make the sale or not, you can substitute another company's logo on the Master Slide for another presentation to achieve a similar effect.

Last-Minute Techniques

Finally, if you can't get insight into the motivating factors directly from your client, online, or in printed or collateral material, your best bet is to get on the phone. Try to locate people who have successfully used the product or service you're presenting about, or to identify the pain, concentrate on those who have had stories of frustration or disappointment with an aspect of the subject that your presentation is addressing.

At a minimum, pay attention to the last chapter of this book (Chapter 8, "Delivering a Killer Presentation") so that you are thoroughly technically prepared when you are presenting to a group. Then you can use the extremely valuable minutes leading up to the event to meet members of the audience and get anecdotal material relating to the subject matter. Ask them pointedly and specifically what their major areas of concern are and target your opening accordingly.

You might try an opening like this one. "While I have a lot of slides prepared, Ms. Jones' experience in purchasing real estate, which we just discussed, brings up a key element of what many buyers and sellers are most concerned about."

WAKE UP THE AUDIENCE To increase interaction and refocus the audience's attention on you (and your message), just hit the "b" button on your keyboard to blank your presentation. This gives you complete attention as you use such a personalized opening, which will make the audience feel more confident that you truly understand their concerns and that what you have to say is relevant to them. To wake them up and create an even more dramatic effect, bring the house lights up at the same time.

Of course, you can't really plan to meet a Ms. Jones prior to your presentation; leaving such a contact to chance is risky. You are better served by planning far ahead of the actual speech or event and by having your dramatic slide elements in place before you even leave for the venue.

Although identifying the emotional hot buttons of the audience and dramatizing your approach to these issues is a big part of the planning process, there are other areas that you will want to consider before you start actually creating slides.

Structure and Organization

After you've homed in on one or more needs and hot buttons for your audience, you should have a good idea of where the presentation is going. But there is still the small matter of putting the concepts down on paper and then actually creating the slides that will help you deliver your message.

You may be inclined to say, "Okay, I've identified some important items that matter to the audience—why don't I just put together a bunch of slides with information relevant to those issues?"

In going down this path, you would presumably create slide after slide of titles and bullets, intersperse a few more creative slides with photos, diagrams, and perhaps video, and come out at the end with the feeling of "Whew, I'm done."

Finding the Ending

At this point, it's probably a good idea to think about *your objectives* for the presentation.

Another point to consider is whether you are creating this presentation for yourself (as the speaker) or whether you are creating a slide show to be presented by someone else (a busy executive or colleague).

If you are the presenter, you have an advantage: You should have a clear idea of what should occur when the last slide has been shown and the lights go up (if you've done the preliminary work of figuring out how the lights work or getting someone else to handle them). Here are some objectives you might anticipate:

- In a sales presentation, you will have gotten the sale, closed the deal, or at a minimum gotten a clear indication of what the next step in the process will be and that it will happen.
- In a training event, you will have seen some "light bulbs go off" as those present have seen the value of whatever you are delivering and have shown excitement and enthusiasm about applying it in their own endeavors. Attendees will come up at the end while you're trying to gather your materials and ask you more questions and want your business card.
- For a motivational speech or sermon, this level of enthusiasm will be even more pervasive and obvious—perhaps you will even receive a nice round of applause.

So in continuing to structure your presentation, the next question you need to ask is: What do I need to do to accomplish this objective?

In sales, this will be a *call to action*; in other circumstances, it may be a subtler message, perhaps summarizing the main ideas or concepts that you want to be sure that the audience takes away.

But in any case, clearly spelling out for yourself (or your speaker) what the final objective will be can put together what an attorney would call a closing argument but what the presenter might consider simply the last slide.

Many presenters make the last slide an information slide about themselves (website and phone number) and then simply conclude with "Any questions?"

This is almost a capitulation at the end of an event that you consider an ordeal. The audience will surely pick up on your lack of energy, and even if the presentation has been a success to that point, you may not achieve your objective.

If you use the ideas in this book and your own imagination to create uplifting PowerPoint presentations instead of bludgeoning your audience with deadly bullets, you should eagerly look forward to presenting and at the end have a surge of energy that will move the audience to see your point of view and either buy your product or service or do things the way you've suggested and taught.

In any event, leave your "information slide" for Q&A or pass out a business card. But end your speech on a high note by asking for the order or otherwise emphasizing your main message in a positive and compelling way.

Now that you've committed yourself to that, you have your ending!

Learning from Hollywood

In the previous Jim Endicott example (OnStar), we saw how compelling an emotional presentation using audio and the audience's imagination can be, particularly in establishing a connection and articulating a value proposition.

Another colleague of mine, Cliff Atkinson, is the president of Sociable Media and another well-respected consultant for corporations and individuals in crafting presentations.

His book is called *Beyond Bullet Points*, so you can quickly see what direction he is going in the use of PowerPoint. He makes a compelling case for moving all of your bullets off your slides (into the Notes panel, which we'll cover in Chapter 8) and using primarily images to supplement your presentation.

If you ever get a chance to see Cliff present, he is an excellent proponent for this technique; with poise and precise timing, he makes the right image appear on the screen just as he verbally makes each point (using a presentation mouse).

His slide shows are full of images, while his notes contain the text portion of his speech that can be referred to later on.

Whether you can accomplish this feat is a matter of your own dedication and commitment to preparation, but I submit that moving at least some of your bullets off the slides and using images with the techniques we cover in Chapter 3 is a great start to adding life to your presentation.

But in terms of planning the presentation and adding a viable structure, I would argue that you probably still need to use text. In *Beyond Bullet Points*, Cliff actually goes along with this in suggesting a "Hollywood" approach to structuring your presentation.

Briefly, this means adopting the conventional three-act structure of most movie scripts to begin to organize the flow of ideas and messages in your presentation.

Enhancing the Three-Act Structure

Having worked as a screenwriter, I would add one other key element to our three-act structure concept: the *inciting incident*.

The way I was taught, every story begins with something along the lines of "this is the day that" something unusual happens to trigger an inevitable and dramatic series of events.

In a PowerPoint presentation, this may not be as remarkable as ET appearing in your neighborhood, but if you go back to the point we made in the initial phase of planning a strategy—finding the pain—I submit that this is analogous to using an inciting incident in a screenplay.

So if we have a three-act structure for our earlier real estate example and have decided that the most compelling emotional message for our audience is that they're running out of time, the inciting incident may just be that:

"We've Just Sold 95% of the Development!"

Our first act would continue with the testimonials or buyers and their reasons for purchasing.

Our second act might be why the units have gone so quickly and inventory is scarce—the features of the property and what makes them compelling.

The third act could be how the audience can participate in this great opportunity—with the close being—obviously—

"Act Today (Don't Be Left Behind) and We May Even Throw in the Closing Costs."

By conceptualizing the value proposition at the beginning and clarifying our objective at the end, using the popular three-act structure makes a story emerge. In fact, besides Cliff Atkinson's Hollywood analogy, many accomplished presenters use the idea of telling a dramatic story as the basis for creating a compelling presentation.

NOTE Another colleague, Terrence Gargiulo, author of Stories at Work, actually defines and describes in detail nine different story types to empower executives in the management and human resources fields. If you're working in these areas, the following Gargiulo story types can help you find your message:

- Stories empower a speaker
- Stories create an environment
- Stories bind and bond individuals
- Stories require active listening
- Stories negotiate differences
- Stories encode information
- Stories act as tools for thinking
- Stories can be used as weapons
- Stories are medicine for healing

Words or Pictures?

Having begun to structure our presentation in three acts, we have, of necessity, used words to create the beginning of an outline.

Many of you (those who favor the menus of computer programs) are mainly *verbal*—in fact, if you're reading this book, that's probably the way you like to organize.

Others, however (those who favor icons on toolbars), are primarily *visual*—and they've been particularly interested in the concepts of dramatizing the message with images, video, diagrams, and other visual tools. Their slide shows will be filled with these elements.

Fortunately, PowerPoint has specific tools that support both of these styles of story building for your slide show.

As you would imagine, for the verbal folks, the Outline panel is a great place to begin structuring your story. (We'll cover this in the section, "Visualizing in Slide Sorter.")

Mastering the Outline

Using the Outline panel is not rocket science, and most computer users have worked with this technique over the years. What will help you in your presentation development, however, is taking a few minutes to actually understand the nature of the PowerPoint and Microsoft Word Outline tools.

If I simply copy and paste the five main ideas for my potential real estate presentation into the Bullet Placeholder of a PowerPoint slide (in Normal view), as done here:

RATIONAL REAL ESTATE

- "We've Just Sold 95% of the Development!"
- Our first act would continue with the testimonials or buyers and their reasons for purchasing.
- Our second act would be why the units have gone so quickly and inventory is scarce—the features of the property and what makes them compelling.
- The third act might be how the audience can participate in this great opportunity —with the close being—obviously—
- "Act Today (Don't Be Left Behind) and We May Even Throw in the Closing Costs."

When I click the tab for Outline, I see the text with the Outline, as shown in Figure 1-4.

NOTE If the Outlining toolbar doesn't open automatically with the Outline panel, click View > Toolbars > Outlining.

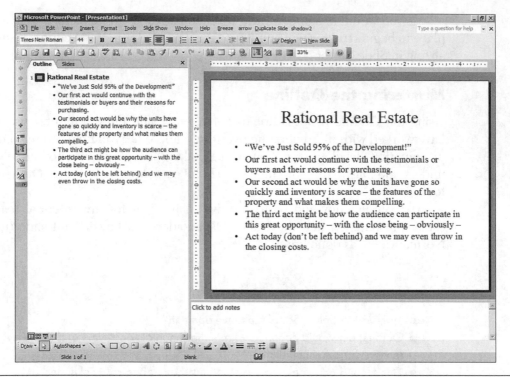

FIGURE 1-4   Putting your main story concepts into a single slide makes them visible in Outline view.

Working with the outline is a matter of understanding promotion and demotion of bullets. If you place your cursor at the beginning of any of the bullets and click the Promote arrow (or SHIFT+TAB), that bullet becomes the title of a new slide, and the presentation takes shape, as shown in Figure 1-5.

- Rational Real Estate (Title Slide)
- 95% Have Been Sold
- Buyers Love Our Community
- Valley Vista Has Everything You Need
- You Can Move Into a Condo Right Away
- Act Today

We'll pay the closing costs.

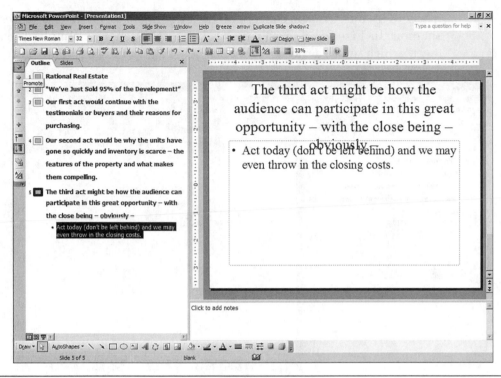

FIGURE 1-5   Promoting the bullets makes them the titles of new individual slides.

But these bullets and slide titles are still wordy—we need to rewrite them.

Here, let me refer again to Cliff Atkinson's *Beyond Bullet Points* in which he argues in favor of making all slide titles action-oriented sentences, including a subject and verb.

If you think back to our first bullet example in the section, "Adding Some Drama," where we showed how to more effectively present the OnStar product, we had a typical title and bullet scenario:

Our Roadside Solution

- Offer instant communication between the customer and a central switchboard
- Bring assistance no matter where you are or what happened
- No cell phone necessary

This is the most common way people write bullets in PowerPoint.

Let's try the Atkinson concept on the titles in our new real estate presentation. In Figure 1-6, each title has been rewritten as a complete sentence, which makes a specific point instead of a general statement.

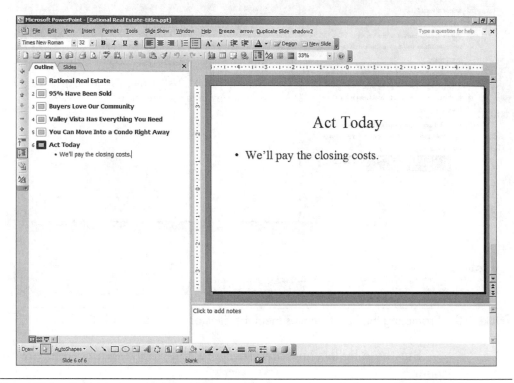

FIGURE 1-6   Rewriting each slide title as a complete sentence helps establish story flow.

As you change the text in the Outline area, the text placeholder in the slide itself reflects your changes. At this point you could add more individual bullets to your slides, as we did here by putting "We'll pay the closing costs" as a bullet in the final action slide to complete the presentation.

NOTE If you're more comfortable working with Microsoft Word, remember that it also has a very *specific Outline view*, which corresponds exactly to the titles and bullets of PowerPoint. If you create your outline in MS Word's Outline view (click View > Outline to change to Outline view in MS Word), you can subsequently click File > Send to Microsoft Office PowerPoint, and it will automatically generate a PowerPoint file similar to what is shown in these figures.

Outline files can be opened, edited, and changed in both programs by using the *.RTF file format; you can save your PowerPoint file as just the Outline portion (excluding images, charts, *textboxes*, and other non-outline elements) by clicking File > Save As > and changing the Save as type dialog box to show Outline/RTF (*.rtf). (For you verbally oriented folks, this is a great way to collaborate on just the text portion of your main presentation structure in a team without having to email huge PowerPoint files loaded with other elements.)

If you populate the slide with more bullet text, use the Collapse All button to see just the slide titles—giving you a clear view of the main story flow of the newly structured presentation.

This gives us the beginning of a three-act structure for this presentation, with an opening needs statement that relates to an audience fear (being left out)—and a closing action slide that hopefully would generate sales.

Visualizing in Slide Sorter

If we click the Slides tab now, we don't get much of a visual view of our story flow—we can barely make out the slide titles unless we zoom in.

To get the big picture and address the concern of more visually oriented presenters, let's switch to Slide Sorter view to simulate the six-slide presentation we have begun to structure, as shown in Figure 1-7.

NOTE With the short presentation shown here, we've zoomed in to 100% to see all of the slides in their entirely; with a large slide show you can zoom out to see more of your slides.

I've added a few images quickly to the first slide of Act 1 (95% Have Been Sold) to show you how the visual elements show up in Slide Sorter view along with your titles.

The main reason to work in Slide Sorter view as opposed to Outline view is to see the visual elements of your slides after they've been added. If you followed Atkinson's concepts, most if not all of your slides would have only a title and perhaps a picture; in fact some of the slides as Cliff actually presents would have *no title at all*.

To see a story flow with these slides, you would absolutely need to be in Slide Sorter view.

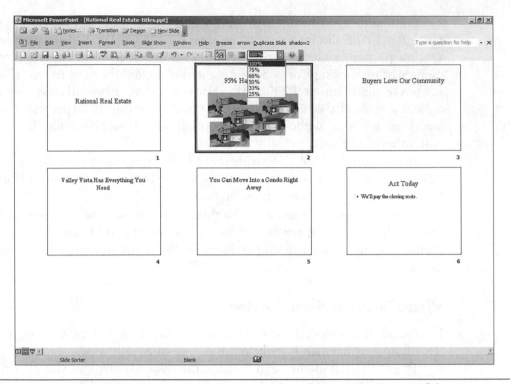

FIGURE 1-7 Slide Sorter view lets us get a better idea of the main concepts of the presentation as they begin a three-act structure.

NOTE Totally eliminating the titles from your slides increases their dramatic impact in some cases when projecting a powerful image—but be careful. It makes these valuable slides more difficult to locate later on if you use hyperlinks or Action Settings (see Chapter 4, "Secrets of Animation and Navigation") or may make it confusing to navigate to a specific slide during the presentation itself—unless you've memorized the slide number.

You might find it a good idea to *hide your slide titles* in this instance, either by putting them behind the picture in the slide (click to select the title, move it over the picture, and then use the Draw > Order > Send to Back command on the Drawing toolbar to move the text behind the picture). Or, you can also zoom out of the slide and drag the title placeholder outside the visible area of the slide.

Using Markers or Bumpers as a Section Roadmap

Many presentation coaches suggest setting off each section of your presentation with a separate slide to give your audience an idea of how much further you have to go (and when you'll finally get to the point or the snacks).

In Cliff Atkinson's book, he simply sets off each section or act with a title slide, "Act 1," "Act 2," and so on.

But we can get more comfortable with one of PowerPoint's most important features by creating a simple Bumper Slide table and then duplicating it for our sections. Tables are a great way to present important text visually (as the attorney referenced in the section, "Other Research Techniques" discovered). Tables can also be used to refine the layout of a slide with images and diagrams.

I can just add a new slide, as shown in Figure 1-8, and apply a *Blank Layout* from the Slide Layout Task Pane. When I click Insert > Table, I can make it a two-column/two-row configuration, and when it is added to the slide, the Tables and Borders toolbar appears. If it doesn't appear when you click on the table, click View > Toolbars > Tables and Borders.

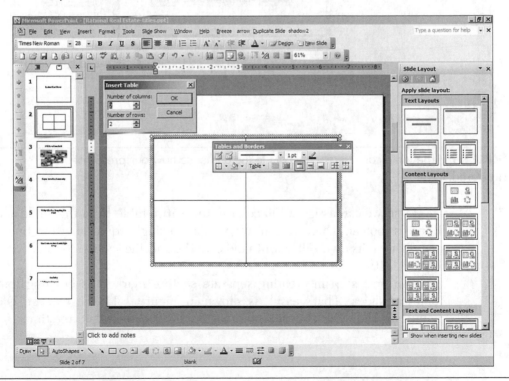

FIGURE 1-8   The standard PowerPoint presentation begins with titles and bullets that may not be compelling.

Using our value proposition and the main themes of our three acts, we can enter the text, as shown in Figure 1-9, drag through to select the cells, and then center them within the squares. We can use the Justify command on the selected text to center it vertically as well.

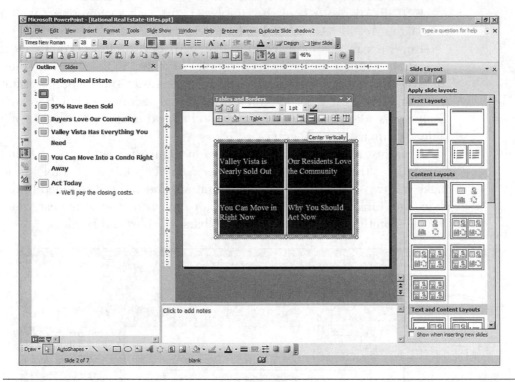

FIGURE 1-9 The table can visually indicate to the audience how our presentation is structured.

First, we can assign a Fill color to the entire table from the Table and Borders toolbar. Then we can differentiate a single square by selecting it and giving it its own Fill color to indicate the specific section to follow (see Figure 1-10).

The next step in creating separate section markers is creating four identical slides. That's easy! As shown in Figure 1-11, we use the Old Duplicate Slide Trick by choosing Insert > Duplicate Slide three times.

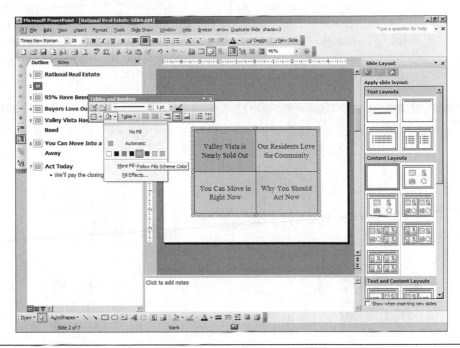

FIGURE 1-10   Selecting an individual square allows us to give it an individual Fill color.

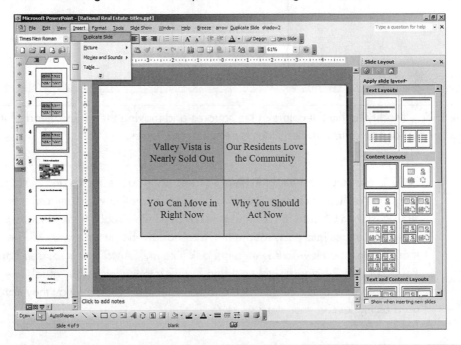

FIGURE 1-11   Inserting duplicate slides enables us to replicate the table quickly and easily.

Then, by modifying each of the duplicate slides—changing the Fill color of the appropriate segment to reflect a new topic—and dragging the slides to the front of the appropriate sections, we have set off each part of our story structure visually, as shown in Figure 1-12.

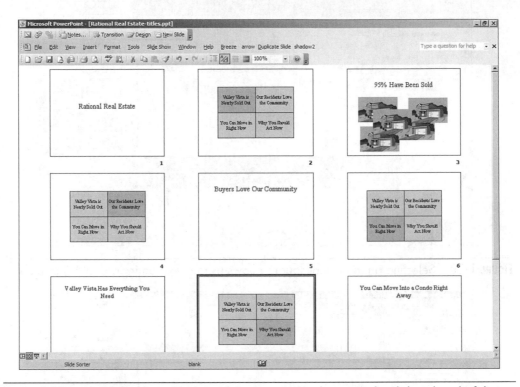

FIGURE 1-12   Modifying the Fill colors of the squares and moving the slides ahead of their respective sections gives us Bumper slides for each of our topics.

NOTE You can select the individual squares and use the Tables and Borders toolbar to make them look nicer than this basic style; we'll cover many aspects of slide design in Chapter 3. For those who really love visuals, think in terms of inserting images into each square that foreshadow the pictures you will use in that section. In a How-To PowerPoint book (like my *SAMS Teach Yourself PowerPoint 2003 in 24 Hours*), we would go further into the intricacies of tables—but this should be a quick introduction and serve to show you one way they can be used as markers in your story structure.

There are other creative ways to structure your presentation and to let your audience know that you have a story flow and that you're on track—you can use a thermometer or temperature gauge to show progress or put slide numbers on each slide—of course, if you get up into triple digits, you might have an audience revolution on your hands.

NOTE Geetesh Bajaj has a free download of such a presentation thermometer on his Indezine website. Geetesh is one of many PowerPoint MVPs that answer questions on the PowerPoint Newsgroups and whose contributions will be credited in this book. The direct link to Indezine and the free add-in is http://snipurl.com/ip95. His website along with links to others referred to in this book can be found in the "Resources" section at the end of the various chapters.

Crafting a Message for Different Presenters

Earlier in this chapter, we introduced Korie Pelka, who works as a communications director and helps executives from various divisions in her company deliver presentations. Korie shared some very valuable insights on how she works with her corporate presenters at Rick Altman's amazing PowerPoint LIVE conference in San Diego. (See the section, "Resources.") Everyone can benefit from Korie's "in the trenches" experience with different corporate presenters, each with idiosyncrasies, strengths, and weaknesses.

Some readers, like Korie herself, are probably working with the actual presenters to enhance their message. Others present for themselves in their chosen field. In each case, there needs to be an assessment not only of the potential audience but also of the style and characteristics of the person or team that is making the presentation.

This may seem obvious, but let's look specifically at some of the presenter "types" that Korie mentions in her description of her work. We can begin this with the way she extracts information from her associates to craft their presentations.

For those she calls the "doodlers," who like to lay out their ideas in quick drawings, she suggests a sketchpad to begin laying out actual ideas and slides. For these folks, she provides a worksheet based on a simple PowerPoint Handout—you can replicate it by printing a set of blank slides (by selecting File > Print) and choosing Handouts as the option, and then selecting the option for three blank slides per page with blank note lines beside each slide (see Figure 1-13).

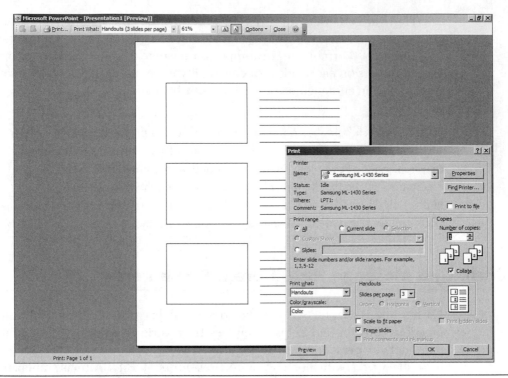

FIGURE 1-13   Printing a set of blank handouts with placeholders for drawings and text can help you create a simple storyboard.

Others she works with have more grandiose visions that may not fit on a sketchpad or handout; she refers to them as the "artists" and provides them with a large whiteboard on which to map out their complex scenarios.

Finally, for the "writers," she uses a planning document similar the one just described to assess needs and extract information about the prospective audience and, in her case, about the presenter him or herself.

Do a Needs Assessment

Korie's main questions to be answered in the document mirror those that Jim Endicott and other consultants use, with a few wrinkles:

- What does the presenter want to achieve?
- What does the audience want to achieve? (What is their profile and level of education?)
- What are the obstacles to (mutual) success?

■ What are the significant logistical issues, important aspects of the venue, and the platform for delivery?

Because Korie's actual "client" is the presenter, she establishes those objectives first.

But then she quickly takes her presenter to the key issue we addressed earlier—and adds an assessment (for her own and the presenter's benefit) of the important characteristics of those who will be in the audience.

Her third question in the planning stage can become a significant second or third act, particularly in a sales (or legal) presentation. Specifically anticipating and mapping out answers to potential objections to the case you or your presenter is making can be an effective strategy.

On the other hand, you may not want to raise these issues until the audience does so—in this instance, you could craft a message in anticipation but set the stage electronically by *hiding those slides*.

This makes you look particularly clever and well prepared if and when the points are raised—"I happen to have a slide to address that very issue"—but you don't have to use the hidden slide(s) if the occasion doesn't warrant it.

In our example of the real estate presentation, we can create an Objection slide ("Interest rates are rising") and right-click on it. By selecting Hide Slide, as shown in Figure 1-14, this slide will not be shown during the normal sequence but remains in our three-act structure.

To show the hidden slide while you're presenting, right-click on the screen (or click the popup toolbar), select Go to Slide, and locate the hidden slide(s) from those with parentheses.

Notice the potential importance of having Titles in your slides to locate the **right one** *if they're hidden.*

To return to your spot in the slide show, repeat the procedure, but instead of Go to Slide, as shown in Figure 1-15, select Last Viewed. You'll go back to where you left off when the question was asked.

Finally, because Korie wants to spare her presenter any surprises, her last question concerns the venue and the technical considerations involved. In her case, this may involve moving a presentation from where it was authored to the laptop on which it is delivered. This can present challenges, which we will cover extensively in Chapter 8.

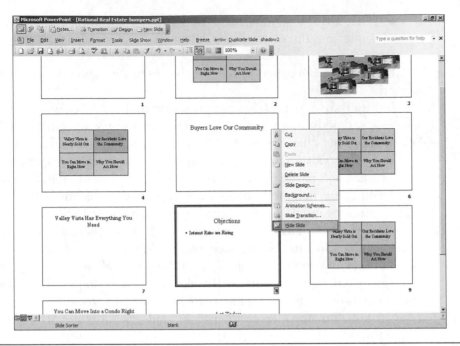

FIGURE 1-14 Hiding slides that you may or may not show in Slide Sorter view lets you access them at any time during your presentation.

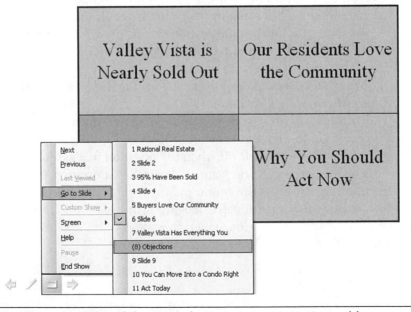

FIGURE 1-15 Using the Go to Slide option during your presentation enables you to locate a hidden slide by its title or the parentheses around its number.

Do an Honest Self-Assessment

Having gotten as much from her presenter about his or her own ideas (and the needs of the anticipated audience), Korie becomes a bit of a shrink. She analyzes the strengths and weaknesses of the presenter (self-described and observed) and creates a profile that helps her in her work.

You can benefit from this as well; if you are the presenter, do a self-assessment. Which type are you?

- **Verbalizer**—This potential presenter has all kinds of ideas and spews them out, quite possibly in a disorganized fashion. The presentation will need to be structured effectively and text either edited out or re-presented using pictures, diagrams, and visual analogies (as we'll do in Chapter 3).
- **Non-Verbalizer**—As the presentation craftsperson, you will need to be persistent to draw out the material because as Korie says, "It's all in there." Use a sketchpad and blank handouts and forms to extract the information on all levels—audience and presenter objectives in particular. This can be a presenter who will have some stage fright—rehearsal will be necessary but may not be an indicator of eventual performance. Because the material is internal, the presentation may shine even after poor rehearsals.
- **Technologist**—This is a fact-based individual who may need to be drawn out in terms of what the emotional payoff of the presentation will be. The good news is that he or she can provide lots of graphs, charts, tables, and diagrams. The bad news is that these visuals may need to be re-crafted to make them intelligible to the audience and focused to be on message in the flow of the presentation. Well-designed animation (see Chapter 4) can help these folks to show processes and simplify the message.
- **Writer**—Similar to the verbalizer, this individual comes armed with lots of extraneous information, probably in the form of copious notes. Korie's tip here is to "show them that white space can be their friend." Use pictures wherever possible to show instead of bullet-ize your message, and don't be afraid to chop up huge chunks of information into bite-sized units (per slide) that the audience can grasp.

In her corporate environment, Korie also has occasion to work with different executive types—perhaps you'll recognize someone among the following:

- **Numbers Guy**—Lots of financials, like the technologist mentioned earlier; the story needs to be extracted—perhaps by goals, by quarters, or by geography. There's a story there somewhere.
- **Slide Counter**—Wants X number of slides per perceived topic but with little or no organization. There's another story there somewhere.
- **Sales Folks**—Hard to get them away from their cell phones to concentrate on the message—think they can "wing it" on personality and charm—if they want to use PowerPoint, they need to craft a strong message and rehearse (no distractions).
- **Top Executives**—Tend to become more self-absorbed without a clear message. Korie suggests steering them (or yourself) clear of unimportant details (features) and focusing on a visionary message. In the movies this is called a "high concept." In presentation language it means keeping it simple but hitting the hot buttons.

To personalize each presentation, Korie then makes it a point to "find the passion" within each individual, which can help her shape a dramatic opening story or elicit one from her colleagues. In each case these can lead to stories that help them (or you) connect to the audience and break through the potentially mind-numbing tendency to just show slide after slide of titles and bullets.

The story, whether it's about a vacation, family member, sports event, or whatever, can and should help illustrate the speaker's emotional connection to the material at hand. Using the real estate example again, a personal story about buying or moving into one's first home would create a connection that facts about property values may not.

Korie keeps what she calls a "story journal" and suggests to her colleagues that they do the same. Stories can also be a great tool for handling the transitions from one part of a presentation to another by offering concrete examples. A good tool for keeping track of stories and organizing them would be Microsoft OneNote, which we cover in some detail in Chapter 6.

Again, hitting the "b" key on the keyboard, turning off the PowerPoint slides, and connecting with the audience on a personal level can help make the entire event a success.

Take a Modular Approach

Obviously, none of us (and no one we work with) fits neatly into any of these categories, but we can learn from these tendencies to help us craft our presentation.

Depending upon what she gets from her interviews with and forms completed by her colleagues, Korie has developed a number of potential story structures, which you may also find helpful:

- **Problem solution**—Graphic solution—scenario building. Solving a problem is the obvious antidote to the "pain," which we identified earlier. It's a grabber.
- **Timeline**—With needs and objectives established, some sort of chronology can help tell your story effectively.
- **Physical**—A map or diagram (referring to demonstration area elsewhere in the case of a trade show) can draw in the audience and explain key issues. Here animation can be helpful, building the venue piece by piece.
- **Issue—Actions (Case Study) (Problems and Solutions; Customer testimonials)**—These are dramatic opportunities and places to use audio and video.
- **Opportunity—Leverage (Corporate IPO)**—These are specialized presentations that call for *numbers*, but they can be presented visually and dynamically. Try what-if scenarios using dashboards.
- **Features, Benefits**—Again, with objectives clearly defined, it's time to talk about what you've got to offer—but always link it to a tangible result that matters to the audience.
- **Law**—Evidence—conclusion (or reverse it—put out your conclusion, put forth the evidence—check off (QED-proven!)—This is a legal scenario, but it can work with logically minded audiences (academics, medical professionals, anyone who needs to establish facts).
- **Rhetorical Questions Answered**—A good technique that lends itself to creative slides.
- **Top Ten List**—When all else fails.

Any of these potential topics can either help you brainstorm your entire story structure or help you populate an "act" within the greater whole.

Keep in mind that the units are not mutually exclusive. If, like Korie, you are in a corporate environment, you may have occasion to use different elements like those just described at different times.

If you are the real estate developer, you might use the Opportunity-Leverage (emphasizing numbers) scenario for prospective large-scale investors, while saving the case studies and customer testimonials for larger presentations to groups of individuals.

The beauty of PowerPoint is the ability to make these components *modular* and strategically move them around in your story after they've been crafted.

Korie makes two other excellent points about effectively using each of these structures or potential modules.

She likes to introduce each one with what she calls a "hook" that specifically links to the objectives for the presentation (preferably the audience's, not yours).

Using our real estate example, a hook might be a Quotation slide—such as "They're not creating any more real estate." This links psychologically to the underlying premise of the presentation—buy our condos while there is still a chance.

It also serves as a *transition* between our segments. Just as our Bumper slide or marker signals the continuity in our story, a good presenter should have a good verbal segue to the next act. This can be a story centered on an image slide or simply an anecdote of some kind that links one act to the next.

For example, in your Notes panel for the real estate presentation (see Figure 1-16), you might remind yourself to tell a story about "how Ms. Gomez contributed her own chaise lounges to the pool area." (The slide itself may show Ms. Gomez or the furniture.) This would transition into a discussion of features or why the residents love your condos.

CAUTION Remember to differentiate the "Notes" that you make for the presenter's benefit in preparation from the "Handouts" you intend to print for your audience. They don't need to see your secrets. Before printing either, save a separate version of the presentation for your Notes and another for your Handouts. We cover more aspects of Notes and Handouts in Chapter 8.

Keep in mind that every aspect of your presentation makes a point, so it becomes a story. To follow what Jim Endicott calls "the Persuasive Message Flow" and see whether it makes sense, there are a number of options:

- **In the Outline**—Collapse your Outline to see just the Slide Titles and read whether they make sense.
- **In Slide Sorter**—Follow the images within the thumbnails and refer to the titles where present—do they follow a logical structure that leads to your conclusion?
- **During Rehearsal**—Use the Slide Show > Rehearse Timings feature and save a version (not your final version) of the presentation for later review to see how much time is allocated to each act or module. When timings are saved, the actual running time will show in Slide Sorter view under each slide thumbnail. This can help you prepare the overall length and flow of the show.

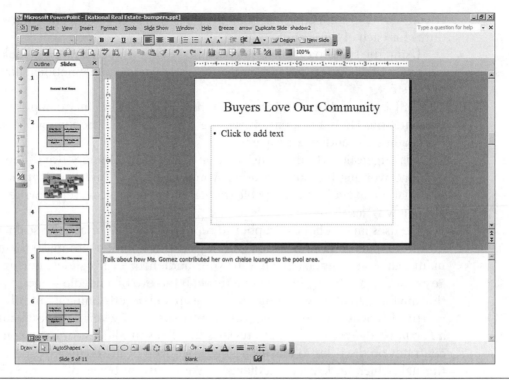

FIGURE 1-16   You can use the Notes panel to remind yourself of stories that help you transition from one part of your presentation to the following segment.

CAUTION Unless you want to be surprised by unintended animations or slide transitions, don't use the version of your presentation for which you saved the rehearsed timings during the presentation. Use it only for rehearsal. Keep a version without saved timings separate for use in front of a live audience.

Use a Script or Storyboard

Depending on the complexity of your project, you may go to the lengths that Cliff Atkinson describes in *Beyond Bullet Points* of actually formulating a complete script for your presentation.

His suggested process is as follows:

- Write a script to focus your ideas. (Use PowerPoint Notes pages.)
- Storyboard your script to clarify your ideas. (Use PowerPoint Slide Sorter view.)
- Produce the script to engage your audience. (Deliver the presentation.)

If you like Cliff's concept, his book provides detailed and specific procedures for each of these steps.

Using the storyboard analogy, which he credits with inspiring his book, Cliff uses Slide Sorter view primarily to test the logical and emotional flow of the story.

Cliff is also ruthless in terms of editing the "chunks" that comprise a presentation. He is a student of learning theory and is a proponent of not overloading the audience's capacity.

His suggestion: Reduce the load on short-term memory—and don't overload working memory. In other words, there is a limit to how much information an audience is capable of retaining, and as some screenwriters also know—"less is more."

He uses an excellent metaphor to represent the importance of scaling down the chunks of information within your presentation—to make them memorable and understandable for your audience. In his slides, he suggests thinking of fitting information through the eye of a needle—and putting anything that doesn't fit into the Notes panel or jettisoning it entirely.

Jim Endicott uses the same sort of story overview when he talks about a *Persuasive Message Flow*. He reviews his slides in Slide Sorter and concentrates on the titles to make sure that each step of the cognitive process through which he leads an audience makes sense in terms of where he's been and where he is going.

As we learned from Korie Pelka, we can use a sketchpad or a more rigorous process when working with a presenter to elicit the key parts of their story, which we can use as hooks with various modules of components.

If you need to have a client sign off on your proposed presentation or get comments from other members of your team, creating a storyboard is a good first step.

You can print your slides in a configuration of up to nine per page using the Handouts option in the Print options dialog box (refer to Figure 1-13).

It's also helpful to know that you can add notes directly to your slides as you review your storyboard in Slide Sorter view. Look for the Notes button that pops up in the Slide Sorter view toolbar when you change to Slide Sorter view as shown in Figure 1-17.

CREATE A REHEARSAL VIDEO Although professional speaker coaches often videotape presenters to fine-tune their speaking skills (as we discuss later), there are now sophisticated tools that enable you to go beyond the Rehearse Timings feature of PowerPoint to watch yourself presenting the actual material you've put together.

Camtasia 3, from TechSmith, offers an add-in for PowerPoint that enables PIP (Picture in Picture) from a camcorder or webcam that lets you record the speaker along with the PowerPoint slides and audio.

Although a major feature of this program is the ability to post a presentation as an online movie (see Chapter 6), distributing such a movie to your team for comments or watching yourself as you prepare (a horrifying prospect) can help you reevaluate your story flow and timing as you familiarize yourself more thoroughly with the material.

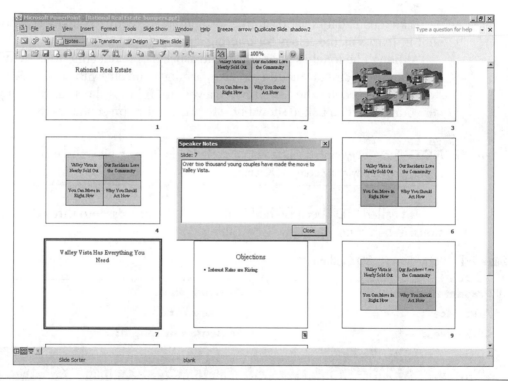

FIGURE 1-17   Whether you're doing a complete script or adding anecdotes, you can also access your Notes pages directly from Slide Sorter view.

Learn from Professional Coaches

In my work with numerous clients, I've had the opportunity to observe experts in the "soft skills" area of presentations—facilitators and speaker coaches. Particularly if you're a seasoned or professional presenter, you've hopefully had yourself videotaped to see your own energy level, eye contact, and tendency to fidget, and you've mastered the art of facing a live audience.

Although many aspects of this endeavor are common sense (smile, establish rapport), becoming proficient obviously takes practice and in most cases also means working with a professional coach. Frequently, these coaches use the analogy of top athletes, who are the most coached people in the world—even Michael Jordan had (and presumably paid attention to) a great coach.

Fortunately, there are lots of books on how to present that stop just short of PowerPoint. One of the most successful recent books on this topic is *Life Is a Series of Presentations* by Tony Jeary (see the section, "References").

Like a comedian's act or a great screenplay, structure is a key component in Jeary's methodology for crafting a presentation.

Although he touches on many of the aspects of connecting to an audience that we've already mentioned, like "arming yourself" with an arsenal of stories and anecdotes, he also provides a very useful worksheet for planning not your PowerPoint slide show but rather the entire presentation itself.

NOTE Tony Jeary makes this template available for free on his website: http://www.tonyjeary.com/3-DOutline.

It's called "3D" because he breaks down the process into three dimensions: What, *Why*, and How (see Table 1-1).

TABLE 1-1 Tony Jeary's 3D Outline

Presentation Title: Audience: Objectives:			Delivery Date: Delivery Time Presentation Length:	
#	**Time**	**What (Dimension 1)**	**Why (Dimension 2)**	**How (Dimension 3)**
		Final prep	Assure everything working	Set up and test
1				
2				
3				
4				
5				
6				

Notice the sections pertaining to the audience and objectives.

Jeary uses the example of "Clara," who is to make a presentation to her garden club and populates the template with the tasks that she needs to perform.

After doing her final preparations (which we'll cover in Chapter 8 from a technical perspective), Clara welcomes her audience and establishes rapport, reminding them of the fun they had at past projects (telling a story). Ten minutes is allotted to this in the worksheet.

Clara then takes five minutes to *identify the pain*. She describes the current condition of the traffic island she proposes to redesign.

Fifteen minutes are devoted to her concrete ideas for a patriotic theme to redesign the area.

Ten minutes are provided for questions and answers.

A final five minutes are earmarked for a summary and close (*call to action*).

What I suggest is that after you've gone through Jeary's process to structure the entire event—not just the slide show—and particularly considered the *Why* column for each entry, using the elements of PowerPoint to work within the *How* column makes a lot of sense.

Let's go through Jeary's example with Clara.

Using a series of bullet slides to "remind the club about their past bonds and experiences, etc." is a no-brainer—don't do it. That discussion and the showing of actual flower samples is a good time to turn off the projector (click the "b" key) and connect directly with the audience.

But showing pictures of the current situation would be a powerful tool and an excellent use of PowerPoint, which we'll cover in Chapter 3.

Scanning her drawings into slides to dramatize her ideas for a patriotic theme would also be a possible use of PowerPoint for Clara, as would having a few hidden slides ready for any objections during the Q&A.

Her most dramatic use of PowerPoint might be in her summary and call to action. She could dissolve the actual photos of the current traffic island into mock-ups or artists' renderings of how she visualizes the results. Using a simple dissolve or fade animation, which we'll cover down the road, would be an effective technique.

In terms of crafting the slide show remember to also use the concepts of presenters who don't even mention PowerPoint in planning for the entire event.

Many of these coaches and experts, like Tony Jeary, use techniques that work with or without technology—because they work with people. But when implemented correctly, as we've already seen and will continue to describe in detail, technology can be a terrific tool.

On another point, Jeary is also very big on being focused on the audience and not your own agenda. We've already mentioned one very cool way to do this: During the presentation, take advantage of the magic "b" button on your keyboard. This blanks the screen and puts the entire focus of the room back on you.

Then, at the end of the presentation you should be ready with a printed evaluation form to solicit the feedback of the audience on your content, your presentation style and effectiveness, and any other aspect of the event that is significant (the venue, food, etc.).

By having a printed form that you distribute during a break, you can motivate the audience to participate by using the forms as a raffle (for your book or another prize).

NOTE Chapter 6 covers other ways to get immediate feedback during the event. For example, use an Audience Response System during the event, and then in your follow-up you can use an online web form. Getting a form filled out is difficult, but it has the advantage of potentially putting the answers (and their contact information) into a database.

NOTE On this book's CD, we have a sample Word Evaluation Form Template as well as a Web Form Evaluation and Database Template.

There are many books besides Tony Jeary's that can stimulate your thinking on how to structure and craft your presentation. (Several are listed in the section, "Resources" at the end of the chapter.) We suggest you refer to them, along with the later chapters of this book, and thoughtfully implement technology where appropriate to make your message more effective.

Consider Facilitation

Remember that PowerPoint is just one widget in your presentation toolkit. Trainers, in particular, know the value of getting their audience involved in an event, a physical activity, or a game.

It breaks up the monotony of a lecture, and the most successful trainers of this type call themselves facilitators so that they can charge more money. You can learn some of these techniques from books like *Games Trainers Play* by Edward E. Scannell and John W. Newstrom. A big part of these kinds of exercises is their debriefing so that participants learn something, and PowerPoint graphics can be very effective during this phase.

If you can anticipate the results of your exercise, you can create slides that describe, for example, the typical group dynamics that your audience has just experienced. Even more effective is eliciting these results directly from the audience and noting them on a flip chart or whiteboard.

Analyzing group behavior together stimulates discussion, creates energy, and provides the audience with the concrete feeling that they have gained substantial insight into a problem or issue.

Using a Flexible Presentation Structure

So far, we've concentrated on developing a cohesive story structure to deliver a message in a *linear format*. But presentations don't always play out exactly as anticipated—for instance, you may want to have hidden slides ready for questions as we've already discussed.

But what if more complex sets of slides may be of value? For example, assume you're a commercial realtor and you won't know until you go into the client's office just which office complex would be the most appropriate to show.

Going back to the modular concept we mentioned, you could have a group of slides for every eventuality within your presentation.

Then, every time you modified this file for a new client, all of those slides would be re-saved, resulting in lost hard drive space and inefficiency.

The way to address this issue might be to create hyperlinks to any number of potential presentations within your story structure to allow you to navigate to these slide shows *or specific slides within them* any time you find the need during your actual presentation.

Hyperlinks and Action Settings

To link to another file or slide, you need a trigger, which can be any selectable object in your slide.

In Figure 1-18, we will use the title of our slide, which we've selected by dragging through it. We right-click and choose the Action Settings.

In the Action Settings dialog box, use the drop-down arrow to select to Hyperlink to Other PowerPoint presentation (see Figure 1-19). Another dialog box will open, allowing you to choose which presentation you want to access during the slide show.

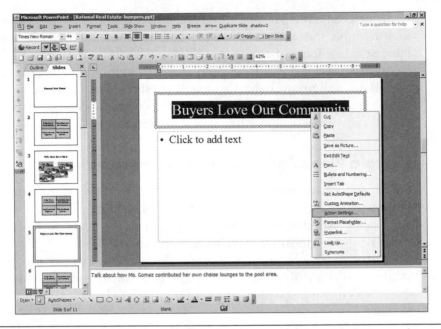

FIGURE 1-18   Locate a trigger or selectable object in your slide to begin to use the Action Settings with a right-click.

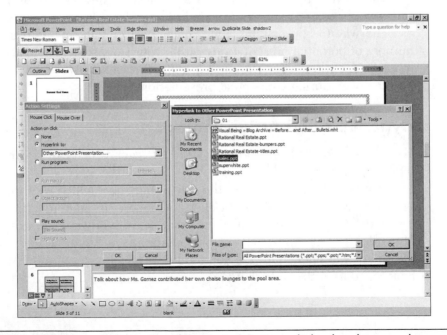

FIGURE 1-19   The Hyperlink to area of the Action Settings dialog box lets you choose to go to several different locations, including Other PowerPoint Presentation.

When you've selected a PowerPoint file, you can even drill down to a specific slide, as shown in Figure 1-20. Here, after we click OK, the slide called Our Strengths will open when the hyperlink is clicked.

Finally, the Action Settings link will be underlined in the slide (if it's text—see Figure 1-21), and during the presentation, when the mouse goes over it, the cursor will turn into a hand, indicating that the link is active.

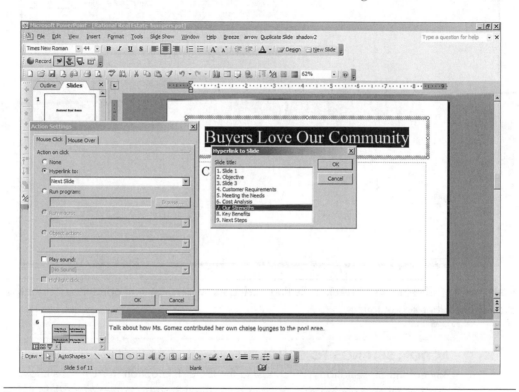

FIGURE 1-20 When you select Other Presentation, you can go inside the file to select a specific slide to show.

Then, you can continue further along in the linked presentation or, after showing the slides desired, simply press the ESC key to return to the last slide viewed within the presentation you were showing.

NOTE There is also an Insert > Hyperlink command in PowerPoint, which should not be confused with the Action Settings. This will ask for a web URL or local file location, but it makes it a bit more difficult to locate specific portions of the designated file or presentation. (You can do it using Bookmarks.) Action Settings offer the most flexibility for linking to other files.

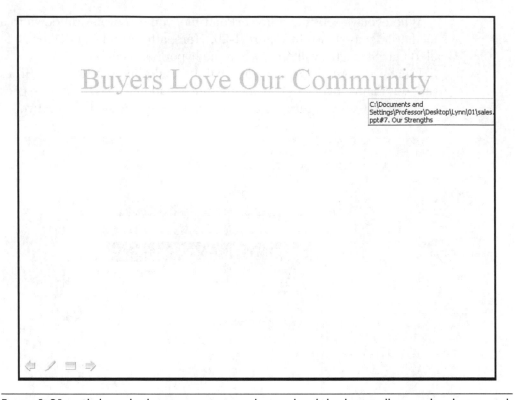

FIGURE 1-21   Clicking the hot Action Setting during the slide show will open the designated slide in the other presentation.

ACTION SETTINGS TO OTHER FILES You are not limited to opening just PowerPoint presentations. By choosing the Other File option in Action Settings, you can open any other document or file using the program that is the default for that file type. This would enable you to access, for example, a lease document using MS Word directly from PowerPoint. Word would open the file, allowing you to navigate through it, and when the window was closed, you'd be back in your PowerPoint presentation. The only drawback is that you would *not have the annotation tools* of PowerPoint available while you were displaying the other file.

Relational Presentation Model

One proponent of Action Settings is Robert Lane of Aspire Communications (http://www.aspirecommunications.com) who presented a model at

PowerPoint LIVE 2005 that proposed using one presentation every time you present and having it link to every other presentation on your laptop. Lane's ubiquitous standard presentation can begin with as few as three slides from which he can drill down through a set of topics to locate any slide in his library with a few more clicks.

This Relational Presentation model would, once again, be of value in a real estate presentation where you did not know which direction the audience (or buyer) wanted to go—and had every conceivable possibility available in a linked set of files.

As you can imagine, this scenario can be daunting for three main reasons. First, you must be thoroughly familiar with your file structure so that you know exactly how to get to any specific topic or slide at any time without fumbling. (Lane has a hierarchical model for this purpose).

The other concern is *breaking links*. If you move linked files without moving the trigger file in the same relative manner between folders, the links will be broken, creating a nightmare scenario for reestablishing connectivity. You need to design your system from the ground up so that files will not be moved and will remain fixed according to a cohesive and efficient folder structure.

Finally, as we'll discuss frequently during the course of this book, you need an *effective backup strategy* because having all of your presentations always "live" makes them vulnerable to the vagaries of travel—theft and loss. In this scenario in particular, you would need to back up all of your files all the time! (We'll talk about backup more in Chapter 8, where we deal specifically with disaster avoidance and recovery.)

Closing Any Time

Proceeding with our real estate scenario, let's look at another common occurrence during a sales presentation—time constraint.

Have you ever seen a PowerPoint presenter run out of time? It's not a pretty sight. He or she glances at the time, panics, and says something like, "Let me go quickly through the rest of my slides."

What follows is a blitz of titles and bullets that generally obscures everything you've already accomplished and confuses the heck out of the audience. Your story flow is completely out the window, and your close is jeopardized.

This issue was addressed by Jim Endicott at a recent seminar when he suggested using the features of PowerPoint to make it possible to go to the summary or closing point of the presentation at any time or at set intervals throughout the presentation.

The easiest way is simply to know the slide number (within the current presentation) of the slide that begins your summary and close. In the example (see Figure 1-22), using Slide Sorter we see that Slide 10 begins a closing sequence of the last three slides, including Financing Options.

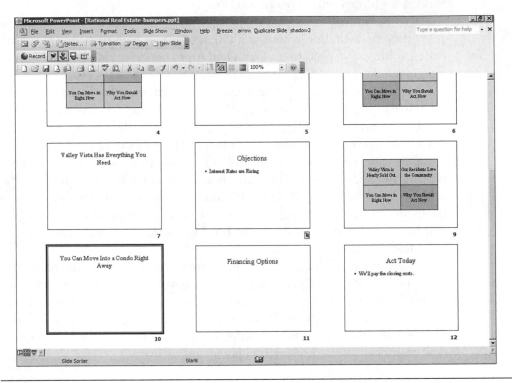

FIGURE 1-22   Slide Sorter view reveals that our closing sequence begins with Slide 10.

If I wanted to close this presentation as I was delivering it, I would simply walk over to the laptop, type the number 10 using the number keys at the top of the keyboard, and hit ENTER.

We would jump right to Slide 10, and with a carefully prepared segue—"So you can see what we have to offer, let's go right to how you can move in today…"—you're ready to close.

You've maintained your story flow, the audience may never know you changed the number of slides you intended to show, and what difference does it make? You're ready to achieve your objective.

Magic of Custom Shows

There's just one little problem with using the slide number—what if you decide to add a slide or take one out just before you speak, and you forget exactly where the close is? You could use the Go to Slide scenario we mentioned before (refer to Figure 1-15), but it's unwieldy in this context—you want to move to this set of slides as seamlessly as possible.

Another alternative, which is also useful for many aspects of restructuring your presentation (shortening it, storing different versions, and so on), is using Custom Shows.

When you click Slide Show > Custom Shows (see Figure 1-23), you are provided with an almost unlimited set of options for revising your story structure.

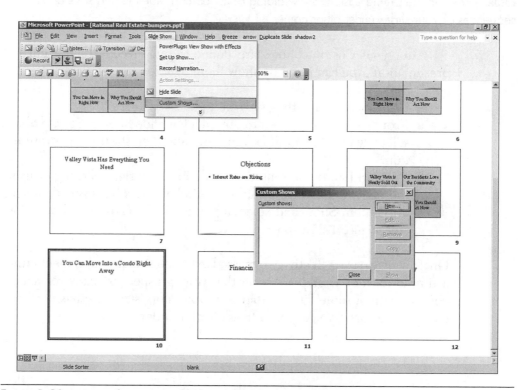

FIGURE 1-23   Open the Custom Shows dialog box to create alternate structures for your current presentation.

When you click New in the Define Custom Show dialog box, you can select and click Add to put one or more slides (in whatever sequence) into a newly named custom show.

Here (see Figure 1-24), we're using our final three slides to create a custom show called "Long Close."

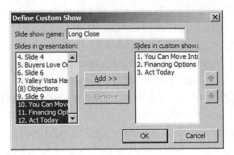

FIGURE 1-24   In the Define Custom Show dialog box, you can redefine and save other sequences of your slides under other names.

After your Custom Shows are defined (and saved with the current presentation), you can instantly show them in at least three ways:

- From an Action Setting or hyperlink.
- From the PowerPoint editor, by clicking Slide Show > Set Up Show, selecting the custom show you want, and then starting the presentation.
- From within the presentation mode itself, by right-clicking or using the popup toolbar as we did with hidden slides but instead clicking on Custom Show and selecting either Long Close or Short Close (see Figure 1-25).

Once again, you've effectively bypassed extraneous material to meet either a time crunch or your perception that your prospect is ready to make a commitment of some kind. Either way, your story structure has not been compromised, and you're ready to ask for the order.

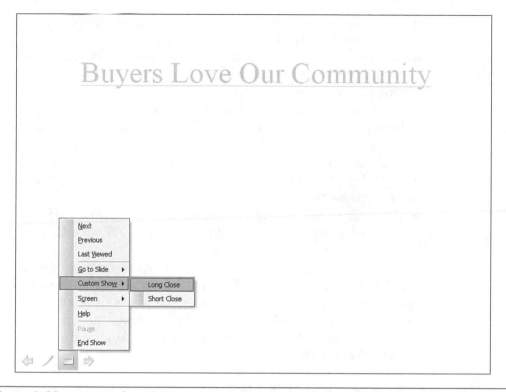

FIGURE 1-25 You can launch your Custom Shows instantly from your current presentation by clicking the popup toolbar or right-clicking on the screen.

Creating a Project Folder

After you've established your main message and structured your story into acts or modules, it's really time to flesh out the presentation. Unless you're going to stick to the title and bullets model that involves simply filling in a set of slides with text, you're going to want to assemble your assets.

By analogy, this would be assembling a cast for a production, and in fact Macromedia Director, a multimedia rival of MS PowerPoint, uses a Cast window or panel to compile the digital components of what will eventually appear on its "Stage."

What are some of these potential components? Here are just a few examples, with the chapter in which we deal with the acquisition and use of these assets noted:

- Spreadsheets and charts with the data that will support your key points (see Chapter 3).
- Documents (transcripts, contracts, email, and letters) that pertain to the subject matter or involve communication with your client and target audience (see Chapter 3).
- Maps and diagrams—even scanned into your computer as images or bitmaps—that you can use to visually direct and describe important issues. Or, these could come in as HTML web page files from MapQuest, Yahoo!, or some other source entirely (see Chapter 3).
- Digital photos from a camera or scanned images from snapshots (see Chapter 3).
- Video clips from a client CD-ROM, captured from a VHS tape or camcorder, or perhaps even extracted from a DVD (see Chapter 5).

You will probably assemble many of these assets as you structure your presentation and begin to outline the flow of ideas. Others may be provided to you over time or may become apparent as you're working, but I suggest that you create a project folder on your desktop to house all of these assets. You can create a new folder and name it by right-clicking on your desktop, as shown in Figure 1-26.

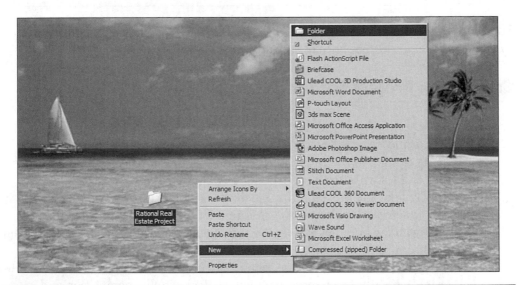

FIGURE 1-26   Right-click on your desktop to create and name a new folder for your project.

With the folder created, you can begin to drag in the various files that you will be working with and save subsequent files into that desktop folder. Although you may need to copy some files, creating a bit of redundancy and using up hard drive space, there are several compelling reasons to work in this fashion:

- You won't waste time as you write the presentation looking for items that you knew from the outset you would need.
- Important linked files (videos and spreadsheets) will be in the same folder with the presentation, so it's less likely that you'll move one without the other and break the links.
- You're less likely to forget to include important pieces of information that you've saved to your project folder as you work on the presentation.
- At the end of the day or session, it's easy to drag the project folder to another hard drive or flash backup drive, *protecting your hard work from corruption, disaster, or mischief.* (This reason is the most useful from my perspective.)

To me, some file duplication is a small price to pay for this peace of mind because as we see in Figure 1-27, the project folder gives us instant access to all of our work product, and by opening My Computer, we can quickly drag some files or the entire folder to another folder or disc.

As we continue to build our slide show components using the techniques in the coming chapters, the underlying source materials (captured video, scanned photos, and so on) will continue to be compiled in the project folder, making subsequent revision easier and lowering the chances of being unable to complete our project and edits in a timely fashion.

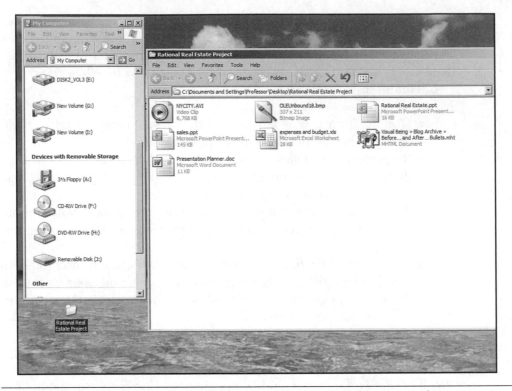

FIGURE 1-27   With a Desktop project folder created it's easy to drag it entirely, or open it and move its contents, to back-up hard drives or external devices.

Case Study: SuperWhite

You are the presentation specialist for a company that makes SuperWhite, a new cosmetic dental product that whitens teeth with a simple clear gel applied with an electronic toothbrush.

Steve, the Marketing Director of the company, comes into your office with Janice, the Vice President of Sales, in an excited state. They have an appointment with the largest Cosmetic Dental Group in Los Angeles for the following week, and they want to blow them away with a knockout presentation. They know you're the PowerPoint expert, but they're loaded with ideas.

The VP of Sales is almost bouncing off the ceiling as he hands you artwork from the graphics department. "Look what we designed!" he says as he hands you the printout of a Superman-styled "S" insignia on a tube of the gel. "This is our new super-hero logo, and we want you to fly it in, twirl it a couple of times, and then blast it into the center of the slide with a neat sound effect!"

"I can do that," you say, and they smile. "But is that really what you want?"

They look at you like you just landed from Mars. What are some of the questions that you need to ask to construct a terrific SuperWhite sales presentation?

(Think about this on your own before you read some concrete suggestions that appear in the next section.)

Key Questions to Consider

You respond by raising these issues:

- To whom are you going to deliver this presentation?
- What are the biggest issues in their practice—What problem are we solving for them? (Remember Jim Endicott's concept of identifying the pain.)
- What would be the best result for them after working with SuperWhite?
- What are the objectives of your company as a result of delivering the presentation?

When you raise these points, Steve and Janice look at each other for a moment and sit back and consider.

Janice says, "Well obviously we want their top executives to replace their current whitening regimen with ours. This should be easy because right now they're propping the patients' mouths open with a rubber stopper and making them sit under the lamp for an hour, drooling into a bib."

Okay, well that's a start, you think to yourself. "But doesn't our treatment cost a lot less, so they'll make less money?"

Steve shoots to his feet. "That's a short-term view. They can do a lot more whitening in a lot less time with less overhead with SuperWhite. Because it's patented and exclusive, they will have a license for a simple at-home solution, and they don't need to maintain extra space with a lot of expensive equipment."

Okay, now you have something to work with. Instead of a flying logo, you open the presentation with two slides showing the problems with conventional teeth-whitening tools (see Figures 1-28 and 1-29).

FIGURE 1-28   "Is This Your Word of Mouth?"

FIGURE 1-29   "Or This?"

There are always going to be some people who just don't get it. The Marketing Director may still have a timeworn idea of how a presentation should begin.

"What about that slide about our company, and how it started and how many employees we have?" Steve asks.

Janice puts up her hand—"You know Steve, I like this. Let's see how it works."

"What about other solutions we're up against?" you ask.

"There are those goopy trays you have to leave in your mouth," Steve says.

"And those yucky strips," Janice adds.

"Let's get some pictures of those if we can," you suggest, reinforcing the other alternatives that are equally unpleasant for your prospects' patients.

You continue the presentation with typical bullets, but in the first one, you list the benefits to the prospective client.

And on the next, you list the benefits to their now much more satisfied patients.

"Wait a minute," Janice says. "This is promising, but what about proving that it works as well as what they're currently using?"

"Or better," Steve chimes in, still not completely convinced.

"Don't we have before and after pictures?" you suggest. "Let's fade a few in and out to show them some typical results."

Janice adds that the manufacturer has a video showing how easy the product is to use. You add a slide for that video in Slide Sorter view (see Figure 1-30).

And for the close, they wonder?

"Well, you'll need to ask for the order," you conclude. "But we can put up some of our corporate slides to show our track record and fulfillment capability."

"And end with the twirling logo," Steve says hopefully.

"Sure," you sigh, but you know that they're finally on the right track.

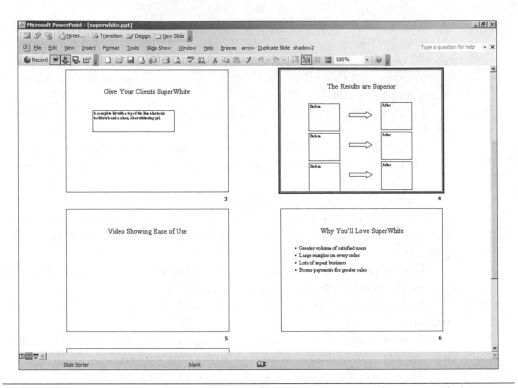

FIGURE 1-30 The next part in Slide Sorter view shows before and after images fading in and a video of how easy the product is to use.

Summary

There's a lot more to a successful presentation than creating a PowerPoint slide show loaded up with titles and bullets. Considering what's at stake should make you acutely aware that a specific strategy needs to be implemented, taking into account the needs and emotional hot buttons of your audience and your own expectations and objectives.

We went through a number of perspectives for planning and structuring our presentation, benefiting from the insights of various experts and experienced consultants and presenters, including:

- Identifying the pain to create a persuasive work flow.
- Assessing the strengths and weaknesses of the presenter and creating modules of slides that can be reorganized.
- Working with the Outline and/or Slide Sorter to see our dramatic story flow.

- Beginning to think about creating visual versions of our ideas instead of using text bullets.
- Learning from speaker coaches and facilitators in terms of connecting to our audience and organizing our entire presentation with PowerPoint as just one potential component.

As we continue, we'll illustrate many of these concepts. Then we'll go on to work with the most important features of PowerPoint and related programs and concepts to create the most effective and compelling electronic visual support for the presentation we have planned and begun.

Resources

I would guess that a majority of readers of this book are not writers. In my weekly web column for InformIT.com, dealing with all of MS Office, I have a section on PowerPoint, and within it I have one section called "What the Heck Do I Say?" (http://snipurl.com/it8c).

Modeling the experts is the best way to learn any craft or profession. Fortunately in the PowerPoint and presentations world, there are resources available to give you ideas on how to approach any project. Here are some of the best:

- Indezine—website by Geetesh Bajaj, PowerPoint MVP—http://www.indezine.com.
- *Presentations Magazine* (particularly Speakers Notes)—http://www.presentations.com.
- InfoComm (particularly the ICIA and Presentations Council)—http://www.infocomm.org/.
- Presentation Samples from Distinction Services—http://www.distinction-services.com/portfolio_main.html.
- Above and Beyond CD—Ten Ways to Avoid Death by Power-Point—http://www.aboveandbeyond.ltd.uk/.
- If you want to build an arsenal of business-related stories, try the book and website of my friend and colleague Terrence Gargiulo (http://www.makingstories.net).
- Tony Jeary's templates and other resources are at http://www.tonyjeary.com.

- Cliff Atkinson's site (author of *Beyond Bullet Points*) is http://www.sociablemedia.com. It includes templates and other resources for planning a presentation and creating powerful visuals from your concepts.
- Ellen Finkelstein's site is http://www.ellenfinkelstein.com/power-point.html. Ellen is a respected PowerPoint and presentation expert who has written for *Presentations Magazine* among other resources in the field.

Reference Books

Here are some great books:

- *Beyond Bullet Points: Using Microsoft PowerPoint to Create Presentations That Inform, Motivate, and Inspire* by Cliff Atkinson, Microsoft Press (March 2, 2005).
- *Life Is a Series of Presentations: 8 Ways to Punch Up Your People Skills at Work, at Home, Anytime, Anywhere* by Tony Jeary, Kim Dower, J.E. Fishman, Fireside (February 3, 2004).
- *The Absolute Beginner's Guide to Winning Presentations* by Jerry Weissman, Que Publishing (March 23, 2004).
- *The Leader's Voice: How Communication Can Inspire Action and Get Results!* by Boyd Clarke, Ron Crossland, Select Books (NY) (May 1, 2002).
- *The Strategic Use of Stories in Organizational Communication and Learning* by Terrence L. Gargiulo, M.E. Sharpe (April 30, 2005).
- *Say It with Presentations!* by Gene Zelazny, McGraw-Hill (2006).

CHAPTER 2

IMPLEMENTING PROFESSIONAL DESIGN PRINCIPLES

I could try to convince you that I deliberately kept the figures in Chapter 1, "Planning an Effective Presentation," ugly, but I doubt you'd be fooled. What I did do, however, was to keep them as simple as possible leading into this second chapter.

For a verbal person like me, what professional designers do is almost like voodoo—they seem to follow some sort of arcane process, and at some point, they transform the ordinary and ugly into something that is astonishing in its clarity and beauty.

If you've sat through a lot of PowerPoint presentations, and most of us have, you've undoubtedly been struck at rare intervals by the thought that "This doesn't look like PowerPoint."

Frequently, this is not the result of some dramatic new template or look for the presentation.

In fact, it is almost certainly the result of *the **absence** of an intrusive look or design.*

The word that most frequently crosses my mind when I have this experience is "clean." Like many presenters, I strive for a clean and clear design for any presentation that I create, but invariably I fall short of what I perceive to be the unmistakable clarity of something designed by a professional.

The quintessence of this level is epitomized, in my estimation, by two regular contributors to *Presentations Magazine* and participants in the PowerPoint LIVE show: Nancy Duarte and Julie Terberg.

Both have carved out a special niche in the world of presentations by mastering the medium of PowerPoint both technically and artistically and by marshalling their own skills along with those of teams of designers to create visually effective presentations.

Again, what both of their samples share is a simplicity.

Nancy's and Julie's respective styles are quite different. I would describe the Terberg method as more colorful and dramatic, while Duarte Design is more corporate and understated. This probably results at least in part from their main clientele; Julie Terberg has written an entire book on doing medical presentations, while Nancy Duarte has created templates and collateral material for some of the world's leading corporations that reflect their brand identity.

Before we even begin to cover a few techniques and processes to attempt to emulate the clean and crisp look of a professionally designed presentation, I encourage you to look at the portfolio samples at Nancy's and Julie's websites:

- http://www.duarte.com
- http://www.terbergdesign.com

What Designers Think About

One of the things that separates professional designers from other people is that they can spend hours and days talking about things like fonts and colors. On the other hand, I am a guy who has used sets of Polaroids from a tailor to dress himself in an outfit of matching slacks, jacket, shirt, and tie.

Can the basic principles of sound design be learned and applied by everyone?

I believe that as a presenter, you would accept this premise at your own peril. You are much better served by using the guidelines and taking advantage of the expertise of someone skilled in the design field.

Even Microsoft doesn't believe it—that's why each version of Power-Point has been released with its own Design Templates that strive to make the implementation of a well-crafted design a no-brainer.

The results have been at best mixed. On one hand, applying a complete Design Template gives your presentation a blended look, along with complementary colors and fonts that seem to work well together…up to a point.

As we'll see, applying a packaged design can greatly streamline the design process, but it comes at a price. Although it does address a key issue—after you have chosen a complete look for your presentation, you can get on with the work of creating your content—it may not be the answer for presenters who want to truly stand out from the pack, represent a unique identity, or communicate a message using the subtleties of color, space, and professional design.

Let's examine the PowerPoint Design Templates more closely before we look more deeply into proven design principles and apply them to our own work.

Using the PowerPoint Design Templates

If we return to the basic Rational Real Estate presentation we worked with in the previous chapter, we see that it has had no design template applied to it.

Notice that the Design Templates that are in use in the current presentation are at the top of the Slide Design—Design Templates Task Pane, and more recently used designs (if you've been working for a while) are in the panel directly below (see Figure 2-1).

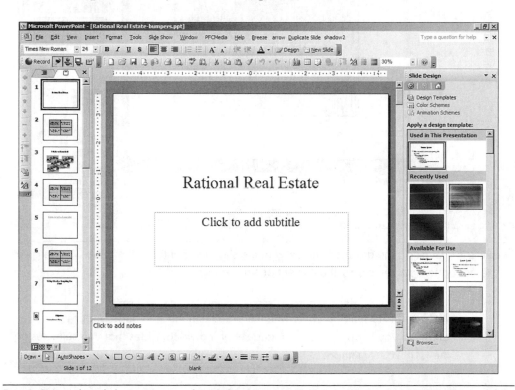

FIGURE 2-1   The Slide Designs in the Slide Design Task Pane are divided into those currently in use, the ones most recently used, and other design templates available in PowerPoint.

We can scroll through the available designs and apply one instantly by clicking on it, and it becomes the template for the entire presentation.

We can also click the drop-down arrow at the right of the design template thumbnail and get other choices, including Apply to Selected Slides—in this case, that would be the one in the preview window in Normal view (see Figure 2-2).

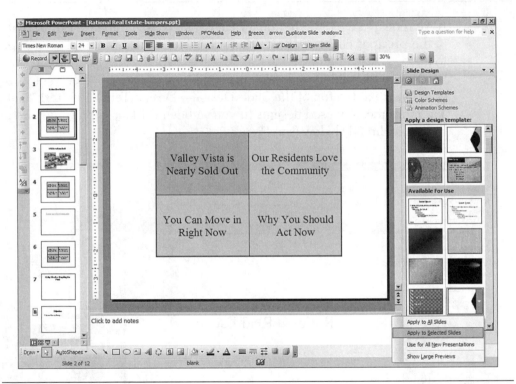

FIGURE 2-2 Clicking the drop-down arrow in the slide thumbnail of the Slide Design gives us the option to apply it to only the current or selected slide.

NOTE This technique works with the slide thumbnails in Slide Sorter view by allowing you to apply a design to a set of individual slides that you select using the CTRL+click method.

If we apply the design to the selected (or currently viewed) slide here, the effect is dramatic. Not only is a design applied to the slide's background, but complementary colors for lines and fonts also replace those that were in the slide before the template was applied (see Figure 2-3).

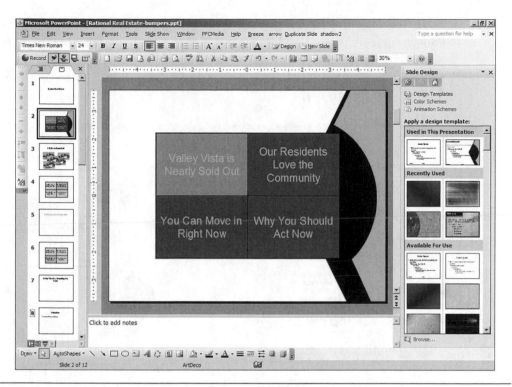

FIGURE 2-3 Applying a Slide Design from the Gallery changes the colors of lines and fonts to coordinate with the overall design.

In addition, if you scroll back up to the top of the Gallery, you see that the new design has joined the basic design as those that are in current use within the presentation.

NOTE We applied the new design to one of the slides *other than* the Title Slide. The Design Templates generally have a slightly modified design for the Title Slide to set it apart. However, it is the slide design for all other slides that is shown in the preview slide design thumbnail.

So the good news with slide designs is that they quickly and efficiently convert one or more slides into color-coordinated packages, complete with common design elements in the background.

The bad news is that these packaged designs generally brand your presentation as just another PowerPoint slide show, and everyone has seen most of these designs a million times.

If you click the Browse button at the bottom of the Slide Design Task Pane, you can open the file folders for the various design templates (including those from previous versions of PowerPoint from which you may have upgraded) and find and preview even more packaged slide designs (see Figure 2-4).

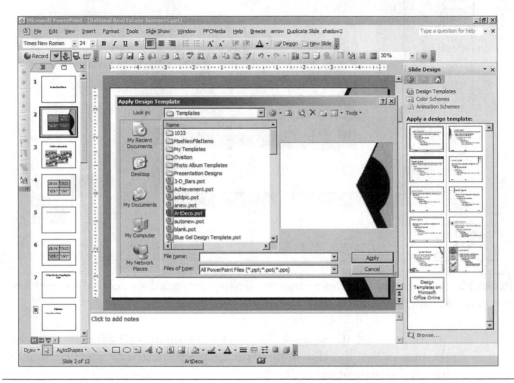

FIGURE 2-4   Using the Browse button to open your actual template file folders provides an even greater selection of pre-packaged PowerPoint templates.

If you click on Design Templates on Microsoft Office Online (see Figure 2-5), you can download yet more packaged designs from the Office Assistance website (http://office.microsoft.com/en-us/templates/ CT011153611033.aspx).

If you find a Design Template that suits the flavor of the presentation you are creating, then using the slide designs makes proceeding with your presentation a snap. The colors you have applied complement each other, and even if you add drawing objects, the lines and fills (or *accents*) will continue to be complementary according to the slide design's *Color Scheme*, which we will cover more extensively in a bit.

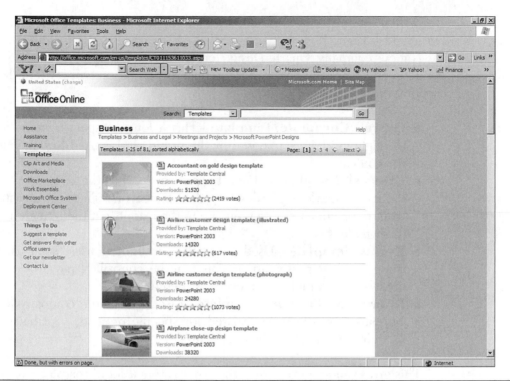

FIGURE 2-5   There are always new categorized templates available for download from the Microsoft Office Assistance center.

But my guess is that after you have familiarized yourself with some of the examples of corporate designs that are clean and reflect a corporate brand, you will want to learn how to create a set of more professional templates for your own presentations.

Creating a Branded Template

I have seen Nancy Duarte, a well-established expert in the area of presentation design, speak at a number of conferences, hoping that her skills will rub off on me and I will no longer need Polaroids to decide what to wear for an evening out.

She has broken the design process for templates into a number of distinct areas and provided some valuable guidelines for constructing a branded corporate template. What is striking about her final results is how clean they are and how different they look from anything in the Slide Design Task Pane.

Nancy's company, Duarte Design, creates a set of templates for its corporate clients that they can use for the main presentation types within the corporation:

- **Overall Corporate Template**—Has a long lifespan, adheres to the tight guidelines imposed by the brand, and is used throughout the company.
- **External Templates**—Used by verticals within the company for their own marketing, sales, or other endeavors. This can deviate from the main corporate template to the extent that the branch has its own identity.
- **Events Template**—Used externally for limited uses, such as a trade show or presentation. This may be controlled more by the artist and might map to an event or theme.
- **Internal or Program Template**—Used within the company for campaigns and may be updated for specific projects. Can have a short lifespan and may be confidential.

This gives you an idea of the scope of creating a set of templates for a corporation from a professional perspective. Depending upon the size and parameters of your own presentations, you may or may not want to create separate templates for these various applications.

But if you want to create presentations with a clear sense of identity relating back to you who you are and what you represent, you may want to continue down this path and think through some specific decisions.

Don't Fear Space

One of the first things that strikes you about a Duarte slide is how easy it is to read and absorb. There is no competition for attention among disparate design elements; even a logo, when present, is unobtrusive and subtle in its effect.

There are no extraneous clouds, dissolving lines, squiggles, curls, or blobs coming at you along with the material. Yet the slides are not bland. In many cases the colors are vibrant, and they are subdued where appropriate, and sometimes you ask yourself why anyone would pay for something so seemingly simple.

This relates directly back to the underlying design choices made about the original template—or blueprint for the presentation.

Analyzing Collateral Materials

If you are creating a presentation for a corporate client or work directly within a large company, you need to focus upon the design decisions that have already been made to promote its corporate image or brand. Duarte calls this auditing or studying the visual attributes of the brand.

A great way to do this is to analyze the website of the company and do a thorough review of their collateral materials. Obviously, the design and positioning of the logo is a key component to any design that may be used in presentations. In addition, the choice of colors and how they are used can best be gleaned by looking at a variety of web pages, reviewing brochures, and even taking a long hard look at business cards.

If you take a look at Google.com, you immediately see the simplicity of the overall look and the unmistakable color choices reflected in the letters comprising the corporate name.

Whether you've ever realized it or not, Hewlett-Packard has a certain shade of purple or dark blue associated with its main logo. An entirely different shade of blue represents American Express. These attributes are immediately obvious to a designer. For those who are not specialists in this field, the use of color and the layout of a page or brochure may become apparent only after time or, in some cases, never.

In Chapter 1, we added some images to a slide for our imaginary real estate presentation (refer to Figure 1-7). Let's pretend that this image represents our corporate logo and use it to illustrate some of the steps involved in creating a simple branded template.

Using a Grid System

Duarte uses a simple spatial grid concept to create a template that is in her words "a container for amazing content." The best way to see how her grid concept emphasizes simplicity is to contrast it to the PowerPoint Layouts in the Slide Layout Task Pane or the numerous placeholders that scream to be filled in within the Slide Master view.

In a new, blank presentation, whenever you open a new slide, the default layout is Title and Bullets, and the Slide Layout Task Pane pops up (see Figure 2-6).

If you switch to the Slide Master view, which represents the true *blueprint* for all formatting for the design template (as we'll cover in more detail later), you get an even more complex set of placeholders crying out for fulfillment (see Figure 2-7).

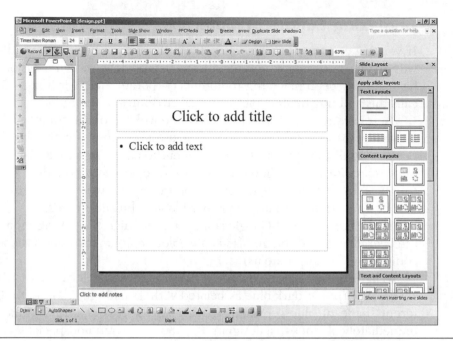

FIGURE 2-6 PowerPoint prompts you to create a bullet slide or choose another layout, most of which have placeholders for content.

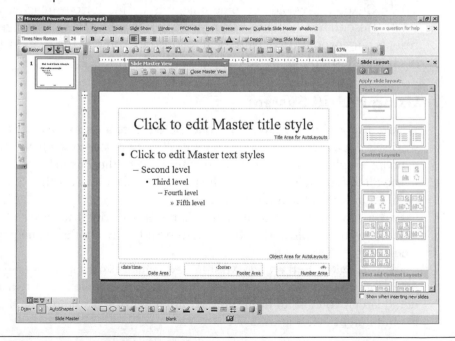

FIGURE 2-7 PowerPoint's Slide Master view, which represents a blueprint for the template, also features placeholders for lots of text to be formatted.

Contrast this with the type of slide a designer like Duarte may create, which really springs from one of the simplest Slide Layouts in the Task Pane: Title only.

For a simple corporate template, she may add only a single thick line in a color coordinated with or central to the corporate logo. Or, she may position the logo beside the slide title.

You can either use the View > Grids and Guides feature directly within PowerPoint or create your own mini-grid system with a table or the Drawing toolbar to further refine the use of space within the template slide.

If you like, you can then Reapply the Title and Bullet Layout and reposition and format the bullets within the grid. Figure 2-8 shows the result.

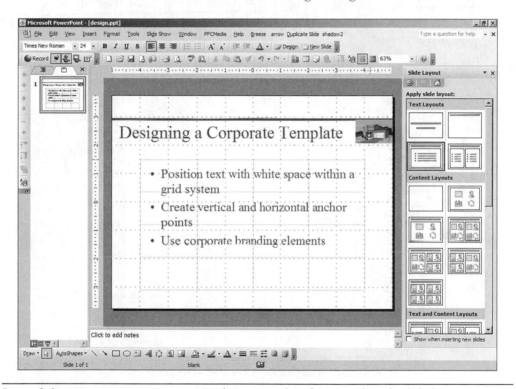

FIGURE 2-8   You can create your own identity template from a Title only slide by using a grid system.

Duarte's team builds the various types of slides that her corporate clients may use by continuing to

- Position text with white space within a grid system
- Create vertical and horizontal anchor points
- Use corporate branding elements

NOTE The slide being created here is for initial design purposes only; to actually implement this design throughout the entire presentation, the design choices made in this phase need to be used in a series of Masters, which can then be applied to a set of slides with content—as we'll see in section, "Understanding the Role of Masters."

Positioning a Logo

The logo's position directly under the simple line or bar is just one possible choice.

As we can see in Figure 2-9, there are at least four other positions where the logo could be located that keep it clear of the main content areas.

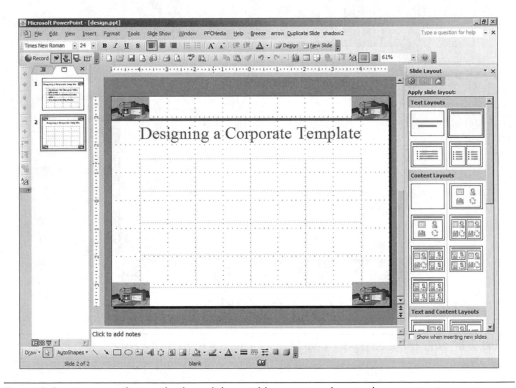

FIGURE 2-9 Using a cleaner look and the grid layout, you have other positioning options for the logo.

Using either the multiple Masters feature of PowerPoint (or by saving any of these logo locations as a separate Design Template), you could create an entirely different "look" within your branded sales presentation or create a different look for a marketing plan, a training session, or any other application or presentation type you may need to create.

To create multiple Masters, you would simply return to Slide Master view, click create New Master on the Slide Master view toolbar, and reposition the logo in the four new locations for each new master (see Figure 2-10).

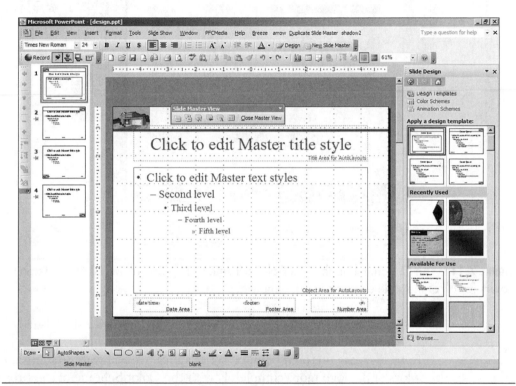

FIGURE 2-10   Four newly created Masters appear at the top of the Slide Design gallery in the Slide Design Task Pane.

Using a Branded Color Scheme

So far, we've only used the eight basic colors of the blank (white background) slides with which we've started. We can see a very basic and bland Color Scheme if we click the Edit Color Schemes prompt at the bottom of the *Color Schemes* part of the Slide Design Task Pane.

If we click the Custom tab within Edit Color Scheme, we can create our own Color Scheme composed of entirely different colors, as shown in Figure 2-11.

But what colors would we choose, and why are they important?

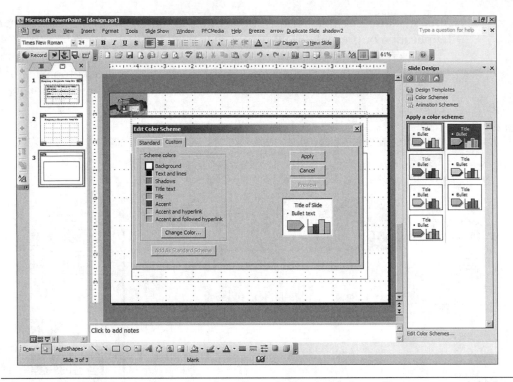

FIGURE 2-11   The Custom tab in the Edit Color Scheme dialog box allows us to set default colors for all of the slide elements in our template.

The ones here seem to complement the logo we are using, but let's examine it more closely.

To truly create our own branded set of slides, we will want to integrate the colors of the logo more completely with the Color Scheme of the presentation template.

WHEN TO USE A BACKGROUND The Background formatting tool in Power-Point is a vestige of a time before templates and Masters, particularly when 35mm slides were still in vogue. It doesn't affect the overall template or Color Scheme when the Background is applied, so it doesn't have much power. What it is good for mainly is to create a conventional two-color gradient of the type that used to be the standard for 35mm slides.

Fine-Tuning Color Schemes

If we type the word "Title" for our new slide in our design presentation and select it to format it with the Font color tool, as shown in Figure 2-12, we see a set of eight color swatches to choose from directly in the Font color tool, along with a choice for More Colors.

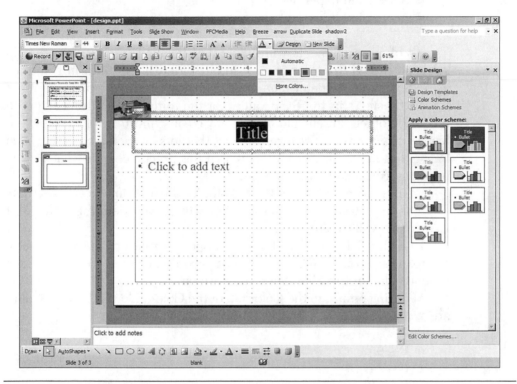

FIGURE 2-12   The Font color tool dialog box shows the eight basic color swatches that are currently set in the slide's Color Scheme.

The default Title text color right now is the darker blue, but we could be sure that if we left this color for a corporate template, someone somewhere would say something like, "That's not exactly the shade of blue we use in our logo!"

We could use these swatches to try to match it visually, but it would apply only to this one slide, and even then, it wouldn't truly be exact.

But for our corporate template, we want to make sure that the major elements in our slide are covered by the Color Scheme:

- Background
- Text and lines
- Shadows
- Title text
- Fills
- Accent
- Accent and hyperlink
- Accent and followed hyperlink

All of these elements will follow the specified set of colors that we select so that all the color choices in our slide will be uniform going forward. So how do we determine these colors with complete precision?

The secret is in the RGB values, or the numerical values assigned to the shade of red, green, and blue in any color. Unfortunately, PowerPoint has no *color picker* or *eyedropper tool* that lets us suck a color out of an image (like our logo) and make sure that this precise color is what we'll be using for Title text in our template.

We need to go outside of PowerPoint for the first time; we'll use Adobe PhotoShop, but any good image editor will let you determine the RGB value of a specific color.

In Figure 2-13, we click the eyedropper over part of the logo's roof in PhotoShop (or the trim below the roof), and that color becomes the Background color for the PhotoShop composition.

More important, in the Color tab of the Color palette, the RGB values are available:

- **R**—9
- **G**—54
- **B**—119

Now you're in business. When you return to the Edit Color Scheme dialog box for our Custom Color Scheme (refer to Figure 2-11), you click on Title text to select it, click on Change Color, and go to the Custom tab in the Title Text Color dialog box, as shown in Figure 2-14.

Now, by entering those RGB values from the logo's trim color into the settings, you will exactly match the color in the logo for the default color for all of your Title text in the new custom Color Scheme.

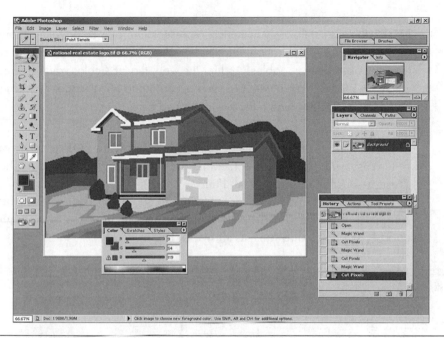

FIGURE 2-13   Most image editing programs, like PhotoShop, enable you to establish the RGB value of a specific color in your logo or other part of your collateral material.

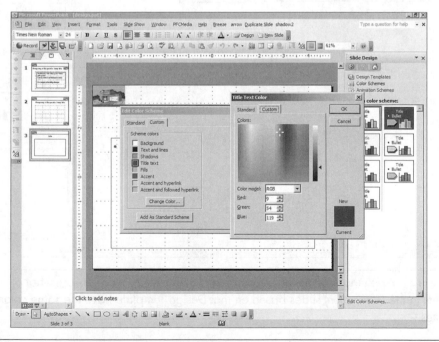

FIGURE 2-14   Entering the RGB values for the color you picked in PhotoShop can assign that color to any of the elements in your Custom Color Scheme.

NOTE RGB is not the only numerical representation of a color value. There is also an HSB (Hue, Saturation, Brightness) value, which defines a specific color in terms of these three variables. And for the web, the HEX color values define specific colors for display in web browsers according to HTML code. Any of these could be used to fine-tune a logo as described here.

We're almost done. Now when we click Apply and OK to close out, the new Custom Color Scheme has taken its place *at the bottom* of the Slide Design—Color Schemes Task Pane.

We can switch to Slide Sorter view to see all of the slides in our new template, click on the drop-down arrow in the new Color Scheme, and choose Apply to All Slides, as shown in Figure 2-15.

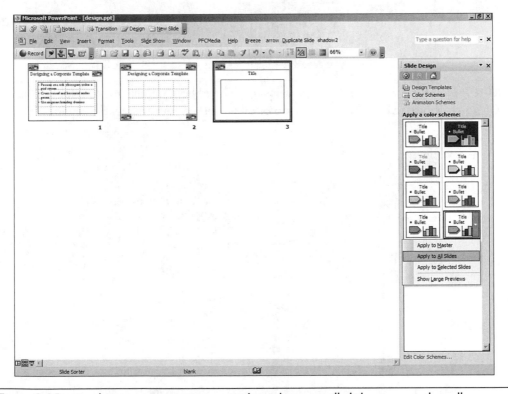

FIGURE 2-15   Applying your new Custom Color Scheme to all slides ensures that all elements in the subsequent slides based on that Design Template have the same color attributes.

In this case, all we've done is apply a slightly different shade of dark blue for the title. To see more dramatic results, apply any other Color Scheme, but remember to Undo (CTRL+Z) after you see the results.

A professional designer would then assign other colors from the collateral material or logo to the specific elements in the slide that should reflect them. This would create complementary colors for fills, lines, and other text.

WHAT'S AN ACCENT? Accents are similar to line colors and would change the main solid block line above the Title text in this template and also the boundary line that highlights the grid.

So now let's imagine that we've matched our colors exactly, assigned them within our Custom Color Scheme according to their RGB values, and applied the Color Scheme to our newly created Design Template.

What we've accomplished is to simulate the process of a professional designer in matching the characteristics of a nice clean template that is not based on any of the PowerPoint templates in the Slide Design gallery.

AVOIDING SURPRISES: ANTI-COLOR SCHEME STRATEGY There are situations where you want to create unique slides within a presentation that will not conform to a Color Scheme or match your template and, more importantly, *will not change the colors in their elements even if they are moved to other presentations.* Many users have had this happen—they design a great chart or diagram, but when it is moved, suddenly the colors change.

The Color Scheme basic eight colors are the key to this issue. Whenever you use the basic eight Color Scheme colors for any element (as shown in Figure 2-12), those colors are subject to change if they find themselves in another presentation ruled by another template with its own Color Schemes.

How can you avoid this problem?

Choose the More Colors setting for any of these elements and then choose other colors for lines, fills, text, or any other items that you don't want changed no matter what.

If you still need to use complementary colors, choose the corresponding swatches under More Colors that match those in the basic eight. To make this a bit easier, whenever you select More Colors and choose a Custom color, it will appear as the ninth, tenth, or successive color in your color swatches under dialog boxes like Text or Fill color. By creating a second row of More Colors that correspond to the basic eight (using the RGB values again), you can get the best of both worlds—match the Color Scheme of your template and make sure nothing happens to the colors if the slide finds itself in another presentation down the road.

NOTE The Goddess of Color Schemes is PowerPoint MVP Echo Swinford. Her tutorials and excellent advice can be accessed online at http://www.echosvoice.com.

Saving Your Design Templates

The only thing left to do is to save our new design as a *new template*.

If we were doing a major project, we might very well save subtly (or perhaps even dramatically) different versions of this color-coordinated template for each of the template types for our corporation—one set for corporate messages, another for special events, one for in-house training, and so on.

If you were creating this template for a corporate client, you might want to save all of these template files in a special folder, which you would deliver upon completion.

But if you are using these templates internally or for yourself, there are some important things to consider.

First of all, template files *are not ordinary PowerPoint files*. When we save the Design Template file, we need to click Save As and then change the Save as Type setting from an ordinary *.PPT PowerPoint file to a *.POT template file, as shown in Figure 2-16.

Now, when you do this, *by default*, you will notice that the destination folder changes to your *Templates* folder.

For most users, simply adding it to the default Templates folder is enough. But because your templates will become quite valuable if you design them for specific uses or take this much time and trouble to fine-tune them, you will want to know where they're located so that you can *protect them and back them up*.

If you were to search for the file design.pot, you would find it in a specific Templates folder *under your User Name* in Windows XP, as shown in Figure 2-17.

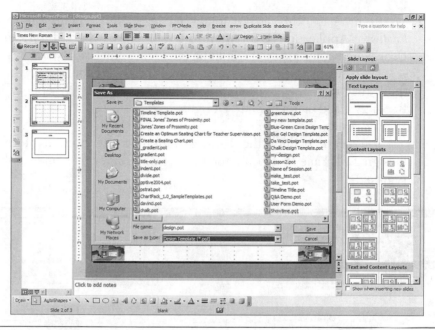

FIGURE 2-16   Saving a Design Template file involves changing the Save as Type setting in the Save As dialog box and noting the destination folder.

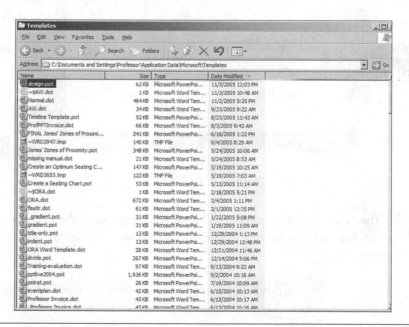

FIGURE 2-17   Saving a Design Template by default puts it into the Microsoft Templates folder under your User Name.

In my case, this is the folder name: C:\Documents and Settings\ *Professor*\Application Data\Microsoft\Templates, where *Professor* is my User Name. Your location would be based on your User Name.

Then, to locate a specifically named template for reuse, you would think that in a new presentation it would automatically appear in your Recently Used panel in Slide Designs.

It doesn't.

You need to click the Browse button at the bottom of the Slide Design Task Pane and locate the newly saved folder by name, as shown in Figure 2-18.

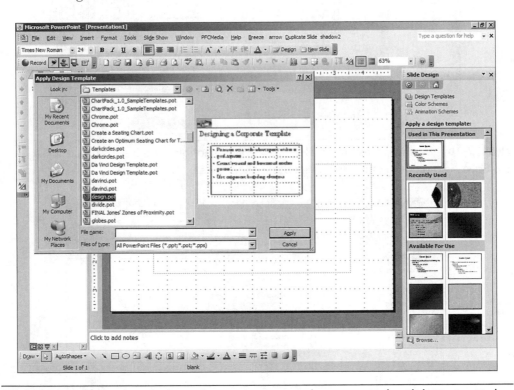

FIGURE 2-18 The newly saved template won't necessarily appear in the Slide Design Task Pane right away. You can click Browse to locate it by its name, preview it, and apply it to a new presentation.

So at this point, we have created a single multi-slide template with a nice clean design that we can reuse or apply at any time to any number of new presentations.

You may or may not want to go to these lengths to fine-tune the Color Schemes of your design templates—you may be happy creating one or more clean templates that you can save in your own Templates folder, back up, and then reuse for the different kinds of presentations you need to create.

You can never go wrong with a clean white background design, and it won't distract from your message.

Design guru Nancy Duarte steers her clients away from anything with lots of red—saying that the audience usually can't handle much of that without getting edgy.

Rick Altman, who runs the PowerPoint LIVE conference and has written extensively on slide design and other PowerPoint-related topics, calls "black the chicken soup of PowerPoint backgrounds," claiming that a template with a black background and contrasting (white or light yellow) text colors is acceptable in a multitude of settings and applications.

Of course, printing a set of slides with black backgrounds in a small business setting can break the bank in laser toner. That's why we will cover design for printing Handouts later in this chapter.

But for now, we're at a point where we can create and apply a template and understand the advantage of designing our own clean look over using the products included with PowerPoint.

If you are creating templates for others, particularly if you are creating a series of them for various types of presentations, you might find it helpful to organize your main Templates folder into subfolders. Obviously, you can do this by right-clicking the main folder and creating a newly named subfolder, just as we created a Desktop project folder in the previous chapter.

Because templates are valuable properties, I strongly suggest saving them to multiple locations and backing them up religiously. If you *really think they're valuable*, and some definitely are, you can also assign a password to open the templates and another to modify them by using the Tools > Options > Security setting in the file, just as you would a normal *.PPT file.

Think back to Chapter 1 where we showed you the AutoContent Wizard; remember that there is another type of template—for *content*.

Just as the example we've been building in this chapter has multiple slides, you can save a multi-slide template file not only to reuse the concepts and language (as the AutoContent Wizard "Presentation Templates" do) but also to maintain palettes of your best diagrams, charts, and even linked videos in a set of template files. That's something to think about as we get into more sophisticated creation of visual elements.

Understanding the Role of Masters

Earlier in this chapter, we mentioned the use of multiple Masters within a single presentation to place a logo in different parts of the background for different slides (refer to Figure 2-10).

With these multiple Masters created, any one or more of them can be applied to one or more slides by selecting them in Slide Sorter view.

Most people use Masters in two ways:

- First, by putting the logo on the Master wherever you choose, you can quickly customize a presentation by applying that master to various slides—they will all share that look.
- Then, by reformatting specific elements within the master, you can quickly make a similar set of changes automatically within of lots of slides at once.

Let's see how and why that works.

As already mentioned, the Slide Master is essentially a blueprint for all slides based on it. And it's very powerful—imagine if in the real world you could build some condos based on a blueprint, and then if you changed the dimensions of the shower in the blueprint, the showers in all of the condos automatically had their dimensions changed correspondingly!

If we click View > Slide Master and return to the three extra Masters we created (but never applied) with the logos in different positions, we should also see that their Title text color is still the blue we created originally—we never changed it to match our template using the custom Color Scheme.

In fact, the Bullet text color is still the hideous black that came with the original ugly white blank template. Remember, we simply created these Masters using the Create New Master button on the Slide Master view toolbar; only the first master has been applied to the actual three slides in our design template presentation.

In Figure 2-19, we can see our current situation, with the third master selected and visible in the preview window and its logo in the lower-left corner.

So just for the heck of it, let's work with this third master.

Let's pretend that your Human Resources director insisted that any slides dealing with his portion of the presentation needed a "totally different look and feel."

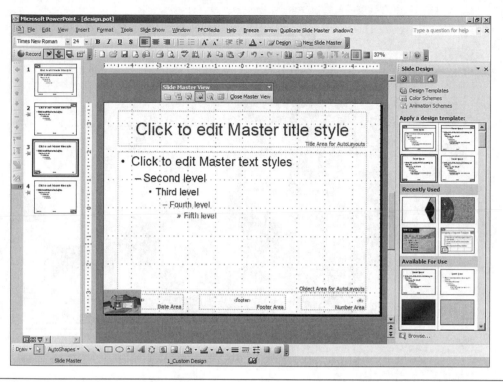

FIGURE 2-19 In this Slide Master view, we have created three new Masters, one of which is selected and previewed. Only the first master has actually been applied in the presentation itself.

You know better than to lock horns with the HR person. Your paycheck could get sent to Pago Pago.

So you go ahead and change the Title text color to a lighter lilac and the Bullet text to a lighter green, both reflected in the logo and loyal to the brand.

Then you use the Format > Background setting (in the Master view, *not in the Normal Slide view*), to change the background of this master to a dark gradient that resembles the older 35mm slides.

You select the Fill Effects in the Background panel and choose two dark colors for a two-color gradient, as shown in Figure 2-20.

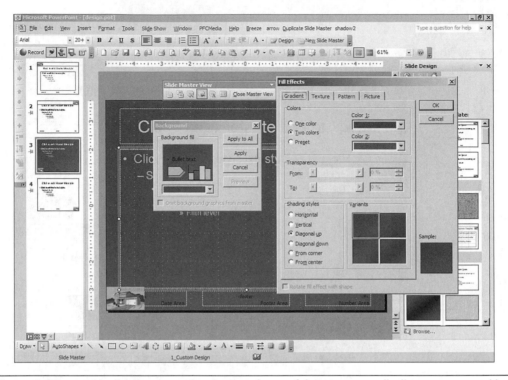

FIGURE 2-20   Manually changing the design of one of the Masters will allow you to quickly reformat a set of slides based on the master.

When you click Apply (not *Apply to All!*), this one radically different Master takes its place in your presentation in Slide Master view.

Just for good measure, let's conform it to the other applied master by giving it a solid light-colored line above the title and confining the bullet area so that it is anchored in the grid to allow for more space around it (see Figure 2-21).

Obviously, our users can always change its dimensions, but not if our Human Resources Director publishes the specification in a policy manual with the template!

So now if we click Close Master View, we can return to the presentation and add a new slide for Human Resources.

Notice in Slide Sorter view that it has the attributes of the main template and the only master that has been applied so far, but all of the possible Masters are still visible in the Slide Design Task Pane.

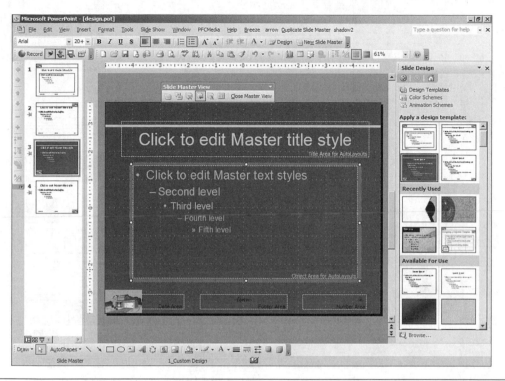

FIGURE 2-21   The Master is refined to conform to the main template, with a solid line above the title and a confined area for the bullets.

This is the situation in Figure 2-22, where we have selected our new Human Resources slide in Slide Sorter view, and in the Slide Masters representing the templates within our presentation in the Slide Design Task Pane, we are about to apply the new master to *Selected Slides*.

TIP In this presentation, we have only one slide representing the Human Resources Department. But if we had more, we could select them all by using CTRL+click in Slide Sorter view.

When Apply to Selected Slides is clicked, the presentation is transformed.

Now the Human Resources Department has its own unique look, based on the newly revised master.

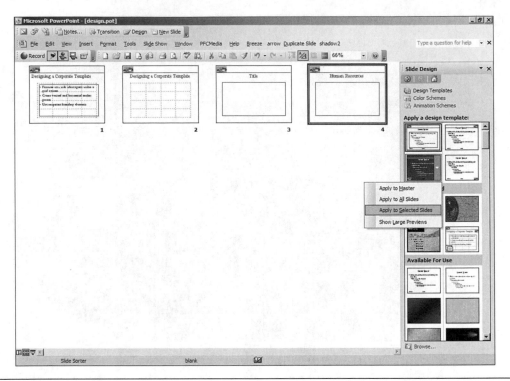

FIGURE 2-22   Slide Sorter view allows us to apply a specific template (based on the Master) to one or more selected slides.

If we return to Normal view, as shown in Figure 2-23, and add another Human Resources slide directly after the one with the new Master, it has the same attributes and is ready for revision.

Obviously, Masters are a powerful way to quickly reformat your presentation.

WHEN DON'T MASTERS WORK? If you have already specifically formatted an area of a slide and then attempt to override it by applying a Master, the affected area won't be revised according to the "blueprint." You would need to Reapply the Slide Layout to enforce the rules of the Master onto the slide (don't ask me why).

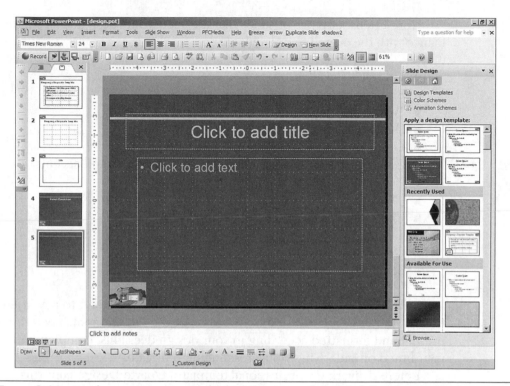

FIGURE 2-23 With a new master applied, slides created directly following it will take on its characteristics.

Final Design Touches

To the extent that you have gone down the path of a professionally designed set of templates for yourself or a client, you should note that your decisions should affect a number of elements, some of which we've now covered, and others that just make common sense.

Now that you understand Slide Masters, you realize that they are the visual blueprints for all of your slides so that different Masters can be used for different types of presentations. According to Nancy Duarte's final checklist, every Slide (and Title) master should conform to the guidelines of the grid and anchor principles and should be checked for the correct font.

Here is a list of types of slides that are specifically designed in conformance with the overall template look:

- Title slide—walk in
- Bullet slides—with and without subtitles
- Two column
- Quote and segue
- Logo format
- Graphic treatment (custom diagrams with shapes and accents)
- Color palette (based on Color Scheme)
- Chart style
- Image, media, and/or video use
- Tables
- Grid system (design slide)
- Screenshots (for training)

But wait. For a completely branded look, you also need to pay attention to your Notes and Handout Masters. All the key elements need to be present and formatted according to your design decisions, complementing your brand or underlying your presentation template.

Before delivering a professional template, Duarte Design confirms the RGB values in the Color Schemes, makes sure they're present in the correct area of the color palette, and deletes extraneous Color Schemes from the template(s).

Duarte makes life easier for her clients by making changes to PowerPoint's default settings, including turning off "Allow Fast Saves." You should examine your own default option settings to see how well they fit your work flow.

Then of course, they test the template by running it in Slide Show mode and check all print versions for glitches. The actual presentation needs to be legible when projected, and you probably need to keep your fingers crossed if you want a given projector to faithfully reproduce your carefully designed and branded colors.

If this is a big issue for you, check the setup hints in Chapter 8, "Delivering a Killer Presentation."

Hopefully, your logo and text will be sharp, clear, and legible whenever and wherever projected.

Losing the Extraneous Placeholders

We didn't really cover the other little placeholders in the Slide Master:

- Date and time
- Footer
- Slide number

What you need to remember is that these placeholders are *only there to format these items* (if you even want them in your slides).

To actually place information into these placeholders, you need to enter it by using View > Header and Footer.

If you want clean-looking slides, you can leave the areas blank, and if you like, you can also select and delete (press Delete) the placeholders from the Slide Master.

But what about the Bullet placeholder?

If you delete the Bullet placeholder from the Slide Master, can you somehow entice your users or inspire the creators of slides based on the cleaner Masters to use bullets wisely, if at all?

Sorry.

Any new slides based on the master will *always* have the default Title and Bullet *Layout*.

You need to talk to the Human Resources person and create a set of policies and recommendations that will enforce or inspire a policy against populating your slide shows with too many bullets or Title and Bullet slides.

The only sure way to eradicate bullets from a slide is to give it a clean Layout—Title only or blank. Generally, the Slide Layout Task Pane opens for every new slide you create by default; if it's not open, press CTRL+F1 to open it quickly, and (re)apply a Title only or blank layout to your slide, as shown in Figure 2-24.

Unfortunately, this is the only way to really get rid of the Bullet placeholder in your newly created slides.

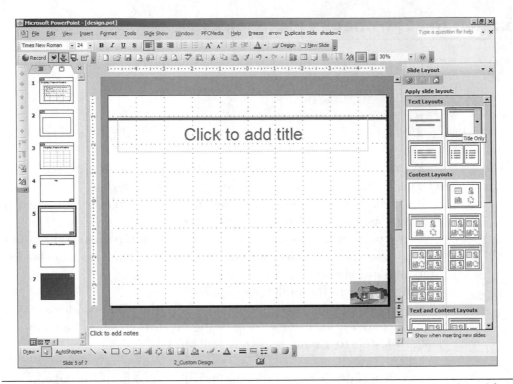

FIGURE 2-24 The only way to get rid of the blank Bullets placeholder is to (re)apply a different slide layout from the Slide Layout Task Pane.

What About Fonts?

Remember the two resources mentioned earlier for design? When I want to work with fonts, I go back to information that I have learned from attending sessions given by Julie Terberg, a frequent contributor to *Presentations Magazine*.

She divides fonts up into five families (no, not those kinds of families).

Serif fonts are considered very business-like and studious—they're the ones that have little extra design elements (or serifs) at the end of the letters. They originally came from the type or print world, and they don't always project very well.

Because we've been talking about creating a clean or more modern-looking design for our presentations, the fonts we might want to concentrate on are the sans serif family (without the design elements, hence cleaner). The good news is that these are also more legible than serif fonts, and as Julie says, "Many professionals consider sans serif fonts to be the best choice for presentation design."

Script fonts, or those resembling handwriting, are a better choice for special effects. Symbol fonts include elements not found in the common alphabet and are sometimes good for special bullets. Display fonts are similar to the WordArt styles, and if you were to design an entire presentation using them, you'd be lucky if the audience just walked out and didn't murder you.

In terms of digital fonts, there are Type 1 (or Postscript) fonts available for higher-end printing, but you really want to stick with the Windows TrueType fonts for PowerPoint and other types of projected presentations.

A rule of thumb is that the farther afield you go in terms of creative fonts, the more trouble you may get into. Besides the design issue, if you download and use an esoteric font and forget to embed it with the presentation, if the file is moved to a machine where that font is not registered, you can have a nightmare on your hands just before you go on. (See the Tip about using Replace Fonts and Adobe Type Manager later in this chapter.)

Figure 2-25 gives you some idea of the representative fonts available in PowerPoint in the Five Font Families.

Serif	Sans Serif	Script	Symbol	Display
Times New Roman	Arial	*Brush Script*	Συμβολ	**Broadway**
Garamond	Century Gothic	*Lucinda Hand*	Wingdings:	*Harlow Solid Italic*
Georgia	**Franklin Gothic**	*Edwardian*		Playbill
Lucinda Bright	Tahoma	*Freestyle*		Curlz MT
Palatino Linotype	Verdana	*Magneto Bold*		Jokerman

FIGURE 2-25 Julie Terberg's concept of the Five Font Families can help you choose the correct one for your presentation or make appropriate substitutions.

Be careful about using lots of different fonts. It's one of the best ways to really annoy an audience because lots of different and weird fonts can make a presentation illegible on the screen and hard to follow.

Having said that, additional fonts are available in MS Publisher, which is now part of many versions of MS Office.

NOTE Additional information about TrueType fonts along with an extensive font library is available at Microsoft Typography (http://www.microsoft.com/typography/default.mspx).

Another source for fonts is http://www.fontgarden.com.

Finally, you can use Google or any Internet search tool to locate more fonts with which to muck up your presentations.

To install a new font, just open Fonts in Control Panel, click the File menu, and choose Install New Font. If you downloaded it, browse to the drive and folder location and add the font to those already loaded on your system.

To figure out just which fonts are currently in use in a given presentation and modify them if necessary, just choose File > Properties > Contents (see Figure 2-26).

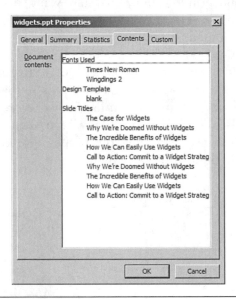

FIGURE 2-26 The Contents panel of Slide Properties lets you see the fonts in your presentation, as well as slide titles and design templates.

TIP A simple Replace Fonts dialog box is also available under the Format menu in PowerPoint that lets you quickly substitute one TrueType font for another throughout your presentation. Presentation professionals who work in "speaker-ready" situations at big events and need more functionality over lots of different fonts that may cause problems use ATM (Adobe Type Manager). This tool can help even if a troublesome "?" appears in the Replace Fonts dialog box by allowing you to quickly substitute an alternative font for a missing one.

Designing for Handouts

Although we will cover the strategies and techniques involved in printing Handouts (and Notes) in Chapter 8, we can and should start to think about these issues in the design phase.

Many of us are printer-challenged; we can't all go to Kinko's or down the hall to a high-speed color printer that will do full-color justice to our PowerPoint masterpieces.

Anticipating the device on which our slides, whether as Handouts or combined with notes pages, will be reproduced on paper is a good design concept to bear in mind from the outset of our presentation planning.

For this reason alone, I would submit that the clean and simple look is preferable for a professional presentation.

In the event that you require a colored background or more significant graphics as part of your overall design, your best bet is to fine-tune some of your main graphics objects in the event that you need to print in either grayscale or black and white.

Two levels of refinement are possible when converting color to grayscale or pure black and white. First, under the PowerPoint View menu, you can instantly transform the current version of your presentation to any of these modes by selecting View > Color/Grayscale.

Then, in any of these modes, you can right-click a graphical object that you intend to use in the presentation and whose design you want to faithfully preserve in the printed Handouts, as shown in Figure 2-27.

Then copy this object for use in the grayscale/handout version of the presentation.

Tweaking the grayscale or black and white settings will be of particular importance if you have chosen a darker (black) background for your slides and want to make sure that more subtle graphical objects are visible in your Handouts.

Going in the other direction, if you know going forward that you will need subtle diagrams in your slides, and they are destined for Handouts, you may want to avoid darker backgrounds and continue to choose cleaner slide designs.

Finally, if your logo will be appearing on all slides using the Slide Master, make sure that it is optimized for printing, and take care to ensure that other graphics and text are not covering up the logo.

This goes back to the grid system suggested by Nancy Duarte and the corresponding choices for placing a logo in the most remote corner of the set of slides with which you will be working.

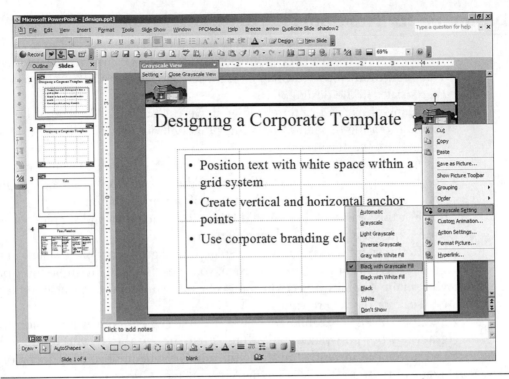

FIGURE 2-27 If you need to print in black and white or grayscale, you can fine-tune your graphics objects to optimize them for Handouts or notes.

Obviously, you can construct one slide set for presentation and another for printing and plan for that from the outset, but coordinating them and making sure that each is synchronized for the latest content may become a challenge.

Considering the ramifications of your design decisions in the planning and design phases can only help in terms of ensuring that both your onscreen and paper versions of the presentations do justice to your message and show you in the best possible light.

Using Third-Party Design Tools

There are so many resources for PowerPoint designers online and for purchase on disc that it would be impossible to list them all here. Font and design specialist Julie Terberg has a bunch of design-related resource sites linked at her site (www.terbergdesign.com).

Prepackaged templates are available all over the place, beginning at Microsoft's Assistance Center. The advantage to these is that they are true *.POT template files that when applied will overwrite your other formatting decisions as Slide Masters in the manner previously described.

Other "PowerPoint templates" are merely nice designs or images. You need to be aware that some of these just put a design into the main slide, while others are savvy enough to put it on a Background. In many cases, if such a picture is all that is supplied, there are no color-coordinated fonts or other elements included, and you will need to re-create them using the principles of the Slide Master.

Then there are companies that offer comprehensive solutions including extra clip media (video and animations) in complete design packages. These include

- **Crystal Graphics**—www.crystalgraphics.com
- **Digital Juice**—www.digitaljuice.com

We'll talk a lot more about using stock photographic images in our slides to communicate ideas and make analogies in Chapter 3, "Creating Dynamic Visuals," but if you want use an image for a customized template, there are two things to keep in mind.

If you put an image on the Slide Master (where it obviously ought to be in order to serve as a background on one or more slides), it is likely to overwhelm the other content that will be added to the slides themselves.

When you insert such an image, as we'll see in the case study at the end of the chapter, you can alter its transparency and then use the Order > Send to Back command on the Drawing toolbar to ensure that the other placeholders remain on the Slide Master and can be formatted in a manner complementary to the image itself.

A good source of templates will do all of this for you. Some that you download may not, so you should be aware of the distinction, and now you have the tools to make the necessary adjustments using Slide Master view in PowerPoint before re-saving the entire package as a template.

Dramatic 3D Animated Designs with OfficeFX

If you explore some of the offerings from Crystal Graphics, they have some animated video backgrounds that will dramatically change the look of your presentation.

But the company that is probably leading the way in this arena is Instant Effects, which publishes the OfficeFX Add-On for PowerPoint.

OfficeFX is probably best employed in scenarios where you have a dramatic live event, perhaps even with multiple screens. Users of this software have included some of the major automotive and pharmaceutical companies. Essentially, OfficeFX takes your PowerPoint design and transforms it into a real-time photorealistic 3D background, with motion graphics and 3D objects that you can move and turn as you present.

Using the toolbar that appears when you install OfficeFX, you can choose from an entirely new gallery of 3D backgrounds and instantly apply them to your slide show. It's an instant design transformation, taking an ordinary set of bullets and putting them into an entirely new environment, like the seascape shown in Figure 2-28, complete with a swimming dolphin and newly shaped bullets.

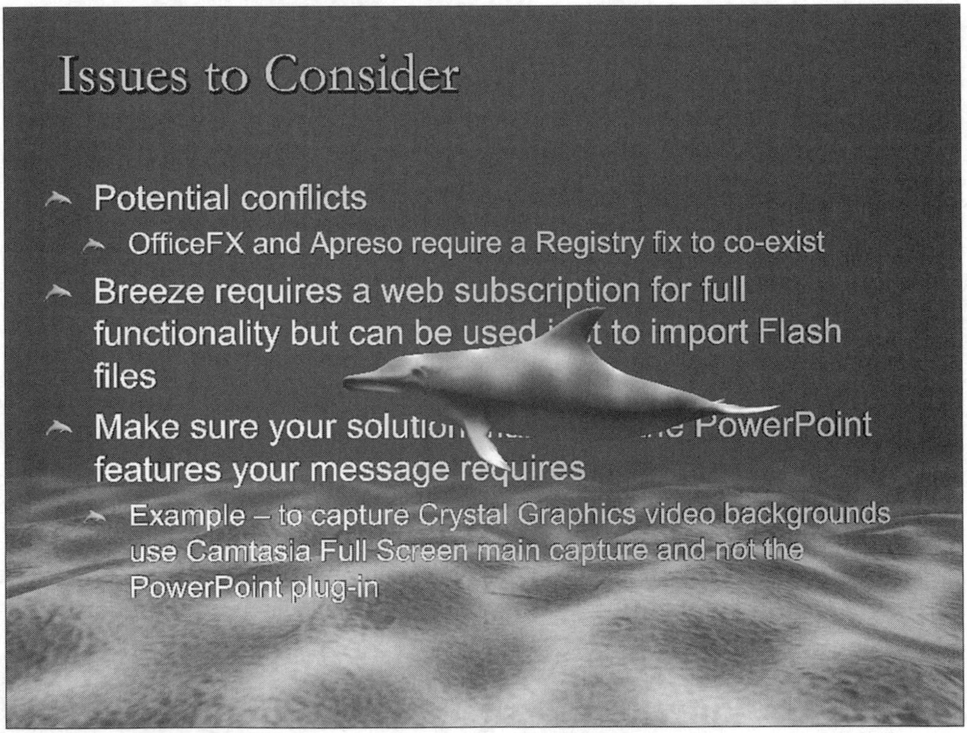

FIGURE 2-28   OfficeFX can instantly give your presentation a dramatic animated 3D design with motion graphics and moving objects.

It all takes place within the OfficeFX tabbed menu, where you first choose a theme from a gallery and then fine-tune it to work with your current content: titles, bullets, and graphical elements. Going slide by slide, you make subtle adjustment to the implementation of the theme as you move through your presentation, as shown in Figure 2-29.

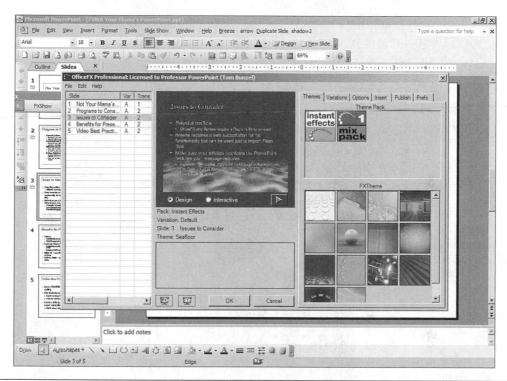

FIGURE 2-29 The OfficeFX menu lets you apply a theme and fine-tune its implementation throughout your presentation, either changing or preserving your text and graphics.

As of the time of writing, OfficeFX recognizes

- Drawing order of all content
- Text fonts, sizes, placement, colors, and bullets
- Content transparency, color, line effects, and bit map inclusion
- Custom animation effects, triggers, and timings for all content and media (with some limitations for Effect Options—currently with respect to sequentially introducing PowerPoint diagrams and charts)

2. IMPLEMENTING PROFESSIONAL DESIGN PRINCIPLES

- Audio and video
- Hyperlinks (within the same PowerPoint file—not externally)
- Slide Masters and Backgrounds (alternately with its own themes, which you determine within the interface)
- Auto Advance slide timings and Kiosk mode

By using the Colors tab of the Options panel, you can decide whether the color you've chosen in PowerPoint or the FXTheme will control the appearance of elements like text, shape fills, and lines.

3D objects created in Autodesk 3D Studio Max can also be imported into OfficeFX slides and manipulated in real time (see Figure 2-30).

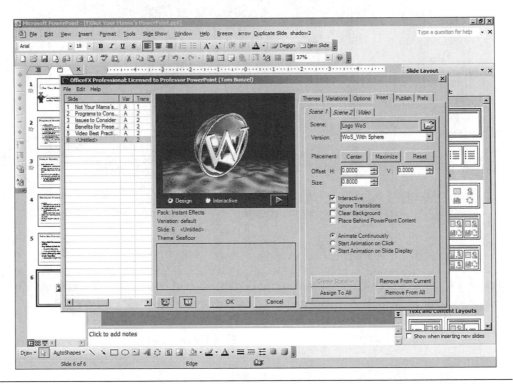

FIGURE 2-30   3D objects created in 3D Studio can be imported into and manipulated in OfficeFX slides.

OfficeFX also really shines with video, which we will cover in greater detail in Chapter 5, "Using Video and Audio Effectively."

But it's worth noting that OfficeFX can map video onto 3D objects and import and export video files as part of its functionality in the Publish tab. A video mapped onto a 3D object is shown in Figure 2-31.

FIGURE 2-31   OfficeFX can map video onto objects as they display in your slide.

Essentially, OfficeFX takes PowerPoint into the production or broadcast arena—printing slides is probably less important to an OfficeFX user than outputting them to video and perhaps posting the video to a web server.

Using the program is obviously an important initial design decision—for one thing, using OfficeFX at a show does require some preparation in terms of hardware. You will need a very powerful graphics card (64MB of video RAM is the minimum recommended) and some other software modifications. More and more laptops are being released that are OfficeFX ready.

It also involves something of a learning curve. Although the menu is straightforward, getting the graphics to perform just the way you want will take you a bit beyond ordinary PowerPoint.

The complete set of OfficeFX hardware and software requirements as well as purchase options and other information can be found at http://www.instanteffects.com.

Here are two things to keep in mind when using OfficeFX:

- Save your OfficeFX presentation within the OfficeFX menu as a separate file.
- Practice presenting from within OfficeFX to take advantage of its capabilities.

You can maintain a prior version of the unaltered PowerPoint presentation to return to in the event that you do not want to use OfficeFX's design decisions later on.

Looking Ahead: PowerPoint 2007

By the time this book is published, a new version of PowerPoint will be available, and some of you may be either using it already or contemplating its adoption. Based on the beta version available at the time this was written, there were several design elements in the new version that are worth noting in terms of producing clean and dynamic presentations.

New Layouts: Setting a Default

The Layout area for new slides has been dramatically streamlined, and perhaps the best news is that creating a new slide will no longer necessitate beginning with a Title and Bullets layout with bullet placeholders.

You can select any layout as a new default, and it will be applied to your new slides, or you can create your own layout to add to the layout gallery and use in subsequent slides.

In Figure 2-32, you can see that a simple Title only layout has been selected in the Layout gallery and is now the default layout for all subsequent slides added to the presentation.

Themes and Colors Enhance Design Templates

Although PowerPoint 2007 will support the older design templates that came with previous versions, and the Color Scheme scenario just described still holds, the central design element for formatting groups of slides is now called a Theme.

Themes are composed of design choices, many of them much nicer and cleaner than the older design templates, colors, and effects. Like the older Design Templates, the new PowerPoint Theme puts an entirely new look onto selected slides, but instead of overpowering them with lots of different graphics and backgrounds, themes appear to be more subtle and clean, as shown in Figure 2-33.

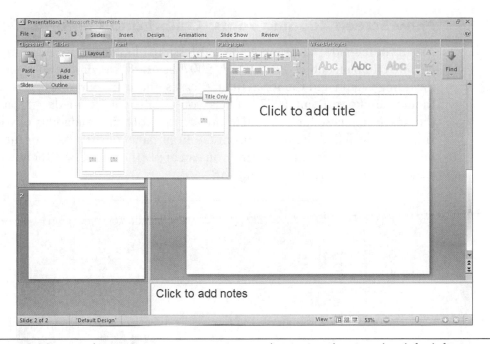

FIGURE 2-32   Any layout, even one you create and save, can become the default for new slides in PowerPoint 2007.

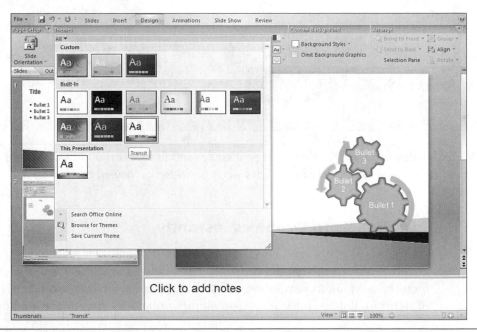

FIGURE 2-33   PowerPoint design decisions in Office2007 will be centered on Themes, which are collections of fonts, colors, effects, and backgrounds that provide a cleaner, more polished look.

New Screen Reading Fonts: Calibri and Cambria

As part of the move to cleaner, more professional-looking slides that can be instantly implemented, PowerPoint 2007 has new screen-friendly fonts, including Calibri and Cambria. In most cases, these are part of the existing themes in PowerPoint 2007, but as you create your own designs and themes, using these fonts should improve the clarity and readability of your slides. You will find the new fonts in the Font panel of the new user interface, as shown in Figure 2-34, and you can apply them and save them with a theme that you create on your own.

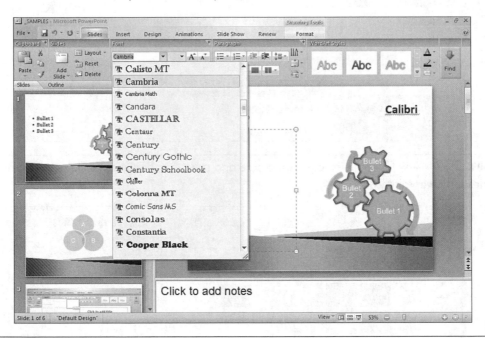

FIGURE 2-34   PowerPoint 2007's new screen-friendly fonts like Calibri and Cambria are designed to enhance the readability of slides when projected or viewed on a computer screen.

Turn Bullets to Graphics Instantly

Although we're going to cover the creation of dynamic visuals in the next chapter, it's worth mentioning here that PowerPoint 2007 enables this technique within its new interface by allowing the user to quickly turn a set of written bullets into a corresponding SmartArt graphic or diagram.

Opening the new diagram gallery with bullets selected can instantly turn the bullet text into any of a host of new diagrams, including Venn diagram, as shown in Figure 2-35.

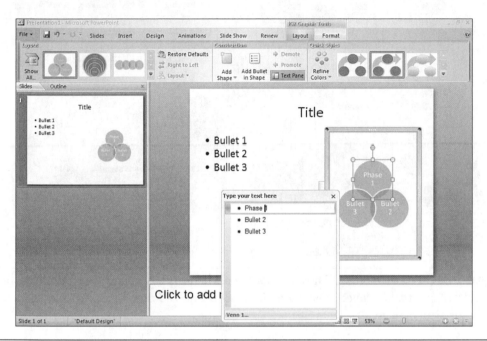

FIGURE 2-35   PowerPoint 2007 encourages the use of visual analogies by allowing the user to transform ordinary bullets into corresponding diagrams from a new gallery.

Use Enhanced Design Effects

Although making a diagram or set of graphics stand out in a professional way with high-end 3D effects or shadows used to involve third-party tools, the new Effects galleries in PowerPoint allow the user to apply glow and bevel effects to the diagrams or graphics they create, as shown in Figure 2-36.

Many of the design techniques that we will cover in the next chapter will be streamlined and enabled in a much easier way in PowerPoint 2007.

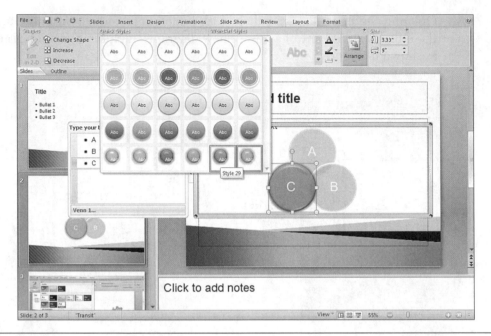

FIGURE 2-36 PowerPoint 2007 has a gallery of new effects including glows, shadows, and bevels that can be fine-tuned, saved, and instantly previewed and applied to new diagrams and graphical objects.

Case Study: Creating Design Templates for a Travel Agency

You are the presentation specialist for a large web conglomerate that has just acquired TravelTime, a full-service travel agency. As part of the acquisition, there will be any number of presentations to be developed for the top executives to take on a road show, for human resources managers to use in training the in-house staff, and for sales and marketing to use as they visit vendors.

The TravelTime executives who have been absorbed into the conglomerate come for their first visit to your office and bring with them the TravelTime presentation template, which they have been using for a while, as shown in Figure 2-37.

They're excited because they've figured out how to put the picture into a rectangle AutoShape and reduce its transparency.

"See, it doesn't really overwhelm the whole slide," the President of TravelTime says. "What do you think?"

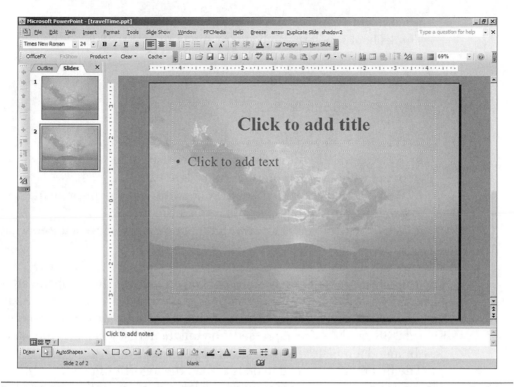

FIGURE 2-37 A common PowerPoint template would use a picture in the background of the text placeholders.

Before you respond, here is the new corporate logo for TravelTime that your major advertising firm has designed (see Figure 2-38).

FIGURE 2-38 This more professional-looking logo is what should be used in the new presentation templates.

What might your response be in this situation?
Think about it before you begin reading the next section.

Key Issues to Consider

You might respond as follows:

- Have we reviewed the overall website of our company?
- We've been asked to redesign the template to fit within our overall brand without compromising your identity.
- We've actually invested some time with a high-power marketing firm to redesign your logo and rethink the brand.
- Why don't you let us work with the elements we have and see what we come up with?

The executives aren't entirely sure, but they're new in the company after all, so they're will to see what develops. Before they leave, you show them the new corporate logo that the advertising agency has designed (refer to Figure 2-38), and they're impressed. You tell them that you'll provide some new branded templates for their division in a week.

The first thing you need to do is to load the logo TIF file into an image editing program and analyze some of the key colors, using the color picker to determine their RGB values:

- The dark brown from the spyglass has an RGB of 93 51 29.
- A darker blue from the map is 94 123 139.
- The gold from the globe and spyglass is 140 116 82.

Then you resize the logo to fit into a slide set so that it won't be overwhelmed. You do this in the image editing program by taking the width and height dimensions down to 15% of their original size and maintaining the original *aspect ratio*. (The aspect ratio of an image is the relationship between its height and width. If one of these dimensions is altered without a corresponding change to the other to keep the ratio constant, the image becomes distorted. Better image editing programs have settings when you are changing dimensions to keep the aspect ratio constant.)

In a blank white slide, you enter the Slide Master view and resize the Title and Bullet placeholders so that they fit into a smaller area to increase the white space. You remove the footer, slide number, and date placeholders and line up the title and bullet placeholders by using the Align Left command under the Order panel of the Draw button of the Drawing toolbar (see Figure 2-39).

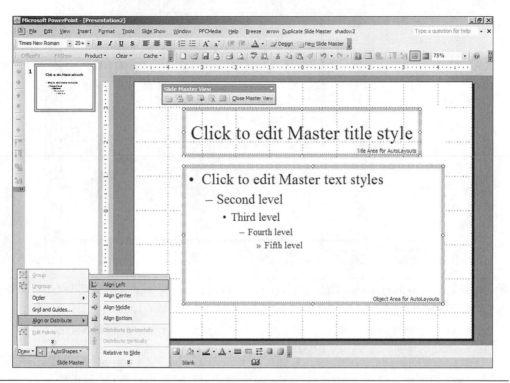

FIGURE 2-39 Clean up the Slide Master by creating and realigning smaller placeholders and removing extraneous placeholders.

Thinking about the logo and its placement for the corporate executive template, you decide to offset it with a thick blue vertical bar. You keep the dark line color but change the Fill color of the bar to be identical to the blue that you selected out of the corporate logo, as shown in Figure 2-40.

Now you bring in the resized logo TIF image by clicking Insert > Picture from File (still in the Slide Master view) and line it up with the colored bar as shown in Figure 2-41.

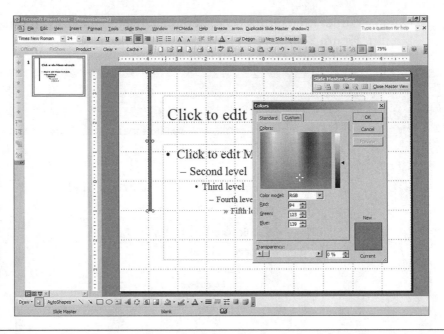

FIGURE 2-40 Use the Custom Colors tab of the Fill color tool to match the RGB values of the corporate logo.

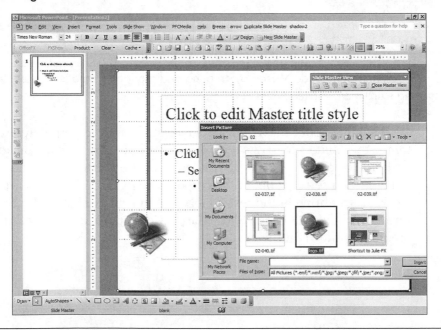

FIGURE 2-41 Inserting the logo into the Slide Master will make it part of the uniform look in the template.

For the Title and Bullet text color, you once again use the Custom tab, this time in the Text Color tool, to match the dark brown from the logo. See Figure 2-42.

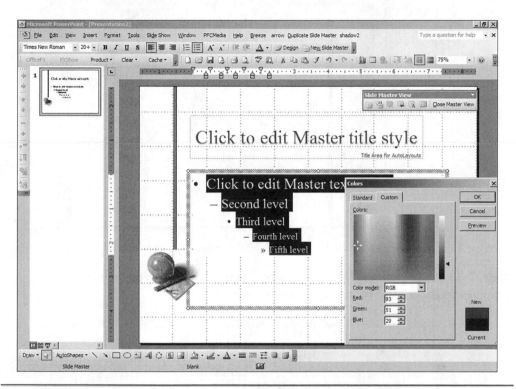

FIGURE 2-42 Refine the text colors in the new template according to the color values of the logo.

You add a Title Master and make it unique by extending the vertical bar all the way to the bottom and adding a larger version of the logo in another part of the slide, resizing the placeholders once again within the grid to allow for more white space, as shown in Figure 2-43.

After leaving the Slide Master and checking the results with a new slide, you enter the Color Schemes Task Pane and use the Custom Color Tab to apply logo-centric colors to other elements in a new Custom Color Scheme based on the slide, including Text and Line colors, Title colors, and Accents, as shown in Figure 2-44.

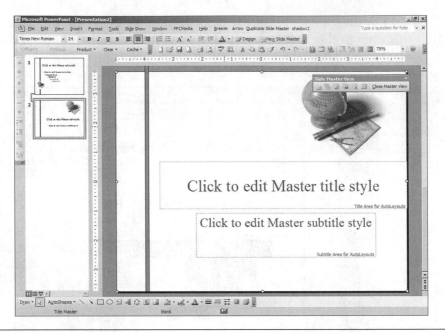

FIGURE 2-43 A unique Title Master can make use of a larger version of the logo and slightly different configuration of the same elements.

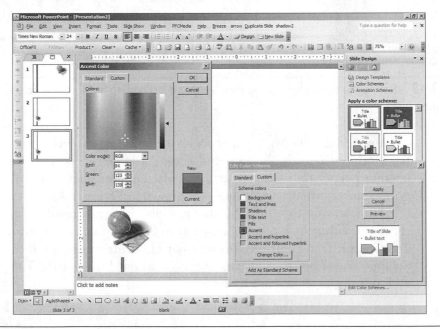

FIGURE 2-44 A new custom Color Scheme will let you use the specific RGB color values for the various slide elements.

Then you exit the Options panel and make sure that you apply the new Custom Color Scheme to all of the slides in the presentation you just created. To round out the set, you add a Quote Slide (without a title) and format the quote box and author reference to coordinate with the template, as shown in Figure 2-45.

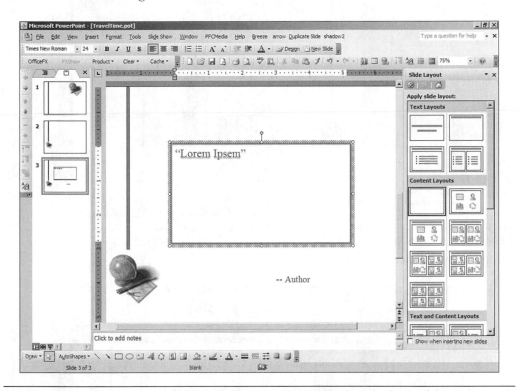

FIGURE 2-45 Different types of slides like a quote slide will adopt the look of the Color Scheme; but they can also be individually refined for their respective types of content.

Just to be sure, you change a layout in a slide for a chart and open a generic column chart to see how it reflects the overall design and look. It looks like Figure 2-46.

Then you save the new presentation as a template file. And then you make slight modifications in the template for HR and sales (see Figure 2-47), saving each as a different template (*.POT) file.

When you bring back the TravelTime executives and present the new templates, they have the usual comments but can see that the new clean look will work as part of their new corporate structure, and they agree to implement the design throughout the new division of the conglomerate.

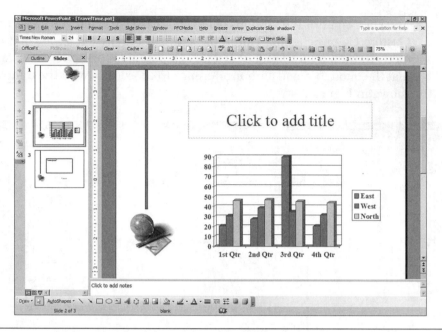

FIGURE 2-46 With the custom Color Scheme applied, all charts and diagrams will also reflect the overall design decisions.

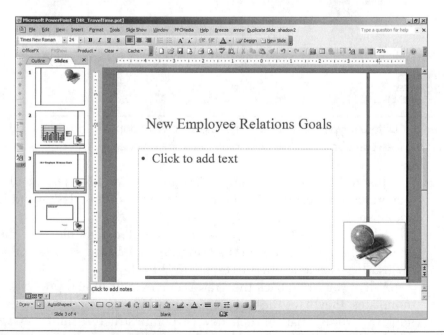

FIGURE 2-47 With some modification, different branches of the company can have their own design looks within the overall brand.

Only one issue may remain: The size of the logo on certain slides may overwhelm the use of images and pictures to tell a story. You agree to make a special picture and diagram slide within the template for the various divisions, where only the solid bars are present, to accentuate any use of images. We'll see how that might work in the next chapter.

Summary

Because such a great part of a successful presentation is its visual effectiveness, in this chapter we picked the brains of some design experts and applied their concepts in PowerPoint and some related programs.

Not everyone has a professional eye, and that's why we analyzed the concepts of using space and branding and created a different template for different corporate divisions and objectives.

Colors are a key component in any design, and we need to understand the various parts of the Slide Design Task Pane, including Design Templates and Color Schemes, and how they interrelate to design properly. We also saw how multiple Masters could help us differentiate parts of our presentation and reformat sections automatically.

The main elements of creating an effective design include

- Thinking like a designer
- Implementing a brand strategy
- Using Color Schemes to fine-tune color choices
- Saving designs as Design Template files
- Choosing simple and effective fonts

We also covered the essential aspects of designing for Handouts and mentioned some third-party design tools. We noted that many design changes will be on the horizon in the next version of PowerPoint and provided a brief preview of some of them.

Now it's time to move from the overall look of the presentation to the individual message components and begin the really worthwhile task of creating individual slides and concepts that visually communicate our most important ideas.

Resources

There is an entire industry devoted to supplementing PowerPoint, and a lot of it is geared to the overall design process. We sprinkled most of the major players in the field throughout the text of the chapter, but here are some other resources that will enable you to manage design elements (like pictures) and your visual elements more effectively.

- Ulead PhotoAlbum—http://www.ulead.com (part of PhotoImpact package)
- ThumbsPlus—http://www.cerious.com
- Desktop Search—Copernic—http://www.copernic.com/
- http://www.visualthesaurus.com/
- Canto Cumulus—http://www.canto.com/
- Presentation Librarian—http://www.accent-technologies.com/

CHAPTER 3

CREATING DYNAMIC VISUALS

The vast majority of PowerPoint presentations are used for speaker support. In Chapter 1, "Planning an Effective Presentation," we discussed the different ways we can craft a talk to appeal to different senses, and hopefully you now have a better idea of the types of messages that will be most effective.

But we still want to use PowerPoint and other tools to enhance this message, and the most dramatic impact we can have is probably visual.

THINKING AHEAD As we work with the visual examples in this chapter, you may want to keep extra copies of the files handy to continue to work with them in the coming chapters; specifically, although we will create static images in this part, in Chapter 4, "Secrets of Animation and Navigation," we will use some of these same elements in animation and navigation sequences.

Using Words as Pictures

One of the best ways to illustrate this point (notice the visual concept) is to have some fun with words apart from their use in titles and bullets.

This idea is not my own. It was inspired by someone known as a "PowerPoint virtuoso," whose presentations are legendary and whose work was first introduced to me through Cliff Atkinson's Sociable Media website.

Larry Lessig is an attorney specializing in intellectual property and is a well-known gadfly in his quest to propound the virtues of open source and to confound the copyright and trademark endeavors of major rights holders. Aside from that, his unique PowerPoint style is worth a look, particularly in the context of trying out new ideas and enhancing communication.

NOTE You can find Cliff Atkinson's interview with Lessig at http://www.
sociablemedia.com/articles_lessig.htm and a sample of his work at http://
randomfoo.net/oscon/2002/lessig/.

Without dwelling on this simple concept, let's create some slides that
we can use to convey a very important modern message.

First, let's create the ordinary Title and Bullet text slide that has graced
or plagued the PowerPoint presentation from the beginning, as shown in
Figure 3-1.

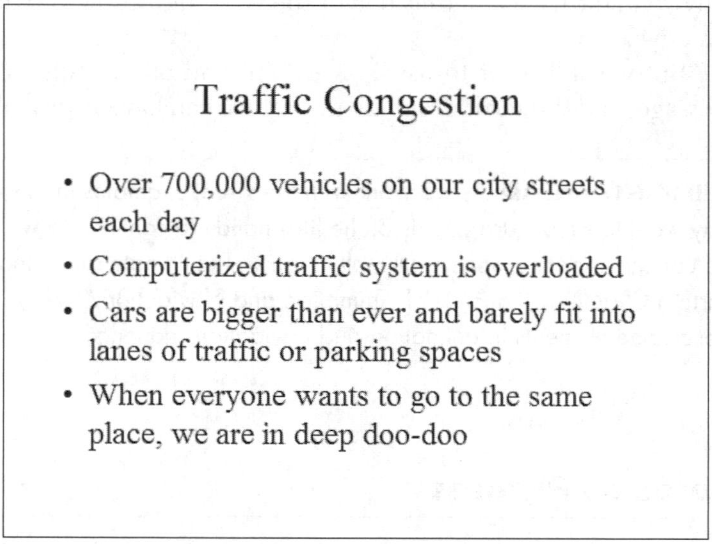

<h2 style="text-align:center;">Traffic Congestion</h2>

- Over 700,000 vehicles on our city streets
  each day
- Computerized traffic system is overloaded
- Cars are bigger than ever and barely fit into
  lanes of traffic or parking spaces
- When everyone wants to go to the same
  place, we are in deep doo-doo

FIGURE 3-1   The common Title and Bullet slide uses language in its most basic form as
though the medium were a book or article.

There are a few bad things that can happen with this slide.

At the top of the list, because the speaker himself (or herself) may start
to fall asleep at the first or second bullet, he or she may well begin reading
it from the screen.

Although the facts themselves may be incredibly important and relevant, if they are shown onscreen at all, they ought to be introduced in a creative and more dramatic way.

Let's try a few different techniques.

If you've looked at the Lessig example online, you've seen the power of a single important word when it is flashed on the screen and used in context with a powerful message.

Let's try it with our example. Take a look at Figure 3-2.

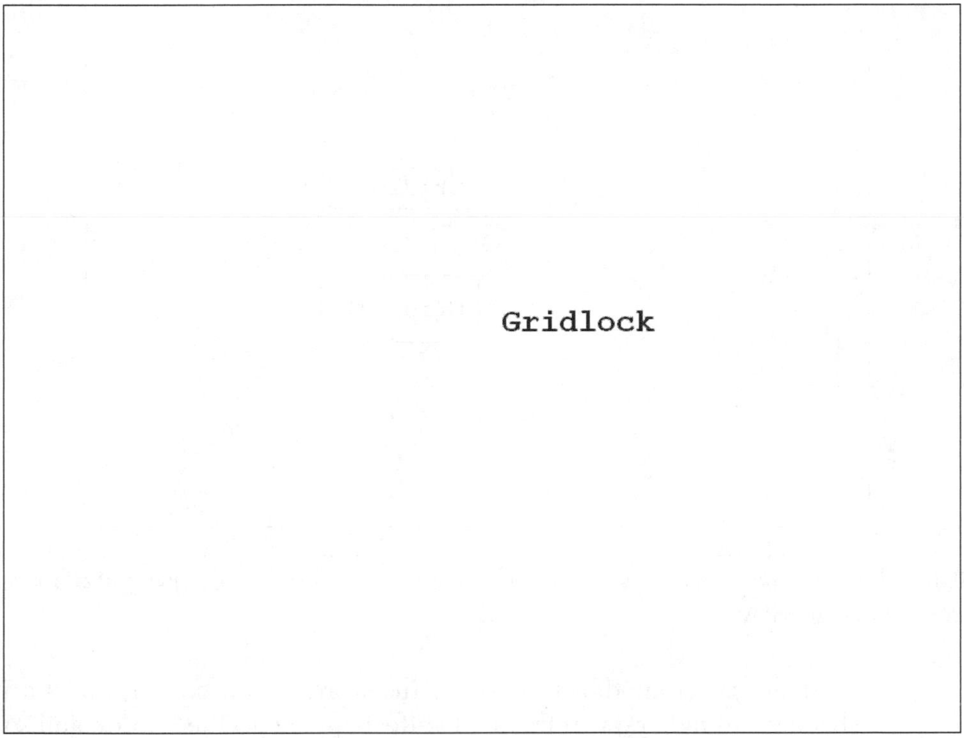

Gridlock

FIGURE 3-2 A single word shown strategically on the screen can convey different levels of meaning.

Imagine this word on the screen with a powerful speaker who has something important to say about traffic congestion. Imagine the power if he told a story about an ambulance that couldn't make it or a fire that blazed unabated because equipment was late to the scene.

By using a *text box* instead of a regular title or bullet, you have the freedom to place this word image anywhere on the slide.

You can right-click the text box and select AutoFormat to give it a border, as you can see in Figure 3-3. The text box at the top has the border as part of its formatting.

The text box below it has a rectangle added to it without a Fill color. By selecting the rectangle and not the text box, a subtle shadow has been applied to only the rectangle. (Applying a shadow to the text box puts the shadow behind the text as well, which detracts from its effect.)

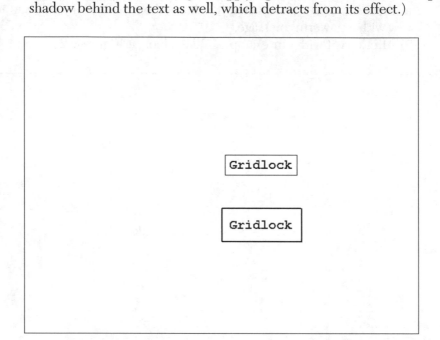

FIGURE 3-3   A bit more emphasis can be added to a simple text box by giving it a border and adding a shadow.

Here is yet another way to use the word with a border, but not just shadow, but rather a wireframe 3D effect applied to the border, and some simple Connector AutoShapes added to the mix.

The message in Figure 3-4 is not as stark as the previous versions, but it does seem to suggest a systematic approach to our problem or a more scientific bent.

We will get into the mechanics of creating these various elements when we get more deeply into diagrams, but for now, be aware that all of the tools for accomplishing this are on the Drawing toolbar docked at the bottom of your screen. We'll go over some of the specific techniques later on.

But let's continue with our visual word exercise and go in another direction, again suggested by Larry Lessig. Here is yet another way to convey the concept (see Figure 3-5).

Here, the Courier font has been colored white and placed on a black background. When strategically used in contrast to ordinary types of slides, the impact is quite dramatic.

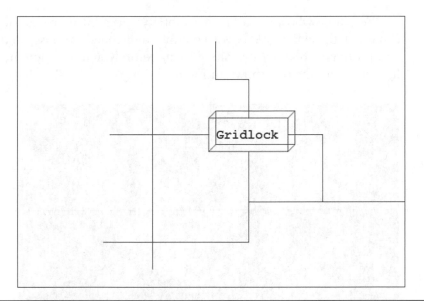

FIGURE 3-4 Visual elements like a 3D wireframe and Connector AutoShapes can provide more context and meaning for the text box.

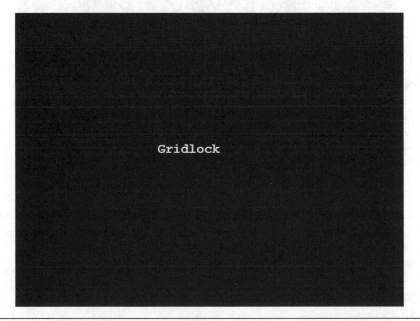

FIGURE 3-5 Using a white Font color on a black background gives the word an even deeper level of meaning.

For those who want a bit less subtlety and a bit more literalism, you can break the letters of the word out into individual text boxes and use the green Rotate tool to twist some of them before you move them into a configuration like the one shown in Figure 3-6.

FIGURE 3-6   Putting the letters of a word into individual text boxes and placing them strategically conveys a bit more literal meaning for the concept.

You can get a bit more imaginative and still continue to work with the meaning of a single word by copying the text box into a more comprehensive diagram, as shown in Figure 3-7.

COPYING AND MOVING THE TEXT BOXES To create this kind of effect quickly, you would create a single text box, add the empty rectangle, and use SHIFT+click to select both. On the Drawing toolbar, click Draw > Group > Group—which makes this a single object.

To quickly copy this shape, you can obviously press CTRL+C when it's selected or hold down the CTRL key and drag out copies or "clones" of the text box.

Finally, you can use the Draw > Align and Distribute command on the Drawing toolbar to straighten out the shapes and space them equally. Or, for this scenario, you might want to accentuate the chaos by also skewing them with the green Rotate tool.

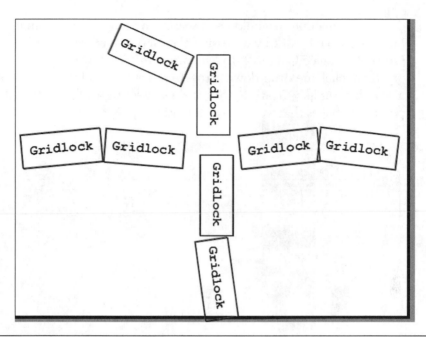

FIGURE 3-7 Expanding the concept into a more literal diagram may or may not enhance the overall effect of your message.

Which (if any) of these techniques you might actually use would obviously depend on the venue, the topic, all of the issues we addressed in Chapter 1, and your own personal style. This exercise is only meant to demonstrate the tremendous range of creativity that is possible within PowerPoint without even going beyond the use of a single word.

Now that hopefully we've got your attention, let's go beyond words and language to the really powerful stuff—images.

Using Pictures Instead of Words

Having played a bit with the word image concept, let's get busy using real pictures.

Probably the best way to dramatize the concept of "gridlock" would be to show it. It would be nice if you had the images you needed available on your hard disk; it is probably more likely that you would need to acquire them—either from prints that you already have or perhaps with a digital camera.

Your other option would be to search an image library online. Let's see how that would work by accessing the Clip Art Library at the Microsoft Office Assistance Center (http://snipurl.com/MSClipArt).

If we click the drop-down arrow to select Search for Photos and put in a search term like "Traffic," we get three web pages full of thumbnails of potential images that we can use. See Figure 3-8.

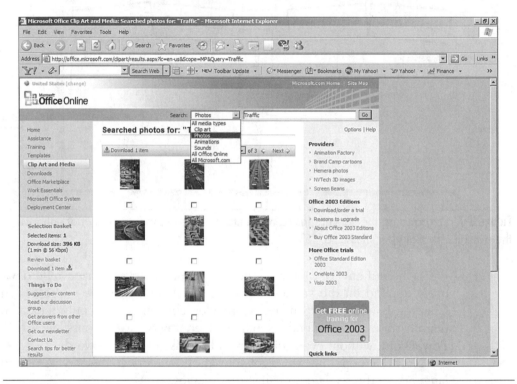

FIGURE 3-8   Putting in a search term on MS Office Clip Art and selecting photos can help us quickly acquire pictures for our slides.

We can quickly check off several potential pictures, add them to our Selection Basket, and click to download them and open the files. As Figure 3-9 shows, after the files are downloaded, you are prompted to open a single reference file.

We can repeat the process with a second term or just open the downloaded file—in this case from Microsoft Office, it's a clip art *.MPF file. When we click to open the file, the Microsoft Clip Organizer opens up, and we see thumbnails of the files we downloaded.

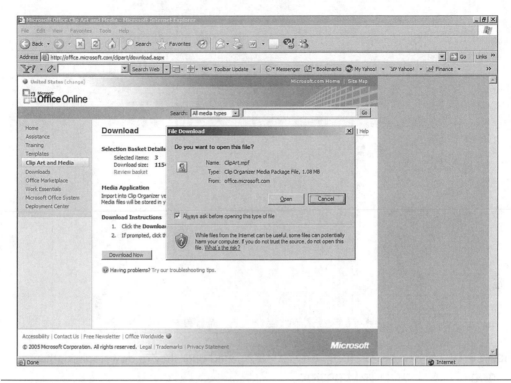

FIGURE 3-9   After selecting several thumbnails from a clip art library, we can download them as a group.

If you examine the Clip Organizer, you will see that it is set up in "Collections," and one of the folders under Collections is called Downloaded Clips. These are then organized into subcategories.

The nice thing about the Organizer is that you can click the drop-down arrow beside any thumbnail and copy the entire image to the clipboard, as shown in Figure 3-10.

Then it's easy to open a new PowerPoint slide and click Edit > Paste (or press CTRL+V) to bring the image into the slide.

You may find that some images dwarf the slide or need to be moved. In the example shown in Figure 3-11, the image was enormous, so to zoom out we changed the View from the drop-down menu to 33%, clicked to select the image, and dragged in a corner to resize the picture within the slide.

Here we left enough room for a title as well. You might find that the image speaks very well for itself and no title is needed.

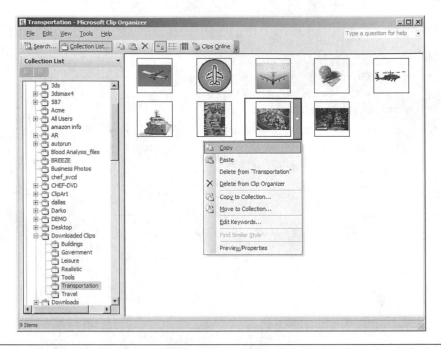

FIGURE 3-10   When Microsoft clip art files are opened after they're downloaded, they are cataloged in Microsoft Clip Organizer.

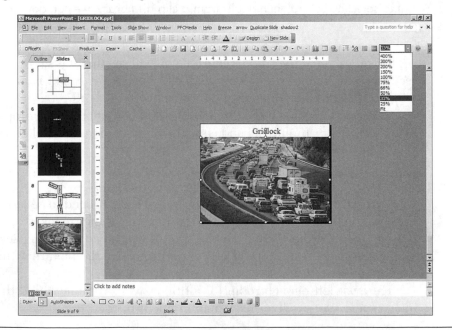

FIGURE 3-11   When the image is pasted from the Clip Organizer into the slide, it may still need to be moved or resized.

Now you have an image that will be displayed full-screen that you can use to make your point beyond words and hopefully appeal to the emotions and sensibilities of the audience.

Thinking in Analogies

The imported figure (Figure 3-11) is dramatic, but once again it is literal. Truly effective communication frequently involves going a bit deeper.

Let's think about what else this same picture could be used to represent besides what it actually shows—traffic at a standstill.

If you're in the computer field, it might be *network traffic*. How about using this same image to dramatize an inadequate network before your solution was implemented?

Remember our planning process in Chapter 1 and the idea of identifying the pain. The pain shown graphically in this image can apply to many different situations.

Let's imagine you are in the medical or dental field and you are selling a system that allows more patients to get care more efficiently. You might use this same image to show the inevitable result of inefficiency in the system you propose to improve.

If we go into the motivational field, we could once again use this very same photo to symbolize being stuck, following the path of the masses, or any one of many different concepts that will dramatize the point we want to make.

A good presenter will want to have a library of powerful images that can be used and reused for different situations. If you are in a specific field, chances are pictures of this kind can be gathered over the course of many projects and then be reapplied in other situations.

So, in practical terms, how is this accomplished?

Image Files v. Clip Organizer

Remember that the actual file we opened was a Microsoft *.MPF file. In reality, this isn't an image or picture file at all.

What do we mean by that?

If you're working with pictures, you actually are storing digital data in a specific file format that the computer's operating system recognizes as an image file.

Computer programs such as Adobe PhotoShop at the high end, Adobe PhotoShop Elements (which is bundled with many digital cameras), Ulead PhotoImpact, and a host of other image *editing tools* recognize scores of image file formats that they can manipulate, edit, and save.

PowerPoint is not really an image editing tool (although we'll take a look at its Picture Toolbar for simple editing tasks later); it mainly projects pictures as part of its storytelling capability within a slide show.

Still, these pictures need to be acquired somewhere, as we just did online using the Microsoft Clip Art site. And then they need to be stored.

To illustrate this point, let's locate the images we downloaded using the Microsoft Clip Art site on our computer. Remember that the Clip Organizer is just a catalog or reference library.

If we right-click one of the images we downloaded in the Clip Organizer and choose Properties, the Properties window (see Figure 3-12) will reveal exactly where the underlying file itself is located.

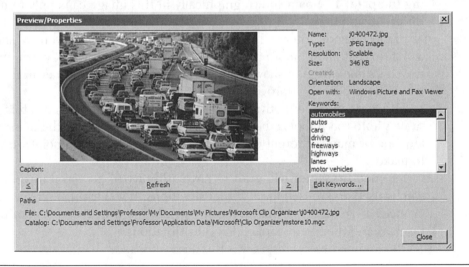

FIGURE 3-12   Right-clicking to reveal the properties of an image in the Clip Organizer shows us where the actual file is located.

The downloaded files are actually within the My Pictures folder inside the My Documents folder, in a subfolder called Microsoft Clip Organizer. This particular image file is actually named j0400472.JPG. (What a useful, descriptive name.)

Those of you who have worked with digital cameras, created websites, or sent pictures as email attachments know that the *.JPG image format is a very common and useful *compressed* format that preserves the quality of an image while reducing its file size. Although it can be viewed in a web browser, it can also work well in a PowerPoint slide, as we see here.

But let's locate the actual file. If we open our My Documents folder and drill down to the Microsoft Clip Organizer subfolder, we can click the drop-down arrow in the View menu and select the option to see all of the images as thumbnails.

Figure 3-13 shows the actual image files we downloaded.

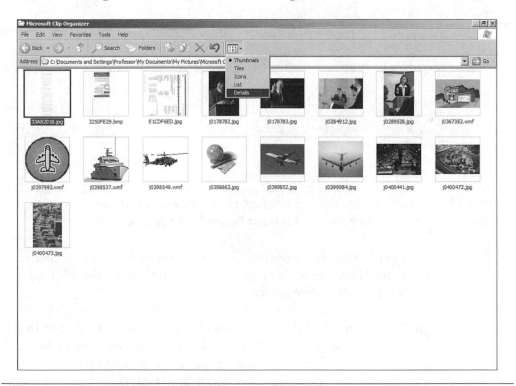

FIGURE 3-13 The actual files referenced by the Microsoft Clip Organizer are located in a subfolder inside the My Documents folder.

If we select the Details option under the View menu (see Figure 3-14), we can see the actual file sizes of the downloaded files, and we can click the column headings to sort them by properties like size, filename, or date modified.

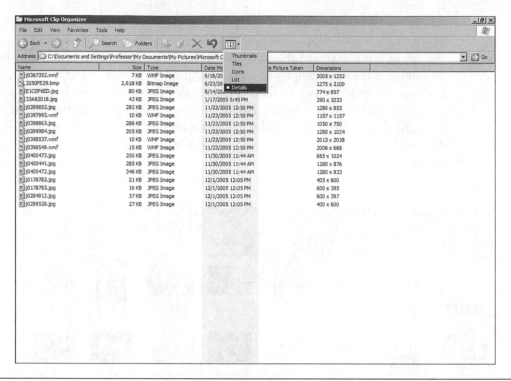

FIGURE 3-14 Viewing the downloaded files by their Details lets us sort them by various properties, and also import them with the Insert Picture from File command.

Although using the Microsoft Clip Organizer to download or search for files on the Microsoft website is nice, knowing where the files actually reside is extremely important for several reasons:

- The files are valuable and should be backed up. Remember that in our earlier scenario, we thought about storing our presentation files in a desktop folder for safekeeping and organization. Now we can also back up our download or acquisition folders for scanned images or those acquired from a digital camera.
- The image files can be searched and moved around. Although the Clip Organizer is a good way to locate them by thumbnail and key terms, as we see in Figure 3-14 they can also be found by other parameters like their size, filename, or date when modified or saved.

■ The files can be reused in other presentations or applications. Knowing where they are located is invaluable in bringing them into other PowerPoint files, editing them with an image editor, or putting them into collateral material (like a Word brochure).

The key point is that there are two ways to bring images into Power-Point.

As we've seen, you can use the Clip Organizer in PowerPoint or click Insert Clip Art on the Drawing toolbar or in a Content Layout within a slide. This opens the Clip Art Task Pane, which lets you search through the Clip Organizer and use a drop-down arrow to insert an image directly into your slide (see Figure 3-15).

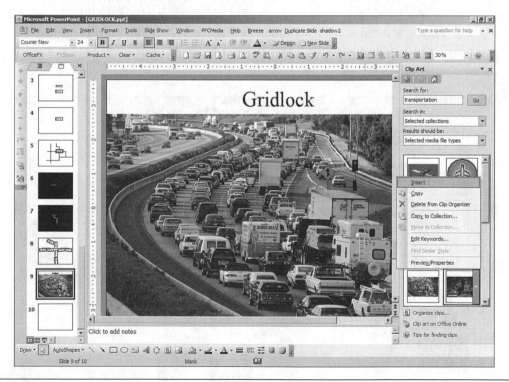

FIGURE 3-15 The Clip Art Task Pane searches through the Collections of the Clip Organizer.

3. CREATING DYNAMIC VISUALS

TIP After you have cataloged your media in the Clip Organizer, you might find it helpful to turn off (uncheck) the search through Web Collections when you use the Clip Art search feature. Otherwise your search may be slowed down by a web search when you already have the content you're looking for locally. Just select the drop-down arrow under Search In > Selected collections and clear the Web Collections option.

Accessing Images from File Folders

But the other option may be more useful if you have your own images that you have either scanned from prints or downloaded from a digital camera. They will be in a folder, very likely in My Documents\My Pictures or another subfolder, and you would bring them into a slide by clicking Insert > Picture > From File (see Figure 3-16). This brings up the Insert Picture dialog box where you can locate the actual image file to insert into a PowerPoint slide.

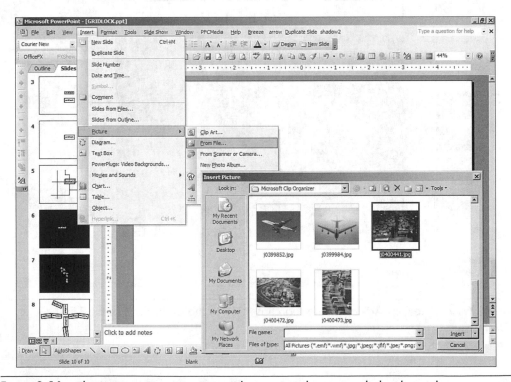

FIGURE 3-16   The Insert > Picture > From File command opens a dialog box where you can select an actual image file directly.

If you click the Files of Type drop-down arrow, you can get an idea of the many different types of image file formats that actually exist and that PowerPoint can accommodate.

FIGURE 3-17 PowerPoint can handle a lot of file formats besides *.JPG. Uncompressed formats with higher resolution include PNG, TIF, and BMP.

NOTE These image file formats are important for other reasons. Image editors like PhotoShop have proprietary formats (*.PSD) that store additional image information in *Layers* to create complex compositions. Other image formats have special characteristics—saving an image in the *.PNG format, for example, allows you to designate an area of the image as *transparent* in the PowerPoint slide (or a web page). This will eliminate the box around the image and make it appear more natural in the slide, as we will see later in this chapter.

When we use the Insert > Picture > From File command, we can select one or more images (using the CTRL+click command), and when we click Insert, they all come into our slide (see Figure 3-18). Selecting each image individually allows us to drag it to another location or resize it.

The Insert > Picture > From File command also does something else that you may notice—when you select an image inserted this way, the Picture toolbar should appear. If it doesn't for any reason, click View > Toolbars > Picture on the main menu.

FIGURE 3-18   PowerPoint can insert multiple images into a slide using the CTRL+click command.

NOTE Sometimes the Picture toolbar is there but is "docked" among other toolbars. If you use a dual monitor setup, it can sometimes appear on the other screen.

Showing Only Part of a Picture

If you've used a scanner or brought pictures in from a digital camera, you generally have used a utility program that is a simple image editor; perhaps you even got PhotoShop Elements or a similar program bundled with the device.

For most people, 80% of the image editing they do involves *cropping* the image. This means selecting just the portion of the image you want to keep and eliminating the rest.

The nice thing in the later versions of PowerPoint is that you can do this directly in the slide with the Picture toolbar.

By choosing the Crop tool on the picture toolbar, different selection tabs appear on the selected image, as shown in Figure 3-19. Now you can drag in the borders of the image to leave only the portion you want displayed in the slide.

FIGURE 3-19   The Crop tool on the Picture toolbar lets you select just the portion of the image you want to display and remove the rest from the projected slide.

Remember that you are not really changing the underlying image, nor are you altering the size of the image that you brought into PowerPoint.

All you are changing with the Crop tool is the portion of the image to be shown.

If you are planning to email your presentation or post it online, image size may become an issue. *Nothing, not even video, increases the file size of your PowerPoint slide show as much as adding pictures.*

NOTE As you'll see in Chapter 5, "Using Video and Audio Effectively," adding video only puts in the first frame of the movie as a reference, sort of like a single picture file that links to the video that will be played within the slide.

Therefore, the other tool on the Picture toolbar you will want to check out is the Compress Pictures button—it looks like four arrows pointing in to the image.

This opens the Compress Pictures dialog box (see Figure 3-20), which allows you to change settings and compress the selected image or *all of the images in your presentation.*

Be careful when you choose this option. Changing the properties of images is the single biggest cause of PowerPoint file corruption.

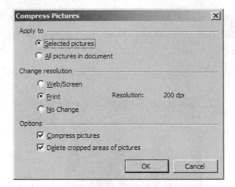

FIGURE 3-20   The Compress Pictures dialog box lets you quickly reduce the size of your PowerPoint file, but you should back it up first.

Having said that, recent versions of PowerPoint have been much better about preserving images in the presentation. Still, when using multiple images, *it is always a good idea to save multiple versions of your presentation* and back them up.

After you've done that, using the Compress Pictures command can be very helpful, particularly to email presentations.

It is important to remember; however, that Undo won't restore the images to their uncompressed state, so if you need them at their best, it is also a good idea to save a version of the presentation before using the tool. This would be the case if you needed to print the slides in high resolution or wanted to project them on a large screen where the lower-resolution images may suffer.

The rest of the tools on the Picture toolbar mostly create straightforward adjustments to a picture's brightness and contrast. The other one we should look at is Set Transparent Color.

Creating a Transparent Image

There are actually two image types that natively support transparency, both in web pages and in PowerPoint—the PNG uncompressed image format and the GIF compressed (256-color) image format. But let's take a look at what can happen if you just try to set a transparent color in PowerPoint with a basic image.

If the color that is to be transparent is not uniform or the image has not been processed correctly, you can get unacceptable results, as shown in Figure 3-21. If you want the jet to be set against a truly transparent color so that it blends with the clouds (and you could later animate it!), you would need a solid transparent background.

FIGURE 3-21   Without a solid color to make transparent, the Set Transparent Color command can be ineffective.

So how do we get around this?

In an image editor like PhotoShop, create a new image with a Transparent Background, as shown in Figure 3-22.

Then open the image for which you want to make a transparent background. Press CTRL+A to Select All, press CTRL+C to copy the image, select the new image with the transparent background, and press CTRL+V to paste the image in.

NOTE Make sure that the new transparent image is the same screen resolution or larger than the one you're pasting in.

Now, use the Magic Wand selection tool (found in most image editors) to select the blue sky background. If areas remain unselected, change the Tolerance setting to lower the precision of the selection (by raising the Tolerance level—see Figure 3-23.)

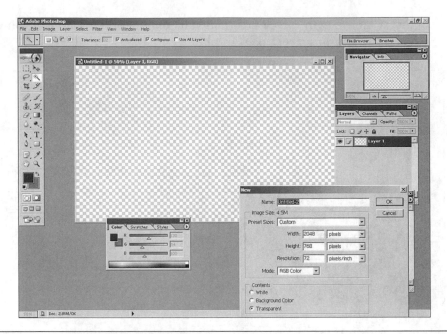

FIGURE 3-22 Most high-end image editors will allow you to add a transparent layer to a new image.

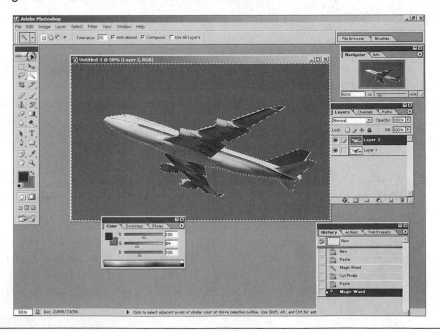

FIGURE 3-23 The Magic Wand selector in PhotoShop and similar image editors can select a color by its similarity to a specific color value.

When the background is selected, press CTRL+X to cut it out of the image. The remaining image will be on a transparent background.

FIGURE 3-24   With the selected color cut out of the image, the background is transparent.

If you want to explore PhotoShop further, now you can see the two different layers that exist in your composition. To make it work in Power-Point, your best bet is to save it as a full-resolution file type that supports transparency. Click File > Save As and change the File Format to PNG.

NOTE In PhotoShop, you will also want to save this as a copy because you will keep your original composition saved as a PhotoShop *.PSD file.

When the resulting file (Plane.PNG) is inserted into the PowerPoint slide, the background will be transparent, allowing you to have your own sky show through.

Now you don't need to Set Transparent Color on the Picture toolbar; PowerPoint recognizes the background as transparent in the PNG file.

NOTE We'll cover custom animation in Chapter 5, which enables us to fly this plane across the screen.

This is a great technique for adding logos to a slide or moving images behind and in front of other images without an extraneous background. Remember that each image is actually a separate object on its own *layer* in a PowerPoint slide. By selecting an image and choosing Order > Send to Back, Bring to Front, Send Backward, or Bring Forward on the Drawing toolbar, you can move any object (like an image or a shape) behind or in front of other objects, creating the illusion of depth.

Acquiring a Folder of Images

Now that we understand the value of knowing the location of a set of image files, we should go through the process of using a scanner or downloading them from a digital camera.

Scanners have been around a bit longer that digital cameras. Like all peripheral devices, they need to connect to your computer through some sort of interface, and in order to work with the device, utility software is generally included.

In addition, most peripheral devices (especially those manufactured for operating systems before Windows XP) come with *device drivers*, or software that allows the operating system to connect to and understand the device.

That's really about all of the technology you need to understand before using a scanner or digital camera to work with PowerPoint.

After a successful setup, your computer will "see" the peripheral in one of these ways:

- The scanner's utility program can be loaded like any other program, and when you place a photograph or other object into the device and scan it, the program creates an image file that you can save in a standard format into a folder on your computer.
- The scanner's program can also load as an add-in to another image editing program (like PhotoShop) so that the finished scan enters the editor to be revised and saved as a standard image file.

■ In the case of a digital camera, no utility program may be needed all; instead the memory device inside the camera may be instantly recognized by a Windows XP PC and be read as though it were any file folder on a regular drive connected to the PC.

Because there are hundreds of these peripherals, each with its own set of software, we'll just look at two representative samples.

In PhotoShop, the File > Import command will launch whatever utility program you may have installed; in the case of Figure 3-25, it's the Hewlett Packard Deskscan utility that comes with many HP scanners.

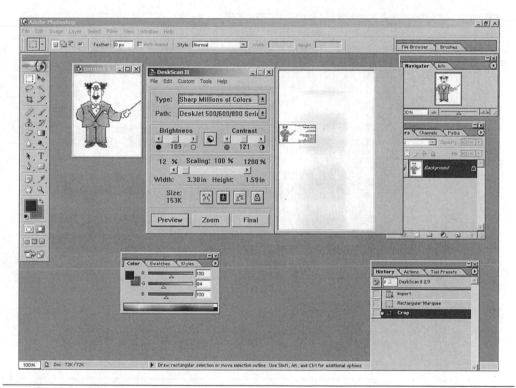

Figure 3-25 The Hewlett-Packard scanner utility can be used inside of PhotoShop or another image editor to acquire a scanned image for editing.

In this example, we're scanning a business card. In PhotoShop, the Selection tool has been used to select only the logo, and then the Image > Crop command has gotten rid of the extraneous text.

Now we can save the file as LOGO.TIF using the Save As command and put it in the My Pictures folder inside of My Documents. (In the case of PhotoShop, we may need to use the Save As Copy command to merge the layers and create a TIF file.)

Connecting to a Digital Camera

When you connect most modern digital cameras to a computer running Windows XP with a USB cable and turn on the camera, the flash memory card in the camera appears on the PC as a file folder. In Figure 3-26, this file folder is shown above the PhotoShop window, with the files on the disk selected to be viewed as thumbnails.

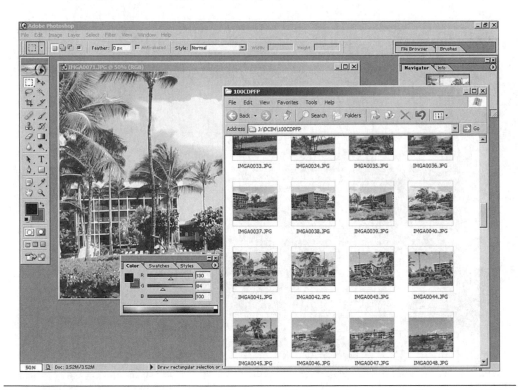

FIGURE 3-26   The contents of most digital cameras' flash memory cards will pop up in Windows XP as a normal file folder.

From here, you can simply drag and drop an image into the PhotoShop window, crop or otherwise edit it, and then save it to another folder, such as the My Pictures folder in My Documents.

Or in most cases (depending upon the file format used by the camera), you can drag and drop or otherwise move the image(s) directly to a local folder.

We'll do both.

First, I drag the picture of a hotel into the PhotoShop window and save it as a TIF image named hotel.tif in the My Pictures folder of My Document; see Figures 3-26 and 3-27.

FIGURE 3-27 With the digital picture in PhotoShop or another image editor, it can be edited and saved in a new location under a new name.

But what if I want to copy a lot of pictures into a newly named folder?

I can create a new folder called "digital pictures" by right-clicking in the My Pictures folder and selecting Folder > New, as shown in Figure 3-28.

Then, with both folders open on my desktop, I can select individual images in my flash memory card folder using CTRL+click (or all of them using CTRL+A) and drag them into the newly created folder (see Figure 3-29).

3. CREATING DYNAMIC VISUALS

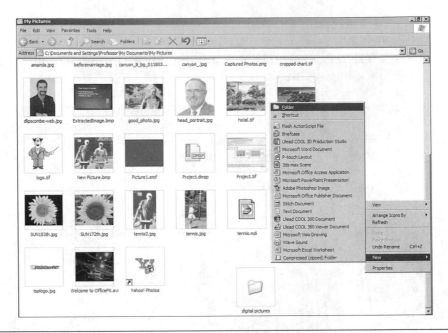

FIGURE 3-28   Right-click in any folder to create a new (sub)folder and name it appropriately.

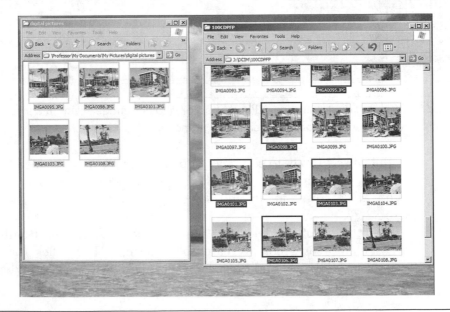

FIGURE 3-29   Opening the flash memory card folder of the digital camera alongside another file folder allows you to easily drag and drop one or more images from one folder to the other.

Now I have a new folder containing multiple pictures from the digital camera.

What are the advantages and disadvantages of each procedure?

If you look at the images in the digital pictures folder, they are named simply as sequential TIF files. The advantage of bringing them individually into PhotoShop, besides being able to edit them, is that I can give them meaningful names, like hotel.tif. (Of course, I could right-click on the images in the folder and rename them as well.)

But as we'll see in the next section, assembling a group of images in a folder like this gives us a lot more than organizational capability in Power-Point. It lets us use the Photo Album tool.

TIP Adding Your Image Files to the Clip Organizer

Because we started with the Clip Organizer as an easy way to begin working with images and to explore its search and cataloging capability, you may be wondering how you can add the pictures you acquire with a scanner or digital camera to the Clip Organizer. (To open the Clip Organizer, use the Clip Art Task Pane in PowerPoint and click Organize Clips at the bottom right.)

There are two basic ways:

- When you first launch Clip Organizer, you are prompted whether you want to automatically catalog all of the media on your hard drive. If you click Yes and go to lunch, when you return, it will have found and organized all of your media files including images into collections for you.
- The other way is to create new Collections that you name appropriately (File > New Collection). Then, when you click File > Add Clips to Organizer (see Figure 3-30), you have three choices:
  - Repeat the automatic cataloging
  - Access a scanner or digital camera
  - Locate the images from existing file folders

After you've done that, you can use the Insert Clip Art feature in PowerPoint to put the newly acquired images into your slides, as I did at the beginning of the chapter.

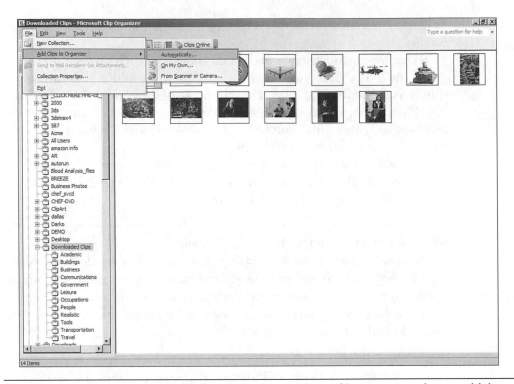

FIGURE 3-30 After you've added images or other media as files, you can always add them to the Clip Organizer to be searched and accessed later on.

Using Multiple Pictures with the Photo Album

Let's take another look at the images I dragged into the digital pictures folder.

Imagine that instead of five images, I had dragged in 50 pictures I had taken of various vacation properties on the Big Island of Hawaii—that I wanted to show to prospective clients of my travel agency.

I could certainly go back and insert them one by one, either using the Clip Organizer or the Insert > Picture > From File features of PowerPoint. But doing that would be time consuming.

Fortunately, PowerPoint has a feature that lets you bring in an almost unlimited number of images automatically and create a new presentation from scratch.

Photo Album became part of PowerPoint in version 2002/XP. You can still download it as an add-in for PowerPoint 2000 at http://snipurl.com/31jg and it's on the book CD.

To open the Photo Album utility, click Insert > Picture > New Photo Album, and the dialog box pops up as shown in Figure 3-31.

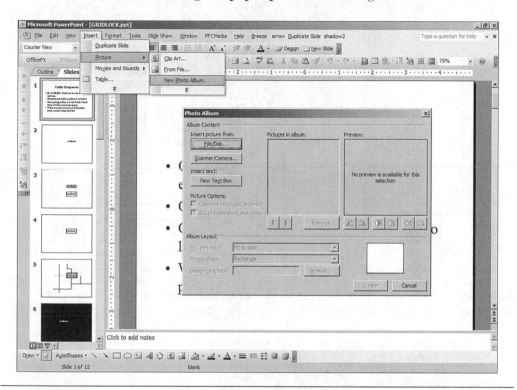

FIGURE 3-31 The New Photo Album feature lets you instantly create a new presentation from many images in a folder on your hard drive or bring them in from a scanner or digital camera.

Click the File/Disk button to access the folder with the images you want, as shown in Figure 3-32. Remember to use the View > Details or Thumbnails option to see the images by their text properties or previews.

Now, you can select multiple images using CTRL+click or select all of the images with CTRL+A and click Insert.

In the dialog box, you can now continue to add more photos from other folders, remove them, or decide how many photoslides you will want in the album (see Figure 3-33).

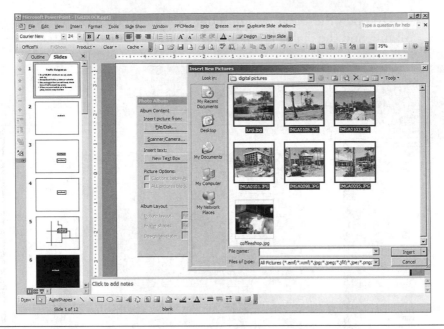

FIGURE 3-32 With Insert New Pictures open, you can select one, several, or all of the images either by their thumbnails or their properties (Details).

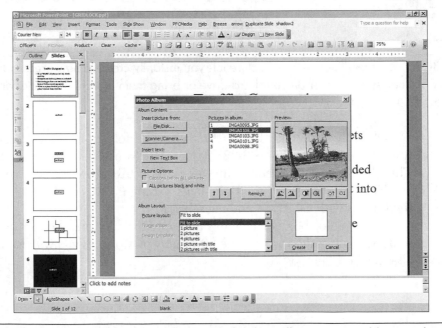

FIGURE 3-33 The New Photo Album feature dialog box allows you to add more photos from other folders, remove them, or configure the slides with one, two, or four images.

Click Create, and a new Photo Album presentation with a title page and your configured images is created. You can either save and work with this presentation on its own, or you can use the Window > Arrange All command on the main menu to drag and drop the picture slides into another open presentation, as shown in Figure 3-34.

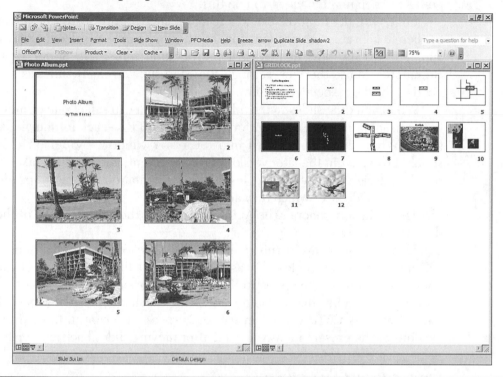

FIGURE 3-34 By opening the Photo Album presentation beside another slide show you can drag and drop the picture slides from one to the other.

USES FOR THE PHOTO ALBUM As we proceed in this book, you will see lots of uses for the Photo Album, including

- As hyperlinked thumbnails for slides in other presentations or slides in a web page
- As image template files for use and reuse in other presentations
- As self-running shows that you can play during breaks or as "infomercials" during your talk
- As potential video clips or parts of DVD projects

We cover the details of these procedures in the coming chapters; you will probably come up with your own uses, too.

Moving Slides Between Multiple Presentations

With many images suddenly on lots of slides, you may see the value of being able to move slides among several slide shows using Window > Arrange All on the main menu (refer to Figure 3-34). There are some points to keep in mind when you do this.

First, with the multiple window scenario shown previously, remember to click to activate each presentation in order to be able to select its slides, and it is usually best to put each presentation into Slide Sorter view. Remember to use the View setting (Zoom) to show as many slides as you need to for the respective window.

When you drag slides to the other window, you can select one or more in the usual fashion—CTRL+A for all slides or CTRL+click for individual slides. When they are dropped into the other window, by default they should be *copied* in the later versions of PowerPoint, and they will take on the slide design template of the destination presentation—or more specifically of the slide after which they are inserted.

They will also generally be AutoFormatted to the specifications of the destination show.

If you want to avoid this, look for the little SmartTag that should accompany the move below the last slide—it looks like a clipboard. If you open it, you will get the option to Keep Source Formatting.

Also, remember that if you don't like the results, you can always click Undo (or press CTRL+Z) to reverse the process. Be careful to save the versions of the presentations you want after moving slides back and forth.

LOOK FOR THE SMART TAG If you don't want slides (with images) to assume the design of the destination presentation after they're dragged and dropped, look for the little Lightning Bolt or Paste Options Icon SmartTag that appears to their lower right. Clicking it will allow you to choose to Keep Source Formatting.

Using the Slide Finder Feature

Now that we're creating slides with complex visuals, we will inevitably want to reuse these slides, often exactly as they've been created and on other occasions with slight modifications.

Although the multiple window scenario is useful, PowerPoint has another feature that you may find even more helpful if you want to preserve the source formatting of the inserted slides.

If you click Insert > Slides from Files, you open the Slide Finder (see Figure 3-35).

FIGURE 3-35   The Slide Finder lets you insert one or more slides from other presentations, save them as Favorites, and preserve their source formatting.

The Slide Finder has a number of useful features, not the least of which is the ability to locate slides by their thumbnails or by their titles (using the toggle button on the display on the right side of Select slide).

After the presentation and the slides are located, one or more slides can be selected in the usual manner—CTRL+A for all, CTRL+click for individual, or SHIFT+click for sequential slides, and then brought into the current presentation.

Notice that there is a clearly defined Keep Source Formatting option available, as well as another tab in which to add and store your List of Favorite presentations for reuse of all or some of their slides.

Using or Hiding Slide Titles

When we added our very first image to a slide from the Clip Organizer (refer to Figure 3-11), we kept the title on the slide ("Gridlock") and briefly mentioned that that was an option we may or may not want to use.

After all, showing a concept without actually naming it can be very effective—particularly if the image is a beautiful full-screen full-resolution file.

Adding the word "Gridlock" or any other title to the slide may dilute its dramatic effect and be superfluous.

On the other hand, in the preceding section on the Slide Finder we saw that sometimes we need a title (or it is helpful to have one) to locate just the slide we want from a presentation we created some time ago.

We will find that this is also the case when we use *hyperlinks* to navigate between presentations in the next chapter.

So let's go through the process of using the important Title placeholder in ways that enable you to use or not use titles most effectively.

In the slide into which we inserted multiple images (refer to Figure 3-18), we currently have no Title placeholder. To make sure of that, we can open the Slide Layout Task Pane (CTRL+F1—choose Slide Layout if it's not there already) and (re)apply a blank layout to the slide.

Now we can reverse the process and give the slide a Title only layout, and type in and fit a title into the slide by resizing its placeholder, as shown in Figure 3-36.

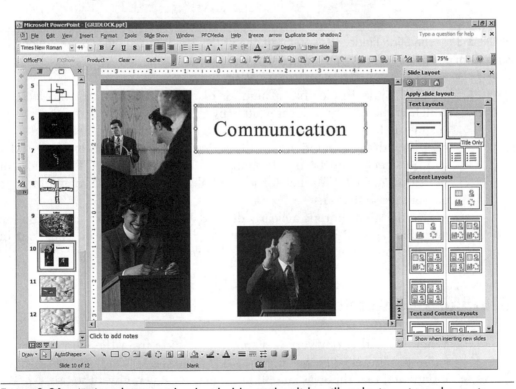

FIGURE 3-36 (Re)applying a title placeholder to the slide will make it easier to locate in Slide Finder or as a hyperlink later on.

But what if we don't want to show the title itself and just want to continue to use it for reference purposes?

In the slide shown here, we could simply give it the same font color as the background—white—and render it invisible.

Our other option is to reduce the *size of the font* and then move the title behind one of the pictures, making it invisible when displayed but, again, available as a reference.

If the title is in front of the image you want to hide it behind, with the title selected, click the Draw button on the Drawing toolbar, select Order, and then select Send to Back.

This technique works very well until we use some of the animation techniques in the next chapter. If we go that route, our best solution is to simply reduce the view size of the slide (Zoom out) and move the title off the visible area, as shown in Figure 3-37.

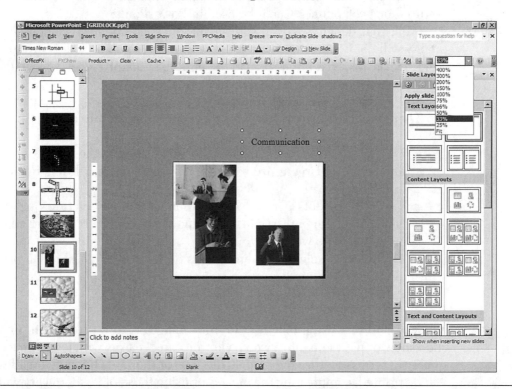

FIGURE 3-37   Moving the title off the visible portion of the slide maintains it as a reference to the slide and may increase the overall impact of the slide itself.

We will find other uses for the off-screen area of the slide in later chapters, and you may have some creative uses for this technique yourself. Keep it in the back of your slide-creating mind.

Digital Cameras and Picture Quality

Before we move on from pictures to charts and diagrams, it's worth going through some of the issues involved in taking and using pictures in the first place.

In discussing digital cameras, let's remember that times have changed—now it's not just the megapixel digital camera that shoots pictures—our digital camcorder that is used for movies (as we'll see in Chapter 5) can sometime provide stills as well, and what about our little camera featured in a cell phone? Can it be used in PowerPoint?

Well, that depends. If the subject matter is compelling enough, any quality will do. Footage of a disaster shot in low resolution could certainly make its way to CNN, but if you had the option, as the producer, you would still choose the one with the best possible quality.

So how do these images compare?

There are three main parameters that determine picture quality:

- The file size or the actual amount of information in the image determines in how large a size it can be displayed without losing quality or clarity.
- The DPI, or dots per inch, is another measure of picture quality, which you frequently see in evaluating scanners or printers and generally has to do with print output.
- The screen resolution or dimensions of the image, measured in pixels, will determine how large an image you can display in a PowerPoint slide or web page.

You will find that if the only use for your images is to present them in a slide show or put them into a web page, you can get away with lesser image quality in terms of either the original file size, or the DPI. But if your slides will be printed, compressing the images or using those of lesser quality will not be an option.

Before we go back into PhotoShop to compare a few images from different sources, let's remember the screen resolution we need to work with. Most PowerPoint slide shows are now projected XGA resolution (or even higher)—that means a screen of 1024 pixels horizontally by 768 pixels vertically.

Some slide shows may still be shown at SVGA or 800×600.

So if you want a full-screen image in these resolutions *without stretching and distorting it*, it will have to be at least this size.

Now let's bring two images into PhotoShop and move the palettes out of the way (see Figure 3-38).

FIGURE 3-38   Image editors like PhotoShop may show larger images in fractions of their original size, making it harder to gauge how they will appear in PowerPoint.

My PhotoShop window for this shot is 1024×768 (XGA), about the size that PowerPoint would normally project. The picture on the right is displayed at 100% size in PhotoShop because it easily fits. This is a highly compressed JPG image taken by the camera in my cell phone.

It is only 25K in size but is still at a screen resolution of 640×480. It would fit nicely into a PowerPoint slide, *but it would print poorly on a high-quality printer*.

The image on the left of the hotel looks smaller, but notice that Photo-Shop is only displaying it at 25% of its original size. It is much larger than the other image in reality, with a screen resolution of 1280×960 (it was taken with the digital image capability of a digital movie camera).

Both pictures are still at a 72 pixel per inch DPI rating, fine for Power-Point but problematic for print.

Now let's bring both images into a PowerPoint slide—*and project it*—and see the results (see Figure 3-39).

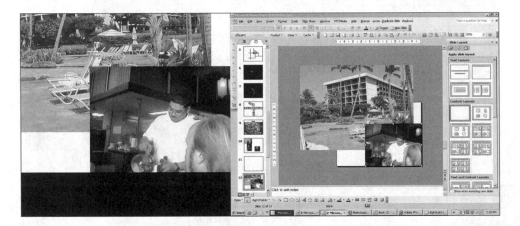

FIGURE 3-39   The original image dimensions (resolution) determine the image size in a PowerPoint slide, while its actual file size will impact print output quality.

Now we can clearly see how the hotel image dwarfs the slide within the PowerPoint editor (on the right) and it will need to be resized downward to fit on the slide when projected (on the left).

At the same time, the 640×480 image will fit nicely on the slide in both the editor and the projected image, although without the clarity or overall quality of the larger image.

So what do you need in terms of *megapixels* in a digital camera? Notice that even the cell phone image is almost adequate for PowerPoint. Any digital camera of two to three megapixels that creates *RAW uncompressed images* in a screen resolution of at least 1024×768 will work quite well for most PowerPoint presentations.

On the other hand, when you print, the higher megapixel rating will translate into much better image quality—if your eventual slide show will be used in a brochure or, God help you, a poster, you'd better acquire images in much higher resolution and DPI.

That's why stock image services charge more for their higher-resolution images than the low-res versions.

NOTE For a list of stock services that you can use to populate your PowerPoint slides, see the "Resources" section at the end of the chapter.

Comparing Data with Tables and Charts

Many presentations are like an episode in the old TV series *Dragnet*, and like Jack Webb, they want to show "just the facts, ma'am."

The good news is that PowerPoint has tools that let you create a table or a chart very easily.

The bad news is that there are better tools available—Word's table tool is superior to the one in PowerPoint, and the Chart Wizard in Excel is a bit better than the MS Graph feature in PowerPoint.

The bottom line, as always, is not getting bogged down in the technology and instead deciding the best way to present information that you deem significant to an audience.

Using Excel for Tables

Some of you are already saying, "Excel, whoa! I thought this was a Power-Point book."

Well, the fact is that if you want to create a table quickly, using the cells in Excel isn't a bad idea.

Even if you've never ventured into Excel and think of it as a giant game of Battleship, you can quickly construct a table like the one in Figure 3-40.

USING COLUMN AUTOFIT The one daunting thing for new Excel users is that items don't always fit into the cells. If you select a range of columns by clicking down through their A, B, C, etc., column headings and then click Format > Column > AutoFit Selection, the columns will allow enough room for your formatted text, and your table will look like the one in Figure 3-40.

If you drag your cursor through the cells, select Edit > Copy (CTRL+C), and simply paste the cells into an empty PowerPoint slide, you're almost there.

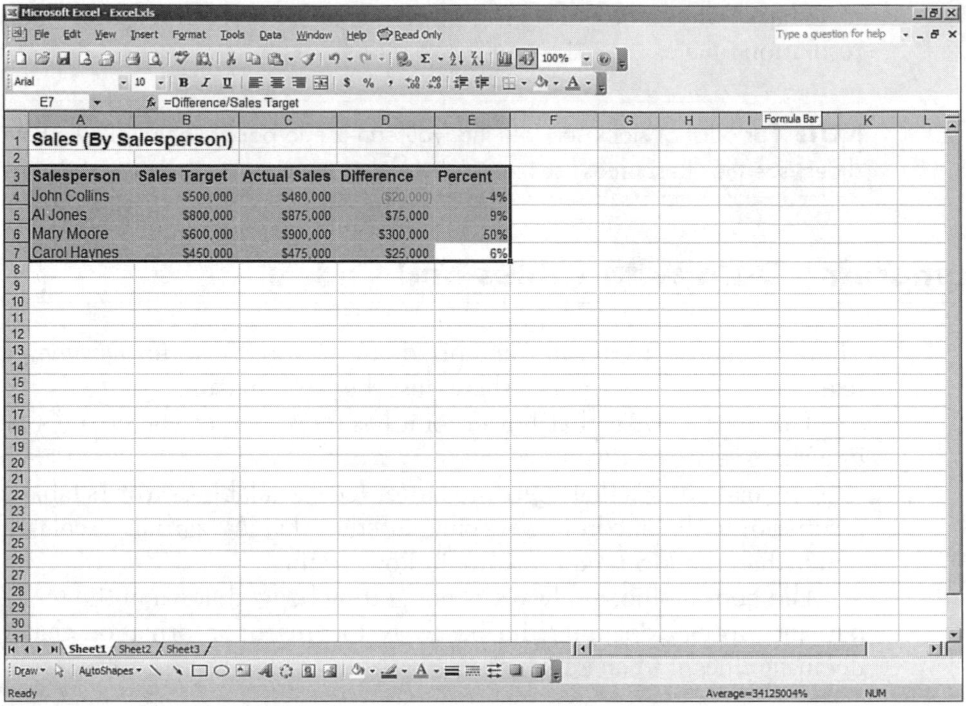

FIGURE 3-40   Using the grid layout in Excel makes it fairly easy to create a simple table.

You get a little SmartTag that you can open up to confirm to Power-Point that this is indeed a table (see Figure 3-41).

Because you have designated this object as a table (as opposed to continuing to use it as an Excel file or a picture), you can now select it and use the Tables and Borders toolbar to edit it.

Click View > Toolbars > Tables and Borders to open the toolbar if it doesn't appear when you select the table. Your first task may be to put in some borders.

The items in the toolbar resemble those in the Drawing toolbar. Notice that you have

- A line color tool that will set the color of the borders
- A border style tool that sets their thickness and appearance
- The border selector box (now set to all borders) that will implement the choices you make (see Figure 3-42)

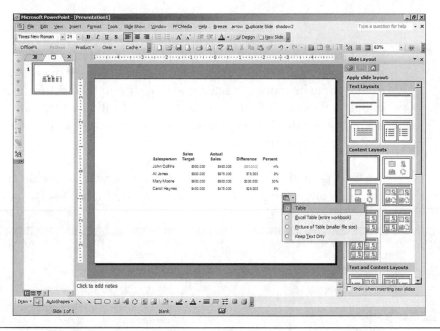

FIGURE 3-41   Pasting a portion of an Excel spreadsheet into PowerPoint is an easy way to create a table.

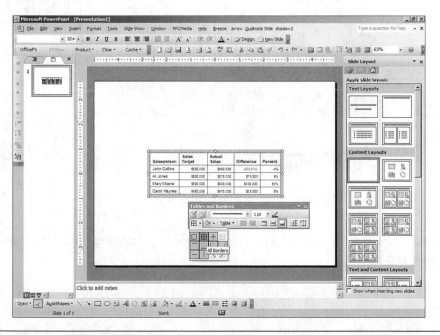

FIGURE 3-42   The Tables and Borders toolbar lets you quickly add and format borders and then revise the rest of the table's appearance.

If we then

- Select the header cells and click Justify > Center
- Click the entire table to select it and then stretch it out into the slide
- Select the header cells again and make them bold with a larger font
- Select the data cells and make them bold with a larger font
- And select the header and data cells separately and provide them with different Fill colors

We end up with a decent-looking table that will be visible from the back of the room when projected full screen (see Figure 3-43).

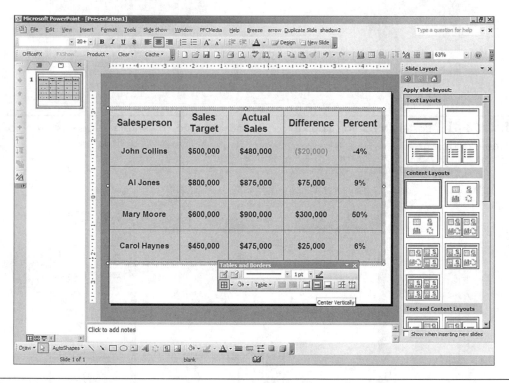

FIGURE 3-43 Use other features of the Tables and Borders toolbar to format the cells and center your text.

If you're determined to avoid Excel and want to create a table directly inside PowerPoint, the Insert > Table command will let you instantly set the number of columns and rows, and when the table is created, you get the same Tables and Borders toolbar. I just find making the modifications and adding the data more time consuming.

The advantage that Word gives you with a table is the AutoFormat feature, but this doesn't always translate very well into PowerPoint. In fact, one of the most annoying aspects of tables is trying to reformat them in PowerPoint if they've been created elsewhere. But using the grid of Excel to create the labels and enter the data is a good starting point.

Now you have presentable data in PowerPoint.

PowerPoint or Excel Charts?

If you have worked with Excel, you know that it is a powerful calculation tool with formulas and functions that create scenarios and help you accomplish financial and other data-intensive goals.

The MS Graph program with which charts are constructed directly in PowerPoint is more limited; it has no calculation capability, and even formula results like sums must be entered manually.

The advantage, however, is that you don't have to struggle with the data twice—once in Excel and then in PowerPoint—to make it work.

So here is a suggestion for deciding whether to use an Excel chart (whether pasted or linked) or a native PowerPoint chart—go with what you have.

If you already have a data table in Excel, you've got the best of both worlds. You can do any of the following:

- Create the chart in Excel using its wizard and then paste it into PowerPoint.
- Open a PowerPoint chart and import the data from Excel.
- Copy and paste the data from Excel into the PowerPoint datasheet.

Quick and Dirty Excel Charting

Without going too deeply into Excel, if we return to the same data table we used in Figure 3-41, we can get a passable chart in Excel in four steps:

1. Select the appropriate data.
2. Click the Chart Wizard.
3. Accept the default chart.
4. Click Finish (see Figure 3-44).

The alternative inside of PowerPoint is to open the MS Graph charting tool by double-clicking the chart icon in a Content placeholder or selecting Insert > Chart.

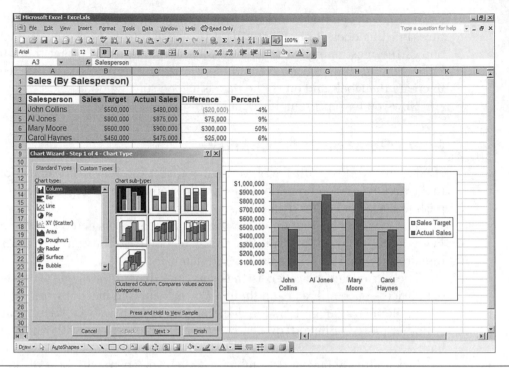

FIGURE 3-44 After you select your data in Excel, the Chart Wizard will lead you the rest of the way.

This is an entirely separate program that brings up extra menu items and toolbar icons to help you create and edit the PowerPoint Chart.

The key here is the data table—you can once again paste the *data you need, and only the data you need,* into the data table and get rid of extraneous columns or rows.

You can also use the Import File option to open the Excel spreadsheet, but you will have to hope that the data you bring in is exactly what you want.

With data in the MS Graph (PowerPoint chart) datasheet, you can keep the default column chart because it may be close to what you want (see Figure 3-45).

If only it were always that easy, right?

What if your boss says, "That's okay, but I want the categories to be the Salespeople and the columns to represent the Target and Actual Sales for each"?

Would you commit murder or suicide?

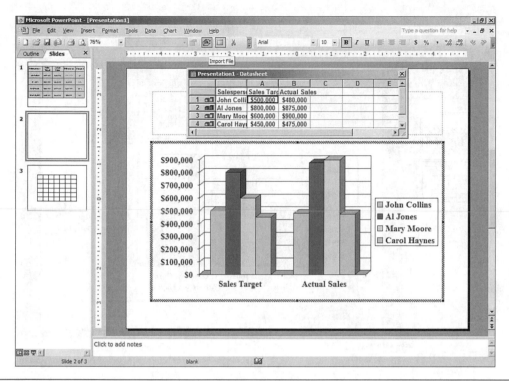

FIGURE 3-45 After you select your data in Excel, the Chart Wizard will lead you the rest of the way.

Actually if charts were your life, you'd know. In this instance you'd realize that the data (it's always the data) that you had in rows should really be in columns, and you would make the appropriate adjustment in the Data tab of the MS Graph/PowerPoint chart menu as shown in Figure 3-46.

But most of us don't make charts our life.

That's what makes charts so difficult for many users—I know that if I am doing a training session of PowerPoint, the one area I always still fear, just a little, is charts. Because even for me, I have a life beyond charts.

The reasons for this widespread confusion are many, but my top two would be the following.

Creating a chart is not that hard, as we've seen previously, but revising it or making it look better is not easy at all. (In fact, many users will start from scratch rather than attempt to revise a chart.)

Deciding which data to select for the chart and what kind of chart to use can lead to nightmares.

Fortunately, there is help available on both fronts.

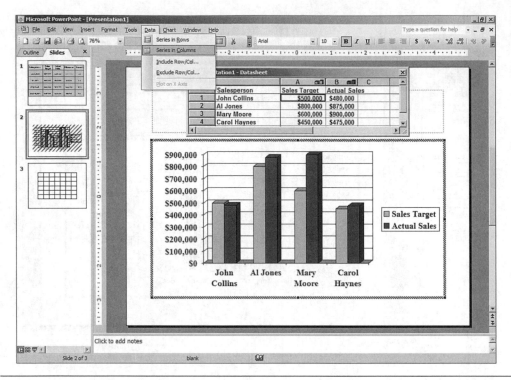

FIGURE 3-46 You can instantly modify how the data is displayed according to whether the series reflects the data in the datasheet's columns or its rows.

Learning from the Zelazny Method

If you look through the Excel Chart Wizard and its Chart Types tab or explore the very similar Chart Types options in PowerPoint (see Figure 3-47), the "hints" they give you as to what type of chart is appropriate are not very helpful.

In addition, as we've seen, it's not always easy to know which data is being plotted and more difficult still to understand how the categories or labels should be laid out.

I said there was help, and it's in the English language. As you click through the wizard or the chart types, one word sticks out—"compare."

Gene Zelazny, a well-respected business consultant and author of several books, including *Say It With Charts* and *Say It With Presentations*, uses this word to help any user select the right type of chart and construct it to his or her best advantage.

The key to the Zelazny method is to *identify the comparison*.

FIGURE 3-47 The Excel chart wizard and the PowerPoint Chart Types try to help you decide on the best type of chart, but they speak in chart-ese.

Zelazny starts his description with a trick question—showing a sample set of data and asking "Which chart is best?" The answer, not surprisingly, is that it depends.

This goes right back to Chapter 1—what is the message you're trying to convey?

The best way to think about this is to phrase your concept in the clearest possible terms. Here are Zelazny's five major modes of comparison:

- **Component**: Percentage of a total.
  "Accounted for the largest share."
  "Share of the market…"
  "Almost half of all…"
- **Item**: Ranking of items.
  "Who did the best?"
  "Rates are about equal?"
  "Who ranks where?"
- **Time Series**: Changes over time.
  "Sales have risen steadily (or dramatically)."
  "Return on investment has trended downward (decreased)."
  "Interest rates have fluctuated."

- **Frequency Distribution**: Items within ranges.
  "Most sales were in the $1000 to $2000 range."
  "The majority of shipments were delivered in five to six days."
  "The age distribution of employees differs sharply from…"
- **Correlation**: Relationship between variables.
  "Sales performance in May shows no relationship between a salesperson's age and experience."
  "Compensation does not vary with the size of the company."
  "The *size* of the policy *increases with* the policyholder income."

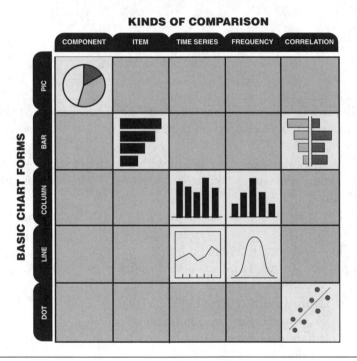

FIGURE 3-48 In *Say It With Charts*, Zelazny identifies five major types of comparison and shows you the types of chart most appropriate for each.

What is very helpful is that Zelazny's chart types conform pretty well to the Chart Types in PowerPoint MS Graph and the Excel Chart Wizard (see Figure 3-47).

The problem can be making the charts themselves behave exactly as they should according to Zelazny's sketches or putting several charts side by side to achieve the types of comparison he describes.

In most cases, the tweaks are pretty straightforward. Zelazny has some specific ideas about clarity of presentation, and he generally suggests

- Removing the legend
- Putting data directly in the chart wherever possible
- Avoiding fancy 3D

Because Zelazny works only with sketches, I took some of his data and imported it into Excel according to several Exhibits that he describes that conform to his comparisons listed previously.

This Excel file with the charts themselves and notes about re-creating them using the Excel Chart Wizard (or revising them in Microsoft's MS Graph) are found on the book CD in the Samples folder as the file Project.xls (see Figure 3-49).

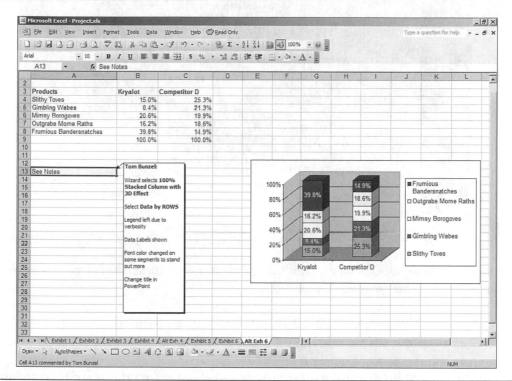

FIGURE 3-49   In Project.xls on the book CD you can find some Zelazny examples created with the Excel Chart Wizard, along with notes on how to best replicate them.

I have also created a set of slides in a PowerPoint presentation in the Samples folder on the CD (Kyralot.ppt) that put some of the charts into PowerPoint and describe some tricks for re-creating them in the Notes panel.

Some of these techniques simply involve combining some chart work in PowerPoint with some drawing tools. For example, to show the remaining unused portion of a Pie Chart, you can leave a blank row in the datasheet in MS Graph (see Figure 3-50).

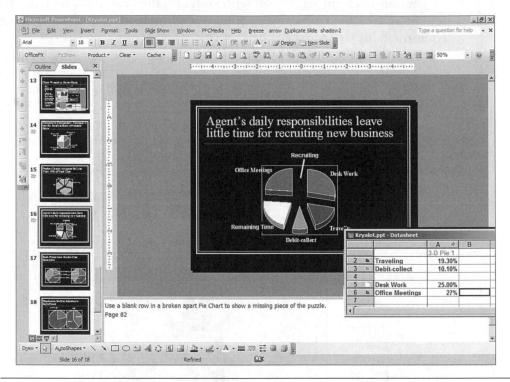

FIGURE 3-50   In Kryalot.ppt on the book CD, the charts are deconstructed in the PowerPoint notes with tips on how they can be created.

Although MS Graph labels the extra pie slice with the same label as the next row, we can add a small text box over the label for the result illustrating the concept in *Say It With Charts*.

When Zelazny and I corresponded about my renditions of his comparisons, he took issue with some of my styles, including the fact that I sometimes like the 3D charts; he feels that they tend to distort the data in some cases.

The main point here is that you can certainly use the models on the CD and your own ingenuity to model some of Zelazny's ideas and create your own.

For several of Zelazny's concepts, two charts side by side are suggested to compare two different sets of data. This is relatively easy to accomplish in PowerPoint:

- Copy and paste the chart
- Revise the second datasheet accordingly
- Remove both legends
- Create a single legend with a text box
- Draw lines with the Drawing toolbar to the legend

An example of this chart is included in the Kryalot.ppt PowerPoint file in the Samples folder on the CD and is shown here in Figure 3-51. Basically, there are two identical charts with similar messages; in PowerPoint each has its own datasheet and its own set of options.

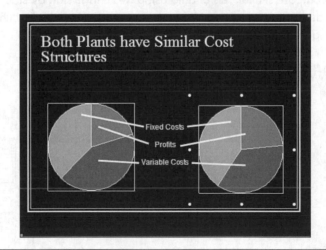

FIGURE 3-50   In Kryalot.ppt on the book CD, the charts are deconstructed in the PowerPoint notes with tips on how they can be created.

To make it easier to size two charts fairly evenly, you can also use the 2-Content Layout in the Slide Layout Task Pane to make room for both charts or to actually create them, as shown in Figure 3-52.

As you begin to work with a specific chart, you may well go through many permutations to get the look exactly as you want. When you have the chart on its way to perfect, you can save yourself some heartache by continuing to work with a *Duplicate Slide* of the chart, thereby saving your hard work in an earlier version.

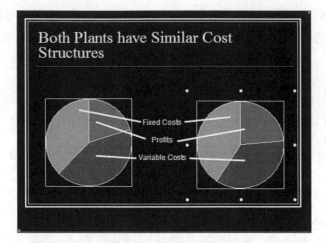

FIGURE 3-51 To compare similar sets of data using two charts side by side, you might want to use a text box as a common legend after copying and pasting the first chart as the second and modifying its datasheet.

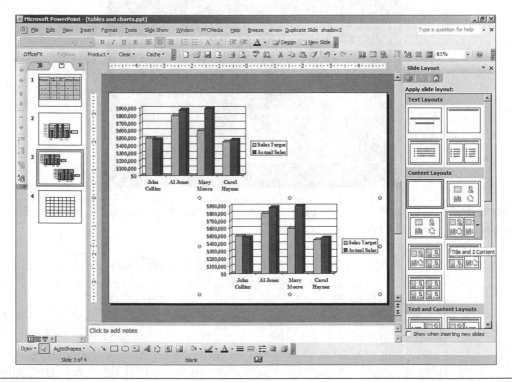

FIGURE 3-52 (Re)applying a 2-Content layout in your slide can make it easier to scale two similar charts before revising their respective datasheets to make a comparison.

When your chart is perfect, if you want to reuse it frequently, consider saving it as User Defined Chart in the Custom tab of the Chart Types dialog box (see Figure 3-53).

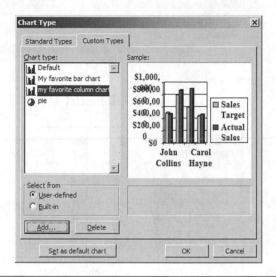

FIGURE 3-53   You can name and save your favorite charts in the Custom tab of the Chart Types dialog box.

WHERE ARE MY USER-DEFINED CHARTS? Unfortunately your user-defined chart settings are not saved with the file or the template. Instead they are saved in a file called *grusgal.gra,* found in the Application Data\Microsoft\Graph folder under your User Name in your Documents and Settings in Windows XP. This is a useful file to back up if you've created a set of user-defined charts, and you can overwrite it in another machine to make these charts available—just remember to put it in the User Name subfolder. In my case the file is in C:\ Documents and Settings*Professor*\Application Data\Microsoft\Graph—my User Name is *Professor.*

Revising a Chart in PowerPoint

Using the MS Graph part of PowerPoint can be tricky.

Remember that when you double-click to activate the chart you are entering another program: MS Graph. Your first task will be to populate the datasheet, import it, or copy and paste it, as described previously.

After you have the data in place, closing the datasheet makes it easier to select other portions of the chart to reformat, as shown in Figure 3-54.

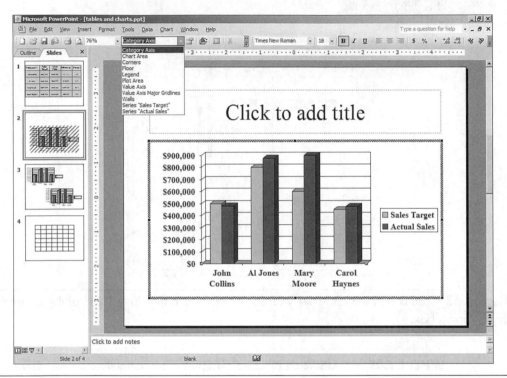

FIGURE 3-54   Closing the datasheet in PowerPoint's MS Graph program lets you access a drop-down list to reformat other portions of the chart.

With the item in the chart selected (Category Axis), you can click to Format the item, and, for example, change its font color (see Figure 3-55).

To clean up the chart, an area to concentrate on is the Scale tab of the Format dialog box of the Value Axis. For example, to show the numbers in the Thousands in the Scale tab, click the drop-down list in the Display Units (see Figure 3-56).

The Alignment tab will also enable you rotate the word "Thousands" by 90 degrees.

My suggestion is to eliminate the labels as much as possible and add them later if necessary—either as Chart Options or as separate text boxes.

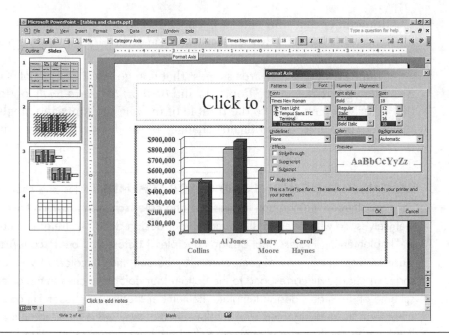

FIGURE 3-55 After selecting the component of the chart to reformat, Format will open the appropriate dialog box to perform the changes you desire.

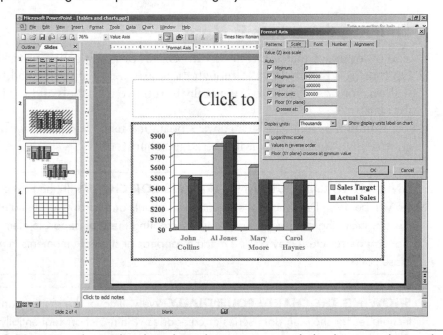

FIGURE 3-56 Using the Scale tab in the Value Axis Format dialog box can shorten the labels by displaying units in thousands or millions.

Remember that your chart will only be as strong as it projects, so don't fill it up with lots of extra verbiage and save that for the accompanying description.

Finally, true chart wizards suggest that you go into the Format > Chart Area dialog box, select the Font tab, and *turn off the Auto Scale* options so that after you have gone to the trouble of making the fonts and labels look the way you want, they will not change if you decide to move, copy, or resize the chart.

REMEMBER THE DESIGNS AND COLOR SCHEMES Tables and charts will vary greatly depending upon the designs and color schemes in which they find themselves, so whenever possible, make your design decisions (refer to Chapter 2, "Implementing Professional Design Principles") before you begin constructing these time-consuming visual components. By default, the Fill colors of your data series in charts will correspond to the bottom four color swatches in the color scheme of the slide's design template. Remember that if you choose Fill colors other than those designated by the color scheme, they *will not change* if the chart is moved to another presentation controlled by another design template.

Chart Options: Less Is More

The other major dialog box of the MS Graph program concerns the Chart Options (see Figure 3-57). Although there are plenty of spots to add information, your best bet here is generally to remove the labels and the legend for clarity.

Remember that labels can always be added using text boxes with more control than you will have with the actual chart tools.

ANIMATING CALLOUTS AND ARROWS FOR CHARTS In the next chapter we will be using Drawing tool elements like callouts and arrows to animate static visuals, including diagrams and charts. By creating these as separate elements that can be selected, they can be made to appear at strategic moments in your presentation.

SHOWING THE CHART SEQUENTIALLY We will cover the strategy and techniques for showing data series or categories within a chart sequentially in Chapter 4.

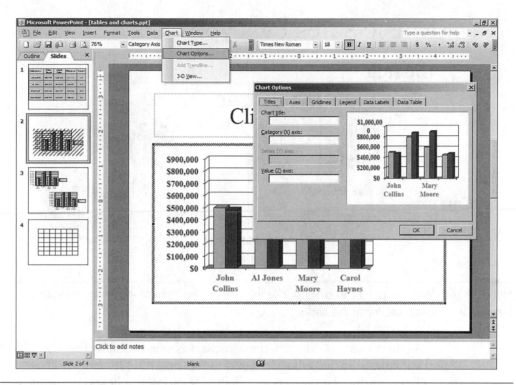

FIGURE 3-57 The Chart Options dialog box lets you add information to the chart but is probably more useful for removing it.

For more about showing financial and other data interactively, see Chapter 6, "Powerful Presentation Tools."

Combining Charts with Imagery

What is the key to the success of any chart or diagram? Obviously it is making the point you want to make, and critical to the success of that endeavor is taking a bit of effort to make the chart *memorable*.

Probably the single most effective thing you can do to set your charts apart from the average set of dull PowerPoint charts is to strip out some of the native components and populate them with a few images. They need not be dramatic. Here are some examples.

Figure 3-58 shows a pie chart that has been enhanced by adding the disc on the right, imported as clip art from the Microsoft Office Assistance Center (refer to Figure 3-8) and placed underneath a "real" pie chart, with the pie slices made empty.

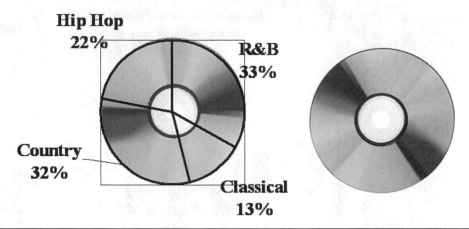

Music Sales by Type

FIGURE 3-58   We can put a clip art disc like the one on the right of the slide beneath an empty pie chart on the left of the slide.

Again, putting it "under" the pie chart is done by selecting the object and clicking Draw > Arrange > Send to Back on the Drawing toolbar.

To empty the data series, we selected it and right-clicked to format it in MS Graph. In the Format Data Point dialog box, we thickened the border to stand out against the disc and made the fill into No Fill as shown in Figure 3-59.

GETTING IT RIGHT Lining up and sizing the disc and the pie chart can be tricky. When the objects are on top of each other, the one underneath is hard to select. Use the TAB key to toggle through the selected objects in the slide and to size and move either the pie or the disc until they are equal and lined up. Use the right, left, up and down arrows on the keyboard to "nudge" the objects closer to where you want them. When you have it right, make sure you save the presentation and back it up so that if you decide you can do better and foul it up, you can always return to the last decent saved version.

What if someone tells me to lose the border around the pie? I need to construct another pie chart from the Drawing toolbar first and keep my datasheet and "real" pie chart off the slide.

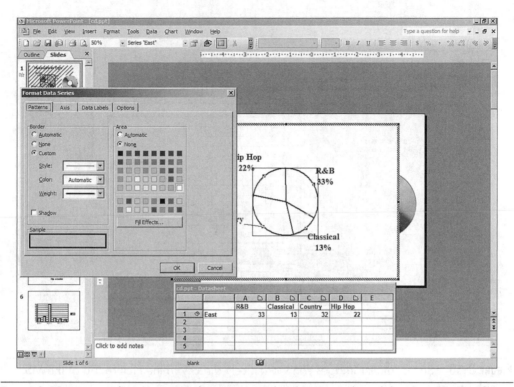

FIGURE 3-59 To get the pie to stand out against the disc, we selected the data series to reformat, gave it No Fill, and thickened its borders.

SHOWING OFF: SPINNING THE DISC Sure, we can make this chart more memorable by spinning the disc. We'll learn how to do that in the next chapter on animation and navigation.

Sometimes after you download a piece of clip art or photo, you can get lucky by placing the image directly into the data series. In Figure 3-60, the cell phone that was downloaded fits nicely into the columns of the chart. To do this, we just right-click to format the data series, choose Fill Effects, and load the image (as a file) into the Picture tab.

When you realize that you can empty the space within the data series as we did in the pie chart (refer to Figures 3-58 and 3-59), you can have a lot more fun. In Figure 3-61, other vector shapes were imported and resized to fit into the data series columns and more or less represent the varying values.

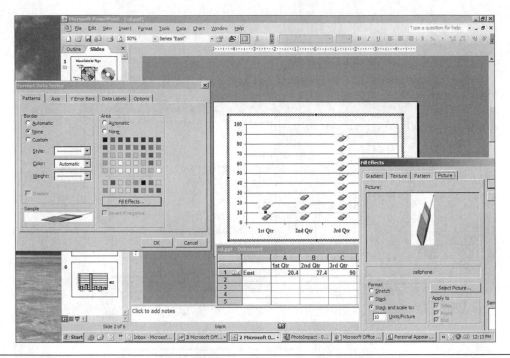

FIGURE 3-60 Some smaller images can work nicely directly in the Picture tab of the MS Graph object.

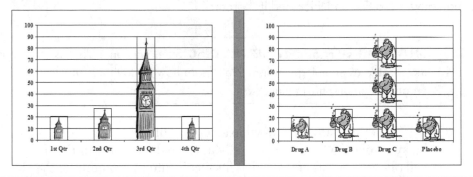

FIGURE 3-61 With the appropriate clip art objects, you can quickly copy and paste them over blank columns or bars and resize them to make the chart more memorable.

Although you can certainly go through the Chart Options and eliminate the gridlines and reformat the axes, sometimes it's best just to create the actual dimensions of the chart from scratch using the Drawing toolbar. In Figure 3-62, the original chart is kept off-screen with the datasheet (in case the numbers happen to change or other modifications need to be made). But by using the chart as a guide, lines and text boxes can be quickly assembled and aligned to make the final chart look a lot cleaner.

VECTOR V. BITMAP Clip art downloaded from MS Office Assistance are usually "vector" objects, which means that they will scale up and down, unlike pictures, which as we saw earlier become blurred if there is not enough information within the file. Because vector shapes are actually just numerical data telling the program the dimensions, colors, and other attributes of the objects, they can be stretched as large as you need them. Many of these shapes can also be selected and "ungrouped" so that you can modify them by getting rid of unwanted portions. In addition, you can combine them with other objects from the Drawing toolbar, including the text box, to give them labels, as we'll see next in the custom diagram.

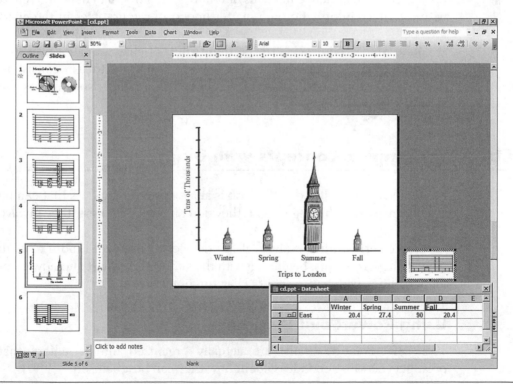

FIGURE 3-62   If you're comfortable with the Drawing toolbar, you can use the graph itself only as a guide and keep the datasheet and original chart off the slide entirely.

LEARN FROM *USA TODAY* *USA Today* uses creative charts called infographics every single day. My colleague Julie Marie Irvin of Keystone Resources in Houston makes it a point to clip these and keep them as a notebook of inspirational ideas for creative ways to present data.

Breaking a Chart into Multiples

Like everything else we've covered, it's important that the glitz doesn't obscure the message. Often it is very important to discuss the actual message behind the graph or chart with the presenter or expert who created it. Some complex tables or graphs have to broken up into smaller components (or "multiples") across a series of slides to truly convey the message. At times like this, a set of six ordinary column or bar charts without any graphics will be more effective in terms of telling your story than one large chart with too much information, no matter how cool the graphics in the chart may be.

Julie Marie Irvin specializes in these kinds of charts, as shown in Figure 3-63. She counsels that it is extremely important to use consistent dimensions, scales, and colors to emphasize the comparisons across the various charts and slides.

Covering Complex Concepts with Diagrams

Sometimes you are faced with obvious analogies or metaphors that can be easily conveyed with images—but they don't involve numbers; they involve ideas.

As PowerPoint has evolved, it has developed more and more tools to convey these concepts, beginning with the simple Org Chart and now coming to fruition with a nice set of "Diagram objects."

Using PowerPoint Diagrams

The PowerPoint diagrams are actually organized into a gallery that prompts you with good ideas about how they can best be used.

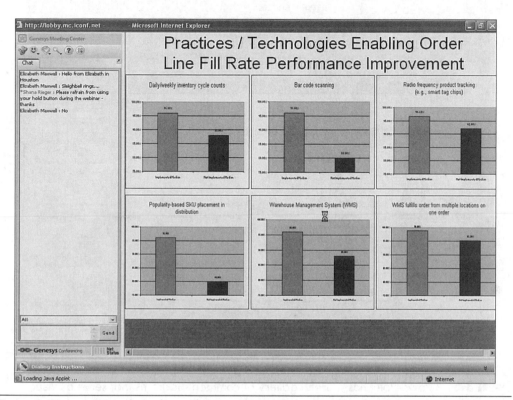

FIGURE 3-63 For complex relationships involving disparate data, it is sometimes more important to break out the charts into individual and consistent multiples.

This figure is from a recent web training that Julie gave on charts, which is available online at http://snipurl.com/lhpe.

Although it's certainly possible to create your own diagram using the Drawing toolbar (which we'll do in the next section) or to use other programs like Visio (which we will also explore later on), there are six commonly used metaphor diagrams available right in PowerPoint.

It's amazing how many users are unaware of the Diagram gallery. To open it, create a slide with a Content layout (using the Slide Layout Task Pane) and click on the little cycle diagram. The Diagram gallery opens (as shown in Figure 3-64).

The Org Chart can be used creatively for more than just the usual organizational structure of a business or institution—it could be a flow chart of ideas, or it could lay out relationships that may be important in other areas, as shown in Figure 3-65.

3. CREATING DYNAMIC VISUALS

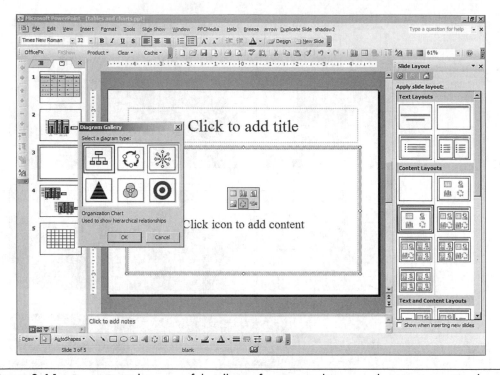

Figure 3-64 PowerPoint has a useful gallery of common diagrams that serve as visual metaphors for concepts you might want to quickly convey.

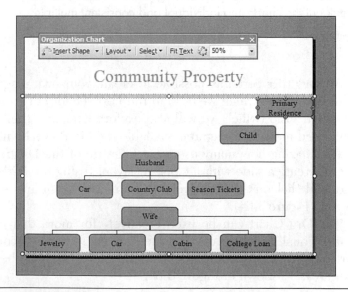

Figure 3-65 You can use the Org Chart in the Diagram gallery to quickly convey a number of different kinds of relationships.

With each diagram, you get a toolbar that allows you to

- Insert Shapes
- Change the Layout
- Select areas for reformat
- Fit (or resize) the diagram
- Open the Style Gallery
- Zoom in or out

The Style gallery can dramatically improve the impact of your diagram as shown in Figure 3-66.

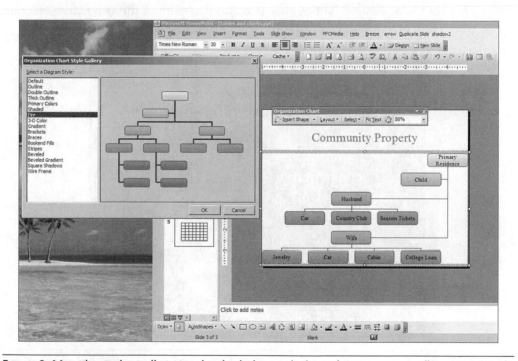

FIGURE 3-66 The Style Gallery (under the lightning bolt) in the Diagram toolbar can greatly enhance the look of any diagram.

INDIVIDUAL FORMATS FOR SHAPES Notice in Figure 3-65 that the Fill color of "College Debt" was changed to a different color to make it stand out. When the Style Gallery was invoked and the Fire style applied, the Fill color of this object was made consistent with the others. This is because by default *Auto-Format* is part of the diagrams, and invoking a style reloads it. To go back and change the Fill color of a shape (or make other formatting changes), you need to select and right-click the diagram and remove the AutoFormat option (uncheck it).

The other five diagram types have interesting attributes.

Figure 3-67 shows a Cycle diagram that has been enhanced with the 3D Color design. Notice that because it is part of the other five diagram types, however, it can instantly be changed into any of them.

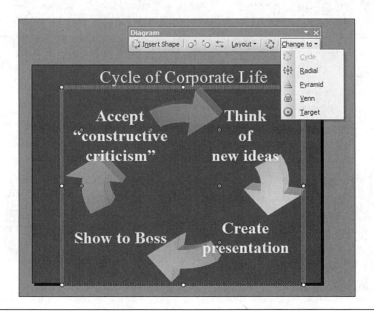

FIGURE 3-67   The Cycle diagram is one of five diagram types that can be instantly changed into any of the other four.

If we deem a pyramid to be more appropriate, we can instantly revise it as shown in Figure 3-68.

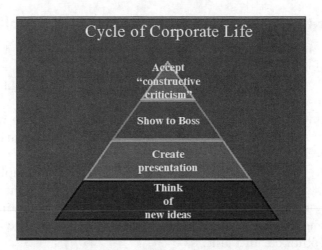

FIGURE 3-68   The Pyramid diagram with the thick outline style.

DIAGRAM ISSUES The unfortunate aspect of the diagrams is that they are "objects" with limited ability to be customized. For example, making large text fonts fit into the placeholders can be a challenge—it frequently helps to use the Shift+Enter command to create line spacing vertically in order to make the text more visible. You can't move the placeholders around, so if text needs to be adjusted, using no text in the diagram and adding it with text boxes may be the only answer.

Although you can easily add a title as part of the diagram (by pasting or dropping it in), adding clip art or images is more difficult—they will always be separate objects and may not display predictably with the diagram, so test them fully.

However, the diagrams have one terrific advantage—they can be shown sequentially using Custom Animation, as we shall see in the next chapter.

The PowerPoint diagrams are terrific quick creation tools to make bullets into images. In fact, as we saw in the preview of PowerPoint 2007 in Chapter 2, the next version will add new SmartArt diagrams for even more concepts.

In the meantime, using the Diagram gallery to fine-tune your thought processes by using the little prompts for each potential metaphor to determine a better way to tell your story and then seeing if the standard diagram types can work is a great way to put your ideas into slides quickly and effectively.

Creating Diagrams with the Drawing Toolbar

Sometimes the PowerPoint diagrams don't quite do the trick or there are concepts that involve very specific parameters. A terrific example of this is the Timeline—a scenario that comes up in many different fields from construction to law.

Unfortunately, there is no Timeline diagram native to PowerPoint—perhaps it will be added to the next version, but we can't always wait for that to happen.

We can tell you that there is a terrific Timeline template in Microsoft Visio, which we will look at briefly in the next chapter. But if you don't have Visio or the time to get comfortable with it, creating a timeline using the Drawing toolbar is a great way to explore this feature and learn how to use it for other creative tasks.

The most basic portion of the Timeline is, well, the actual Timeline shape itself. We could use a long boring rectangle, or we could go with something a bit more creative like the Can 3D cylinder found in the Basic Shapes palette of the AutoShapes panel of the Drawing toolbar.

We'll need to use the green Rotate tool to change its orientation from vertical to horizontal and the yellow carat to make its edge more circular.

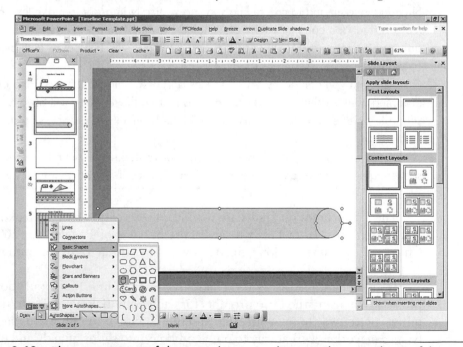

FIGURE 3-69   There are scores of drawing shapes on the AutoShapes palettes of the Drawing toolbar.

The key to working with these objects is to click them to *select them and modify them in any way* and then click elsewhere to de-select them and do something else. We could instantly name this timeline by typing inside it when it is selected, but that would make it harder to work with.

To create a fairly accurate scale representing a year of twelve months, I'm going to create a table with one row and twelve columns below the timeline and fill in the names of the months.

Eventually I drag the table beneath the timeline by using the Draw > Order > Send to Back command, as shown in Figure 3-70 (similar to what we did with the disc and pie chart in Figure 3-58).

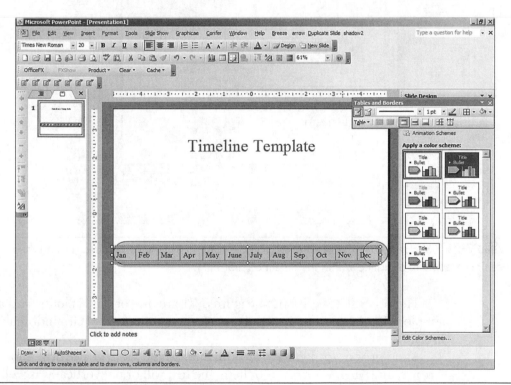

FIGURE 3-70   We can use a simple table to put equally spaced markers within the timeline.

A timeline will need to be populated with markers like milestones.

The Decision shape in the Flowchart AutoShapes palette will make an excellent "deadline." We can drag it out under the timeline and have it point to a month and day where something must take place. We can give it a red Fill color, drag through the text to make it bold, and give the entire shape a moderate shadow, as shown in Figure 3-71. To name the shape, just start typing with it selected; to rename it or format the text, drag through the text and retype its name.

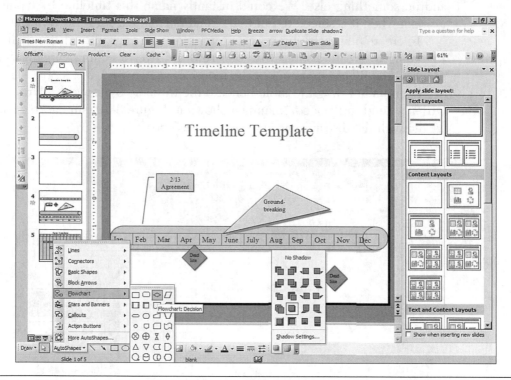

FIGURE 3-71 We make a red deadline shape and copy it elsewhere to reuse again while naming a specific deadline within the timeline ("Permit").

The other shapes shown in Figure 3-71 are one of the Callouts, and a simple triangle can be renamed for another milestone ("Groundbreaking").

Another way to populate the timeline would be with vertical Block Arrows, and when you type into them, the text will orient vertically as well.

To keep the diagram consistent, you can do a number of things:

- Copy and paste the shapes so that they're identical
- CTRL+drag out "cloned" copies of the shapes
- Use the Format Painter to pick up and apply attributes from one shape to another
- Save the shapes to the Clipboard Task Pane or other slides to (re)use them

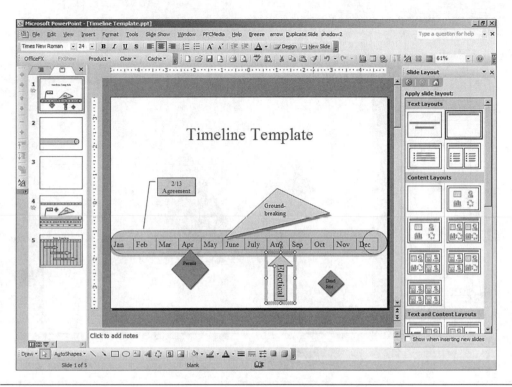

FIGURE 3-72   A vertical Block Arrow can also be used as timeline marker.

You can instantly thicken the borders of a selected shape by using the Line tool popup toolbar and change its Fill color with the Bucket tool.

In this manner, you can expand on the Timeline, reuse the elements in other slides, and save the finished slide as its own presentation or template (*.POT) file.

To improve the quality of the graphics, you might want to hire a designer or take advantage of the tips provided by Nancy Duarte in her articles for Presentations Magazine (http://snipurl.com/kmbm) "Creating PhotoShop Graphics in PowerPoint," InfoComm's Super-Tuesday sessions, and PowerPoint LIVE.

With her permission (www.duarte.com), here is an example of Nancy's use of perspective (Figure 3-73).

Whether you try to do it yourself or let a designer use the Drawing toolbar, it can greatly add to the visual impact of your slides and serve your storytelling cause very well.

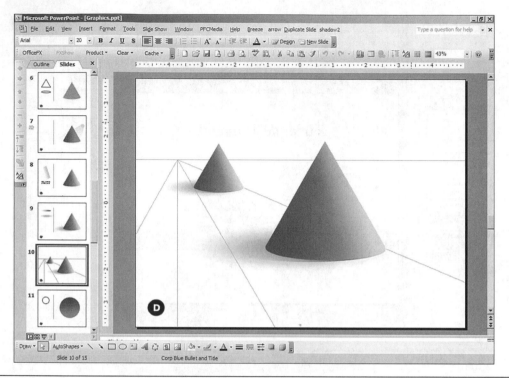

FIGURE 3-73 Having a professional designer use techniques like shading, perspective, lighting, and shadows can make your drawing objects look a lot better.

TIMELINE TEMPLATES If you press F1 (Help) in PowerPoint and do a search for Timeline, you get some useful results. First of all, you get some hints on the Advanced Animation Timeline, which we'll cover in the next chapter.

But you also get links to a series of at least six Timeline PowerPoint Templates at the Microsoft Office Assistance Center. The main page for these (Schedules and Planners) is http://snipurl.com/knch. Some of these can be easily replicated by creating a table for the Timeline grid and placing block areas within it for a project with parallel tracks, but why reinvent the wheel? You can easily customize them now that you understand the ins and outs of the Drawing toolbar.

Using a Visio Timeline

Although we will be working with a number of third-party programs in Chapters 6 and 7 (including a deeper look at Visio), this is a great time to quickly explore the Timeline template in Visio and compare it to what's in PowerPoint.

If you have Visio 2003, you owe it to yourself to explore the extensive set of diagram templates that will greatly enhance your PowerPoint slides. Figure 3-74 shows the template gallery that opens automatically with Visio and the contents of the Project Schedule templates folder, including the Timeline.

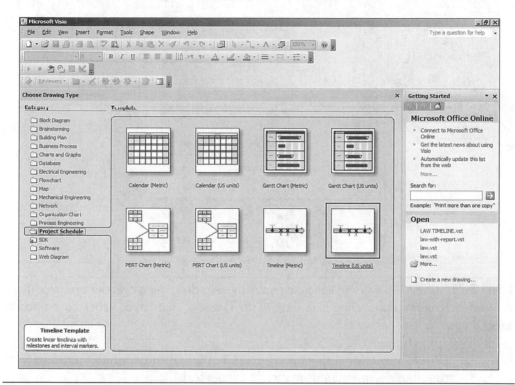

FIGURE 3-74   Visio provides an astonishing array of templates with stencils containing diagrammatic shapes for a wide assortment of functions.

When the diagram opens in Visio based on this template, you get a set of Timeline shapes on a Visio *Stencil* that you can drag into the diagram. Using a cylinder diagram allows you to configure it exactly, as shown in Figure 3-75.

The Visio timeline can be copied and pasted into a PowerPoint slide (Ctrl+A (Select All) Ctrl+C (Copy) in Visio—Ctrl+V (Paste) in PowerPoint), or imported as an Insert > Object > Visio file. It can include a number of different milestones and intervals, along with other shapes showing elapsed time.

Incidentally, you can import a timeline sequence from an Excel spreadsheet or a Microsoft Project file, and programmers can use VBA

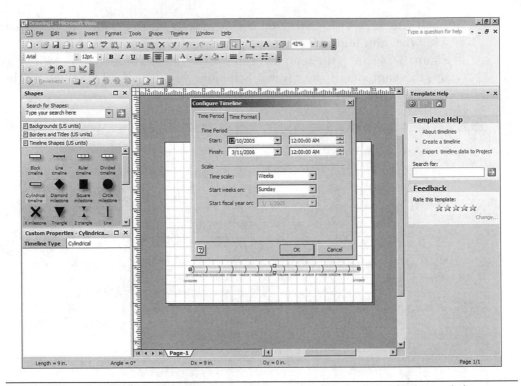

FIGURE 3-75 The Visio timeline template enables you to drag out a cylinder and slice it up in exact increments representing time slices of days, weeks, months, or years, configured to exact dates.

(Visual Basic for Applications; see Chapter 6) to generate an entire Visio timeline document automatically from a text file.

VISIO FOR ATTORNEYS Timeline files are particularly useful in the legal environment, and if that is your field, you should look on the Microsoft Assistance Templates area for a Crime Scenes template created by a private firm called Visimation, a specialist in Visio shape and stencil design. The template is available for download at http://snipurl.com/kmce.

USING THE VISIO TIMELINE IN POWERPOINT A more complete explanation of how to use the Visio Timeline in PowerPoint can be found in an article I wrote for InformIT, online at http://snipurl.com/d8ay.

We will also explore some of the more powerful presentation uses of native Visio files in Chapter 6.

Case Study: Conceptualizing, Creating, and Animating a Diagram to Tell a Story

I'm fortunate to be able to use a real-life case study to introduce the animation techniques that we'll cover in the next chapter.

Imagine that you are the presentation professional working for or hoping to land the account for a pharmaceutical company with a new product that treats sleep disorders.

You've probably seen a number of commercials for these products on TV, but you don't have the budget for a big-time video production or media campaign. Nonetheless, your client expects you to put together a presentation that effectively convinces physicians and psychiatrists that your particular medical remedy is the best one to use.

Although your client comes armed with lots of facts in the form of clinical studies and charts, you are convinced that to truly influence the decision of professionals in this field, you will need to tell your story in a more compelling fashion.

Considering the use of analogy as a key element to your final decision, what might your response be in this situation?

Think about it before you begin reading the next section.

Key Issues to Consider

You might respond as follows:

- What are the real dynamics of the waking and sleeping states?
- What sets your product apart from others in this field?
- Specifically how does your product induce the desired effects?
- What might be the personal experience of people who struggle with sleep disorders?

Finding the Analogy

In thinking about this same issue, a friend of mine, Dr. Leslie Lundt, who practices in this field in Boise, Idaho, came up with an interesting metaphor.

In her mind, the struggle between wakefulness and sleep represents a psychic "tug of war." So Dr. Lundt found two appropriate images and created the image sequence shown in Figure 3-76.

FIGURE 3-76   By visualizing a tug of war between waking and sleep, Dr. Lundt conveys the message of what a product will relieve.

Dr. Lundt's actual single slide is shown in Figure 3-77. Those who took our advice and checked out the presenting style of Larry Lessig will see his influence. She begins with white words on a black background and then adds the images that symbolize the conflict.

How is it done in one slide? If you look at the right panel of the screen, you will see PowerPoint's Custom Animation Task Pane, which will time the entrance of all of the slide elements so that they make their appearance sequentially.

You can see the numbers representing the order of the elements in the slide:

- The word "Sleep"
- The woman struggling with the rope
- The word "Wake"
- The man pulling against her

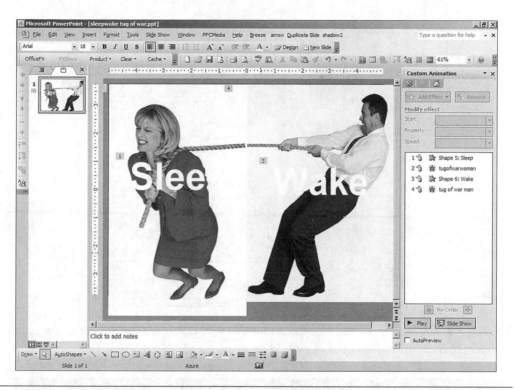

FIGURE 3-77 By visualizing a tug of war between waking and sleep, Dr. Lundt conveys the message of what a product will relieve.

Dr. Lundt chooses to show this slide by controlling it with her mouse, having each event happen as she clicks.

Another way this could be used is to have it run automatically by changing the timings of each "event" to happen After Previous by a brief interval. Then using the Slide Show > Set Up Show dialog box (see Figure 3-78), the show could be set to Loop Continuously, letting the tug of war continue for a few sequences in front of the audience.

What if you had this idea but not the images? A search on the Microsoft Office Assistance Center in the Clip Art area under images with the search term "tug of war" would provide the image shown in Figure 3-79.

In this case, we used a path animation, which we'll also cover in the next chapter, to move the picture to reveal the concepts.

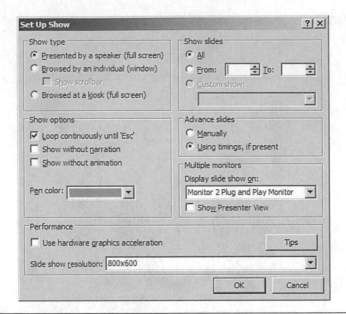

FIGURE 3-78 By letting one slide loop continuously with automatic timings for a few cycles, the relentless aspect of the tug of war could be dramatized.

FIGURE 3-79 By using a simple path animation to move the image to reveal the words "WAKE" and "SLEEP" as the struggle continues, the message can also be delivered.

Finally, if we want to continue thinking in terms of metaphors, and if there is an eternal struggle between waking and sleep, my colleague Zelazny might have another idea—if you visit his website, you will see his fascination with chess. In his honor, I will show you another use of the Fade Exit animation: making a white chess piece fade out to reveal waking and making a black piece fade out to reveal sleeping (see Figure 3-80).

Again, these were easily obtained from the Microsoft Office Assistance Center in the Clip Art area under images.

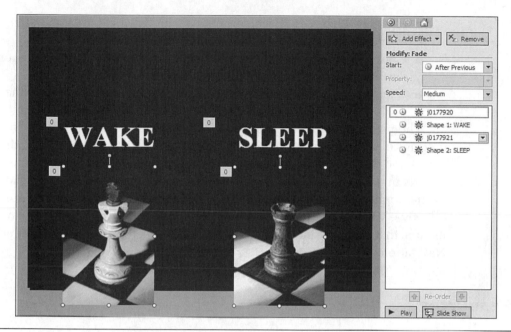

FIGURE 3-80   Fading out white and black chess pieces to reveal the words "WAKE" and "SLEEP" also creates an analogy to dramatize the struggle.

Summary

This chapter was really about going beyond Title and Bullet slides and creating the type of visuals that can take PowerPoint to the next level.

We started by using "words as pictures" to demonstrate how the visual capability of PowerPoint can even make language evocative. Of course, the real power of analogies comes through with the use of actual images, which we cataloged and imported first as clip art using the Clip Organizer and then compiled and inserted from actual picture/document folders. We pointed out how picture quality is determined by file size and resolution and what sorts of images work best in PowerPoint under various circumstances.

The essentials of creating powerful visuals are

- Using Pictures and the Picture toolbar
- Cataloging images and media in the Clip Organizer

- Creating charts in Excel or natively in PowerPoint and adding images to them where possible
- Conveying complex concepts with native PowerPoint diagrams or custom diagrams created with the Drawing toolbar
- Using other programs like Visio for strategic concepts like timelines

The main objective of this chapter is to get your creative juices flowing in terms of creatively using analogies to tell your stories and expanding dry charts and diagrams with more imaginative symbols. We called upon some experts in this area like Gene Zelazny for hints on conceptualizing our data in memorable charts and then adding images to make them even more effective. We concluded with a case study that featured some creative animation that takes us into our next topic: The Secrets of Animation and Navigation.

Resources

Stock photography (rights-managed and royalty-free images) is a great source of images for PowerPoint slides and also can serve as inspiration for using pictures as metaphors and analogies for business and other communication tasks. A partial list of stock image websites includes

- Able Stock—www.ablestock.com
- Corbis Image Library—www.corbis.com
- Jupiter Images—www.jupiterimages.com
- Liquid Library—www.liquidlibrary.com
- PhotoObjects—www.photoobjects.net
- Stock Layouts—www.stocklayouts.com

Besides Visio, other third-party tools can help you create more compelling visuals. These companies concentrate on various types of business diagrams and help you select the content and make it look professional:

- Business Graphics—Graphicae—www.graphicae.com
- SmartDraw—http://www.smartdraw.com
- Storyboard Quick—http://www.powerproduction.com
- Rich Chart Builder—http://www.blue-pacific.com
- Crystal Graphics Charts—http://www.crystalgraphics.com

- 3D directly within PowerPoint—http://www.perspector.com
- Visual Complexity—data driven visuals—http://www.visualcomplexity.com/vc/
- PowerPoint Extreme Image Manipulation Add-In—http://snipurl.com/sbon

3D imagery can be a terrific asset for legal, medical, and architectural presentations. If you think it would be helpful for your own endeavors, here are some companies that specialize in authoring in 3D and generally outputting into a still image or video format:

- Ulead Cool 3D Production Studio—http://www.ulead.com
- Autodesk 3D Studio Max—http://snipurl.com/phgy (Autodesk also has acquired Maya and Alias—other 3D tools with info at the website.)
- Carrara 3D—http://www.eovia.com
- Ngrain—3D for equipment and machinery—http://www.ngrain.com
- Ventuz—3D products—Designer, 3D Realtime, Presentation—http://www.ventuz.com/

Reference Books

Check out these sources from Gene Zelazny (www.zelazny.com):

- *Say It With Charts: The Executive's Guide to Visual Communication* by Gene Zelazny, McGraw-Hill (February 22, 2001).
- *Say It with Charts Workbook* by Gene Zelazny, McGraw-Hill (August 24, 2005).
- *Say It With Presentations: How to Design and Deliver Successful Business Presentations* by Gene Zelazny, McGraw-Hill (December 21, 1999).

Gene Zelazny just informed me that the latest update of his book, *Say It With Presentations*, has two new chapters: "Say It With Imagination" and "Say It With Animation." I fully expect that these will stimulate your creative sides to come up with memorable and insightful metaphors and analogies in your visuals.

3. CREATING DYNAMIC VISUALS

Websites with Cool Sample Charts and Diagrams

Visit these websites to get some ideas for charts and diagrams:

- www.terbergdesign.com
- www.duarte.com
- http://www.tlccreative.com/ppt_examples.htm (download showcase)
- Dan Roam—http://www.milliondollarchart.com
- Photo Album Add-In for PowerPoint 2000—http://snipurl.com/31jg

The following sites have plug-ins for PhotoShop to enhance your images:

- Luce (Light)—http://snipurl.com/sfdg
- Flaming Pear (Commercial but free at the bottom)—http://www.flamingpear.com/index.html
- Polaroid Dust and Scratch Removal—http://snipurl.com/sfdn
- Virtual Photographer—http://www.optikvervelabs.com/
- Bordermania—http://www.pluginfilters.com/bordermania/
- AutoFX Mosaics—Also check out Dreamy Photo and the rest of the Dreamsuite products http://snipurl.com/sfds
- Harry's Filters—http://snipurl.com/sfdw
- Also check out—http://thepluginsite.com
- The Little Inkpot—http://snipurl.com/sfdx
- Vanderlee Plug-Ins—http://snipurl.com/sfdz

CHAPTER 4

SECRETS OF ANIMATION AND NAVIGATION

There are many reasons for the popularity of electronic presentations and digital media:

- They're relatively easy to create, save, and revise, making it possible to reuse resources effectively and efficiently.
- They can be projected to large audiences and transported easily on a laptop (and also on a DVD player, as we'll see in Chapter 7, "The Latest Technologies: Beyond PowerPoint to the Future").
- They can incorporate motion, which was missing in 35mm slides.

In many ways, the ability to introduce motion is the feature that has truly enabled electronic presentations to take advantage of the metaphor of stage and film production. Elements can be introduced as they are needed in groups or as individual components. In some ways, the reason for so many bad PowerPoint presentations may well be the power of the program itself—everybody is suddenly a director.

We've all witnessed presentations with whizzing bullets accompanied by meaningless and annoying sound effects—remember the camera click that was popular years ago as an accompaniment to every bullet and slide transition? Horrible.

But in this chapter, we'll investigate the legitimate uses of motion to create emotion—or at least stir and maintain the interest of the audience.

We'll examine the various ways in which using animation and navigation techniques can make us better storytellers.

Importance of Timing

If you've ever seen a series of comedians perform back to back, you've intuitively realized what sets the great ones apart from the average performers. If you really examine the material closely, frequently it is on a par. But what makes one entertainer stand out, particularly in the area of telling a story, is timing:

- Elements of the material are withheld and introduced at key points.
- Tension is maintained.
- Climaxes are set up and paid off.
- Conflict is articulated and resolved.

Speaker coaches frequently have presenters tell a personal story to engage the audience before they begin what may be a dry, boring presentation.

The idea is that hopefully the energy that they can convey in the course of relating a meaningful anecdote will translate into the whole talk. First, it will build empathy with the audience, then it will foster confidence in the speaker, and finally, hopefully some of the same elements of dramatic effect may actually work in the slide show and accompanying speech.

For example, in Chapter 1, "Planning an Effective Presentation," we talked about identifying the pain as a way to set up your talk and build interest in your topic.

Presumably at some point, the speaker will also provide the antidote to the pain.

When and how this solution is presented will determine the success of the presentation, and in terms of using visuals along with words, PowerPoint and other electronic media let you control the all-important *when*.

In his book, *Multimedia Learning*, Richard Mayer makes the point that we use two primary channels for processing information; he calls them the verbal channel and the visual channel. This combination is what he defines as *multimedia*, setting it apart from what one might call "monotone" or "monotonous" learning—where only a single channel, usually the verbal, is engaged.

He maintains that when both of these channels are used strategically there is more retention of information.

Mayer's seven principles of multimedia development are

- **The Multimedia Principle**—Students learn better from words and pictures than from words alone.

- **The Spatial Contiguity Principle**—Students learn better when corresponding words and pictures are presented near to rather than far from each other on the page or screen.
- **The Temporal Contiguity Principle**—Students learn better when corresponding words and pictures are presented simultaneously rather than successively.
- **The Coherence Principle**—Students learn better when extraneous words, pictures, and sounds are excluded rather than included.
- **The Modality Principle**—Students learn better from animation and narration than from animation and onscreen text.
- **The Redundancy Principle**—Students learn better from animation and narration than from animation, narration, and onscreen text.
- **The Individual Differences Principle**—Design effects are greater for low-knowledge learners than for high-knowledge learners and for high-spatial learners than for low-spatial learners.

Although you might not think of a sales presentation or an inspirational talk as an educational event in which learning theory is involved, I'm sure you would agree that when information is retained, the speaker's goals are more likely to be achieved.

In addition, going back to the analogy of the dramatic production, if the audience is fully engaged, the presentation is far more likely to be successful.

Mayer's main point is that this duality of processing information is what potentially sets multimedia apart from more traditional forms of communication.

But what sets good multimedia apart from bad multimedia is how these elements are *strategically combined*—and the key to that process inevitably comes down to *timing*.

Types of Animation in PowerPoint

Animation in PowerPoint is not a Disney production. It is mainly a way to introduce elements sequentially:

- **Within a slide**—Bullets and other elements
- **Between slides**—As timed transitions similar to video effects
- **Animation Schemes**—Pre-set Entrance effects for bullets and sometimes slide titles

■ **Custom Animation**—Using an advanced Timeline to sequence effects for Entrance, Emphasis, Exit, and even more complex Paths

Let's see how these features can be used practically to enhance our message.

Breaking Up Your Bullets

The classic animation technique in PowerPoint is to have your bullets (and possibly the slide title) appear as you mention them—sort of like "hitting your mark" in a dramatic production.

In a small setting, this is can be accomplished simply by hitting the down arrow on the keyboard to advance to the next "event" or "build"; as we'll see in Chapter 8, "Delivering a Killer Presentation," in a more sophisticated venue, the presenter would use a portable mouse to allow mobility and accommodate a large screen.

Generally, you can make the point that the effectiveness of visual bullets is inversely proportional to their length.

Go back to Chapter 3, "Creating Dynamic Visuals," Figure 3-1, which is a conventional slide with four long expository bullets.

We know that you probably wouldn't want to use these kinds of bullets, which would have your audience reading while you're trying to make your point or, even worse, have you reading the bullets themselves as your audience falls asleep.

But your boss might insist that this material be included.

The easiest way to break it up into presentable chunks is to use the *Animation Schemes* in PowerPoint.

In the Animation Schemes Task Pane, you can instantly click to apply any animation, such as Appear, to a slide in the Window as shown in Figure 4-1.

When it's done and this slide is presented full-screen, each chunk of information is withheld until the presenter is ready to deal with it, as shown in Figure 4-2.

At the bottom of the Animation Schemes Task Pane is a button that lets you apply a simple animation like this to all the slides in your presentation. But bear the following in mind.

Animation Schemes only affect the bullets and in some cases the title placeholders of affected slides…and if there are lots of slides like this in your presentation, you are in big trouble.

This is simply the lazy presenter's way to work—filling up your slides with masses of information and hoping that it comes across.

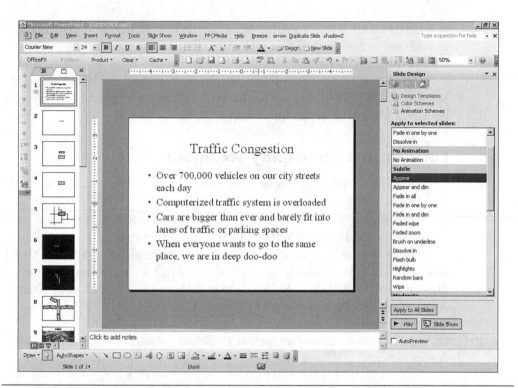

FIGURE 4-1   By opening the Animation Schemes Task Pane and clicking to select the Appear Animation, you apply it to the slide shown in Normal view.

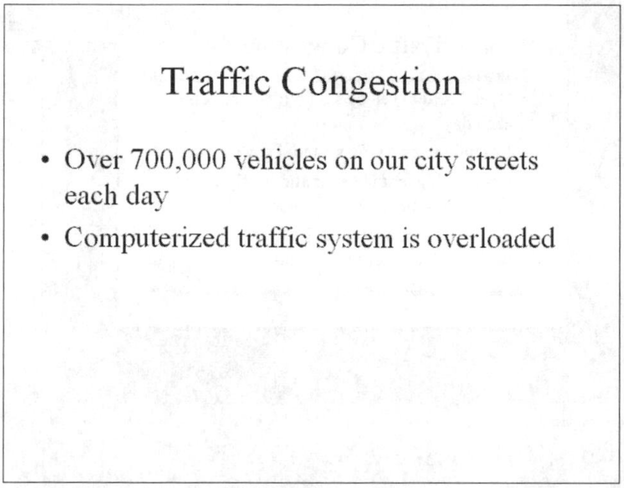

Traffic Congestion

- Over 700,000 vehicles on our city streets each day
- Computerized traffic system is overloaded

FIGURE 4-2   With an Animation Scheme applied, the bullets are broken up into "builds."

Unless your subject matter is highly technical, and you are very animated and accomplished as a presenter, this way of presenting material is deadly dull and ineffective.

Worst of all, it tends to make most presenters read the bullets from the screen, which predictably can lead to a significant attrition rate of any non-captive audience after the first break.

Fade In: The Screenplay Technique

If you've ever read a screenplay, you know that it opens with two words: FADE IN.

Presumably, this effect adds drama to the production, and if you must animate a set of bullets, it's probably the best way to go.

There is a Fade Animation Scheme, but instead let's Undo the previous set of bullets to which we applied the Appear Animation Scheme or choose another Title and Bullet slide and then go directly to the Custom Animation Task Pane as shown in Figure 4-3.

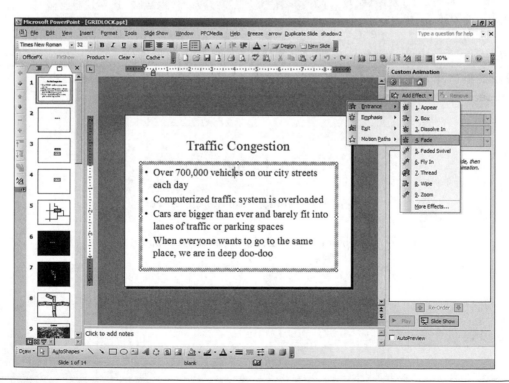

FIGURE 4-3   With a Fade Entrance effect applied in Custom Animation, the bullets will also be controlled by an individual mouse click.

Now, when we select the entire bullet placeholder, we can choose to apply an Entrance effect—and among those we can apply is the Fade effect.

But what if you didn't want to get lulled into the rote click—show bullet—talk routine and absolutely needed to show this information? You could use a staggered automatic Fade in command that would serve three purposes:

- Introduce all of your subject matter dramatically
- Let your audience absorb it for a few moments before you began your commentary
- Let you compose your thoughts and perhaps take a breath and a drink of water

Several aspects of this technique will further reveal the vistas of the Custom Animation Task Pane.

Open the Advanced Timeline

Now, before we go any farther, we need to click the drop-down arrow and open up (show) the Advanced Animation Timeline (see Figure 4-4).

You'll want to drag the border of the Task Pane to the left to give yourself more room and see more of the Timeline.

TURN OFF AUTOPREVIEW PowerPoint is so proud of its animation capability that it wants to show you how it's going to look each time you add a move. This can get a bit annoying—so uncheck the AutoPreview option at the bottom of the Custom Animation Task Pane before creating complex animation sequences.

Next, click the drop-down arrow again and change the selection for how the bullets should be launched from On Click to With Previous (see Figure 4-5).

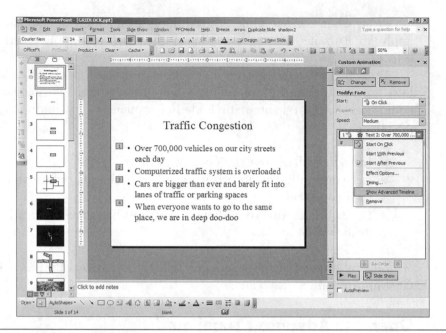

FIGURE 4-4   Click the drop-down arrow to the individual effect to show the Advanced Timeline.

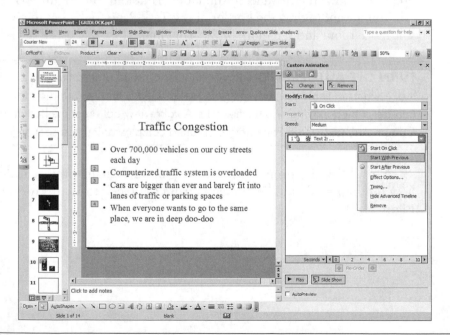

FIGURE 4-5   The drop-down arrow lets you modify how the Bullet Entrance effects are launched.

Now click the Expand/Collapse arrow to Expand the Contents of the Bullet Entrance effects as shown in Figure 4-6.

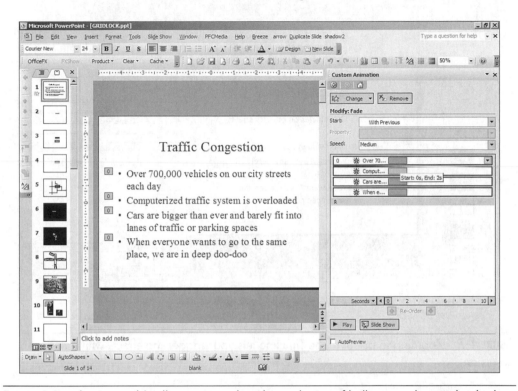

FIGURE 4-6 The Expand/Collapse arrow breaks up the set of bullets into their individual components.

Notice that with the bullets broken up, a two-second span of time (the default) represents each individual bullet entrance—in this scenario, all four "actors" would enter at the same time.

If you hover your mouse at the end of each individual span, you can drag to extend the length of time for each entrance (Fade) to longer than two seconds.

If you hover your mouse over the span itself, you can *drag each span of time to a position further down on the Timeline*, staggering the Entrance effects. If you want to further refine these intervals, you can click on the Seconds drop-down arrow and Zoom In or Out of the Timeline, as shown in Figure 4-7.

You can stagger the intervals of timed automatic entrances by moving the With Previous effects out on the Timeline so that they overlap one another, and you can use the Zoom command to refine the technique.

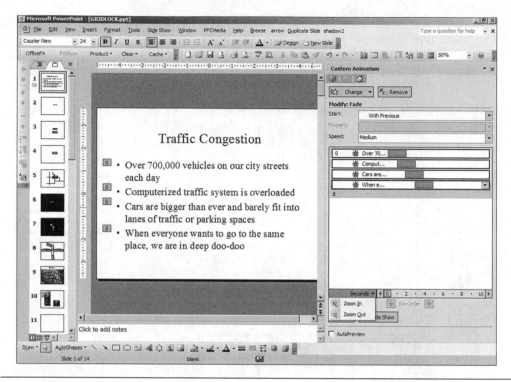

FIGURE 4-7 Zooming in or out of the Timeline lets you stagger the effects with more precision.

Now you have a nice, effective slide that will interest your audience in some complex information, and you can expound upon it after waiting a few seconds to let them absorb it.

CREDIT IS DUE This technique is one of many I learned from working with Rick Altman at his fabulous PowerPoint LIVE show in San Diego. To learn more, visit his website (www.altman.com).

There are other ways to use the staggered fade entrance:

- If you automate everything in the slide, it can make a self-running infomercial or kiosk application.
- You can duplicate this slide and simply replace the bullets to reuse the staggered fade entrance in other slides or presentations.
- Having broken up the bullets, you can now intersperse other effects for other objects in the slide between the bullets.

SELF-RUNNING SHOWS Completely automated and self-running shows can be used as trade show exhibits, tabletop displays, or they can be run at breaks during your speaking engagements. The easiest way to create a self-running show is to use the Rehearse Timings feature under Set Up Show. This lets you run the show manually in real time, and there is a step at the end which allows you to save the timings of the rehearsed show with all transitions and effects set to run automatically. You can then tweak and refine these saved automatic timings in the Transitions and Custom Animation Task Panes.

If you want to continue to use the show as speaker support and control the timings, save it first under another name. This issue is also covered in "Three Gotchas to Avoid" in Chapter 8.

Making Images Appear Strategically

Now that I've got my text bullets animated, let's explore this Custom Animation Task Pane a bit further.

With my bullets broken up, what if I want a picture to appear between the third and fourth bullet?

The first thing I would do is to change the Task Pane to Slide Layout and (re)apply a Text and Content layout to the slide, as shown in Figure 4-8.

Now I can click the Clip Art button in the Content panel to open the miniature version of the Clip Organizer (See Chapter 3 for more information on the Clip Organizer) and search for "Traffic". Having located an image I want to insert, I click OK, as shown in Figure 4-9.

With the Content layout placeholder in the slide, the picture is automatically resized for me into the slide.

As it currently stands, the title ("Traffic Congestion") and the picture would appear with the slide in the presentation. But I want the picture to make a more dramatic entrance, following the third bullet.

I can click the Back button on the top of the Task Pane to return to Custom Animation and add another Fade Entrance effect to the *selected Picture* (see Figure 4-10).

The Fade Entrance for the Picture comes with the On Click launch command by default.

Now I need to move it above the fourth bullet in the Order List.

I can either drag it up one level or, with the Picture Entrance effect selected, click the Up Re-Order button one time.

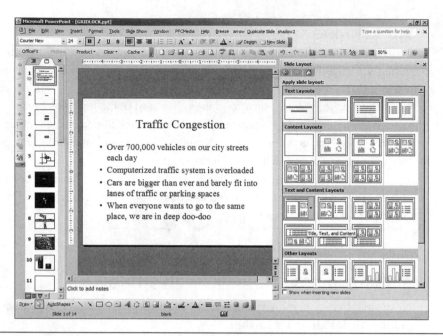

FIGURE 4-8 (Re)applying a Text and Content layout is the easiest way to make room for a picture within the slide.

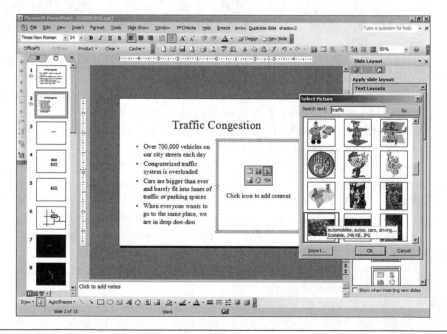

FIGURE 4-9 With the Content panel open, I can insert either a picture from Clip Art (the Clip Organizer) or a Picture from File.

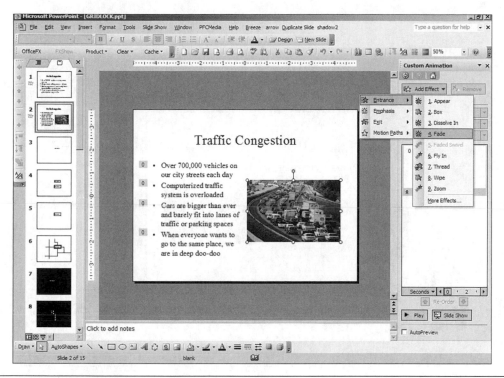

FIGURE 4-10 With the Picture selected, it can be given its own Entrance effect.

But here's the remaining issue—the fourth bullet is still set to Fade in With Previous. It needs to have its launch command changed to On Click, as shown in Figure 4-11.

Now the story will happen as we want:

1. The title and first three bullets fade in automatically.
2. The speaker has time to elucidate and set up the picture.
3. The speaker clicks, and the image appears.
4. One last point remains to be made.
5. The speaker clicks, and the last bullet appears.

Depending upon the message we now want to craft, we have the tools to refine the entrance and launch commands for our selected objects within the Custom Animation Task Pane.

We've also learned something else: *Any object that can be selected in your slide can be animated.*

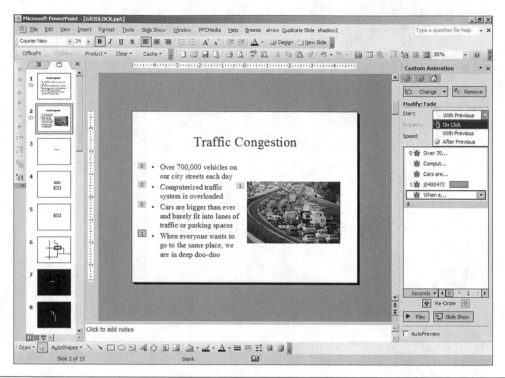

FIGURE 4-11   To control the appearance of the Picture, change its start setting to On Click.

In going beyond the Larry Lessig example (refer to Chapter 3), this can be very effective. If you viewed one of his presentations, you would see a series of words appear as he says them, accentuated by their sudden appearance and his practiced and distinct elocution.

Now we also have the tools to accomplish this within a single slide.

If we wanted to return to the concepts of Chapter 3 and use some of the "word pictures" in text boxes to present a similar (and perhaps more effective) message, the original slide might look like Figure 4-12.

Now we have the tools to make these text boxes appear in any order we want.

With a minimum of effort, we can follow the procedure for the simple bullets to make the entire story unfold in staggered fades automatically, as shown in Figure 4-13.

Remember that the word "Gridlock" is composed of eight individual textboxes.

By dragging a box around them, I can select them all as a unit and apply a Fade command to them all at once. Then I can zoom out of the

Timeline and stagger the appearance of all of the letters, following the appearance of the beginning of the "formula."

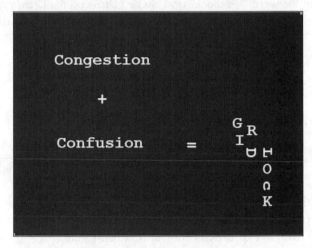

FIGURE 4-12   Using a set of text boxes as word images can convey an effective message.

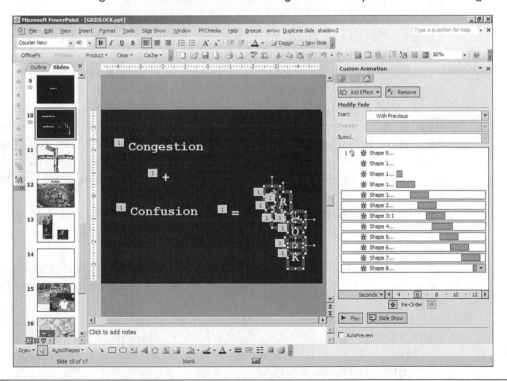

FIGURE 4-13   By using the With Previous command and staggering the entrances, we can animate the entire formula as a story unto itself.

4. SECRETS OF ANIMATION AND NAVIGATION

GROUPING THE LETTERS If we were lazy, we could have selected all of the letters in the word "Gridlock" and clicked Draw on the Drawing toolbar and selected Group. Then we could have made them fade in as a unit with less work.

What's useful about this slide is that all of the information is in one place, which is helpful for handouts.

Taking Advantage of Transitions

But that isn't really how Larry Lessig works, is it?

He achieves his effect by having words strategically *replace* other words.

Although you can certainly do this within a single slide by using an Exit effect prior to another Entrance effect between bullets or text boxes, this is a good time to explore another animation technique—Transitions.

As we saw in the previous chapter, putting a single word on a slide can be very effective.

But is there really a difference between using a Fade Entrance effect for a single word in a slide and using the Fade command for a Transition between slides with individual words?

This is the type of philosophical debate we might have at PowerPoint LIVE, but actually, I would submit that the answer is probably no.

Figure 4-14 shows what I mean. Here, there are three consecutive word-picture slides in Slide Sorter View. Although we could go to Custom Animation to make each individual word Fade in, we can do the same thing at the slide level by using a Smooth Fade transition and instantly applying it to three *selected slides* by clicking each while holding down the CTRL key.

Other transitions can also more *naturally* animate certain storylines.

For example, let's go back to the text table we created in the last chapter (Figure 3-43).

As a PowerPoint table, there is no way to animate this object as a unit (as opposed to the charts and diagrams, which we'll see in the upcoming section).

So what if you wanted to set it up by showing the parameters (categories) first and then revealing them for each salesperson?

Look at Figure 4-15. It shows the original table and five *duplicate slides* that were created from it.

In each subsequent slide, we have deleted one row fewer than the slide before, revealing another row of the slide.

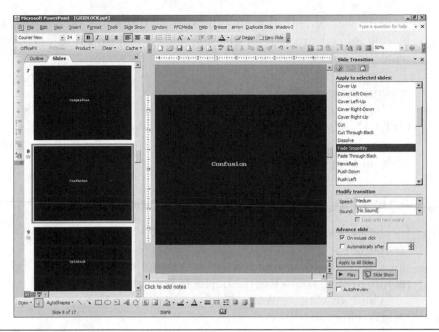

FIGURE 4-14   Using Transitions between slides can be an easier way to quickly create a Fade or other effect, and it can be applied to multiple slides in Slide Sorter view.

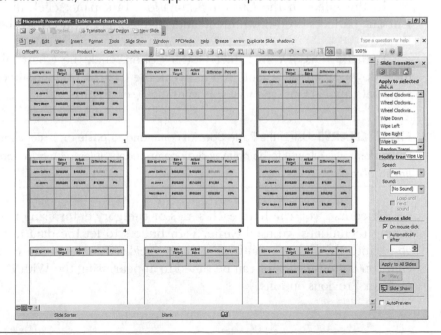

FIGURE 4-15   Using a set of duplicate slides and adding a Wipe transition allows you to build a table in stages.

This was done by dragging through each row and then hitting Delete, leaving a blank area within the table into which to "bring" the next set of data.

Now by using a natural Wipe Up motion in the Transition, each row appears to be climbing into the table.

In the next set of slides, you can see that we have actually used the CTRL+X (Cut) command to completely delete any part of the table. Either way, using transitions between the slides allows us to "build" the table and complete our story.

Animating PowerPoint Charts and Diagrams

Unlike tables, PowerPoint charts and diagrams can be animated by their components.

This works the same way as we've seen with bullets, text boxes, and pictures—first, you select the object to animate.

Then, in Custom Animation, you give it an Entrance effect such as Dissolve in.

Of course, now the entire chart will dissolve in when you click your mouse.

In the effect in the Custom Animation Task pane, click the Chart Entrance effect's drop-down menu and select Effect Options, as shown in Figure 4-16.

With the Dissolve in Effect Options open, click the Chart tab. The drop-down menu will enable you to tweak the Chart Entrance effect until your data appears just the way you want it to (see Figure 4-17).

EXCEL CHARTS Using the Paste Special command to paste an Excel chart into PowerPoint will allow it to be animated by components *unless you have made it a linked object.*

Of course, you can have each series or category enter using the same timing techniques we used earlier with bullets to let the data in a chart come into the slide elegantly and automatically. Elements can enter the chart on a mouse click or can be timed to appear using the With Previous or After Previous options.

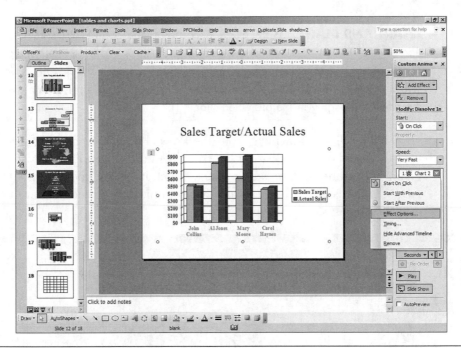

FIGURE 4-16   After applying an Entrance effect to a chart, select the animation's Effect Options from the drop-down menu.

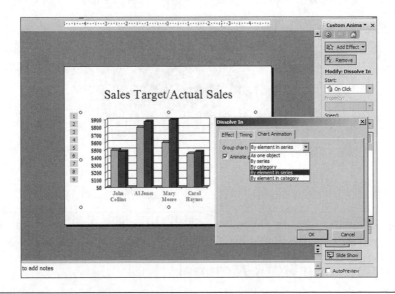

FIGURE 4-17   In the Effect Options dialog box, you can choose to have a category or data series enter the chart sequentially.

CHART AND DIAGRAM EFFECTS Because of their complexity, some animation effects will not work with charts and diagrams; for example, their components cannot Swivel—I know that's really a shame. Choose simple effects and you should have no trouble. If you're not sure, use trial and error, and preview the effect thoroughly in the projected slide.

This is what is also nice about the PowerPoint diagrams (refer to Figures 3-67 and 3-68 in Chapter 3). By selecting them individually and first giving the entire diagram an Entrance effect, it can be opened into its own Effect Options dialog box to make, for example, a Pyramid appear in up or down segments, as shown in Figure 4-18.

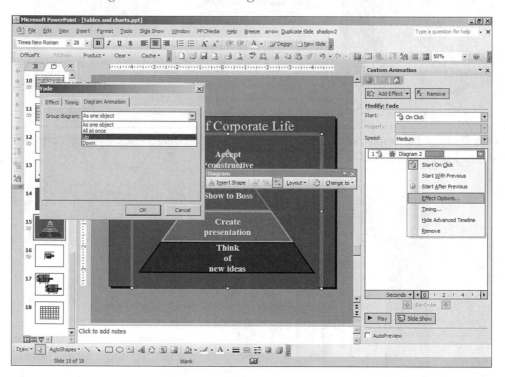

FIGURE 4-18   The Effect Options dialog box will also let you fine-tune the Entrance effect for the PowerPoint diagrams, like the Pyramid.

Animating Static Material

Sometimes you don't have a great deal of choice about your subject matter—it's just thrust upon you by the nature of the presentation itself.

Let's say you're a physician and you have to present a finding based on x-rays or some other specific set of data.

To get the material into a slide, you would first scan it into an image file, as we covered in Chapter 3.

But after the individual image is your slide, there are limits to what you can accomplish.

Or are there?

In Chapter 3, we also explored the Drawing toolbar in our project to create a Timeline. As we worked, we learned that by selecting the objects we dragged out from the AutoShapes palettes, we were able to revise them by changing attributes like Fill color and Line thickness.

Now we also know that with an object *selected*, it can be animated with an Entrance effect, an Emphasis effect, an Exit effect, or a Motion Path.

This gives us quite a bit to work with in calling attention to parts of a static photograph, chart, or graph.

We don't even need to go into AutoShapes to create our first graphic. In Figure 4-19 we have an X-ray that is showing extensive heart disease. We've selected the Oval tool on the Drawing toolbar, and by holding down the SHIFT key, we've dragged out a circle.

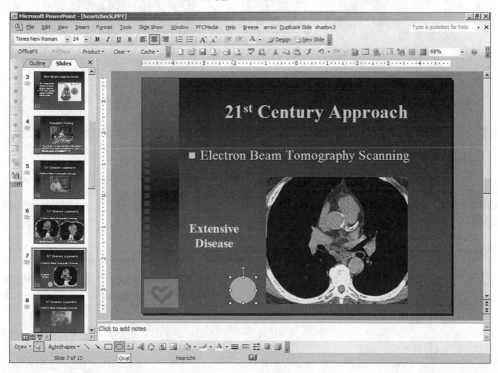

FIGURE 4-19   To call attention to parts of a static image, we can use various Drawing tools, including the Oval.

(Image courtesy of HeartCheck America.)

We make this ordinary circle into something very useful by

- Moving it over the area we want to highlight
- Changing its Line color to red
- Changing its Line thickness to 6 pt
- Changing its Fill color to None, as shown in Figure 4-20

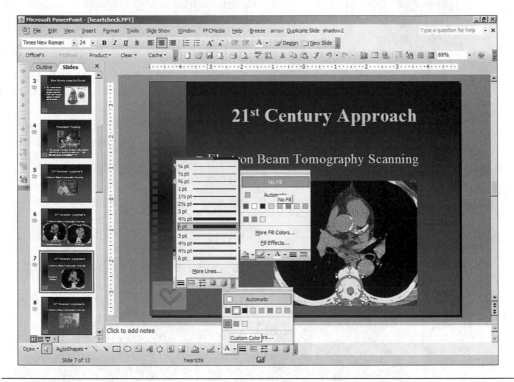

FIGURE 4-20   To call attention to parts of a static image, we can use various Drawing tools, including an empty Oval.

Then, by animating the Entrance of the circle directly over the area we want to highlight with a Fade Entrance effect (see Figure 4-21), during our presentation we can call attention to this important issue at any time with a click of the mouse.

We can continue telling the story of the x-ray with some more elements.

If we want text as part of the message, we can use a Block Arrow, as shown in Figure 4-22. Here the Block Arrow chosen is pointing to the left to highlight the areas of disease. With the arrow still selected, we can type the word "Disease" into the arrow itself.

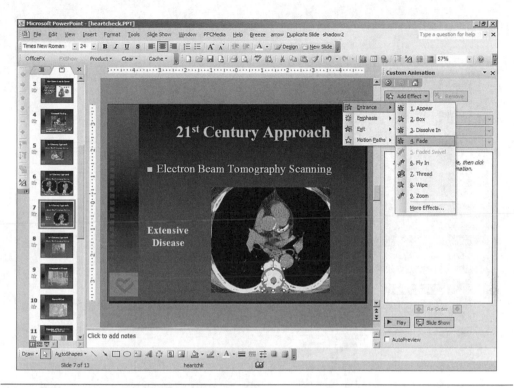

FIGURE 4-21   With the circle given an Entrance effect, it will Fade into the photo and call attention to the area on the click of a mouse.

We may need to change the Fill color of the selected Block Arrow to contrast with the slide.

If needed, we can drag through the text to select only the text, change it to bold, and make its Text color contrast with the arrow.

Finally, with an arrow pointing left, we can give it an Entrance effect where it flies in at Medium speed from the right of the slide. This will now be the second item to which we can call attention with the click of a mouse.

Finally, if we need text and a finer line to call attention to more detail, we might consider a Line Callout, as shown in Figure 4-23. Once again, we can revise its Line color and Fill color to conform to the slide and add a text label ("Problem Areas").

To create your Line Callout, click near the area you want to highlight and then drag in another direction. The result is a text box and a line leading to your destination. It's easy to revise the pointer line by selecting the Callout and moving an end point of the line, and you can use other Drawing tools like Line and Fill color and thickness to revise the other elements.

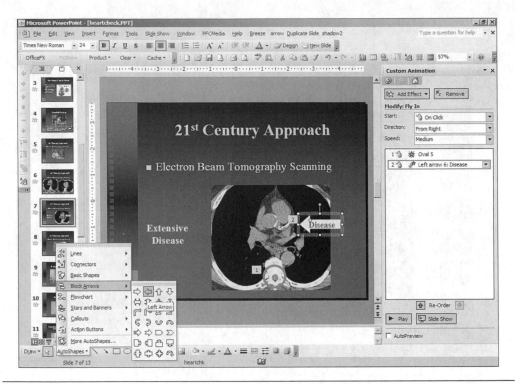

FIGURE 4-22 A Block Arrow animated to fly in can also be used to call attention to a significant area in a static image.

With the Callout selected, we can add another Fade in Entrance effect, giving us the third part of the slide we want to emphasize during the presentation (see Figure 4-23).

Remember that depending upon the presenter's style, he or she can control the entrances of these elements with the mouse click or, if he or she prefers, use the staggered animation effects we covered earlier by using the Advanced Timeline and timing all three animations using the With Previous option.

AUTOMATIC OVALS AND DRAWING TOOLS We will cover techniques for recording macros to make these kinds of drawing objects come into the slide with a single mouse click in Chapter 6, "Powerful Presentation Tools," in the section "Macro Recorder for Presentation Authoring."

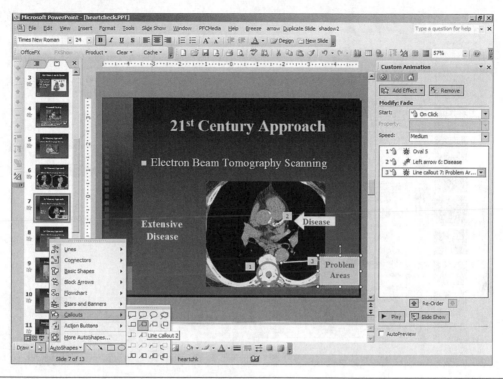

FIGURE 4-23   An animated Line Callout gives you the ability to call attention to a more precise area of the slide and also the ability to use text labels.

Depending upon the complexity of the slide and the message it conveys, you may even want to revisit one of the highlights and give it an Emphasis effect. Like the chart animations, these are limited by the nature of the shape involved; here under More Emphasis Effects we might preview several and perhaps choose the Grow/Shrink effect (see Figure 4-24).

MULTIPLE ARROWS OR OBJECTS Remember that you are not limited to a single Drawing object; to highlight a particularly important area of a static image, you could also use four arrows pointing inward and then use the Draw > Order > Group command on the Drawing toolbar to make them one single object. Then an effective Entrance effect is Zoom Out (even though they're pointing in). Try it.

Also, you can always group a text box with any other shape to give it a text label and animate them as one unit.

FIGURE 4-24 An Emphasis effect can be timed to call additional attention to an area that has already been highlighted.

With the effects in the Custom Animation Task Pane, you may need to reorder their sequence, by either dragging a selected effect up and down in the panel or clicking the Up or Down Re-Order arrows at the bottom of the pane (see Figure 4-25).

EXIT AND PATH ANIMATION EFFECTS Although you can certainly use the Exit effects with these kinds of symbols, it will just complicate your slide; you'll find a better use for this effect in the next section.

Path Animation was shown briefly in the Chapter 3 case study. It is an interesting technique to keep in mind for moving through photographs (similar to the Ken Burns effect) or perhaps moving a Timeline through your slide.

FIGURE 4-25   After the effects have been set up, you can still change their order in the Custom Animation Task Pane.

Triggers for Increased Interactivity

Although this section can certainly be used in presentations for speaker support, corporate trainers and educators will find it particularly interesting for interactive kiosks, CDs, or other learning applications.

Although a simple mouse click can "trigger" an Animation effect, up until now, we've used the word "launch" for a very particular reason.

Triggers have a meaning of their own in PowerPoint animation, and they can be very handy.

Using a trigger means that not just any mouse click will launch a specific animation (or group of animations). Rather, similar to a web page hyperlink, a trigger is the result of a mouse click *directly on another selectable object* in the slide.

Although we could make a visible area of the slide "clickable" as a trigger, in this section we'll take it a step further and create an *invisible button* or *hot area*.

This technique is perfect for a simple interactive game or training exercise.

If we use another x-ray diagram, we can add the two Block Arrows, one designating an area called "Disease" and the next pointing to an area we'll simply call "Other".

In this situation, we want the correct arrow to make an Entrance only when the user clicks on the appropriate area of the screen.

To create the hot area or invisible button, we've simply used a rectangle and given it no Fill color and no Line color, as in Figure 4-26.

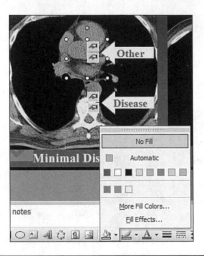

FIGURE 4-26   The selected object in the slide shown here is an invisible rectangle with no Fill or Line color.

Now it's time to assign the Entrance commands and the Triggers.

First, as we've seen, we select the object (Disease Left Arrow) and give it an Entrance effect. With the effect selected in the Custom Animation Task Pane, we click its down option arrow and select Timing (see Figure 4-27).

In the Timing tab, we select Triggers and click the radio button to Start effect On Click of the correct object as a Trigger.

Then we need to find the Trigger from among the objects in the drop-down menu—these are all of the objects we've added to the slide, with numbers in the order in which they were created. Fortunately in this scenario, there are only two rectangles. We'll try Rectangle 7 (see Figure 4-28).

In a scenario like this, we might want to distinguish one area from another and keep coming back to them. In addition, we won't necessarily know in which order they will be clicked—that's what makes this interactive.

Therefore, for each entrance of one Block Arrow, we will add an Exit for the other. In the Custom Animation Task Pane, the Entrance effects are designated with a Green Star, the Exits with a Red.

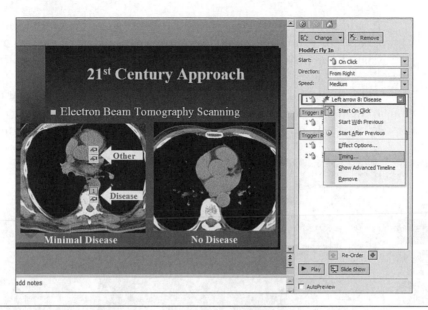

FIGURE 4-27   The selected Entrance effect has a drop-down option for Timing.

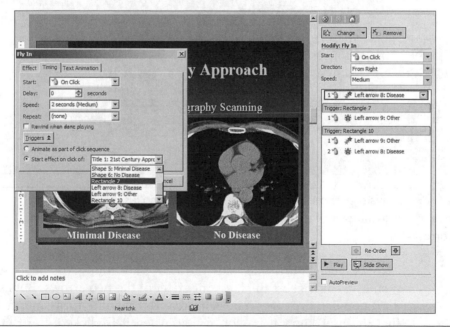

FIGURE 4-28   Instead of remaining part of a normal click sequence in a slide, the effect is now linked to a specific trigger, which needs to be clicked for it to happen.

In addition, we don't want the two triggered objects on the slide when it appears, so at the top of the Custom Animation Task Pane we give each an Exit > Disappear command With Previous (the appearance of the slide itself).

Then we assign triggers to both the Entrance and Exit animations and make them all With Previous.

When we're done, the two triggered objects are shown in Figure 4-29.

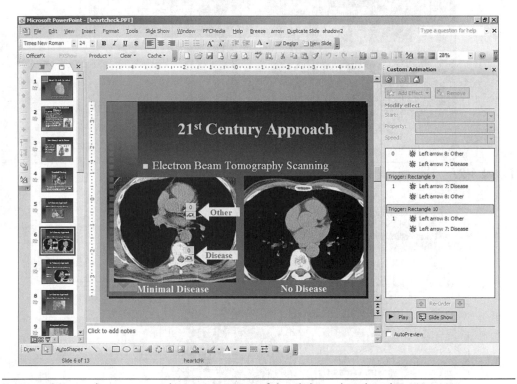

FIGURE 4-29 In this scenario the appearance of the slide makes the objects Exit (disappear), while the click of any trigger make the correct arrow Fade in and the other arrow Exit.

Now whenever the slide loads, the arrows are gone—you might say the new slide event triggers the first Exit effect of the two arrows. But as soon as the mouse moves over one hot area, the pointer turns into a hand, letting the user know it is "hot." Then, when it is clicked, the Entrance effect is triggered, and the correct arrow appears and identifies it. Then if the other area is clicked, the first arrow disappears and the correct one Fades in.

FINDING, SELECTING, AND LOCATING INVISIBLE OBJECTS After you've created your invisible object, it sometimes gets lost in the slide, especially behind other objects. First, use the Draw > Order > Bring to Front command to make sure it's on top of all other objects (so that it can be a hot zone). Then to select it, you can select any object and hit TAB to toggle through all of the selected objects in the slide.

Then, when you want to select the object as the Trigger, you will have to know its "name" in the slide as designated by PowerPoint. In the case of these objects, which are Rectangles, one is Rectangle 7 (the seventh object created), and the other is Rectangle 10.

Needless to say, the more complex your trigger slide becomes, the more important it will be to keep these names handy and noted.

If you get interested in VBA or learn how use the VBA Editor (see Chapter 6), you will find some tools to identify the objects in the slide. You can also find some tools for creating PowerPoint macros at www.rdpslides.com, the site of Power-Point MVP Steve Rindsberg. Chapter 6 also has some sample code that refers to objects by their names within the PowerPoint *Object Model*.

Triggers make your slide a truly interactive composition, whether presented in front of a group, presented to a set of users, downloaded from a web page, or even presented with a touch-screen monitor in a kiosk.

TRIGGER-HAPPY AUSSIE A master animator and PowerPoint MVP is Glenn Millar, another regular at PowerPoint LIVE. His example of triggers is a stripped-out column chart whose data series individually trigger text boxes explaining the various data points. You can find many of his excellent animation examples at www.pptworkbench.com.

Elegant Entrances and Exits

Now that we've covered the basics of using the Advanced Timeline, the With Previous option for staggered animation effects, and the use of Triggers for interactivity, we should think about how to use these tools for good rather than evil.

First of all, you might want to discard a lot of the "Exciting" effects for professional presentations; Boomerangs and Pinwheels probably won't do much to enhance communication with a group focused on your annual report, sales figures, or legal position.

On the other hand, certain Transitions can be effective for making a slide seem larger than it really is.

For example, what if you create a series of Timelines because there will be a lot of detail on each, and they won't easily fit on a single slide?

If you spread the Timelines over several slides—like the three slides for three years shown in Figure 4-30—the most elegant and natural way to move from one to the next is the Push Left Transition.

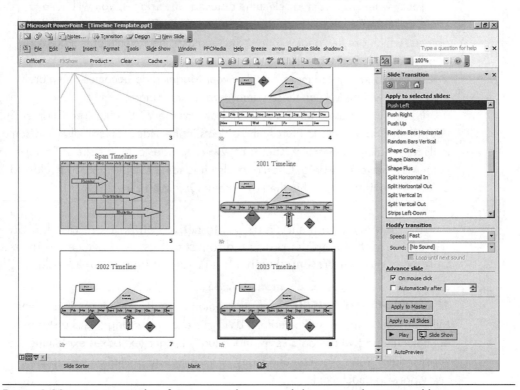

FIGURE 4-30   Using a Push Left Transition between slides can make it seem like you are moving seamlessly through the Timeline or any object that spans multiple slides.

(How do you move back seamlessly? Stay tuned for the section, "Navigation: Movement of Ideas," which is coming up.)

Finally, we've seen how nice it can be to have timed Entrances to create a flow within a slide, and we've also seen how an Exit animation can make a difference—it can obviously give the next object the entire stage (slide) to itself.

This brings up the scenario of timed entrances, almost like a curtain call.

You could also use this to create a timed scenario of steps in a process.

For example, in Figure 4-31, we go through a very simple three-step process using a series of text boxes: Get Ingredients, Mix it Up, Bake the Cake.

Although we could make these bullets, we'd rather show the sequential aspect in a more animated way, so we give the first text box an Entrance Animation, combining a Faded Zoom and Fly in from the Top, and let it sit in the slide for a moment. Then as it flies out to the bottom, the next bit of information is timed to follow it in. The same effect follows for the final stage of the process.

If we had illustrations to go with the three steps, these could be concurrently timed as well.

NOTE To differentiate the text boxes in the screen shot, they're separated here, but if you want, after duplicating them to create the effects in the slide, you could use the Draw > Align and Distribute > Relative to Slide commands to put one exactly over the next.

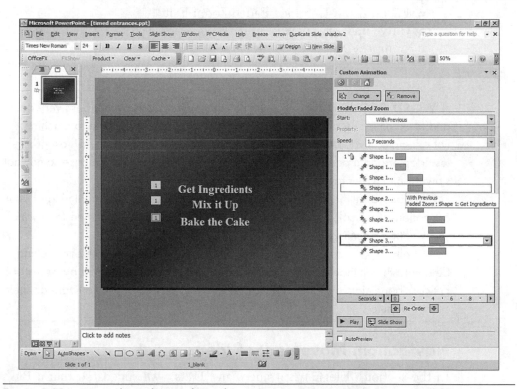

FIGURE 4-31   Using the Advanced Timeline in Custom Animation we can coordinate the Entrance effect of one object or text box with the Exit effect of another.

COPYING EFFECTS WITH OBJECTS If you went through the previous scenario, you noticed that as you duplicated the first text box (after animating it), the animation effects were automatically copied with it and added to the Order panel in the Custom Animation Task Pane. Keep this in mind when creating complex animated sequences; duplicating (or CTRL+dragging out a copy) of your already animated objects also duplicates their animation effects.

What you probably also noticed in this sequence is that the Fly out from bottom Exit is nicely coordinated with a simultaneous Fly in from Top.

Although Fly in/Fly out makes a nice pair of Entrance/Exit effects, there are others you can try:

- Ascend/Descend
- Expand/Contract
- Rise/Sink
- Faded Zoom Entrance/Faded Zoom Exit
- Curve up/Curve down
- Compress/Stretch

A WORD ABOUT TIMINGS Although the Advanced Timeline looks very cool and is extremely useful, the actual timings may vary from machine to machine. For example, if you develop a presentation on a desktop with a very fast graphics adapter and processor and lots of RAM, you may find the response somewhat slower on an older laptop.

Just as we will find with video and audio, to the extent that the timing of your animations is critical, you should test them thoroughly on the machine *from which you will be presenting*.

Finally, if you intend on using these techniques in a web conference setting, be aware that in that situation, the timing will be adversely affected by issues of network bandwidth and the number of attendees, as well as the software on their client computers.

Navigation: Movement of Ideas

In the section, "Elegant Entrances and Exits," we suggested that a Push Left Transition can help you move naturally through a series of connected slides, like a Timeline.

But what if a question from the audience or simply the nature of your presentation requires you to go back to the previous slide?

Unfortunately the Transition will not play in reverse—the same Push Left Transition repeats to the previous portion of the Timeline. This might not be very effective.

It is also important to understand what happens to the various animated elements that you may have had appear sequentially in the prior slides.

One way to take care of that is to use the Action Button AutoShapes as shown in Figure 4-32. Here, the Previous Slide and Next Slide buttons have been dragged onto the subsequent slides of the Timeline. By clicking them, the presenter can instantly go back and forth between slides.

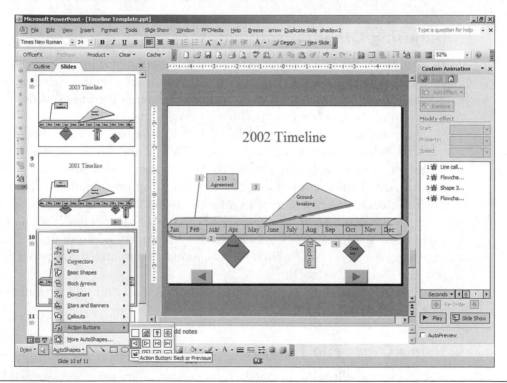

FIGURE 4-32   Using Previous and Next Slide Action Buttons can enable the presenter to move back and forth through a series of Timeline slides.

Note that when you return to a slide with Custom Animation effects, as shown here, the effects will not repeat; the slide, having been shown already, appears in its entirety.

Avoiding Ugly Action Buttons

There are alternatives to using these clunky button AutoShapes.

As we'll soon see, any selectable object can become a navigation trigger to the next or previous slide.

In addition, as we'll learn in Chapter 8, during the presentation itself, a savvy presenter can navigate back and forth quite easily; but using the up or back arrows will cycle back through every event, including the animations. But there are right-click commands that enable more sophisticated movement.

Finally, remember that to instantly add navigation elements or buttons to the entire presentation, you should put them on the Slide Master, and they will appear in the same position on every slide based on that master.

(Re)using Other Presentations

In Chapter 1, when we discussed planning the presentation ("Hyperlinks and Action Settings"), we suggested that as you think about reusing other presentations, you use the Action Settings to launch individual slides or entire presentations from a hyperlink.

As an example of the potential of this technique, we described the work of Robert Lane of Aspire Communications and his Relational Presentation model, in which just a few preliminary slides are used with hyperlinks to launch any number of other slides and presentations, digging deeply into a complex structure in response to audience requests.

Just as a reminder in Chapter 1 ("Magic of Custom Shows"), we mentioned that Custom Shows, which also may be launched from an Action Setting, are subsets of our current presentation reorganized for a specific purpose.

So what else can be accomplished with an Action Setting? How about leaving PowerPoint entirely.

Using Other File Types

For all its versatility as a media platform and its ability to import many different file types directly into its slides, PowerPoint does have some limitations.

For example, what if you wanted to show a document that represented a piece of evidence in a court case? You could scan the document into an image file, but it might not present very well, and it would be incapable of being navigated very easily.

Or suppose you had a PDF document that you wanted to show using Acrobat Reader?

Perhaps someone had sent you a video file in Real Player format—while you might be able to convert it to a PowerPoint-friendly video file using some of the tools we'll cover in the subsequent chapter, it would be easier to just have Real Player launch and play the file.

There are actually two different ways to accomplish these tasks, and both involve a key issue—your determination of the *program* that is the default on your computer for opening the specified file type.

We will cover the use of complementary programs to PowerPoint in Chapters 6 and 7, but if you've already used another tool and need to show a file that has been created outside of PowerPoint, it's a navigational issue.

For example, if you know that Microsoft Word (not Word Perfect or Open Office) is the default program on the machine on which you're presenting to open a *.DOC file created by any of these programs, you can launch it directly from an Action Setting, as shown in Figure 4-33. Right-click on the object you want to launch the file and choose Action Setting > Hyperlink to > Other File.

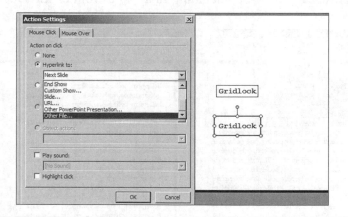

Figure 4-33 Using the Other File setting under Hyperlink to in an Action Setting can launch any program that is the default for a designated file type, with that file open in a separate window.

Next, choose the file you want to open—in this example, we want the Gridlock text box to launch the Highway Transportation Bill that might be the solution to the problem—in Microsoft Word.

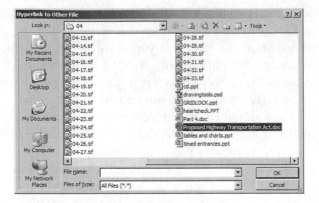

Figure 4-34 With the Hyperlink to Other File dialog box open, you can click on any file type to have the default program open it in another window.

When the presentation is projected, the text box is "hot," and clicking it opens the document in a Microsoft Word window. You can bring this up full-screen and use any of the Microsoft Word Views or Navigation tools, as shown in Figure 4-35, including Reading Layout or the Document Map.

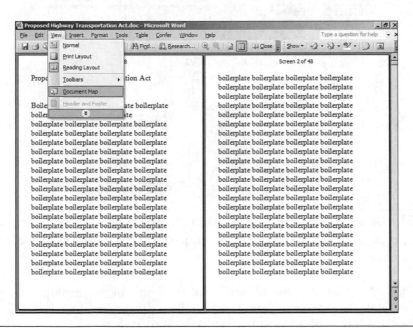

Figure 4-35 By using a hyperlink with the Other File option, you are able to use the features of the default program for that file, like Microsoft Word.

If you had linked to a Real Player video file or an Acrobat PDF file, if these were the default programs on your computer to open these files, the same thing would have happened with these respective file types.

WHICH PROGRAM WILL OPEN THE FILE? In some cases, you may not be sure exactly which program is the default to open a given file type. In this situation, you can open any Windows Folder, click Tools > Folder Options, and click the File Types tab. Now you can select any Registered File Type and click the Change button to alter the program that is the default to open that specific type of file, as shown in Figure 4-36.

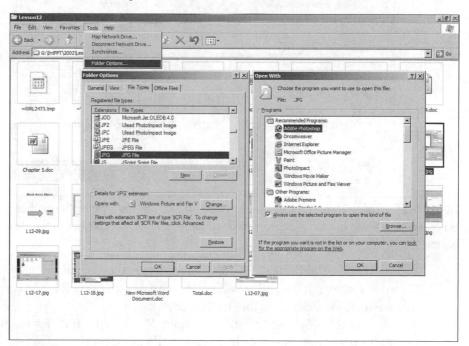

FIGURE 4-36 With the Tools > Folder Options dialog box open, you can select a file type to change the program that will be the default to open it on that particular computer.

Be careful, however, because if you move the presentation, the registered program for the designated file type on the new machine may be different. For example, Word Perfect may open the *.DOC file.

Using the Insert Object Command

There will be those among you who will say, wait a minute, I can put lots of different files and objects directly into a PowerPoint slide using Insert > Object (refer to Figure 4-36).

It's true; among the objects you can insert in this fashion are Acrobat PDFs, Microsoft Word DOCs, and even Shockwave Flash animations. But the results are mixed depending upon the Object type selected, as shown in Figure 4-37.

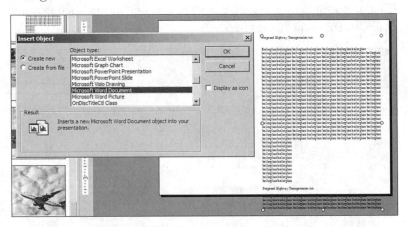

FIGURE 4-37   Using Insert Object also lets you embed the file type from another program in a PowerPoint slide, but the program itself will only function completely in the PowerPoint editor.

In the Word DOC example here, when the slide is actually projected, only the text in the slide itself will be visible—there will be no scroll bars or navigation ability available to the presenter.

Double-clicking the file will open MS Word—but not in the *Power-Point presentation*—only in the PowerPoint *editor*.

This is not very useful, compared to the Action Settings alternative.

The problem is that each Inserted Object behaves according to the peculiarities of its compatibility with the PowerPoint presentation engine. So, for example, a Shockwave file will play—usually—but other files will not because the programs are trying to work *inside PowerPoint slides*.

The beauty of the Action Setting is that the full power of the program is available—not just the visible representation of a portion of the file in the slide or a partial version that may or may not play.

If you need the full power of another program, launching a file that opens it automatically from an Action Setting is generally easier and more effective.

What About Shockwave Animation?

In many cases, your company may have access to excellent animations in the Shockwave format. They may also be referred to as "Flash" files because Macromedia Flash is the most popular program to produce the SWF (Shockwave) format.

I had one client who had an artist who created excellent 2D animation files using Flash and exported them into Shockwave. For simplicity her company converted these files into MPEG *video files* to play them in PowerPoint. (We will cover using video formats inside PowerPoint slides in the next chapter).

But essentially Shockwave was created by Macromedia (now part of Adobe) to "live inside" a web page.

So the easiest way to show a Shockwave file is to link an Action Setting or Hyperlink directly to a web page, and launch the native browser (such as Internet Explorer) to show the animation.

For example, in Figure 4-38, the title placeholder has been selected and right-clicked to create an Action Setting Hyperlinking to the NAPOLEON.HTML file.

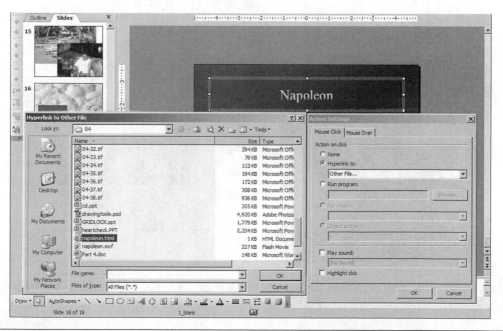

FIGURE 4-38   You can also use the Action Setting Hyperlink to link to a web page with a Shockwave file.

Now, during the presentation, if the hyperlink in the slide title is clicked, the web browser opens, and the page with the Shockwave file is displayed (see Figure 4-39).

FIGURE 4-39   Pointing an Action Setting Hyperlink to a web page file will launch the web browser with that file and a Shockwave file linked to the web page.

What would have happened if we'd linked directly to the NAPOLEON.SWF file (see Figure 4-40)?

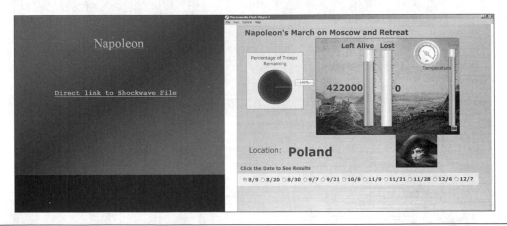

FIGURE 4-40   Pointing an Action Setting Hyperlink to an SWF file will open it in the Macro-media Flash Player.

The Macromedia Flash *Player* would have opened the file, again in another window.

Why or when is one preferable over another?

One issue to consider is whether the Shockwave file is interactive and has controls.

The reason my client converted its Shockwave to MPEG video was that it only needed to start and stop the animation—which is easy to do with a movie.

Other Shockwave files like the one shown here (which is actually created as an Infommersion Xcelsius dashboard, which we'll also cover in Chapter 6) are fully interactive with sliders, buttons, and other features. These should be accessed as true Shockwave files.

Another is the screen size of the Shockwave file. It may look better in the player at full screen. If you have the Macromedia Player configured properly, using it to play the Shockwave file directly also gives you the player controls under its own File menu.

If you're unsure of the player's installation on your machine, or if the file plays fine on its own, you can link to the web page containing the Shockwave file, as shown in Figure 4-40. *The other advantage to this is that using the Back button in the browser takes you back to the PowerPoint slide with the Action Setting or hyperlink.*

If the Shockwave file fits into your PowerPoint slide, you can use the Insert > Object > Shockwave command to insert the file directly into PowerPoint. Unfortunately this isn't always that easy to do; for one thing, if the Shockwave object isn't available, you can't do it.

Sometimes the object is called the Shockwave Active X control (see Figure 4-41); in other installations, it can be the Shockwave Flash Object.

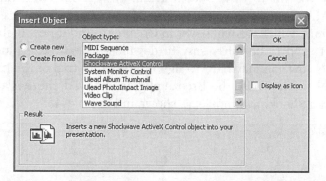

FIGURE 4-41   If you have Macromedia Flash or download the Shockwave Active X plug-in, you can install Shockwave as an object directly in PowerPoint.

Even if the Shockwave object is available, you need to right-click it, select its Properties, and point it to the Shockwave file (see Figure 4-42).

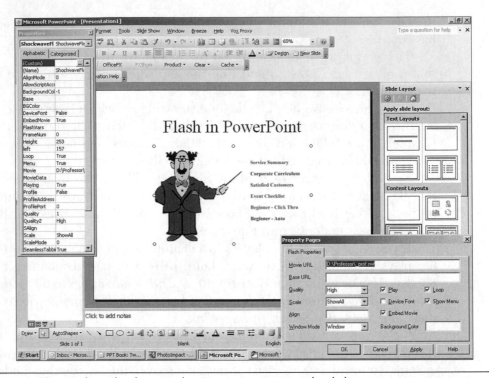

FIGURE 4-42   With a Shockwave object in PowerPoint, right-click it to open its Properties and make sure that the Movie URL points to the Shockwave file you want to play in the slide.

If you want to use Shockwave in PowerPoint, your best bet is to load the Macromedia Breeze plug-in. Macromedia Breeze is a conferencing program, which we will cover in Chapter 7 under new technologies.

It used to be fairly easy to download the Breeze plug-in for PowerPoint; now you may have to sign up for a free trial of the product, which is useful anyway. With the Breeze plug-in installed, there is a menu option to insert a Shockwave movie, as shown in Figure 4-43.

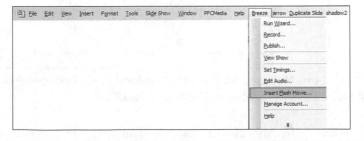

FIGURE 4-43   With the Breeze plug-in for PowerPoint installed, you get a very easy way to insert a Shockwave movie directly into your slide.

Use a Hyperlink or Action Setting?

What you may find a bit confusing is the distinction between the Hyperlink to feature in the Action Settings, which we've been concentrating on, and the Insert > Hyperlink option on the PowerPoint main menu (or the Hyperlink button on the Standard toolbar).

Inserting a "real" Hyperlink will still enable you to do some of the functions of the Action Setting hyperlink function, as shown in Figure 4-44, but for example, it won't allow you to link directly to a specific PowerPoint slide in another presentation.

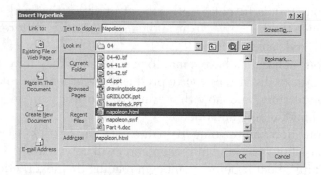

FIGURE 4-44   The actual Hyperlink feature in PowerPoint is best used when linking to a web page or specific document.

What it will enable you to do is to maintain hyperlinks that will work if and when you convert your PowerPoint file to a web page or post it to a website. We'll cover those techniques in more detail in Chapter 7.

LAUNCHING A PROGRAM OR A MACRO Advanced users may have occasion to use the Hyperlink to part of Action Settings to launch an actual program or application or to activate the Run Macro button to run some code during a presentation. (We will cover the use of macros in Chapter 6.)

What would be an example of running a program? One might be an application actually built in Visual Basic or .NET. Another might be if you were using PowerPoint to train users on a program, like MS Word. Then opening Word as a program, instead of a given Word document, might be something you'd want to do.

Case Study 1: Introducing a Corporate Team

As the presentation specialist for a large conglomerate, several executives come to your office with an important project. Having acquired a new subsidiary, the company will want to introduce the executives at the next shareholders meeting and also to prospective institutional investors.

The key to this presentation is flexibility. On some occasions when the presentation is given, one or more of the executives will be present at the event to speak in person.

At other times, they may be introduced through a series of videos.

Your task is to put together a set of slides that will serve to visually introduce the executives to an audience at events of different size and to do so with style and elegance.

Your colleagues have come to you because they have been impressed with some of the visuals you've produced for other presentations to tell the corporate story, and now they want you to use your ingenuity to create something exciting and effective.

You know you're going to go into your bag of tricks to use Custom Animation—but what kind of presentation will you create?

Think about it before you begin reading the next section.

Key Issues to Consider

You might want to think about the following:

- Using a series of Motion Paths to give photographs of the executives an interesting entrance
- Using AutoShapes to hold the images in order to duplicate them easily
- Coordinating the appearance of text boxes that provide additional information
- Creating hyperlinks to slides with video for occasions when the executives are not available (we'll cover video in the next chapter)

Reusing Animations for Important Concepts

Although you know that you can use a simple Fade animation to introduce images and integrate them with bullets, you decide that this occasion warrants something a bit more dramatic.

You zoom out of the slide to a View of 50% or less to give yourself some room outside of the slide (off-stage).

First, you create a simple rounded rectangle AutoShape and move it out of the actual slide at the top right.

(*You use the View menu to turn on the Grid and Guides on the slide and enable Snap to Grid.*) This will make the next step a lot easier.

You open Custom Animation, select the first rounded rectangle, and give it a Motion Path > Draw Custom Path and Select Freeform.

With the Grid and Guides Snap enabled, you can trace a straight path down into the slide, fix the first point with a click, go to the left to the middle of the slide, fix a second point, and complete the move of the rectangle with a third click.

(It may take you a few attempts to get this perfect—but you will find that Snap to Guide will fix many of the flaws that may mar your efforts. See Figure 4-45.)

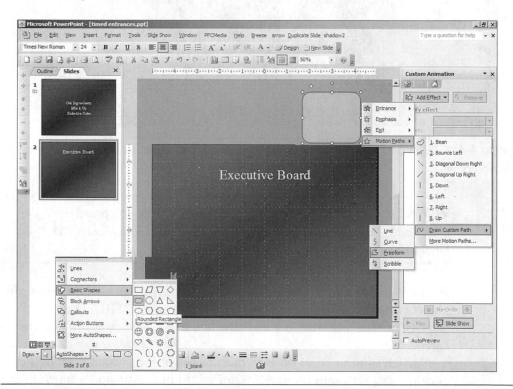

FIGURE 4-45   Using Snap to Grid and Guides, it is easy to trace a straight set of Motion Paths for the selected object down into the slide.

With the move completed, the first animation should be in the Custom Animation panel as shown in Figure 4-46.

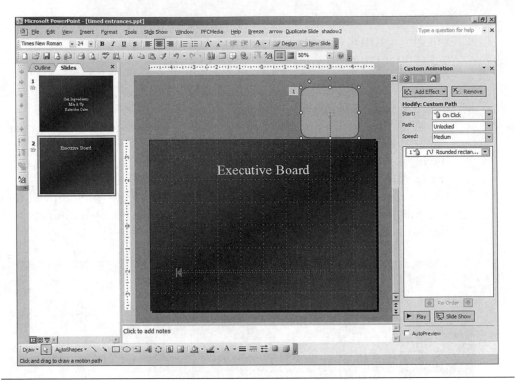

FIGURE 4-46   With the Freeform path created, there is a first animation in your Custom Animation panel.

WORKING OFF-SLIDE By creating the object off-slide, you avoid having to create an Entrance effect prior to the Motion Path effect. The Motion Path bringing the object into your slide is the entrance.

Because we're introducing three executives, we can now duplicate this object two times. With the rectangle selected, press CTRL+D twice.

Notice that the Motion Paths attached to the rectangle are also duplicated.

Now all you need to do is to click to select the second rectangle and click the last set point on its Motion Path to make it stop its move in the middle of the slide.

Finally, click the third rectangle to select its Motion Path and click its last two points to make it stop at the bottom of the slide without moving to the left. The final Motion Paths are shown in Figure 4-47.

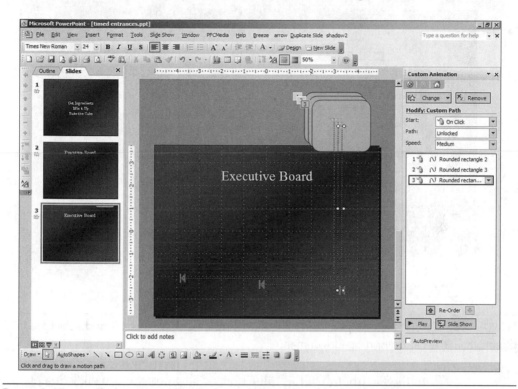

FIGURE 4-47 With the rectangles duplicated, the second and third Motion Paths can be shortened so that the final move will result in the rectangles side by side.

Now it's time to put the pictures in the rectangles. Click the first one to select it (you can do this in the Order column of the Custom Animation Task Pane) and right-click to select Format AutoShape.

In the Format AutoShape dialog box, click the Fill Color drop-down arrow and select Fill Effects, as shown in Figure 4-48.

4. SECRETS OF ANIMATION AND NAVIGATION

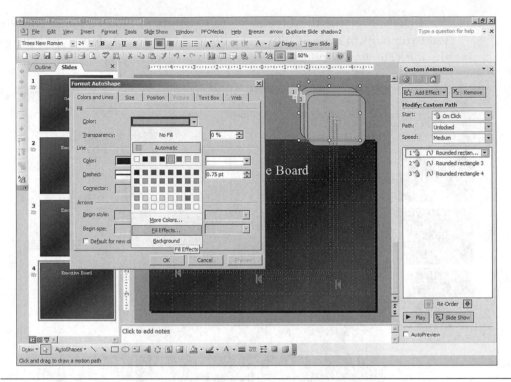

FIGURE 4-48 To put photographs inside the AutoShape, you right-click it and select the Fill Effects from the Fill Color drop-down menu.

In the Picture tab of the Fill Effects dialog box, we can click Select Picture, and from a file folder on our computer, we can select the picture of the first executive to appear. Clicking Insert will bring the image into the Fill Effects panel. Click to select Lock picture aspect ratio, and click OK (see Figure 4-49).

We can repeat this process for each of the remaining two rectangles, filling them with the pictures of the other executives. We can play the current slide by pressing Shift+F5 to test the sequence, and we can see the executive board members enter the slide one at a time and line up, as shown in Figure 4-50.

To make the AutoShapes line up perfectly, you may need to play it several times and use the arrow keys on your keyboard to "nudge" the AutoShapes to be right on top of each other prior to their entrances.

To coordinate the introductions, you'll next create three text boxes in the slide above where the pictures will move in with the names, titles, and ages of the officers.

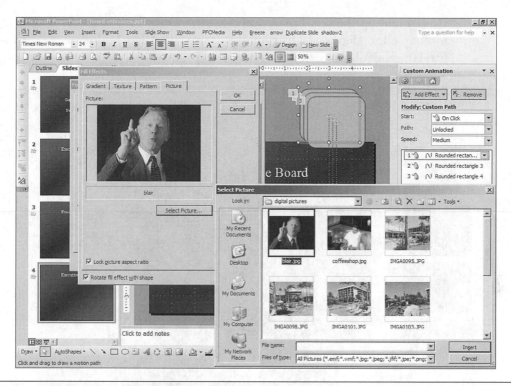

FIGURE 4-49   Within the Picture tab of the Fill Effects dialog box, use Select Picture to put the photograph inside the AutoShape.

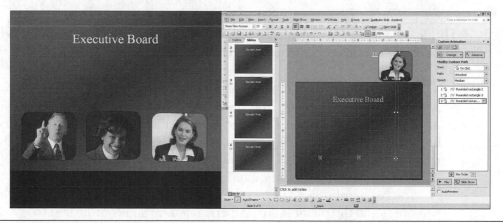

FIGURE 4-50   Playing the current slide will test the Motion Paths and show how the AutoShapes with pictures look and line up.

To line up the text boxes, you click the Draw button on the Drawing toolbar, click Align and Distribute, and use the Align Middle and Distribute Horizontally commands, as shown in Figure 4-51.

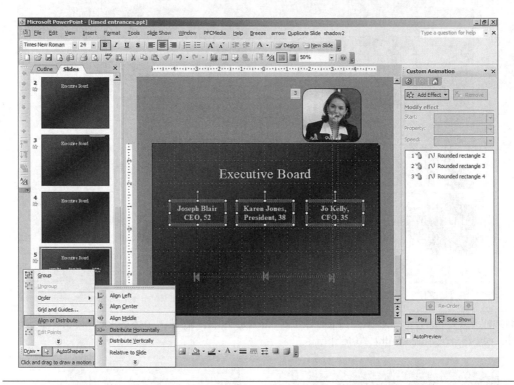

FIGURE 4-51 To accompany the appearance of the images, text boxes can be coordinated with the Align and Distribute options to appear in their proper positions.

Now it's time to coordinate the animation of the text boxes with the appearance of the images. You open the Advanced Timeline in Custom Animation and give each of the text boxes a Fade In Entrance effect that begins With Previous—tying each to the mouse click event that begins the respective path animation for the image to which it's connected.

The final Timeline is shown in Figure 4-52.

You're almost done! You test the slide once more to make sure that the text boxes and the pictures are properly lined up and coordinated (see Figure 4-53).

Now you're still going to need a "Plan B" if the executives are not present to speak as they're introduced. After dropping a video slide into the presentation and naming it for the executive in the video, you can use the text boxes to trigger hyperlinks to the respective video slides.

FIGURE 4-52   You can time the appearance of the text boxes to closely follow the arrival of each image to coordinate the introductions elegantly.

FIGURE 4-53   Testing the slide to play at Full Screen is the best way to check that the Entrance effects are properly coordinated.

4. SECRETS OF ANIMATION AND NAVIGATION

Right-clicking the text box for the first executive, you select Action Settings and Hyperlink to Slide, as shown in Figure 4-54. With the titles of the slides in a dialog box, you can select to hyperlink to the video slide for the first executive.

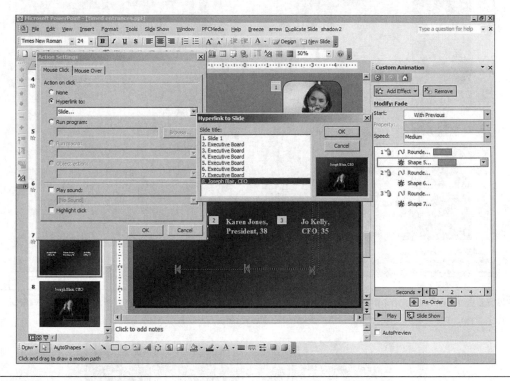

FIGURE 4-54 Creating an Action Setting to move to a video slide can give the presenter that option if he or she clicks on the appropriate text box.

Now your presentation has a number of scenarios. The presenter can introduce either the whole team at once (with three mouse clicks) or the members one at a time. If one or more of the team members is present, they can come up and speak. If not, the presenter can click on the hyperlink to the video slide of the missing team member and let the audience watch a video.

If necessary, additional Action Settings and Hyperlinks can be created directly from the images themselves to other supporting pages with the curriculum vitae of the executive or other biographical or important information.

When you present this slide to your colleagues, they see the possibilities. One presentation provides the flexibility they need to serve various purposes, depending on the venue and the circumstances.

"What about a DVD that does it all automatically that we can distribute to attendees?" one of them asks. "Can we get the video to play on a DVD or a web page?"

"Sure," you reply, "but you'll have to wait 'til one of the next chapters."

Case Study 2: Using a Memorable Metaphor

You can think of this as a "bonus" case study because I had intended to just include one in every chapter. But let's go back to the thought processes we discussed in the previous chapter on creating powerful visuals; we discussed the power of analogy or metaphor in telling our story.

In the course of my work, I have had the opportunity to see two absolute masters of animation, whose websites are found in the "Resources" section: Troy Chollar and Glen Millar.

Audiences at PowerPoint LIVE literally applaud when these two PowerPoint MVPs show some of their samples and are kind enough to deconstruct them for mere mortals.

So, as a bonus for this chapter, I will re-create some of Glen Millar's techniques as the next step in the "Gridlock" scenario. We saw how much more powerful the image of gridlock can be than a series of bullets.

And we have gone through the steps of alternating the Entrance effect of a picture with explanatory bullets and presenting a series of images instead of text.

In this short sequence, I will demonstrate how you can work with an image by placing it on the Background of a slide and then hiding and revealing (in essence, masking) the image with a series of simple or complex AutoShapes.

The first thing we need to do is to put our main image not in the slide itself but rather on the Background of the slide with which we'll be working.

We click Format > Background and select the Fill Effects from the drop-down menu. As we did with the AutoShape, we now can click the Picture tab and add an image as the Background for the current slide (see Figure 4-55).

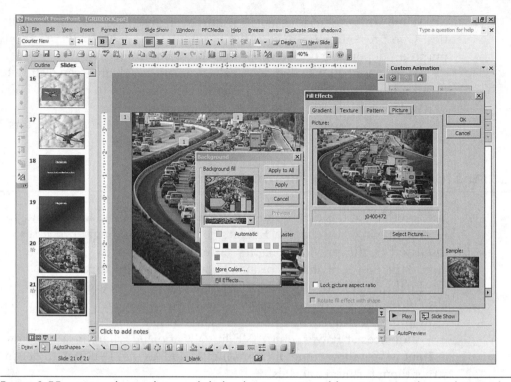

FIGURE 4-55 Using the Background dialog box, we can add an image to the Background of the slide.

The next two items I will add to the slide are two AutoShapes that will look like they're the main message of the slide itself. I create a red rectangle and an octagon that resembles a Stop sign (see Figure 4-56).

Formatting an AutoShape with a Background Image

I want to create a more complex effect, so on top of the rectangle and octagon, I place three fitted triangles—two right triangles and an isosceles triangle in the middle. It may take a little twisting, rotating, and resizing to get them to fit perfectly, as shown in Figure 4-57.

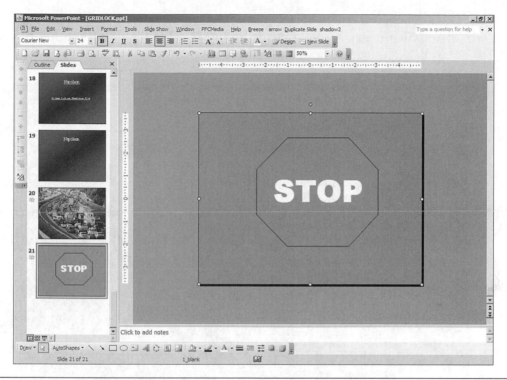

FIGURE 4-56 Using a rectangle and an octagon that fill up the slide, the background is obscured or masked with a simple message.

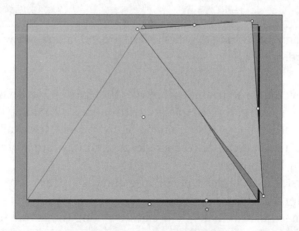

FIGURE 4-57 Covering the message with three fitted triangles can help us set up a nice animation sequence.

Then, for each of the triangles, we right-click it, select Format AutoShape, remove the Line or Border (No Line), and set the Fill Effect to Background, as shown in Figure 4-58.

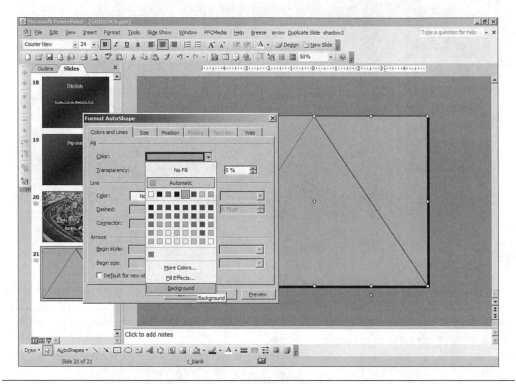

FIGURE 4-58 By filling the rectangles with the Background image, we will make it look like a single static image.

Now the three triangles look like they're a single image in the slide; you could create greater complexity with more AutoShapes—Glen Millar has used a set of images resembling a jigsaw puzzle, for example.

But now we can have a single click in Custom Animation triggering a series of Exit effects.

First, the triangles will collapse and disappear.

After a slight delay, the main message components—the rectangle and octagon—will also make their exit, revealing the actual image on the Background (see Figure 4-59).

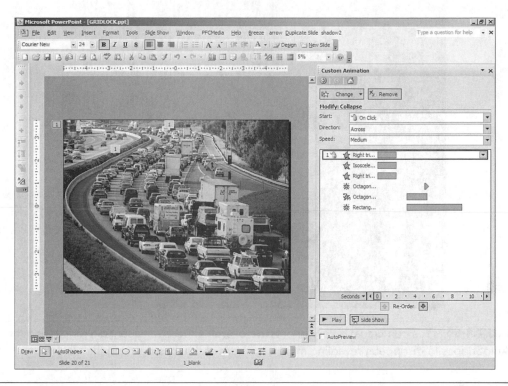

FIGURE 4-59   As the objects disappear with respective effects on the Advanced Timeline, they reveal first the message and then once again the main image.

NOTE Setting the effects to music, which we'll learn in Chapter 5, "Using Video and Audio Effectively," can make the message conveyed by the slide even more powerful.

A quick shot of the final sequence projected full-screen is shown in Figure 4-60.

To the extent that you build a complex sequence of AutoShapes in this manner and have them leave the scene with a properly timed series of effects, you will leave an audience with a lasting memory of your message.

FIGURE 4-60   You can create a very impressive overall effect by sequentially animating the AutoShapes to disappear, revealing more and more of the message and then the image.

Summary

In many ways, what sets PowerPoint apart from older presentation formats like print and 35mm slides is the ability to create movement and simulate a dramatic production or film.

These techniques should be used not haphazardly but rather to enhance the connection with the audience; just as actors get a proper entrance, the elements that are of particular importance in your slide show should be introduced in a sequence that makes sense and enhances your message.

We looked at the main techniques to add movement and effects to PowerPoint slides:

- Bullet Animation
- Transitions
- Animation Schemes
- Custom Animation

And we went into some depth to fine-tune the movement of elements by using the Advanced Timeline. We also went through the use of Triggers to increase interactivity and make specific objects launch the effect or entrances of other elements.

A big part of the strategy of movement is also navigation—the ability to move around within a presentation or roam outside the slide show to introduce material in other PowerPoint files or even in other formats. We showed how this can be done using Action Buttons and Action Settings.

Finally we covered some advanced animation techniques that set slide shows apart by reviewing the craft of some master animators. The result is the ability to add movement to our slides in a way that dramatically enhances our storytelling ability.

In the next chapter, we go even further into the movie analogy by working with video.

Resources

An academic approach to the issues of cognitive learning theory and multimedia can be found in

- *Multimedia Learning* by Richard E. Mayer, Cambridge University Press (April 23, 2001).

Master Animation Websites

More samples from the master animators covered in this chapter as well as in-depth tutorials are available at

- Glen Millar, www.pptworkbench.com
- Troy Chollar, www.tlccreative.com/ppt_examples.htm

CHAPTER 5

USING VIDEO AND AUDIO EFFECTIVELY

If we were just writing a simple book about PowerPoint, we could probably stop right here. We've pretty much covered the features of the program itself in terms of how they can help convey a message.

In the second half of this book, as Paul Harvey might say, we'll cover the rest of the story. PowerPoint by itself can do quite a bit, but it can also

- Use advanced media like video and audio
- Use the work product of other programs, including the rest of MS Office
- Integrate with new technologies like the web and DVD
- Take maximum advantage of the potential of a speaker, facilitator, or subject expert

These topics comprise the second half of this book.

In terms of advanced media (video and audio), here's what we'll cover in this chapter:

- How to capture and edit your own video and present it in Power-Point
- Troubleshooting video and audio so they work (almost) flawlessly
- Using narrative and CD music as audio enhancements to a presentation
- Understanding and integrating complementary formats like DVD and HD

Of course, true to our mandate, it's probably worth asking, why use video at all? Is it just to add the "Aah" factor, or can it truly enhance communication?

Power of Video as a Metaphor

There's a reason why more people currently watch television or play video games than read books. It's the same reason that the motion picture industry is so huge.

Pictures that move with synchronized sound and music are compelling storytelling vehicles.

Until very recently, the technology to produce movies was beyond the means of all but the largest studios with very expensive equipment.

With the computer, the microprocessor, and new developments in digital photography, all of this has changed.

I wrote my first book on using digital video in 1996 (*Digital Video on the PC*), and the main project in that book was creating a postage-stamp-sized video with passable audio that we could burn to CD.

Now anyone with a camcorder and a video capture card can import and edit video on a PC or Mac and distribute it any number of ways.

Because of its ability to play many different video file formats and to display video among the many other visual components we have already covered, PowerPoint is a great way to play one or more video files.

Our own video files don't have to be of Oscar quality. If they support the storyline of our presentation, whatever its subject, movies can go a long way toward moving an audience.

Perhaps the most powerful example I have seen of video as a communications tool in PowerPoint was at a pharmaceutical conference.

One of the topics was the purported efficacy of a product to treat Alzheimer's disease and slow the debilitating process of cognitive degeneration.

While several speakers produced graphs and charts, and obviously numerous bullet slides on the topic, one practitioner showed a series of video clips.

In each, the subject was asked to recall a series of simple terms several seconds after being given them to repeat.

This test was apparently in somewhat widespread use among the practitioners at the conference. What made the video so much more powerful than the publication of the findings in some kind of statistical table of results was that the audience could feel the humanity of the subjects.

In the first set of video clips, the subjects struggled to remember even the most obvious terms that had just been said to them.

In the "after" set of clips, the subjects were demonstrably more alert and could recall any number of terms; in addition their energy and delight at the experience were manifest on their faces and touched the audience, even though it was made up of jaded professionals.

Other speakers I have worked with have used video as an icebreaker or simply to set the mood for a conference or event.

One motivational speaker used actual movie clips from Hollywood before most DVDs were copy protected. I never really encouraged this, but he would use the scene from *The Matrix* where Neo is offered the choice of two different colored pills. Naturally this is a perfect metaphor for just about any important decision in virtually any field or endeavor.

What is so amazing is how easy it is to get video that tells a story.

Acquiring Video

Before we go into shooting your own video for a presentation, we need to back up a minute and go through a few technical issues.

If you remember in Chapter 3, "Creating Dynamic Visuals," we worked extensively with pictures. Although we used the Clip Organizer to catalog our pictures, we found that there were advantages to inserting pictures From File, directly from folders on our hard drive where we had stored them.

A big part of this was knowing the *file type* and *file extension* for picture files. We found JPG images, which we acquired from digital cameras, TIF images, which may come from scanners or stock photography, and PNG images, which had the attribute of supporting transparency high full resolution. While these were all image files they had different properties and uses.

So what are the main *video file types*? They are as follows:

- .MOV (or QuickTime) is the Apple format. Unfortunately Power-Point doesn't like most QuickTime files (we'll get into why and the exception later on).
- .FLV is the Macromedia Flash video format, and it won't work in PowerPoint directly.
- .AVI is the basic Windows format.
- .MPG is a compressed format for movies and DVD.
- .WMV is the newer Windows format for web streaming.

These last three video formats are easy to insert as a video file into a PowerPoint slide, and they will *usually play*. (If they don't, there are two major reasons, which we will get into later in this chapter.)

But first, let's work with the type of video you may already have. Perhaps

- Someone in your organization has already shot corporate video for other presentations or for a CD or web project.
- You are connected with a client or colleague whose video is distributed on CD (like the pharmaceutical companies), which you could use in your own presentations.
- You are good at searching the Internet or can use stock libraries (listed in the "Resources" section) to acquire video.

Now that you know the file types associated with video, you should be able to transfer your video to your computer and insert it into PowerPoint.

But sometimes when you put a CD into your PC that has video (for example, an encyclopedia), its own *player program* pops up, and you can play the video, but you have no idea where to locate it and how to use it.

The key is to use the *Explore* feature of Windows XP.

Open the My Computer window and locate the CD or DVD drive with the disc that contains the video you would like to use.

Right-click the icon for the drive and select Explore as shown in Figure 5-1.

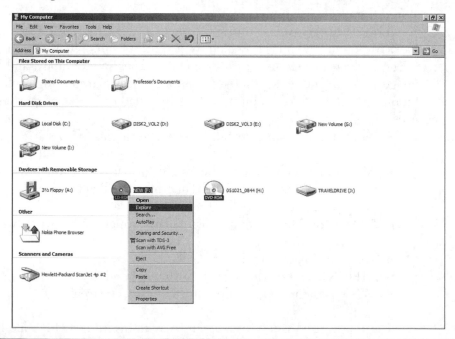

FIGURE 5-1 By choosing to Explore a CD or DVD disc, you can examine its native folder structure and see its actual files.

By opening the folders on the CD and choosing Details from the drop-down menu, as shown in Figure 5-2, you can click Size to sort the files and see the largest ones. They will be the movie files stored in whatever format on the disc (hopefully .AVI, .MPG, or .WMV).

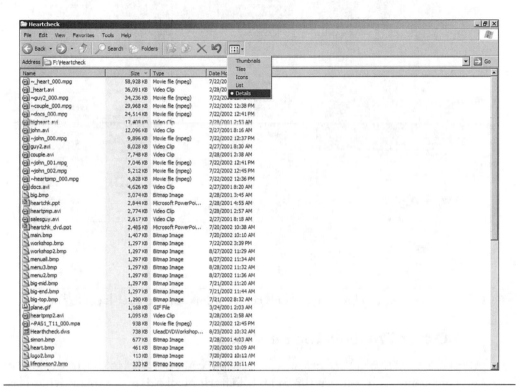

FIGURE 5-2 With files sorted by size, the movie files will be the largest ones.

With the video files on the disc located, it's easy to create a folder (on the Desktop or elsewhere) and drag the files you need from the disc to the PC. See Figure 5-3.

Be patient. Sometimes these files are huge and take a while to transfer.

5. USING VIDEO AND AUDIO EFFECTIVELY

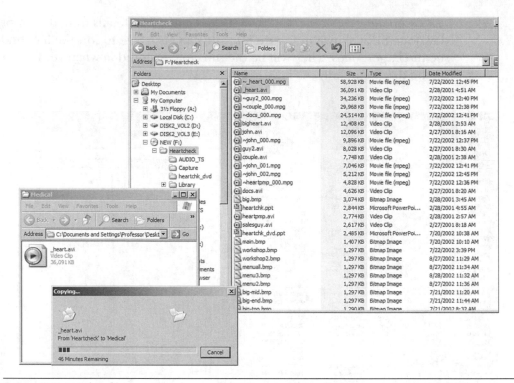

FIGURE 5-3   Video files can be dragged and copied from a disc to your local folder.

Other Ways to Locate Video

With a CD or DVD in your drive, after you open the folder to explore its contents, you can use the Search feature by clicking the magnifying glass on the toolbar and designating that the search be for Pictures, Music, or Video and check to enable Only Video. This is a good idea if you don't know in which subfolders video may be located.

You can also open the Clip Organizer from the Clip Art Task Pane in PowerPoint and choose File > Add Clips to Organizer.

If you select On My Own, you can Browse to the disc and have the Organizer search for media files on the disc for you. If you click Automatically, the Clip Organizer will take a lot longer but will include the media files on the CD or DVD as well.

ACCESSING VIDEO FROM A DVD I get this question all the time, and it depends upon what kind of DVD.

Some DVDs are like CDs—they're just data discs with movies in the formats shown earlier. In this case, the same technique will work.

However, in most cases, DVD discs are movie DVDs, meaning that an interactive interface has been burned on the disc and they have been formatted to play in commercial DVD players.

You *can Explore* these discs, but you will find two main folders on them: VIDEO_TS and AUDIO_TS. If you open the VIDEO_TS folder, you will *not find MPG or any other PC-friendly video file type.*

(This has nothing to do with copy protection. That is another matter entirely.)

In order to use video clips from a movie DVD, see the section "Getting Video from a DVD" and make sure that the DVD is not copy protected.

Playing Video in PowerPoint

With the videos transferred to a local folder, playing them in a PowerPoint slide is easy. Click Insert > Movies and Sounds > Movie from File and choose the video clip from the folder into which you transferred it (see Figure 5-4).

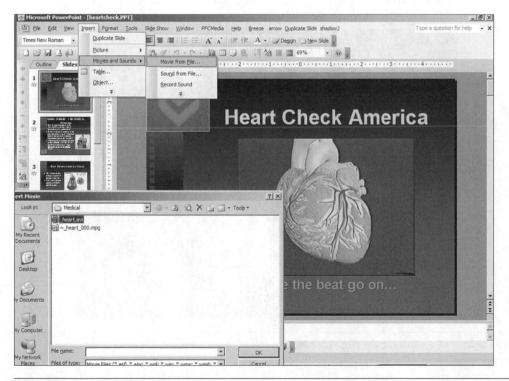

FIGURE 5-4 Click to insert a movie from file, locate the file and folder you want, and choose OK.

Before the movie is placed in the slide, you are asked whether you want it to play Automatically or When Clicked. Choosing When Clicked gives you maximum control over the clip and the ability to set it up before showing it. Selecting Automatically might be an option for a self-running show (in a kiosk). You can also change this setting by selecting the clip in the slide and using the Effect Options in Custom Animation as we covered in the previous chapter.

Finally, when you make your choice, the first frame of the clip is placed as a reference in the slide. The actual clip remains in the folder from which you accessed it.

This is very important. Video is never embedded into PowerPoint, and one of the main reasons video doesn't play is that the actual file is no longer available or has been moved to another location on the hard drive. (See the section "Troubleshooting Video Problems.")

Now, with the video reference in the slide, when the presentation is shown Full Screen, moving the cursor over the clip turns it into a hand (it's active). Clicking the clip once plays it, clicking it again *pauses* it, and so on (see Figure 5-5). Clicking outside the clip advances the slide.

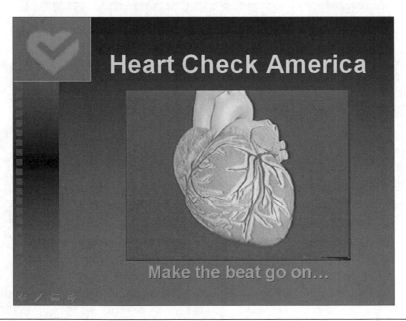

FIGURE 5-5 With the movie clip reference in the slide, you can click to play or pause the clip.

This kind of control is particularly useful in the scenario we described earlier. In the Alzheimer's example, the situation could be set up by the speaker with a similar slide, and both the "before" and "after" clips could be stopped and started whenever the speaker was ready.

PLAYING VIDEO DIRECTLY FROM DISC Theoretically, you don't need to transfer the video to your PC; you could insert the movie directly as a file from a CD or DVD, but you probably shouldn't. First of all, playback will be slower, and you don't want to risk that during the presentation. More importantly, if you lose the disc or forget to bring it, the movie won't play at all. You're much better off doing the transfer, letting the movie play from the hard drive, and using the disc for backup.

Video Window Size

The window size of the video playback is a function of its quality when it was "captured" or downloaded from a camera, edited, compressed, and saved—a process we describe in this section.

The results are analogous to the picture quality from a digital camera; the more megapixels in the camera, the better a photo's resolution, and the larger its dimensions in the slide. (See "Digital Cameras and Picture Quality" in Chapter 3).

In the early days, PCs were slower; you were lucky to be able to get a clip of 320×240 screen resolution. Now 640×480 or 720×480 (DV) resolution clips are much more common.

Although you can stretch some video files, the results can be unpredictable, particularly with AVI or WMV movies. (MPG-compressed video typically stretches into a larger resolution with less distortion.)

But generally, it's not the size of the video that matters—it's the message. The Alzheimer's clips did not need to be large; they would have been effective in a smaller window.

However, you can use some strategies to make older, smaller video clips work better in your slides. First of all, you can put them inside drawing objects, like rectangles with shadows, and combine them with bullets or text boxes as labels.

You can also use multiple video clips in a single slide, as shown in Figure 5-6, which has five smaller video clips set up to play when they're clicked.

FIGURE 5-6 Smaller video files can be placed together into a single slide and controlled with mouse clicks.

Although these files can all be played at once, the presenter is well advised to play each one and stop it before continuing. This scenario is also great for an interactive situation where the presenter can tell the audience about the four or five videos in the slide, ask which subject area they want to know about the most, and then play only those videos.

Using Your Own Video

Now that we know the PowerPoint-friendly video formats, we can begin to think about creating, editing, and inserting our own movies.

The good news is that if you are using Windows XP, you already have a video editing program on your computer.

The bad news is that you still need a special peripheral, known as a *video capture device*, to bring video into your computer.

It's actually quite possible that if you have a newer PC or laptop, you already have a video capture device: a *Firewire port*, sometimes known by the catchy phrase IEEE 1394 or, as Sony refers to it on its notebooks and PCs, iLink.

A Firewire port accepts a simple cable that attaches to a digital camcorder and simply downloads video directly to your computer. Generally, these digital camcorders use a special videotape cassette called mini-DV.

You can differentiate the types of digital cameras or camcorders and ports on a computer, VCR, or video device by the cables they use. Figure 5-7 shows the three main types of connectors you may find:

- Analog video (and stereo audio)—yellow (video), red, and white
- Firewire
- USB

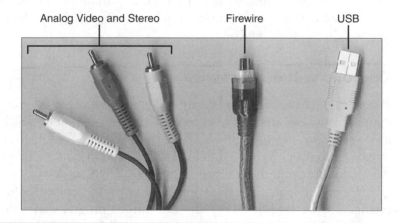

Analog Video and Stereo   Firewire   USB

FIGURE 5-7 The three main types of connecting cables between peripherals and the PC for video are analog (yellow), Firewire, and USB.

FIREWIRE VS. USB If you have a digital camera, chances are, you are used to transferring still images from the camera to your PC or laptop using a USB cable. In some cases, digital cameras can also create small MPG movies, and the USB cable can also transfer these to the computer.

In addition, there are also USB video capture devices that you can purchase that will connect externally to your PC and that will accept *analog video* from an older camcorder or VCR.

FIREWIRE PLUG SIZES The Firewire plug shown in Figure 5-7 is a four-pin plug that goes into the camera, and the other end goes into a notebook or laptop. A similar plug with six pins on the other end is typically used to connect a Firewire camcorder to a desktop PC with a Firewire card or port.

A digital camcorder uses small videotape cassettes that record in a special digital format called DV. The videocassettes are called mini-DV.

If you have such a camcorder (or a version that records on digital Hi-8 cassettes called digital 8), a Firewire cable, and a Firewire port on your Windows XP desktop PC or laptop, you're in business.

This cable and peripheral combination supports excellent-quality video and audio. Generally, it doesn't result in errors or dropped frames, and it has a terrific feature that we'll see in a minute—*Device Support*—which means that it can control your camcorder directly from programs like Windows Movie Maker.

Capture without Firewire

If you do not have Firewire but are using an older camcorder or VCR, you connect it to an external video capture device (generally USB) using the analog cables (refer to Figure 5-7) and then use a USB cable to connect the device to your PC. You need to load software to make sure that the device is functioning properly and is recognized by Windows XP.

If your camcorder or digital camera (with the ability to film movies) connects directly only by USB, your utility program with the camera should enable you to transfer and save in a PC-friendly video format, generally MPG.

Some camcorders or digital cameras record directly to a flash memory card, internal hard drive, or DVD. Once again, you should be able to transfer the movie files to your PC using the utility program included with the device.

Finally, there are some high-end graphics cards (like ATI's All-In-Wonder series and other graphics cards from nVidia) that directly capture analog video to your hard drive using analog cables (refer to Figure 5-7).

After the video is transferred using the appropriate cable or media (flash cards, DVD, or USB cable to the hard drive on the device), the video can be imported into Windows Movie Maker to edit further, if necessary.

Using Movie Maker

You can find the Movie Maker video editing program under Start > All Programs > Accessories > Entertainment > Windows Movie Maker in Windows XP (see Figure 5-8).

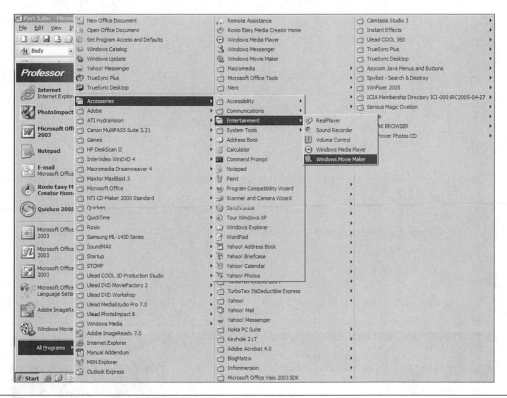

FIGURE 5-8 Windows XP includes the Microsoft Movie Maker program under its Accessories.

OTHER VIDEO EDITING PROGRAMS There are several higher-end video editing programs other than Movie Maker, notably Adobe Premiere (and Premiere Elements), Ulead VideoStudio, Pinnacle, and Sony Vegas. All of them have the basic features of Windows Movie Maker and use the same basic metaphor of a Timeline or Storyboard to edit and save video in various other formats.

We will use Movie Maker here as an example of the most basic techniques and export a file that can be projected in PowerPoint.

Following the same basic steps in the other programs will be easy when you follow along using Movie Maker.

Camtasia Studio 3.0 is similar to Movie Maker as well, and it has some extra features that we will cover in Chapter 7, "The Latest Technologies: Beyond PowerPoint to the Future."

The Windows Movie Maker interface is like almost all video editing software, with the following included:

- A Clip Area where imported or captured movies are referenced
- A Preview window where editing changes can be monitored
- A Timeline or Storyboard where clips are assembled with titles, effects, and other elements before being saved as a new file in their final video format

Movie Maker makes the process even easier by putting the major tasks on the left panel:

- Capture Video
- Edit Movie
- Finish Movie

The program is shown as it is opened for the first time (see Figure 5-9).

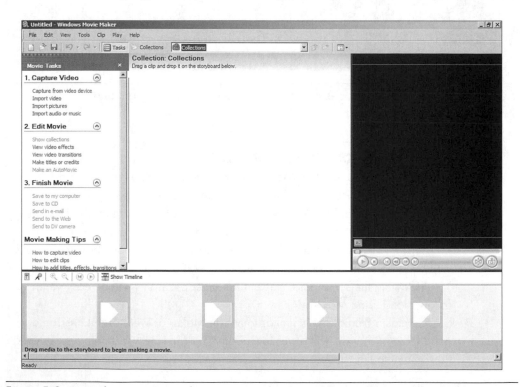

FIGURE 5-9 Windows Movie Maker is a typical video editing program with all of the major components.

First Video Capture: Travelogue

If you have Firewire enabled on your PC, and you connect a Firewire camcorder using the cable, all you need to do is turn it on in VTR mode. (Most camcorders have at least two modalities: Camera for filming, and VTR (resembling a VCR) for playback, dubbing, and editing.)

FIREWIRE POPUP WINDOW When you first connect and turn on a Firewire device, a popup window will appear in Windows XP with the options available for use with the device; among them will be Capture with Windows Movie Maker. You can use this to open the Movie Maker Capture Window, or you can close the dialog box to capture and work directly from within Movie Maker. As you add other programs that work with the device, you can use the popup window to open those applications in their respective capture modules as well.

With Movie Maker open, the screen shown in Figure 5-10 appears when you turn on the camcorder. This is the same as clicking Capture from video device in Movie Maker.

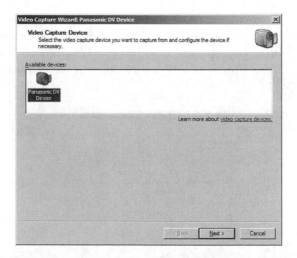

FIGURE 5-10   Windows Movie Maker is a typical video editing program with all of the major components.

The Capture Wizard should show your properly installed Firewire device and any other capture peripherals on your system. Select the camcorder and click Next.

We'll name the first clip we will capture (download from the camcorder) "travel" (see Figure 5-11). We note that the default folder where the file(s) will be saved is the My Videos folder inside My Documents.

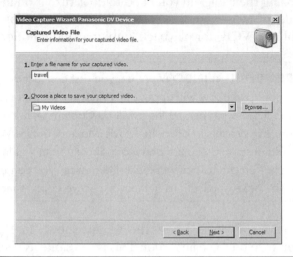

FIGURE 5-11   Windows Movie Maker provides a default clip name and folder location that you can change.

Click Next to choose Video Quality. Keep the default, Best quality for playback on my computer (see Figure 5-12). We can always save the other options under Finish Movie, which we will cover under that section (see Figure 5-21).

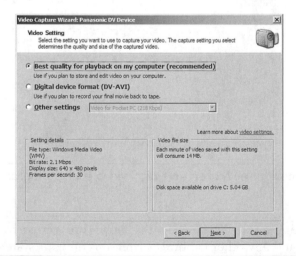

FIGURE 5-12   Windows Movie Maker asks for the video quality in which you intend to capture. The best quality will provide the maximum versatility for other functions.

Click Next, and you get the option to save the entire tape automatically. Because we want only the travel segments, we select to Capture parts of the tape manually (see Figure 5-13).

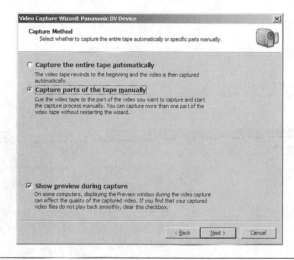

FIGURE 5-13 Windows Movie Maker can capture automatically, but it's usually better to locate the segments you want to avoid wasting time and hard drive space.

Click Next, and we're in the Video Capture module (see Figure 5-14). Notice that the VCR-like controls are *active* with a Firewire camcorder on and properly connected. These are device controls.

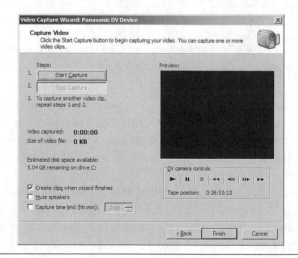

FIGURE 5-14 In the Video Capture module Firewire devices can be controlled directly by Movie Maker.

When you click the Play button, the video plays from the camcorder (see Figure 5-15). Notice that with the VCR-like controls, you can also pause, stop, or fast forward the video to the segment you want. (Hold down the Fast Forward or Reverse buttons to move the tape rapidly in either direction.)

Figure 5-15   Windows Movie Maker lets you fast forward or reverse through your footage to locate the segment you want to capture.

A few seconds before the segment begins, with the video playing, paused, or stopped, click Start Capture. The video runs, but you will also see the time elapsed and the hard drive space used in the left panel of the capture module as the footage is transferred as a clip into your PC (see Figure 5-16).

When you click Stop Capture, the segment is saved, and you can continue to add more clips or click Finish to exit the Capture window.

When you click Finish, the clips you captured are assembled in a Collection within the main area of Movie Maker (see Figure 5-17).

FIGURE 5-16 Windows Movie Maker uses the Start Capture command to begin download-ing video to your PC.

FIGURE 5-17 Windows Movie Maker saves references to the clips you've downloaded in its Collections window.

The Default view of Movie Maker favors the Storyboard. Click Show Timeline to make Movie Maker resemble most other video editing programs.

Drag and drop a clip into the Timeline and click Play in the Preview window to watch it (see Figure 5-18).

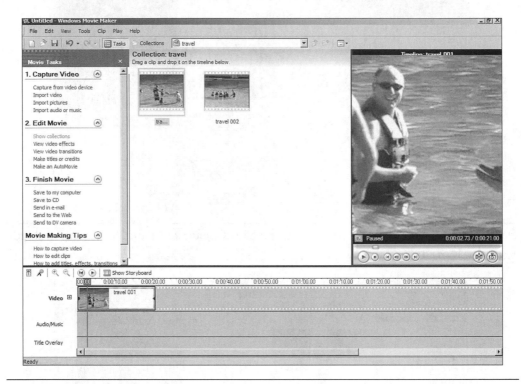

FIGURE 5-18   With a clip added to the Movie Maker Timeline, you can change its start and end points or add effects.

Just as we cropped a scanned image (that is, an image we acquired from a scanner), the most common function we will perform with captured video is to *trim a clip*. This means deleting unwanted portions at the beginning and the end so that the segment on the Timeline is exactly what we want. So either play or drag the slider on the Preview window to where you want the segment to begin and click Clip > Set Start Trim Point (see Figure 5-19).

Continue to the end of the clip and repeat the process, but select Clip > Set End Trim Point.

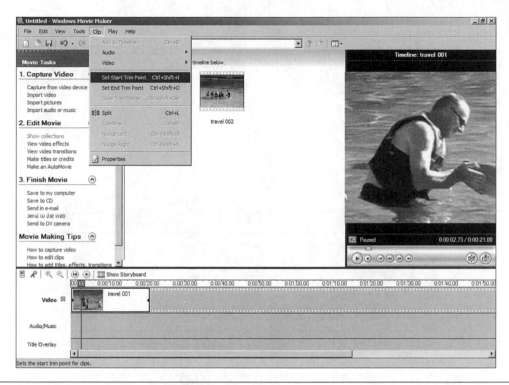

FIGURE 5-19   Click Clip > Set Start Trim Point where you want your final movie to begin.

Now the segment in your Timeline is exactly the movie you want to present in your travelogue in PowerPoint. Trick question: Where is it saved?

Answer: Nowhere.

Click File > Save Project As and name the project "travelogue" (see Figure 5-20).

NOTE Important: You still haven't saved the movie. Saving the project is simply creating a tiny file that takes Movie Maker back to the same state.

To save the final version of the movie in the Timeline, click Finish Movie > Save to My Computer (see Figure 5-21). Once again, you get a chance to name the final movie and decide where it will be saved. (For our project, it will go into a Desktop folder named "Travel.")

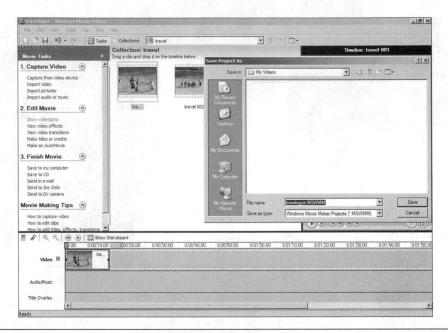

FIGURE 5-20 Saving the project saves the clip references and your editing decisions.

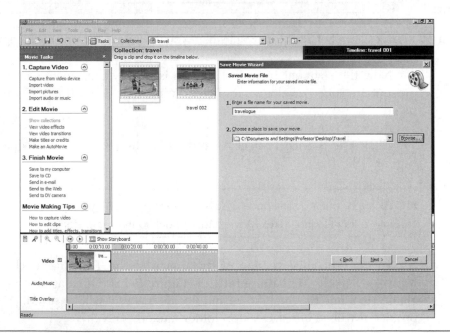

FIGURE 5-21 By clicking Save to My Computer, you open the Save Movie Wizard that begins the final "encoding" process.

Click Next and choose Other Settings. Click the drop-down arrow and select High quality video (large) (see Figure 5-22). Notice the other selections for web or portable device playback; we want only the best for PowerPoint.

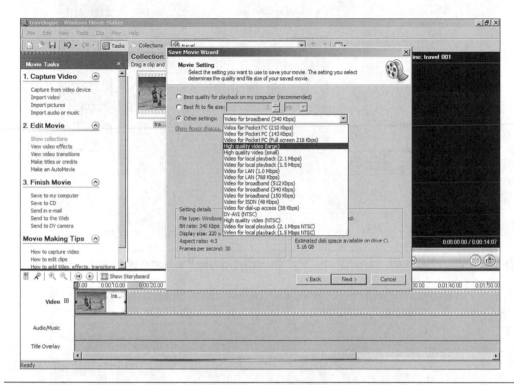

FIGURE 5-22 Finishing the movie gives you lots of output options.

When you click Next, the movie is simply saved in its final form in the folder under the name you chose (see Figure 5-23). If you used the Timeline to combine multiple clips, add titles or transitions, or create a complicated new movie, this might take a bit of time.

Don't bother to watch the movie now. Uncheck the option and click Finish. Let's examine the final movie by inserting it into PowerPoint. (Remember the folder where it was saved—in our case, Travel on the Desktop.)

In a slide created to hold the movie (with the title "Travelogue"), click Insert > Movies and Sounds > Movie from File, as we did in Figure 5-4. This time, select the new movie we created, travelogue.wmv, and click OK (see Figure 5-24).

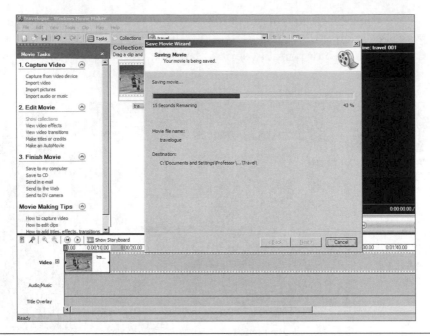

FIGURE 5-23 The final movie is saved to the folder under the name you chose.

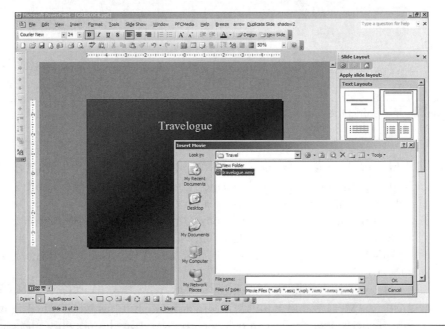

FIGURE 5-24 With the movie file saved locally, you can insert the video into a PowerPoint slide.

Once again, you have the choice to make it play Automatically or When Clicked.

Pick either, although we prefer When Clicked, and the movie is inserted into the slide. Because of the quality we chose, it is a large 640×480 sized video that we can move below the slide title. If we play the slide Full Screen, we can watch and control the video with a mouse click (see Figure 5-25).

FIGURE 5-25   The final movie can be played in PowerPoint in the same fashion described earlier (Figure 5-5).

Did you notice the *file type* that Movie Maker used to save the final video? It was a *.WMV file, the latest Windows Media Video file format. This is the only output file format for Windows Movie Maker 2.0—it is possible that later versions will also support an MPG format for DVD production.

What if you needed it in another format? Take a look at the disc that may have come with your video capture device. It is very likely that you were provided with a light version of one of the aforementioned editing programs, or another one entirely.

Now that you know the basic theory of video editing, you can use another program to import the WMV file and convert it to another format like AVI, MPG, or possibly MOV (QuickTime).

Troubleshooting Video Problems

Earlier, we mentioned that one of the main reasons video may not play is that the actual video is not embedded into PowerPoint. Never, ever. It is always a *linked* file, and the image in the slide is simply a reference to it.

So what happens if you click on a movie and it just doesn't play?

Unfortunately, the Edit > Links command, which you can use to fix links to charts and other hyperlinked documents, won't work with video.

What you can do is to right-click the video object in the slide and select Edit Video (see Figure 5-26). This will reveal two important facts: the actual name of the video file linked to the slide, and the location where PowerPoint expects it to be.

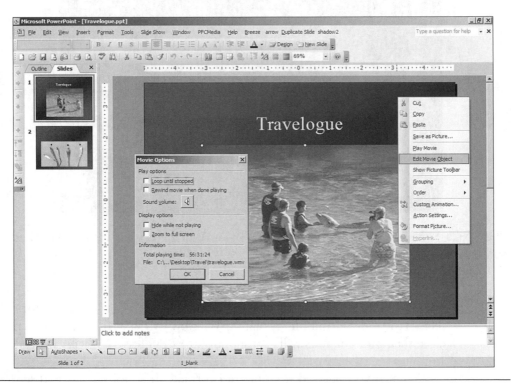

FIGURE 5-26 Right-clicking and selecting Edit Video will tell you the filename and expected location of the video file.

You now have two choices:

- Locate the actual file on your hard drive and move it to the folder where PowerPoint wants it to be.

- Delete the current video object, locate the video file, and repeat the process of Insert > Movies and Sounds > Movie from File.

So how do you maintain the links between your media files and presentations? Read the following two tips.

KEEP YOUR VIDEOS WITH PRESENTATIONS This should convince you to keep your video files in the same folder as the PowerPoint presentation as much as possible. If you must use a \Video or \Movies folder to conserve disk space, be careful about moving your PowerPoint files, and if possible, use the root C:\ drive to store the common media folders because if the files have to be moved to another PC, the root C:\ drive location will not be relative to a user name or other variable parameter.

MOVE YOUR FILES WITH PACK TO CD PowerPoint 2003 introduced the Pack to CD option under the File menu. Although you can use it to move your presentation *and linked files* to a CD or DVD, you can also move them to another local folder. Using this intermediary step before moving the presentation elsewhere will ensure that linked files and their hyperlinks are correctly preserved.

Understanding Codecs

There is one more potentially vexing issue for users of video in Power-Point, and this has to do with *codecs*, which stands for compression-decompression.

What this means is that just because a file is saved as an AVI, WMV, or MPG video file, it may not play correctly on your PC.

To understand this, let's go back to the capture process in Movie Maker. Remember that our original clips were downloaded using a specific peripheral—probably the Firewire device—and saved in their original form in the My Videos folder in My Documents.

You might well have asked, "If I didn't need to edit these videos, why not play them directly in PowerPoint?" After all, they were saved as Best quality on my computer.

Well, truthfully, you could, but you'd have to be very careful. If you *only used the files on the same computer on which they were captured,* you would not have a problem.

But those files were saved on the capture PC using the specific com-pression-decompression software that works with the capture peripheral.

If that peripheral (and its software or *codec*) is not present on the machine where the video will eventually need to be played (in PowerPoint or even in Media Player), it won't play correctly. (Sometimes the audio will play without the video; sometimes it will just result in an error message telling you that the codec is not present.)

That is why there is a Finish Movie step in Movie Maker—not just to allow you to edit and combine clips with titles and effects, but also to give you the opportunity to use the Other Settings output option (refer to Figure 5-22).

And that's also why saving the final version of your edited video in Movie Maker or another program is sometimes referred to as *encoding*—as referenced in the caption for Figure 5-21. By going through that extra step, Movie Maker is actually changing the codec for the WMV file from the one used for capture to one that is ubiquitous on Windows XP computers.

To learn more about this than you probably want to know, you can open the System Properties in Control Panel, open Sound, Video, and Game Controllers, and right-click to open the Properties of Video Codecs (see Figure 5-27). This will open the Video Codecs Properties panel; click the Properties tab and look at the various codecs registered on your PC.

If you continue to use only the Other Settings options for finishing your movie in Movie Maker, you won't need to know anything about these codecs.

But if you move on to more sophisticated video editing software, such as Pinnacle, Ulead, Adobe Premiere, or Sony Vegas, you will need to learn how to set specific codec options for your final movies.

Figure 5-28 shows the Make Movie codec options in Adobe Premiere 6.5.

Notice that the interface resembles Movie Maker, but in the video output dialog box, you can select a specific output codec. The ones to avoid are capture codecs. Typically, Sorensen, Indeo (from Intel), Microsoft, and Cinepak codecs will work on most machines.

In any video editing program, look for output options or settings for your final video file to reveal the codec choices.

PLAYS FOR CERTAIN PowerPoint MVP Austin Myers has created an Add-In for PowerPoint that converts almost any video file into a PowerPoint-friendly codec. It's free to try for two weeks and then costs $49.95, which includes a year of free email support. The site is www.pfcmedia.com.

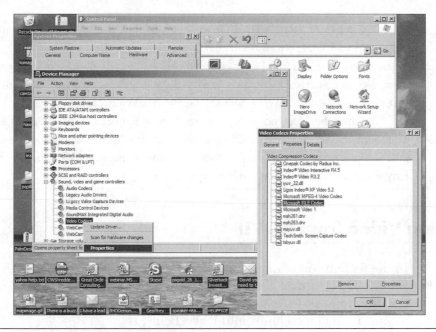

FIGURE 5-27   The video codecs registered on a Windows computer determine which types of AVI, MPG, and WMV files will play properly.

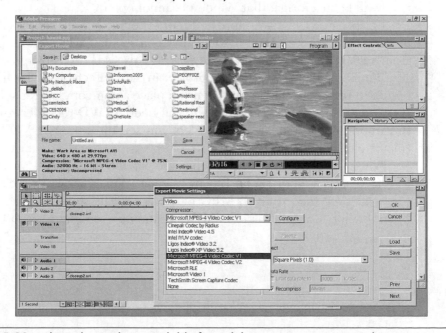

FIGURE 5-28   The video codecs available for Adobe Premiere appear in the options panel within the video output settings.

A NOTE ABOUT QUICKTIME The only QuickTime (MOV) file that will ever play in PowerPoint is a movie with the Cinepak codec. Even that is iffy. If you need to use QuickTime files in a PC PowerPoint presentation, you will want to bring them into an editor like Pinnacle, Ulead, Adobe Premiere, or Sony Vegas and convert them to an AVI, WMV, or MPG format with a Windows-friendly codec.

The other thing you could do is to make sure the QuickTime Player is enabled on the machine, link to the QuickTime file using the Action Settings (as described in Chapters 1 and 4), and let the audience see the movie play in the QuickTime Player before closing it and continuing to present.

Getting Video from a DVD

In the section "Acquiring Video," we mentioned that if someone gives you a movie DVD instead of a DVD disc with movie data files, and you explore the disc, you won't see any MPG, AVI, or WMV files that you can transfer to your PC and then insert into PowerPoint.

Remember that a movie DVD has a special format that enables it to play on consumer DVD players with an interactive menu, and the movie itself will be in a format that Windows cannot open.

But because there are more and more programs available for creating movie DVDs, there are also some that can extract MPG video directly from a DVD movie disc. One of the easiest to use is Ulead MovieFactory 2.

When you open a new DVD project in MovieFactory 2, you have an option to Import DVD Video. When you place a non-copy-protected DVD movie disc into your DVD recorder (you need a DVD recorder for this), the Import DVD Video command lets you see the various DVD "titles" (movie clips) on the disc (see Figure 5-29).

When the clips are extracted, they are actually placed into MovieFactory to create another DVD. But by placing your mouse over a clip, you can see where the extracted MPG movie is actually stored (in the Ulead MovieFactory Capture folder in My Documents—see Figure 5-30.)

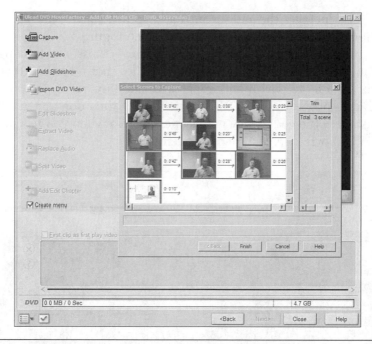

FIGURE 5-29 Some DVD authoring programs like Ulead MovieFactory 2 let you capture video segments from a DVD disc as MPG movie files on your PC.

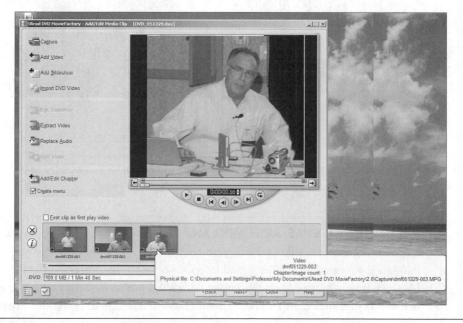

FIGURE 5-30 Ulead MovieFactory 2 expects to use the extracted video to create another DVD movie disc.

5. USING VIDEO AND AUDIO EFFECTIVELY

By locating the movies in that Capture folder, you can easily insert them directly into a PowerPoint slide (see Figure 5-31).

Remember, however, that if you move these movies—particularly if you break the links to the PowerPoint files that reference them—you will not be able to play them properly. In addition, some laptops may not be able to play extracted DVD movie files (if they don't have a DVD player installed, the codec may not be present). So when you use movies from a DVD movie disc, test them frequently.

FIGURE 5-31 Movies extracted from a DVD with Ulead MovieFactory 2 can be brought into PowerPoint and played in a presentation.

PROJECTION ISSUES WITH MPG MOVIES Sometimes when you try to play large-format movies in PowerPoint, particularly MPG files, an anomaly may occur that lets the movie play only on the laptop, or only on the projector, but not both. (A black box will appear on the screen where the movie isn't playing.) This is the result of a graphics card that is not quite powerful enough to pump the video to both screens.

To work around this issue, when projecting such a movie, toggle your display options to send it *only to the projector* and do not play it on the laptop, then return to a dual-display scenario when the movie is done playing.

We cover the setup procedures of laptops and projectors in Chapter 8, "Delivering a Killer Presentation."

Using DVD Instead of PowerPoint

Now that we understand the relationship between DVDs and PowerPoint and realize that they both use movies, you may be wondering if there isn't a way to burn a PowerPoint presentation to DVD.

There are several reasons why you might want to do this:

- To provide or sell a value-added takeaway to a client or audience
- To create a viable backup of your presentation
- To be able to play the presentation in a pinch on a consumer DVD player without a laptop or projector

The two main things you will need for this are a DVD recorder and a DVD authoring program—even something as simple as MovieFactory 2 can do it, but the more sophisticated the program, the better the final results.

The DVD authoring program assembles final movies *and individual images* into an interactive menu that can play back the movies or a slide show.

The easiest way to do this is to use a program like TechSmith's Camtasia Studio 3.0 to capture your PowerPoint presentation as a movie file. Then the final movie of one or more presentations can be assembled in a DVD project in an authoring program and burned to disc.

The alternative is to create a simulated presentation using the DVD program with an interactive menu that launches both the original videos (burned to DVD) and a slide show based on one or more PowerPoint projects.

Getting Your Slides to DVD

Because the DVD program accepts individual images as components of a slide show (or as backgrounds for interactive menus), you need to merely reverse the project of bringing images into your slides by exporting your presentation as a set of images.

You do this by using the File > Save As command and, from the Save as Type drop-down menu, selecting an image file format, like TIF (see Figure 5-32).

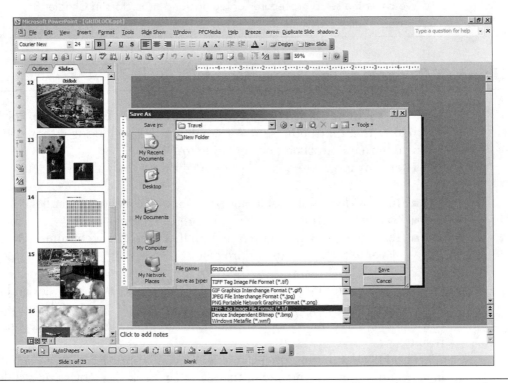

FIGURE 5-32 You can save one or more PowerPoint slides as still images by changing the output Save as Type option to an image file.

When you click Save, you are prompted whether you want to save only the current slide or All Slides in the Presentation. Chances are, for a DVD, you will want the entire slide show.

When the images are stored in a folder, you can generally find a Create Slide Show option in a DVD authoring program to use your PowerPoint slides on a finished DVD (see Figure 5-33).

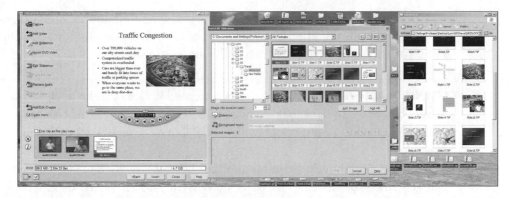

Figure 5-33   Even an inexpensive DVD authoring program like MovieFactory can create a DVD that mixes video and slide shows composed of exported PowerPoint slides.

Preserving Features

If you take the easy way out by assembling the DVD in an authoring program, you will lose many PowerPoint features, like hyperlinks, transitions, and animation, although the DVD authoring program may also provide some of these in its own functionality.

(To maintain animation and transition effects, save the PowerPoint show as a movie before burning it to DVD by using a tool like Camtasia Studio 3.0.)

If you want to build slides (sets of bullets or any other sequence), you can break them up by using the Insert > Duplicate Slide feature and removing the unwanted portions from successive slides, as we did to animate the table in Chapter 4, "Secrets of Animation and Navigation" (refer to Figure 4-15 in Chapter 4).

Now you can have four images representing the various "builds" in a sequence and show them in succession on your DVD.

(We cover more aspects of DVD authoring and using DVD instead of PowerPoint in detail in the case study at the end of Chapter 7.)

Using 3D Animation

One of the most fertile sources of movies for presentations is photorealistic 3D animation. Many of you have certainly seen simulated 3D walkthroughs of buildings that have yet to be built or medical simulations of parts of the body.

The key to using these kinds of files is knowing that animations (unless created in Flash) are almost always ordinary movie files and adhere to the same principles and file types that we've been discussing.

USING FLASH ANIMATION Animation created in Flash can be published as Shockwave and inserted into PowerPoint as described in Chapter 4. Newer versions of Flash also use a special FLV file format that as of now is not usable in PowerPoint.

You can publish a Flash project as a QuickTime MOV file and then convert that to a PowerPoint-friendly AVI, MPG, or WMV in another video editor.

But because Flash is essentially a web animation and video tool, using it to publish a Shockwave file in a web page and then linking to that web page in PowerPoint is probably your best bet. We will cover using PowerPoint on the web in Chapter 7.

For a utility that helps insert Flash files into PowerPoint, consider Microsoft MVP Shyam Pillai's toolbox at http://skp.mvps.org/toolbox/.

If you get a 3D animation on a CD or data DVD, transferring it to your hard drive should allow you to play it within PowerPoint. Many animation files from high-end 3D programs like 3D Studio Max (from Autodesk) or Lightwave are saved as AVI or MPG. In some cases, they may be Quick-Time (MOV) or WMV.

A great way to get your feet wet with 3D animation is another Ulead product, Cool 3D Production Studio (see Figure 5-34).

Notice that a 3D program has many of the elements of a video editing program: a Timeline, a clip panel (in this case, a set of attributes to apply to objects), and a playback or preview window.

The main difference is that what you are creating is *objects* in a three-dimensional world that can be navigated and viewed from all angles. After objects are created, they can be given attributes like texture or lighting (similar to the 3D options for selected objects in PowerPoint). In addition, by making changes to size, position, or other parameters at specific frames in a Timeline called *key frames*, the program has the ability to calculate the *in-between frames (called "tweens")* and render an animated movie of the results.

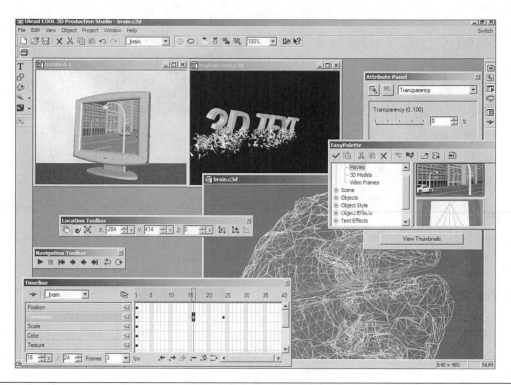

FIGURE 5-34   An inexpensive animation program like Ulead's Cool 3D Production Studio can enable you to create simple 3D movies for use in PowerPoint.

In my 3D workspace, I can rotate, resize, or move the object with the Location toolbar and eventually apply an effect (like an explosion) from the Easy Palette. Finally, I can save the entire animation as a video file (File > Create Video File), and when I look at the output to AVI option, I can see the same compression codecs available to me as I did in my Adobe Premiere 6.5 video editing program (see Figure 5-35).

As you can imagine, learning to use a 3D animation program, even one as basic as the Ulead Cool 3D Production Studio, takes an investment in time. The important takeaway here, however, is that the final output is viewable and presentable in PowerPoint as a video file using the same principles we have already covered.

FIGURE 5-35 Ulead's Cool 3D Production Studio creates animation as AVI movie files with the same compression codecs as other video editing tools.

Working with Audio

Although video might be the "star" of many PowerPoint presentations, sound is what engages yet another sense, as hearing joins sight in terms of the audience's attention.

If the presentation is used for speaker support, the use of audio can be superfluous and even annoying—as it is when used to accompany gratuitous animation or slide transitions. Whoever first put a camera "click" with a bullet or dissolve should be in the Presentation Hall of Shame.

On the other hand, readers of Richard Mayer's book, *Multimedia Learning*, know that research has shown that audio accompanying a strong visual reinforces retention dramatically. This is the result of the second sense (or "channel") being engaged—which is not the case when written bullets or text boxes accompany a visual because they are a second visual and generally a distraction unless used effectively to supplement the speaker's remarks.

Again, the timing of the audio is critical, but for presentations that are *not for speaker support*—those distributed on DVD or CD or via a kiosk—having an audio "track" accompanying the slide show can be a very effective tool.

In PowerPoint, you can employ various strategies to play audio during a slide show.

Creating a Sound File in Windows

Just as we saw that certain video file formats were Windows-friendly and could be easily used in PowerPoint, there are three main audio file types that will work well in a slide show:

- **Windows *.WAV**—Full fidelity, and the standard.
- ***.MP3**—Compressed format mainly for music downloads.
- ***.WMA**—Highly compressed Windows web audio format.

Once again, the Windows Accessories > Entertainment folder provides a way to create your own *.WAV audio files for use in Windows and Power-Point and even a way to edit them simply. Make sure a microphone is properly installed and connected to your PC, and you can use the Windows Sound Recorder in Windows 95, 98, Me (may the Force be with you), and XP (see Figure 5-36).

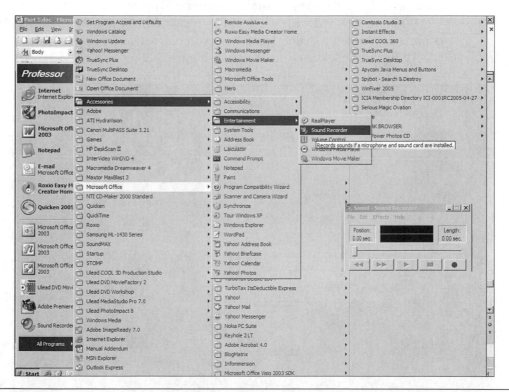

FIGURE 5-36 Windows Sound Recorder makes it easy to record, edit (on a basic level), and save *.WAV audio files for use in Windows and PowerPoint.

To record an audio file, hold the microphone near your mouth, click the red Record button, and speak clearly (see Figure 5-37).

FIGURE 5-37 With a microphone connected and configured, you can see the audio level in the Sound Recorder as the file is recorded.

When your statement is complete, click the Stop button. Click Play to listen to your sound file. Click Record again to *append more audio to the segment*. Click File > New if you don't like the results and want to create a new "take." (You will be asked whether you really want to lose what you've done, and if you click Yes, Sound Recorder will open a new blank file.)

If you're satisfied with what you've recorded, use the File > Save As command to open a dialog box where you can select a folder, name your *.WAV file, and click Save, as shown in Figure 5-38.

FIGURE 5-38 With a completed sound file in Sound Recorder, you can save it to a folder like any other computer file, in the WAV audio format.

After you get a bit more familiar with Sound Recorder, you will be able to fine-tune segments by deleting portions before or after the slider, copying and pasting portions, and even mixing with a file. These options are under the Edit menu, as shown in Figure 5-39.

FIGURE 5-39 The Edit Menu of Windows Sound Recorder allows you to delete, copy, and paste audio segments before you save them as *.WAV audio files for use in Windows and PowerPoint.

SOPHISTICATED SOUND EDITORS Sound editing programs that let you visually select, copy, and modify sounds are available with many sound cards and are part of many digital audio packages (such as Roxio, Sonic Solution, and Nero). As we did with Windows Movie Maker, after we get used to a simple editing system, we can move up to more complex versions if the need arises.

The other advantage of more sophisticated sound editors is the ability to convert one sound file type to another and compress the size to move it to portable devices like MP3 players. If you have a sound file that is not PowerPoint-friendly (QuickTime MOV, for example), these other programs can convert it to *.WAV, *.MP3, and perhaps *.WMA.

OPTIMIZING SOUND RECORDER The main limitations of Windows Sound Recorder are that it opens and saves *only* in *.WAV file format and that it is mainly connected to the Windows XP microphone input.

If you right-click on the speaker icon in your System Tray (the lower-right of the Windows interface), click Open Volume Control and then Options > Properties, change the Properties to Recording (from Playback), and click OK, you can select Line In instead of Microphone (the default) as the sound system's input device (see Figure 5-40). Line In is for a stereo plug on your sound card, and you can now use Sound Recorder (or another sound editing program) to record from an analog source like a tape recorder or a VCR. Just get the appropriate cables and plugs from Radio Shack.

5. USING VIDEO AND AUDIO EFFECTIVELY

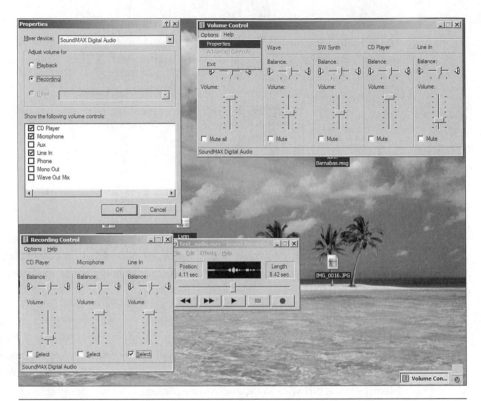

FIGURE 5-40   Right-clicking the speaker in your System Tray allows you to adjust the Windows system audio properties, including selecting a different Recording input source for your sound card.

Inserting a Sound as a File

Now that you've saved the sound file as a simple *.WAV file in a folder, you can reference it in your slide the same way that you did with the movie clips and control its playback. When you select Insert > Movies and Sounds, choose Sound from File (see Figure 5-41), and you get the dialog box that allows you to select your just-recorded (or another) sound file.

Unfortunately, inserting a sound file in this way puts an ugly speaker icon into your slide (see Figure 5-42). But notice that the audio file also goes directly into the Custom Animation Task Pane, where its Effect Options can be modified. Drag the sound icon out of the slide's visible area and then click its Timing in the drop-down list of Effect Options to open the Play Sound options dialog box, and you can assign any object to play the sound when clicked, like an Action button or even a text box. (For more on using triggers, see Chapter 4.)

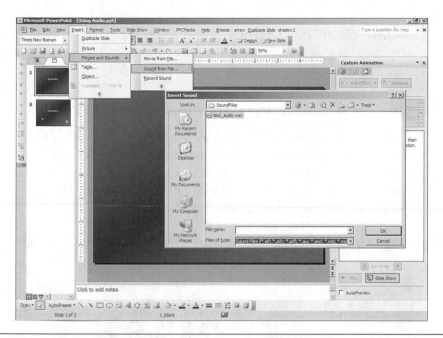

FIGURE 5-41 Insert Movies and Sounds lets you put a sound file into your PowerPoint slide just as you did with a video.

FIGURE 5-42 You can modify the trigger for the sound object in Custom Animation to allow you to start the sound file with another object in the slide.

AUDIO VS. VIDEO CONTROL Although PowerPoint lets you start, pause, and continue video, clicking the trigger for the audio object, whether the sound icon itself or another object, will simply restart the sound file.

Use an Action Setting to Play a Sound File

Now that you understand the nature of audio files, you can also access them directly using an Action Setting for any selected object. For example, drag through a slide title as shown in Figure 5-43 and right-click to open the Action Settings. Change the Action Setting from Hyperlink to Play Sound and choose Other Sound.

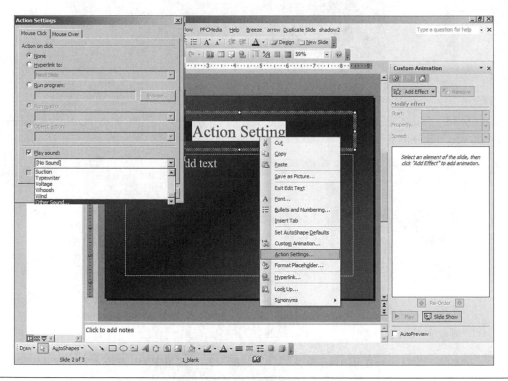

FIGURE 5-43 You can use the Action Settings dialog box to make a selected object play a sound file directly.

A dialog box opens, and you can choose the sound file you want to play from within a folder on your PC.

The Action Settings feature changes the text to a hyperlink (it becomes underlined—see Figure 5-44); now when the slide is played, clicking the text will also play the sound file, and you've avoided Custom Animation and the ugly speaker icon.

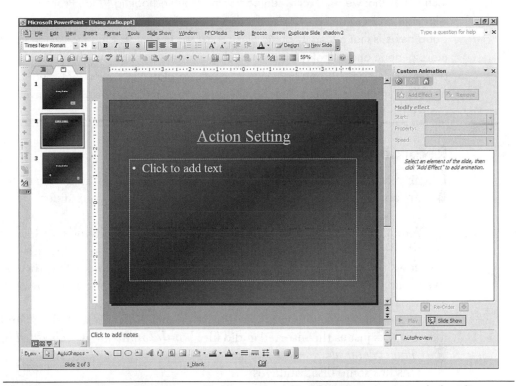

FIGURE 5-44 The Action Settings will play a sound file when the trigger (underlined) text is clicked during the slide show.

OTHER SOUND FILES When you open the Action Settings, you see a list of sound files (most of which are sound effects rather than music) that come with PowerPoint. Use these at your own risk.

Using "hot" zones like an Action Setting or a Trigger to play sound files can really enhance a kiosk or interactive PowerPoint presentation by providing clues or prompts for right and wrong answers.

You can also control sound files programmatically with Visual Basic for Applications (VBA), which is a macro language that we will cover later on (in Chapter 7).

LINKED AUDIO FILES Just as with video, audio files used in the fashion described here are generally *linked* to the presentation, and if the links are broken, they will not play. You can repair broken audio links using the same techniques that we used for video earlier in "Troubleshooting Video Problems." Although codecs can be an issue if video is acquired from another source, the good news is that generally audio files are saved in compression types that are more generic and will play on most machines. The exception may be if you move an audio file from the web or a Mac computer to play it in PowerPoint. Here again the more sophisticated sound editing programs can be helpful in converting the file to a usable Windows *.WAV audio file.

Recording Audio within PowerPoint

I hear readers out there saying, "Wait, can't you record audio inside of PowerPoint or set up narration that is linked directly to your slides?" Yes, you can—but there are issues.

When you use the command Insert > Movies and Sounds > Record Sound (see Figure 5-45), you get a similar interface as you do with the Windows Sound Recorder. And, you can start and stop recording successive audio files—but without the versatility of editing the sound or saving it as a separate sound file.

When the speaker icon is put into your slide to represent the sound file, it works just as the inserted audio file, *but the audio file is embedded in your PowerPoint file*.

This has some disadvantages:

- The PowerPoint file will get very big with lots of sound objects.
- It's hard to keep track of the sound object, which you may later want to edit or delete.
- The sound objects are difficult if not impossible to edit or reuse.

On the other hand, using recorded sound files that are linked from another folder allows you to edit them or delete them more easily and reuse them for other presentations or applications. For example, in a training application, recording a statement like "Almost, but good try" or "Please try again" allows you to use the same sound file on different occasions.

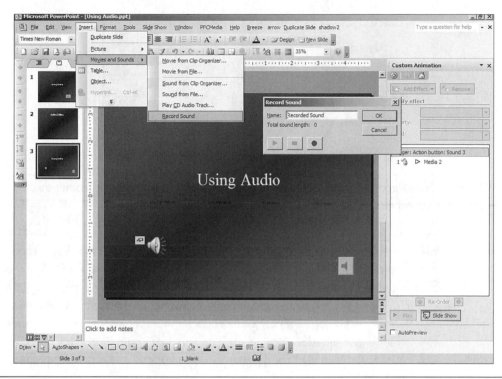

Figure 5-45 The sound recorded directly within PowerPoint is embedded in the presentation and referenced by the speaker icon. It can also be triggered by another object using Custom Animation effect options.

Using the Record Narration Feature

The Record Narration feature under Slide Show in the PowerPoint main menu gives you the best of both worlds.

First, you don't have to leave PowerPoint to record using your microphone, and the option lets you test your microphone level and recording quality.

In addition, by checking Link Narrations In within the dialog box to set up narration, you can designate a folder to save your recorded audio as separate sound files for each slide in *.WAV format (see Figure 5-46).

The other aspect of this technique is that the sound plays automatically with each slide for which you record narration, so for a self-running presentation, this can be quite useful, but for a presentation with speaker support, it is probably inappropriate.

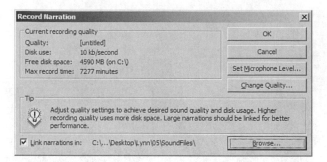

FIGURE 5-46   The Record Narration dialog box provides the option to link (rather than embed) your sound files, keeping them in a separate folder for reuse.

MICROPHONES MATTER Most microphones for PCs plug into the sound card of the computer. A few more powerful and professional units use the USB connector. If you are going to do a lot of narration, video blogging, or podcasting (covered in Chapter 7), investing in a high-end microphone is probably worth the cost. Samson Technologies (http://snipurl.com/m4uo) makes an excellent model, while even higher-impedance mikes from dealers like Radio Shack will improve audio quality significantly. (For a figure showing various audio connectors, refer to Figure 8-24.)

Using CD Audio for Backgrounds

It's amazing how often clients have asked me about using an audio CD for musical background or to accompany a series of slides. If you've opened the Insert Movies and Sound feature in PowerPoint, you've probably noticed the Play CD Audio Track option (see Figure 5-47).

With an audio CD in your computer's CD or DVD drive, you can arrange to have one or more tracks play successively over a series of slides—or you can have them play before you even begin the presentation, which is very nice.

The only difference is that a CD audio icon is put into the slide instead of the speaker icon for a sound file, but you can change the trigger just the same way by using the Effect Options for the CD audio event in Custom Animation.

Needless to say, the audio CD must be in the PC when you present with this option.

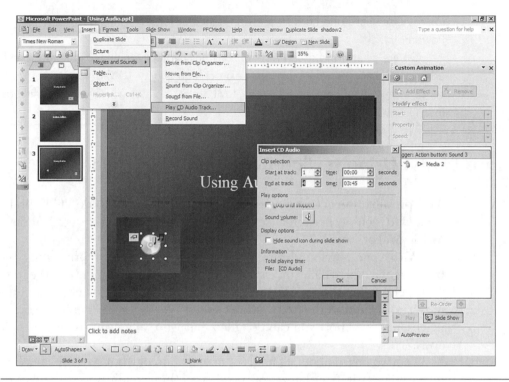

FIGURE 5-47 The Insert CD Audio dialog box provides complete control over a music disc in your optical drive.

USING "RIPPED" AUDIO FILES Everyone knows that there is a music revolution going on in which users are extracting audio files from their CDs or downloading songs from the web. Generally these are saved as *.MP3 audio files, and the good news is that PowerPoint can insert this type of audio file into your slide using the Insert > Movies and Sounds > Sound from File option.

Here again, the location of the files becomes significant because they will be linked to your presentation, so although you can insert references to the music from the My Music folder in My Documents (where ripped music is frequently stored), if you move the presentation, you will need to adjust the links accordingly.

Can you use music downloaded from iTunes or another pay service? The rights management of the service will determine the answer. Certainly your iTunes library folder is visible on your PC and makes the songs accessible if they are saved in *.MP3 format, but generally the proprietary versions are impossible to play elsewhere and hard to convert to another format if they don't play in PowerPoint.

On the other hand, good ripping software (typically included with the sound editing program just referenced) can extract high-quality *.WAV versions of songs from CDs or compress them as *.MP3 files, both of which will work fine as inserted audio files in PowerPoint.

Case Study: Using a High-Definition Video File

As a presentations consultant, you've figured out how to do video pretty well, and you've mastered some video editing tools beyond Windows Movie Maker.

With your newfound fame, a client comes to you representing the travel agency for which you captured the dolphin video mentioned earlier in this chapter and says, "We want to do something really spectacular at the next Travel Show at the Convention Center. We've got tours going to exotic places, and we know you can do video, but we really want to blow people away."

They've heard about all kinds of new technology but have no idea how to implement it. You know you need something really special—what do you come up with?

You decide you're going to try to project in high definition.

Key Issues to Consider

You might want to think about the following:

- Where can you get high-definition video content?
- What kind of video files will play in PowerPoint?
- What kind of projection equipment will you need to project Hi-Def?
- Can you use PowerPoint to make it work?

The first thing you do is to go to the Windows Media website to see what Microsoft is doing with high-definition video: http://snipurl.com/5rpy (dolphins on Microsoft Windows Media in High Definition WMV file wformat).

You're in luck: two clips of dolphins at incredible quality and high resolution are available for download. One is 720p (high definition and more common to project), and the other is 1080p (super high resolution).

The smaller clip is at a resolution of 1280×720 (width/height); the larger one is 1440×1280! What the heck can you find to play this kind of video full screen?

Your first stop is www.projectorcentral.com.

A projector search finds 107 projectors that can handle 1280×720 (WXGA). (A search for QXGA, an even higher-definition format—2048×1536—yields a JVC projector selling for $225,000.)

Although the site is full of reviews, there is an editorial commentary devoted to WXGA (1280×720) projectors. Although many of them are extremely expensive, they are available for rental, so you're in business. But how are you going to project this puppy?

You're going to need a graphics card that can rock at 1280×720. You're going to give it a try on a Sony Vaio that you've got set up for Instant FX software. But its native resolution is just XGA—1024×768. You wonder whether it can pump a bigger image using a DVI output (high definition converter) (see Figure 5-48).

FIGURE 5-48 To project true high-definition digital output from a PC, you need a DVI output or plug with a special pin configuration.

The next thing you do is to use the Extended Desktop feature of your graphics card. Right-click on the Desktop and choose Properties > Settings to configure your PC for 1280×960 (maintaining a 4×3 aspect ratio) and change the secondary display (the image that will go to the projector) to 1280×720 (see Figure 5-49).

But what happens in PowerPoint? Even at the higher resolution, the movie overwhelms the slide (see Figure 5-50).

FIGURE 5-49 To go to a 720p projector, the secondary display on the Extended Desktop can be manually set to the proper resolution.

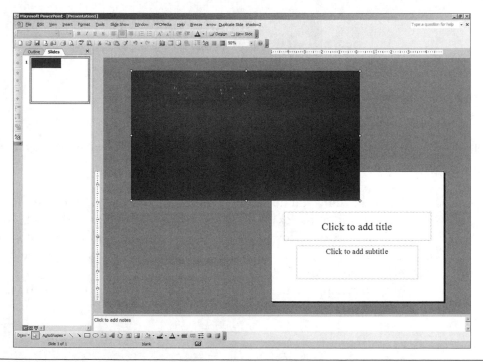

FIGURE 5-50 The standard PowerPoint slide size won't accommodate the giant movie.

But with a bit of ingenuity, we fool PowerPoint by using the Custom setting for Page Setup to simulate the dimensions we want at 12.8" by 7.2" (Landscape) (see Figure 5-51).

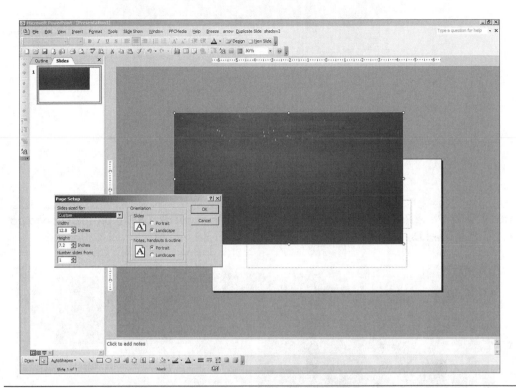

FIGURE 5-51   By customizing the PowerPoint slide, its size now accommodates the movie.

To move the movie to the projector along with the slide show during the presentation, we're going to use Presenter View, which requires the Extended Desktop. We can set this up under Slide Show > Set Up Show (see Figure 5-52).

When the show is actually presented Full Screen, the movie is projected in the proper resolution to the 720p projector and can still be controlled in PowerPoint (see Figure 5-53).

The tricky part will be adding other slides with elements that are not distorted in this resolution, but you can get around that by using the hyperlink navigation techniques shown in Chapter 4.

In the meantime, you will need to invoice your client for the rental of a high-definition projector and perhaps a more powerful laptop to show the movie without a hitch. Then again, you may find it easier to just set up your desktop PC with a high-end graphics card for this particular occasion.

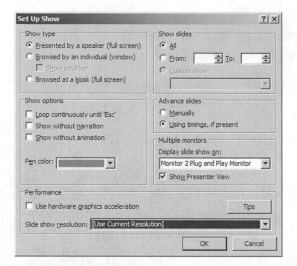

FIGURE 5-52   The Presenter View in PowerPoint Set Up Show allows the presentation to go to the Extended Desktop—in this case, it will be the projector.

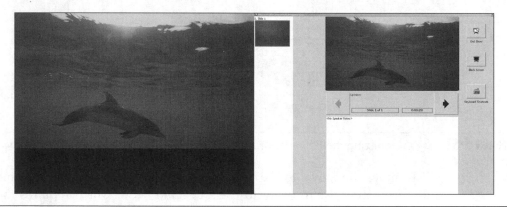

FIGURE 5-53   PowerPoint shows the movie in proper resolution on the projector while you control the show in Presenter View.

Summary

Video and audio are features that can truly make an ordinary presentation into a "multimedia production"—and from the standpoint of content, movies, narration, and music can do a lot to enhance the impact of your slide show and deliver your message.

In a medical presentation, showing the effects of treatment on patients as they move and talk can do a lot more than most tables and charts. For a motivational speech, a rousing soundtrack or integrated success stories can bolster enthusiasm and add credibility.

The problem with video and audio files is that they require additional hardware and software to prepare them for PowerPoint. In this chapter we described the essential process of capturing, editing, and saving both video and audio formats so that they will behave properly in your slide show. Two main reasons for glitches are broken links and wrong codecs; remember to keep your linked media files with your presentation and to save your final versions in a format that will play on any computer.

Finally, we covered some of the emerging technologies that you may want to integrate with your presentation, including DVD as a source of footage or even an ultimate output destination, and high definition for those occasions where you really want to take advantage of a the ultimate projection hardware.

In all cases, using video will require some extra effort to make it work properly, but it will pay off in setting your presentation apart from the ordinary.

Resources

Here are some websites and a book that will help you decide the proper way to use video and audio in your presentations and also help you to use the latest hardware for the best-quality audio:

- *Multimedia Learning* by Richard E. Mayer, Cambridge University Press (April 23, 2001).
- My webinar on using video in PowerPoint—http://snipurl.com/l651.
- USB Microphone—Samson Technologies—http://snipurl.com/m4uo.

Video Stock Footage Websites

These sites provide source video files that you can insert directly into PowerPoint presentations; some charge while others are free.

- Stock Footage—stockfootages.net
- Royalty Free Footage—www.stockfootage4less.com
- www.movieclip.biz—Buy a yearly membership for only $149.00, and you can purchase any movie clip for only $.99 a movie.
- FootageFirm Stock Footage—www.footagefirm.com
- A Luna Blue—www.alunablue.com

5. USING VIDEO AND AUDIO EFFECTIVELY

- Artbeats—www.artbeats.com
- Global Cuts—www.globalcuts.com
- Ulead Pick-A-Video—www.ulead.com/pav/catalog.htm

PowerPoint to DVD and Other Helpful Programs

Although I haven't tried them all, here are some potential utilities for turning PowerPoint slide shows into DVD formats and working with Flash video. See Chapter 6, "Powerful Presentation Tools," for more about using Camtasia Studio 3.0 and additional resources.

- Camtasia Studio 3.0—www.techsmith.com
- www.powerpoint-to-dvd.com/
- www.tomdownload.com/dvd_software/powerpoint_dvd_maker.htm
- www.allformp3.com/powerpoint-dvd-maker/
- www.convertzone.com/net/cz-PowerPoint%20DVD%20Burner-1-1.htm
- www.softforall.com/Multimedia/Video/1st_PowerPoint_DVD_Creator07070167.htm
- http://skp.mvps.org/toolbox/

CHAPTER 6

POWERFUL PRESENTATION TOOLS

By now, you've surely realized that PowerPoint has become a multimedia *platform* and that a successful presenter can take advantage of many supporting programs to convey his or her message. Sometimes PowerPoint is like the quarterback of a presentation team (or if you don't care for sports analogies, it's like the conductor of an orchestra).

The slides are the spine that can link to video, charts, diagrams, and other programs that may convey a specific message better than mere text or even graphics.

Examples of how to use these programs comprise most of this chapter and are included in the "Resources" listings at the end. We'll cover a few of the more powerful applications that can help you present more effectively, with or without PowerPoint.

Most of these programs would justify an entire book on their own, but as we have seen, the power of many of these techniques is best experienced with concrete examples. So in this chapter, we'll try to present the potential for more effective communication offered by these programs with scenarios of how they can be used.

But obviously, to use a program like Visio truly effectively, you will need to dig deeper than we can in this chapter. The same would be true for all of these resources, each of which comes with extensive documentation. But in the following examples, you will get an idea of the many ways with which to expand the world of PowerPoint with tools that can dramatically enhance the depth, scope, and reach of your message, whatever it may be.

Taking Advantage of Visio's Intelligent Diagrams

In many ways, Visio is the "missing link" between PowerPoint on one hand and Excel and Access on the other. For the most part, PowerPoint is the platform for visual communication, while Excel and Access are repositories of specific information (in the form of spreadsheets and databases) that we may want to present.

Visio is somewhere in between. In the Timeline example we covered in Chapter 3, "Creating Dynamic Visuals," we just opened the door slightly to the possibilities of Visio and suggested a closer look at the many types of Visio templates, many of which contain design elements in their Stencils that can be effective in PowerPoint slides.

What we saw with the Visio Timeline is that the shapes themselves literally represent the mathematical relationships that they convey. When a milestone or interval is placed on a Visio Timeline, it is exactly of the duration and in the position that its date and time represent compared to the entire span of time.

This concept of *parametric shape design* extends to the entire program. Whether you use shapes from a Visio Stencil or create your own, you can use them to visually and spatially represent exactly what you intend to convey in a way that PowerPoint cannot.

Custom Properties for Visual Databases

If you use one of the Building Plan templates to lay out some office space, you will get Stencils with objects like cubicles, doors, and furniture, along with equipment like PCs and monitors, as shown in Figure 6-1. More importantly, with a shape selected, like the PC, it may have one or more *Custom Properties* with which to keep track of specific information in a database.

This information can be imported from or exported to an Excel spreadsheet or an Access database, and several Visio macros allow this to be dynamic—that is, as you add another item to the diagram and fill in its Custom Properties, the underlying database (Excel or Access) has the proper table updated with the information. For those of you familiar with Access, Visio becomes a *visual form* for adding to the database.

More significantly, from a presentation standpoint of communicating ideas, this potentially becomes a very powerful tool:

- The diagrams themselves visually represent exactly what you may need to show an audience.
- You can build the diagram in front of the audience (as we'll see in a project planning session shortly), and the entire story takes shape visually, spatially, and with the details saved.
- A report of the final set of objects (across one or more pages of the diagram) can be generated to give the "big picture" of overall cost.
- From the reports, scenarios can be run to predict cost structures and results.

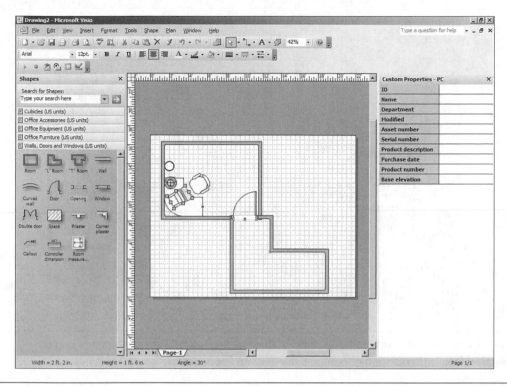

FIGURE 6-1   When you select the desk shape in the diagram, its Custom Properties are available to be filled in to store specific information about the shape.

For example, consider a set of building plans for a technical office space that is populated with different sets of equipment, and as each item is added or removed from the total inventory, the cost and investment can be recalculated and analyzed according to the new parameters.

Figure 6-2 shows a different set of Custom Properties being filled in for shapes that are dropped into two columns of a legal diagram: one representing Prosecution facts and the other for the Defense.

It's easy to generate a simple report of the latest status of the evidence, just as we might of the inventory of the office building (see Figure 6-3).

In the case of the legal scenario here, the report could be filtered to separate Defense and Prosecution facts or put into a sequential format (like a timeline) to see how the events played out.

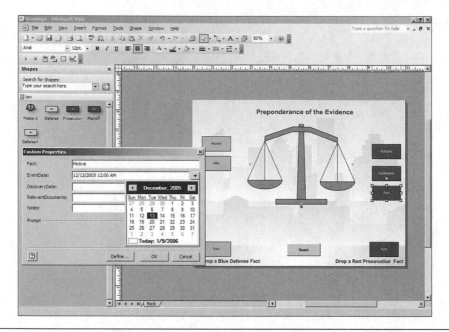

FIGURE 6-2 As facts are assembled on both sides of a case, their parameters can be entered into a database that contains the Custom Properties.

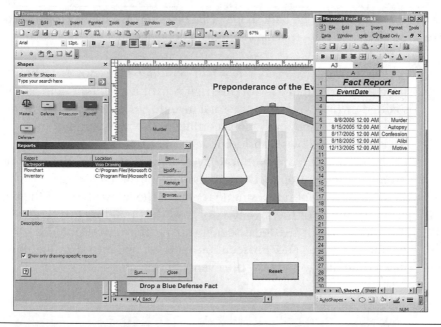

FIGURE 6-3 A report in the form of a spreadsheet can be generated from the Custom Properties within the various shapes of the document.

If you wanted to present directly from within the diagram by dragging and dropping more "facts" onto the page, you could get the scales to physically tip in one direction or the other (see Figure 6-4).

What's happening here is that the angle of the scales (which by default is set to an even level) is actually being controlled by a user-defined cell in the Page's ShapeSheet, which is a spreadsheet that keeps track of the properties of all of the parameters of a selected object; with no object selected, the ShapeSheet for the page is accessible.

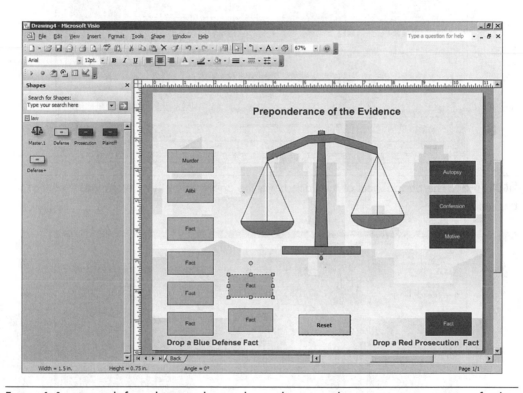

FIGURE 6-4   As each fact object is dropped onto the page, the appropriate amount of "tilt" is added to the angle of the scales.

In Figure 6-5, you can see that the angle in the user-defined cell named "User.Angle" is now set to .82, tipping in the direction of the majority of "facts."

The Drop command in the ShapeSheet of the fact object uses a function (SETF) to change the value of the user cell in the Page ShapeSheet by increments, thus changing the angle of the scales (see Figure 6-6).

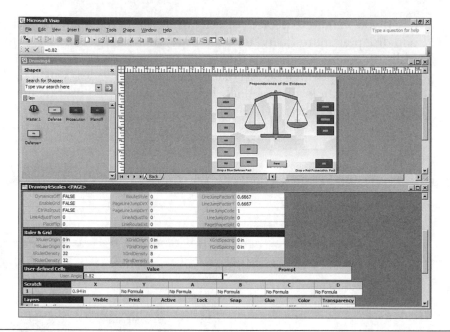

FIGURE 6-5 The ShapeSheet of the Page holds the angle value that determines the tilt of the scales.

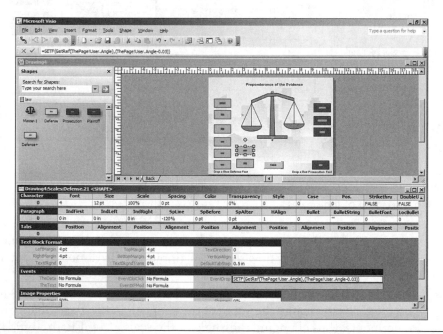

FIGURE 6-6 A command entered into the ShapeSheet of the dropped object changes the value of the user-defined cell of the Page ShapeSheet, thus changing the tilt angle of the scales.

This kind of programmed functionality takes a while to learn, to be sure—but it represents a different kind of presentation strategy in terms of "real time" scenarios. Off the top of my head, ideas include

- A nutritionist dropping meal combinations into a set of menus and calculating caloric content
- A dentist keeping track of the cavities and dental work in patients' charts and subsequently presenting the information
- An architect laying out tracts of land, dragging and dropping "units" into place, and evaluating environmental and geographic consequences

Layers for Visual Interactivity

Another aspect of Visio that makes it a powerful presentation tool is the ability to put items on Layers and make them visible or invisible by programming a few simple buttons.

Figure 6-7 shows a home office inventory with different components put on different Layers, indicated by the Layer properties panel. Besides generating a report compiling the assets and their value, Figure 6-7 can also be dynamically used by a presenter to Hide and Show different sets of cables or wires (audio or video).

We're about to begin our first foray into the world of automation or *code*. By toggling between the Design and User modes of Visio, we can select a button and alter its command sequence for a Click command.

Figure 6-8 shows the selected button and the lines of code associated with its Hide command.

The first time I saw this technique, it was applied to a subway map of London; depending upon the destination selected in a drop-down list, only the appropriate subway line was shown, and the irrelevant routes and stations were hidden. It was obviously far more complex than this example.

This may well be where you get off—programming is an entirely different level of expertise that requires a lot of attention to detail. But, now that you know what is possible within a tightly controlled environment like Visio and how it can affect visual presentations, you're ready to also think about it with other programs, including PowerPoint. (More on code in the case study at the end of this chapter, as we program Access to control PowerPoint.)

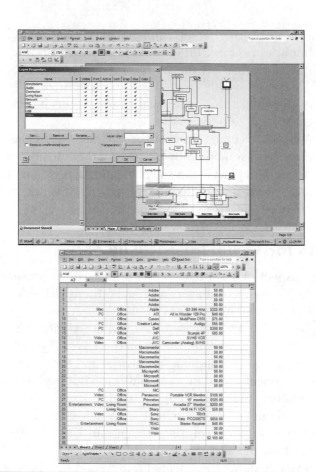

FIGURE 6-7 By taking advantage of Visio Layers and placing different sets of items on various Layers, you can quickly make some elements invisible while showing others.

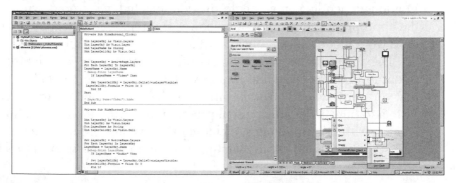

FIGURE 6-8 The Click command code determines which Visio Layer(s) are hidden, affecting all objects on that Layer. The Show command will reveal elements on a Layer that had previously been hidden.

Remember that to use Visio as Visio, it cannot be imported or copied into PowerPoint. When copied, a Visio diagram becomes a static image or in some cases a grouped piece of clip art—but without the Custom Properties and Layer capabilities that really make Visio shine. You are advised to hyperlink to a Visio document from PowerPoint to open it as Visio (refer to Chapter 4, "Secrets of Animation and Navigation") and work with the diagram using its Visio capabilities before returning to PowerPoint if you need to work from a slide show.

Presenting with Excel Pivot Tables

As discussed in Chapter 3, sometimes you can't get away from figures. Although charts can convey data and trends effectively in many instances, they are still static.

What if you are in a situation that calls for instant responses to different kinds of questions about your data?

A familiarity with Excel pivot tables can truly make you look like a genius; although pivot tables are among the most powerful tools Excel has to offer, they are widely ignored and misunderstood as too difficult.

Take a look at the typical spreadsheet shown in Figure 6-9.

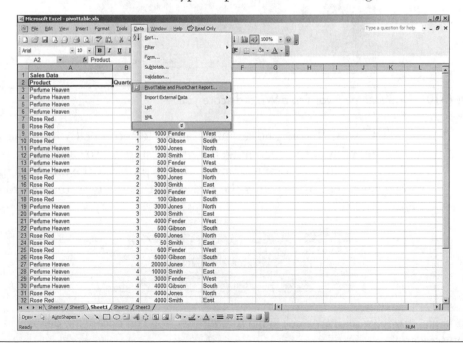

FIGURE 6-9 A typical spreadsheet will have data entered in various different categories.

You can see this disparate data as representing information about Who, What, Where, and When, all relating to How Much.

The problem is that the type of information someone may really need, such as who sold the most in the East during the First Quarter and which product did the best, is very difficult to extract.

With a little bit of *courage, you can make sure you've selected the first cell in the spreadsheet*, and then click Data > PivotTable and PivotChart Report (see Figure 6-9).

What discourages lots of people is the appearance of a potentially confusing wizard (see Figure 6-10). Accept the defaults in the first screen of the Pivot Table Wizard with a cell inside your table of data selected—unless you are an experienced user and want to isolate a subset of your data.

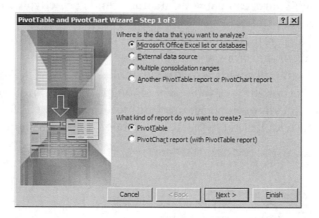

FIGURE 6-10 Don't let the Pivot Table Wizard scare you.

Click Next. If you paid attention and selected a cell within the data itself, preferably at the beginning, the second step is also easy. You're being asked which data you want to analyze, and it's probably the only data in the spreadsheet, and by selecting the first cell, it's already in the wizard (see Figure 6-11).

FIGURE 6-11 If you've selected a cell in the spreadsheet, you can accept the defaults in the second screen.

Click Next. Okay, you'll probably do better by putting it all into its own worksheet (see Figure 6-12).

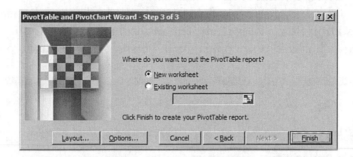

FIGURE 6-12   Accept the defaults in the third screen to put the pivot table into its own worksheet.

The Pivot Table Report grid opens in a new page (see Figure 6-13).

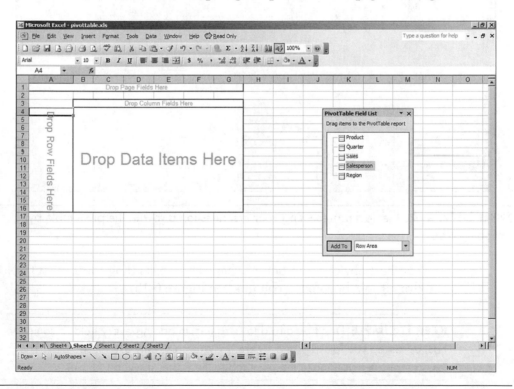

FIGURE 6-13   The Pivot Table Report is a place to ask your questions of the data and extract just the information you need.

Let's think about the question someone may be asking you, like a "who" question.

Who sold what or how much where?

Take the Salesperson field from the Fields list and drop it into where it says Drop Row Fields Here. The result should look like Figure 6-14, with your "who" field now populating the first set of rows in the pivot table.

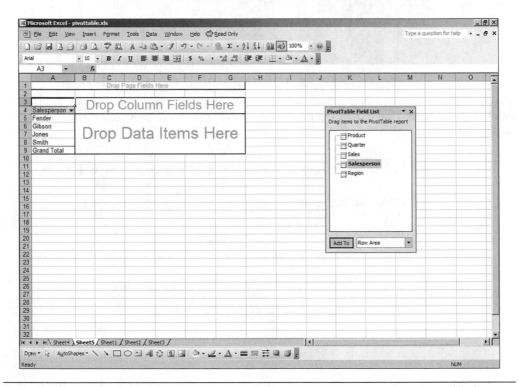

FIGURE 6-14   Make the field representing your first question a row in the pivot table by dropping it in.

The next obvious question is what was sold, so drag the Product field and drop it so it becomes a column (see Figure 6-15).

KEEP IT SIMPLE Don't be afraid to refrain from adding every field. If someone has just asked you for who and where, for example, only use those fields. The less complicated you make the pivot table, the easier it will be to use.

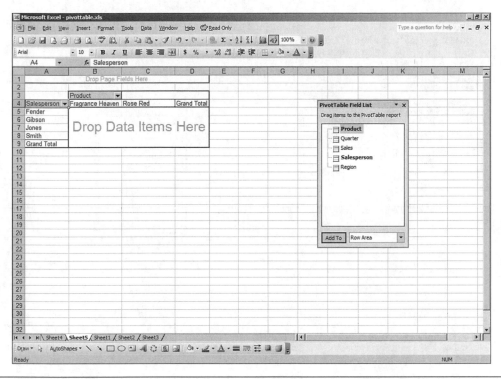

FIGURE 6-15   Make the field representing your next question a column in the pivot table by dropping it in.

You get the idea. Now it's time to add how much (this is usually the actual *data*; in this case it's the "Sales" figures) to the middle (the Data Area) and place the sort items (the where information—Region, or the when parameters—Quarter) into the Page tabs at the top (see Figure 6-16).

Now the fun begins. Notice the drop-down arrows that enable you to sort the following:

- Where—Region
- When—Quarter
- What—Product

Clicking any or all of these arrows lets you isolate information—such as which product did the best in a particular region, or when it sold the most units.

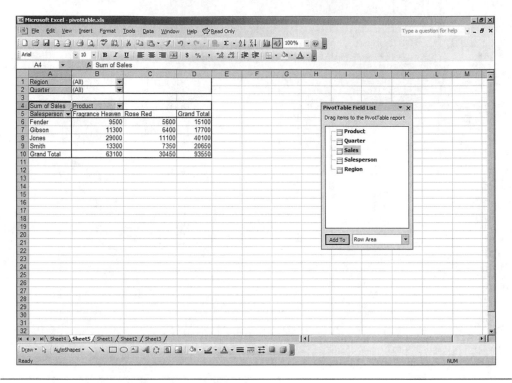

FIGURE 6-16 Add the data to the middle of the pivot table and use the Page tabs for additional sort items.

Because you can revise the fields—just drag them out of the pivot table to remove them and then drag them back into the other positions—you can easily see the data by Quarter (When) and use the Sort Fields (Pages) to isolate a salesperson.

"Hey Gibson, how come you only sold 100 units of Rose Red in the second quarter?" (see Figure 6-17).

Questions like these are now a lot easier to answer.

But the real power of the pivot table, like the Visio diagrams we looked at previously, comes by *keeping the material in Excel*. If you copy the table, and even if you Paste Special in PowerPoint, you will only get a static representation of the entire table or the last sort option you selected.

So how do you work with this effectively in a presentation?

Remember that you can use an Action Setting or hyperlink to a document or file, as we discussed in Chapter 5, "Using Video and Audio Effectively," so you can open this Excel spreadsheet to the worksheet with the pivot table and manipulate the data using your sort Pages to answer any questions posed by your audience or to make additional points or analyze results.

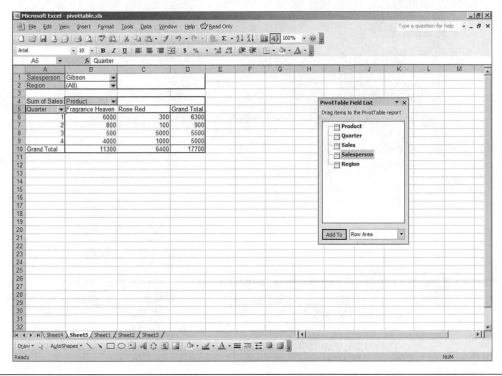

FIGURE 6-17   Use Page field(s) to sort your data by parameters to break it down further.

As we will discuss in Chapter 8, "Delivering a Killer Presentation," during your presentation, you can also toggle between the open Excel file, your presentation, and other programs by using the Alt+Tab command, but it takes some practice.

Finally, you could also save the Pivot Table *as a web page* and use your hyperlink capability to open it during the presentation. Make sure you check Interactivity and the option to publish or republish only the pivot table, and you can get a web page with the full interactive features that you can post online or link to in a presentation (see Figure 6-18).

ONLINE PRESENTATIONS We will be covering the aspects of presenting online more fully in Chapter 7, "The Latest Technologies: Beyond PowerPoint to the Future."

6. POWERFUL PRESENTATION TOOLS

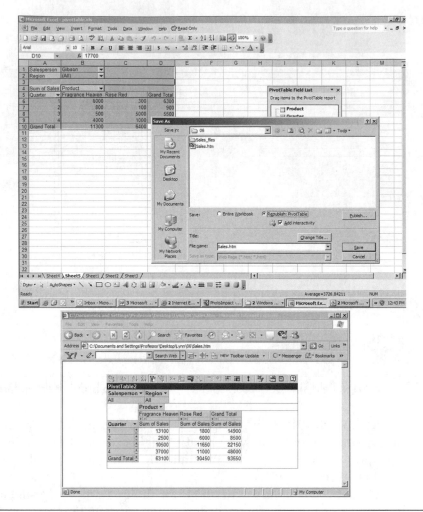

FIGURE 6-18   Saving your pivot table as a web page may make it easier to access and work with during a presentation and will also allow you to make it available online.

Making Excel Interactive with Crystal Xcelsius

If you want to take the interactive model for data even further, think about creating dashboards. These are user interfaces with controls that take the underlying data of a spreadsheet or database, display it visually, and allow the user to interact with it intuitively.

For example, look at the simple mortgage calculation spreadsheet in Figure 6-19. In the selected cell, the principal for a given set of parameters (payment, interest rate, and term) is calculated based on an Excel function, but this could be any formula.

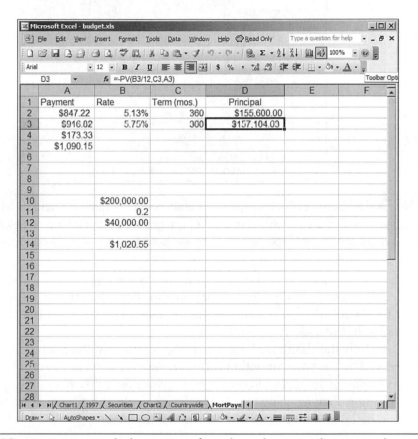

FIGURE 6-19   A mortgage calculator uses a formula to determine the principal amount that can be borrowed based on the interest rate, term, and monthly payment.

Using this spreadsheet, you could keep plugging in different payment amounts, change the interest rate or the term, and see how the final payment would be affected.

Another formula (in cell A2) determines the payment required for a different set of parameters, with a variable loan amount (principal). Again, you could try different loan amounts and interest rates and see the resulting payment. Or, you could create a *dashboard*, as shown in Figure 6-20.

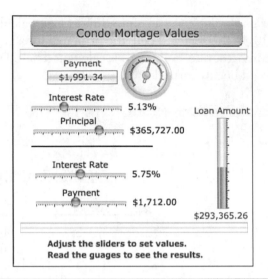

FIGURE 6-20 A dashboard of the mortgage calculator uses the same formula as found in the spreadsheet but displays the values in a set of gauges with different inputs determined by sliders, and the results are displayed interactively based on the underlying formula.

In the dashboard, the variable amounts are represented by *sliders* that let the user manually increase or decrease the value; this is the equivalent of manually doing the same by increments in the cells within the proper range in the underlying spreadsheet.

With the dashboard set up properly, the resulting amounts are displayed in text boxes or within various creative gauges in the dashboard. For example, as the user chooses a higher interest rate or monthly payment, the thermometer gauge on the right increases the principal amount that can be borrowed. It is more visual and immediate.

AWARD-WINNING DASHBOARDS This dashboard was created with a tool called Crystal Xcelsius by a company called Infommersion. The product won Best in Show at the last COMDEX in Las Vegas and has since been acquired by Business Objects. You can explore it further at www.xcelsius.com/Learning/Center.html.

Briefly, the way the dashboard works is as follows. Figure 6-21 shows the mortgage calculator in the Xcelsius interface. The underlying budget.xls spreadsheet with the formula has been loaded as the data model.

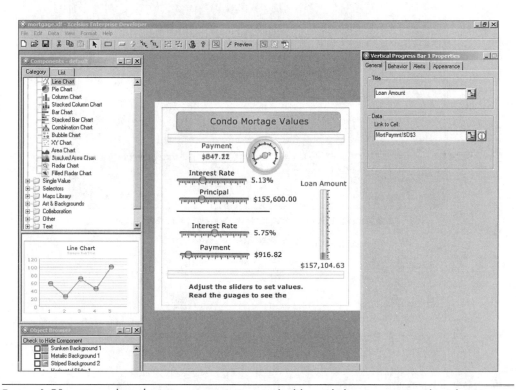

FIGURE 6-21 Crystal Xcelsius creates interactive dashboards by connecting directly to an Excel spreadsheet as a data model and linking controls to the cells and formulas.

By selecting an item from the Components panel, like the vertical *progress bar (thermometer)* that will represent the principal amount, it can be placed in the dashboard. With the component selected and right-clicked, its properties can be set to the appropriate cell in the spreadsheet (see Figure 6-22). When the Data selector is opened in Xcelsius, it opens the linked Excel file and lets you choose the cell that contains the resulting formula.

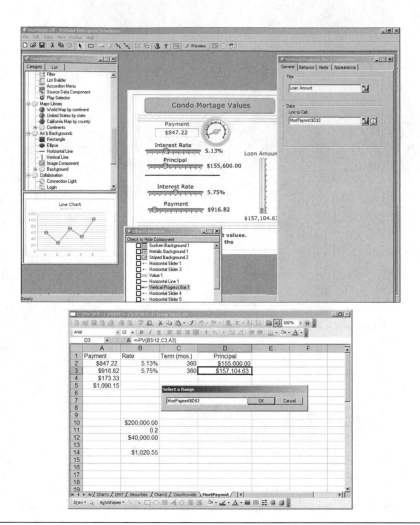

FIGURE 6-22 Crystal Xcelsius links its component to a cell in the spreadsheet containing a formula, the result of which will change according to the values controlled by the user as he or she moves the sliders.

To change the values of other items, like the payment amount or the interest rate, sliders are linked to those cells (see Figure 6-23). When the Data selector for the slider that represents the payment amount is clicked, it opens the linked Excel file and lets you choose the cell that contains the controlling cell.

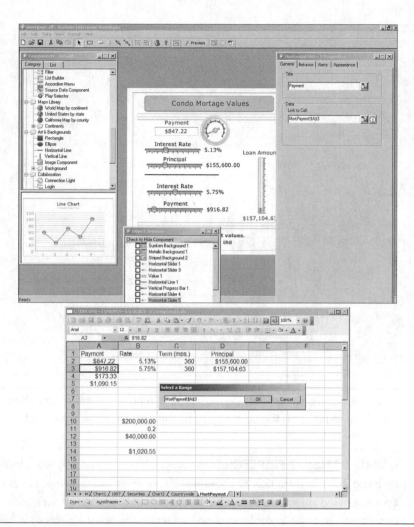

FIGURE 6-23   To create a variable amount that will affect the result in the vertical progress bar, Xcelsius' data selector lets you locate the appropriate Excel cell.

When you're done creating a dashboard, Xcelsius first lets you preview the functionality. Notice how the example in Figure 6-24 is similar to a pivot table but more visual; four different products' revenues are compared, toggling between their respective column chart by clicking in the dashboard.

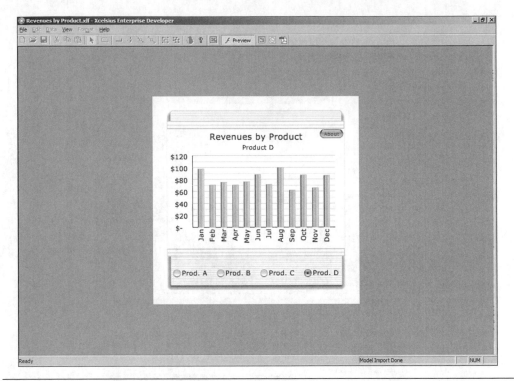

FIGURE 6-24   Xcelsius can also simulate a pivot table by changing the results shown over a series of values depending upon the category or parameter selected from a list.

USING XCELSIUS SELECTORS The way selectors generally work in Xcelsius is by using items in a list box or check box to move an entire range of cells within the underlying spreadsheet to a blank range in the same worksheet. Then the component (such as the column chart) reflecting the resulting values is linked to the target area. Each time the list box is clicked, new values are placed in the target range, and they are displayed in the dashboard.

Obviously, going through all of the details of this program here would be impossible, but hopefully you can see its potential for creating a dynamic dashboard to compare data based on input from an audience or user.

Finally, Xcelsius can output the dashboard as a Shockwave file (see Figure 6-25). It can be exported directly to PowerPoint, HTML, simple Shockwave (Flash), or several other formats.

For more about Shockwave, refer to Chapter 4.

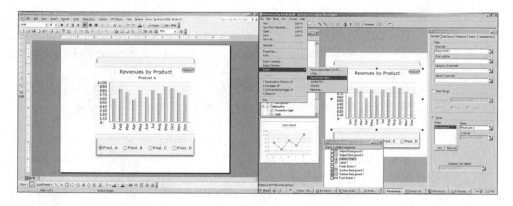

FIGURE 6-25 Xcelsius can export a completely interactive Shockwave version of the dashboard directly into PowerPoint (left) or a number of other formats.

Probably the best way to learn Xcelsius is to download one of the complete tutorials from the learning center (www.xcelsius.com/Learning/Center.html), which contain both the Xcelsius file as well as the Excel spreadsheet to which it can be linked and take you through the process step by step. The cost of Xcelsius varies depending upon which version you select; for most users, the basic version should have most of the controls you need and will suffice.

Using Camtasia Studio 3.0 for PowerPoint Video

In Chapter 5, we mentioned that one of the components of a DVD project with PowerPoint would be to export the presentation as a complete video. This has been available for the Mac version of PowerPoint for a while, but just recently, a PowerPoint add-in has been created by TechSmith Camtasia that lets a user capture an entire presentation as it is presented, with all of the animation, transitions, and even the video.

The production is saved as a standard video file in a Windows format, generally .AVI or .WMV.

Camtasia Studio 3.0 takes this a step further, allowing the user to appear with the presentation in a "video in a window." This has a variety of applications:

- If you can't physically present—sending a video of the presentation along with yourself in a window and your actual message as an audio track is probably the next best thing to being there.

- If you want to rehearse or get comments from colleagues—using the video version of the presentation gives the audience (and you) the best possible idea of how you intend to present the visuals and convey your message, and adjustments can be made.
- If you want to post the video on a web page or burn it to a DVD—we will cover these techniques more completely in Chapter 7.

Unfortunately, Camtasia Studio is not cheap—as of this writing, the full version was around $300. This makes it comparable to higher-end video editing programs, and in truth, that is exactly what the full program looks like (see Figure 6-26). The full portion of Camtasia resembles Windows Movie Maker, but it has other features (like a separate video and audio timeline) and can be used as a full-scale video editor. It also supports a wide range of output formats, with the exception of MPG; however, if you combine it with a DVD authoring program, you will have the ability to create MPG files for DVD production as well.

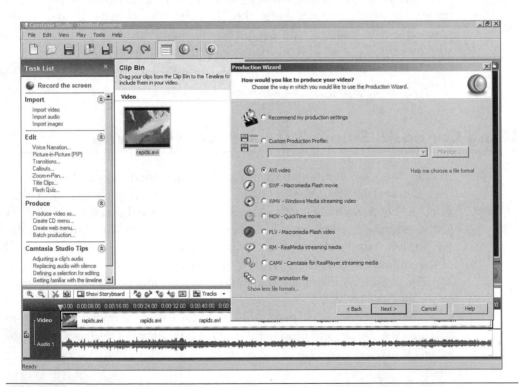

FIGURE 6-26 Camtasia Studio works as a complete video editing package, with the ability to separate audio and video tracks.

We want to concentrate on the Camtasia Add-In for PowerPoint, which is a toolbar that appears in PowerPoint's editor. (If you've loaded the program and the toolbar doesn't appear, click View > Toolbars > Camtasia in PowerPoint.) On the toolbar, you can first check your recording options (see Figure 6-27).

T........on

- Over 700,000 vehicles on our city streets each day
- Computerized traffic system is overloaded
- Cars are bigger than ever and barely fit into lanes of traffic or parking spaces
- When everyone wants to go to the same place, we are in deep doo-doo

FIGURE 6-27   Camtasia Studio installs a special toolbar directly into PowerPoint.

The recording options let you set your microphone level (it works with the microphone jack in your soundcard, not in the camera). Then you can also configure either a webcam or a Firewire digital camcorder for the video in a window component (see Figure 6-28).

CAMTASIA FOR TRAINING The Camtasia toolbar also features the ability to add a highlight of the cursor movements so that students can watch a trainer go through various steps when demonstrating software.

IF NECESSARY, USE MOVIE MAKER TO CONNECT FIREWIRE Sometimes, Camtasia favors a USB video camera over the Firewire connector. You can work around this by first setting up to capture Firewire in Movie Maker (as described in Chapter 5) and then configuring Camtasia; it usually will locate the Firewire digital camcorder after Movie Maker or another application has connected to it.

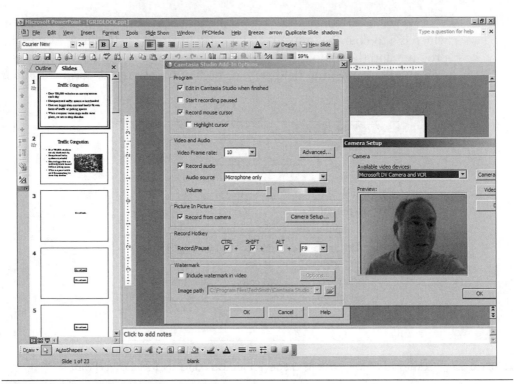

FIGURE 6-28   Camtasia Studio's toolbar in PowerPoint lets you configure your microphone and a video capture device.

With the camera and microphone configured properly, all that's left is to press the red Record button. A popup screen will determine when recording will actually start and will prompt you on "hot keys" for pausing and stopping the recording process. The presentation will play full screen as usual (you won't see your video image during recording).

When capture is completed, the project is opened automatically in the Camtasia Studio Editor. You have the option to export it immediately or review it first, which is usually a better idea. As you can with most video editors, you can "scrub" (drag) through the timeline with the green marker arrow to view portions of the video in the preview window (see Figure 6-29).

If you like, you can add a title or transition to the masterpiece but the main point here is probably to export it in a video format that will work for the application you have in mind.

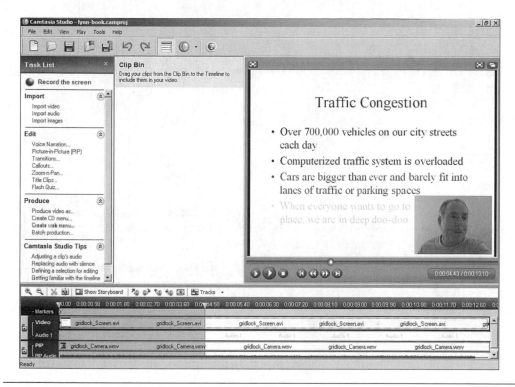

FIGURE 6-29 Camtasia Studio's video editor opens with the PowerPoint capture project.

We'll export this as an AVI movie file in a screen resolution that will allow us to use it in a subsequent DVD project in the next chapter. Clicking Produce > Produce video as in the Task List opens the Production Wizard, essentially a step-by-step process that culminates in the *rendering* of your project in the video file format you selected. Depending upon the complexity and length of the production, this can take minutes or hours. The important panel is the Video Output options (see Figure 6-30). Here, you can choose a full-screen resolution and a codec that will work for your purposes. (For more about codecs, refer to "Understanding Codecs," in Chapter 5.)

WEB PAGE OUTPUT One of the Camtasia output options is to link it to an HTML web page. To take advantage of this and have the movie stream or play within a web browser, *do not* use the AVI format; the WMV format will work with the proper scripting in most web browsers, and Camtasia does that authoring for you with this option. We will discuss web output in more detail in Chapter 7.

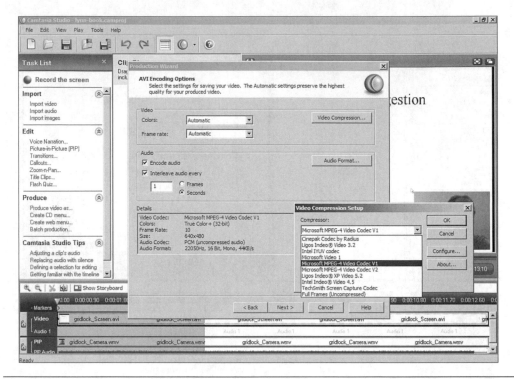

FIGURE 6-30 Camtasia Studio's Production Wizard lets you export your movie in a variety of formats, compression options, and screen resolutions, depending upon its final purpose.

With a Camtasia movie saved to a local folder, you can use it the way you would any other video file. In this case, you could even make a presentation movie inside another presentation (for training purposes). Just go to the Insert > Movies and Sounds > Movie from File command and put the final AVI file into a PowerPoint slide (see Figure 6-31). When you play the slide, you will see the video in a window that you recorded with Camtasia.

WINDOWS MEDIA ENCODER If you don't want to buy Camtasia, you can achieve some of the same results (without the video in the window) by using another screen capture utility available for free from Microsoft. Windows Media Encoder can also capture all of your PowerPoint presentation at different frame rates along with your builds, transitions, audio narration, and even video (if your system is powerful enough). It is not quite as user-friendly as Camtasia and is limited to creating the WMF video file format only. You can download WME at http://www.microsoft.com/windows/windowsmedia/forpros/encoder/default. mspx (we will go through an encoder broadcast session in the section, "Online Video Solution 1—Broadcasting with Windows Media Encoder" in Chapter 7).

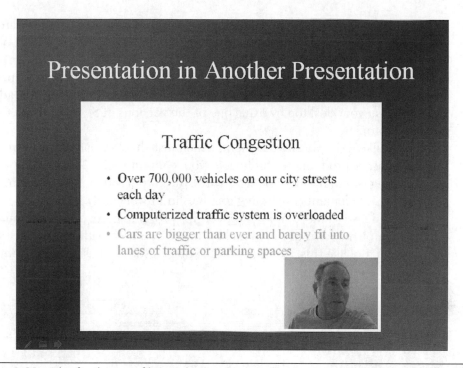

FIGURE 6-31   The final movie file can be used in another PowerPoint presentation just like any other video, resulting in a presentation within another presentation.

Serious Magic Communicator as a Presentation Broadcast Studio

We discussed creating, editing, and inserting video into PowerPoint in the previous chapter, but it simply involved acquiring video that was already shot and trimming it.

As we saw in the previous section, video can also be captured from a computer screen and combined with a live video in a window to create a new digital video file.

Any of these movies can be shown within PowerPoint, burned to a movie DVD, or posted or streamed on the web (we'll cover the latter two issues in Chapter 7).

But how do you create really compelling professional-quality video?

You can conceivably obtain high-quality camcorders (3-chip), hire a lighting specialist and a sound expert, and go out into the field and shoot your footage.

But if you think about it, most of the professional video you watch is created in a professional broadcast studio. If your business, school, or church has such a facility, you're in business.

But what if you don't? Whether it's to show in PowerPoint, burn to DVD, or post or stream online, you can simulate a full-blown broadcast studio on your desktop by using one of the versions of Serious Magic Communicator.

Unlike a simple video camera, which just shoots whatever is in front of the lens, a production studio lets you combine "live" shots (of people speaking or other video footage) with stills, other video, graphics, and any number of elements (including graphics in PowerPoint).

Again, we can't completely cover this program here, but you should get an idea of the kind of functionality that is available with a broadcast production tool like this. In Figure 6-32, you can see the basic Visual Communicator interface.

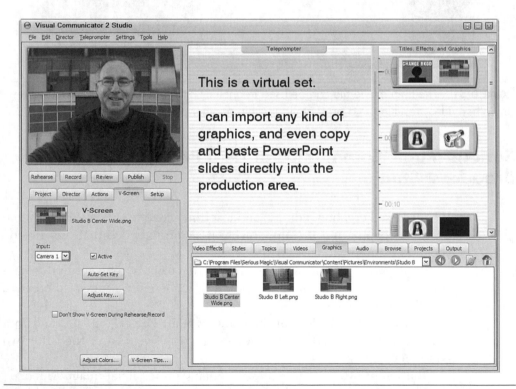

FIGURE 6-32 Serious Magic Visual Communicator gives you a complete video production facility on your desktop.

Notice that one of the features is the ability to use a *virtual set*. As I appear in the preview window, I am not in such a fancy studio at all, but rather in the den of a one-bedroom apartment in Los Angeles.

All versions of the program come with a green screen—a large green sheet that you can tape into your "studio" to serve as a backdrop for "virtual" camera shots. Within the V-Screen effect in Communicator, the backdrop becomes transparent in the same way that professional photographers and videographers use the device to put anyone into any background they want. Also included is a high-quality microphone for narration and voiceovers.

The other feature of note here is the *teleprompter*. This gives the "broadcaster" the ability to write out a complete script, which is integrated on a timeline (on the right) with a series of titles, effects, or graphics.

Figure 6-33 shows one way to insert graphics into the effects panel—by copying a slide directly from PowerPoint and pasting it into an effect. You can also import entire PowerPoint presentations to narrate and combine with other video.

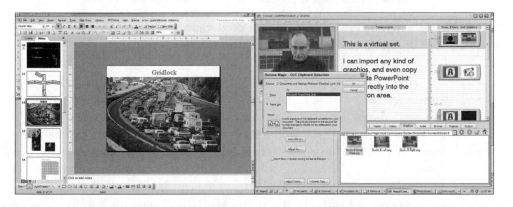

FIGURE 6-33 Serious Magic Visual Communicator lets you drag and drop or copy your PowerPoint slides into a production.

With the production assembled in the timeline (or Actions panel on the right), you are ready to rehearse and eventually record, combining the camera footage with the effects in the "Action Trays." As you can see in Figure 6-34, effects like fades move between footage of the broadcaster and the graphics that need to be displayed.

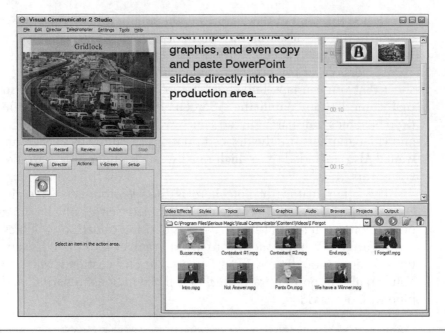

Figure 6-34 As you rehearse and record your production in Serious Magic Visual Communicator, you can preview all of the effects and transitions.

The studio accepts other video as well—we can drop the video we previously created with Camtasia directly into an Action Tray, and it will play as a segment in the overall production (see Figure 6-35).

Finally, with the production recorded, it can be published (or exported) as we have seen elsewhere. Visual Communicator's "Wizard" gives you many of the same options we saw with Camtasia in terms of video formats and applications. The final video can be streamed from the high-end version, combined with an HTML (web) page, or simply saved as a Windows video file to use in PowerPoint or to burn to a movie DVD (see Figure 6-36).

There are three different versions of this product (more information is available at www.seriousmagic.com):

- **Visual Communicator 2 Web**—$189.95—Output for the Internet or CD
- **Visual Communicator 2 Pro**—$289.95—Output for broadcast resolution; drag and drop PowerPoint, more templates and effects
- **Visual Communicator 2 Studio**—$489.95—High-end professional video output including up to three cameras

These versions are also discounted for educational use.

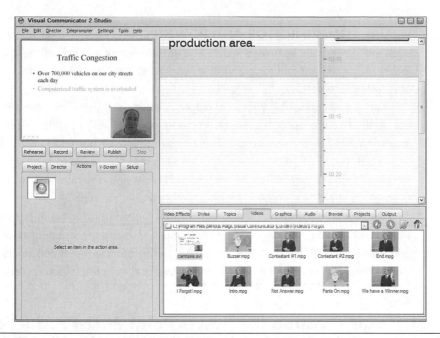

FIGURE 6-35   Other video segments input into Serious Magic Visual Communicator play in the proper sequence in the timeline.

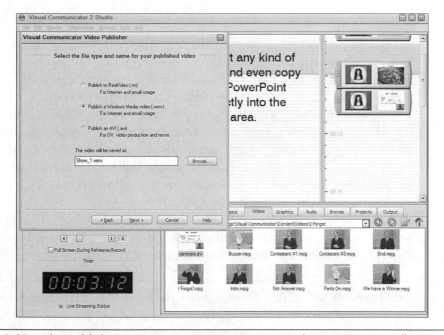

FIGURE 6-36   The publishing options in Serious Magic Visual Communicator allow you to create the usual Windows video formats in many different resolutions.

VISUAL COMMUNICATOR AND POWERPOINT Visual Communicator complements PowerPoint in several ways. If your final output is a PowerPoint presentation, VC is a great tool for creating video files to display in your slides, as we covered in Chapter 5.

But as you can see, if your final output is video, VC gives you complete control of all of your graphical elements to create a video file for multiple uses: importing into PowerPoint, broadcasting or streaming, or burning to DVD. In this way it can be a PowerPoint alternative for situations where video is all you need, with the flexibility to reuse your PowerPoint content and any related graphics (in a standard Windows image file format) within the video itself.

You should also be aware that you are not limited to bringing in just one slide at a time into the timeline. You can import an entire presentation at one time and then work with it by interspersing your own graphics and effects, including video of yourself and the underlying narration read from the teleprompter.

Serious Magic Ovation for PowerPoint Post-Production

In Chapter 2, "Implementing Professional Design Principles," we spent quite a bit of time creating a clean, professional look for our PowerPoint presentation.

A new product from Serious Magic is similar to some of the commercial templates and backgrounds we noted in the "Resources" section because it also provides help during the actual presentation itself. In video terminology, it's almost a post-production tool for PowerPoint.

When you import a PowerPoint presentation into Ovation from Serious Magic, the slides go into a bar at the bottom of the interface, and several libraries of "Power Looks" are available to reformat your slides (see Figure 6-37). Notice that the bland title and bullet slide about traffic congestion is now projected over a background of animated clouds.

With your background selected, Ovation enables you to present directly out of its Present tab. Here, you can make large text notes to accompany the slide show and also track the timing. It is a combination of PowerPoint's Rehearse Timings and Presenter View (see Figure 6-38).

DUAL-MONITOR SETUP Ovation resembles PowerPoint's Presenter View in taking advantage of a dual-monitor setup on an extended Windows Desktop. This requires setting up a second monitor or projector—a procedure we cover in detail under "Presenter View" in Chapter 8.

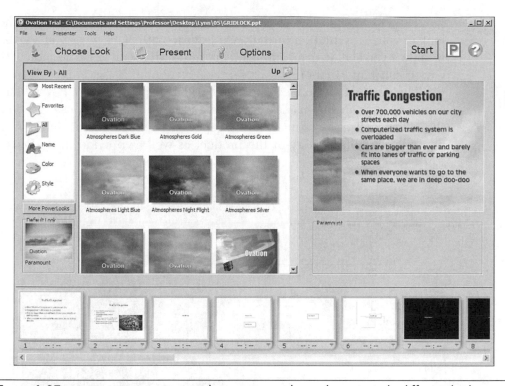

FIGURE 6-37 Serious Magic Ovation lets you instantly apply an entirely different look to your presentation from a library of professional designs.

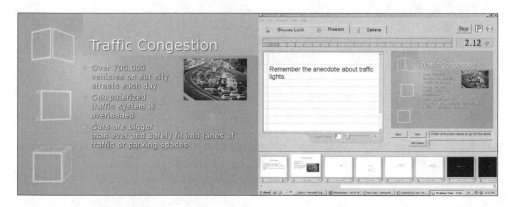

FIGURE 6-38 Serious Magic Ovation's Present tab lets you keep track of the timing of your presentation as well as refer to notes during the show.

The Options tab lets you save default information and customize the look of your presentation further (see Figure 6-39). This gives you a walk-in slide if you like, with an animated background as well as a title slide with your contact information.

This product, although brand new, will certainly set your PowerPoint shows apart from the masses. As more and more presenters use Ovation, the effect will abate somewhat, except that Serious Magic intends to upgrade the functionality of the product as well as provide more Power Looks to its users.

FIGURE 6-39 Serious Magic Ovation's Options tab provides additional ways to customize your look and integrate professional introductory and intermission slides.

UPDATING FROM POWERPOINT Ovation has a PowerPoint button on the upper right that lets you go back to your original presentation to make updates and changes. Then, under the File menu, Ovation lets you refresh the current Ovation version to make sure that it has accepted your changes prior to presenting.

Microsoft OneNote as a Presentation Resource Center and Mini-Conferencing Tool

As you create presentations, whether in PowerPoint or in another format entirely, you begin to accumulate tremendous amounts of source material. Some of this is via email or telephone with your client or subject expert, some is from the Internet or published magazines and books, and still others can be little scraps of information that come in from any number of sources.

Keeping this disparate information saved and *organized* is a tremendous challenge.

My first attempt to organize this kind of information came in junior high school when I got my first loose-leaf notebook. I remember pages sticking out from all of the sections because I had to also keep track of tests, mimeographed notes, magazine articles, and other material, in addition to the actual notes that kept slipping out of the binder.

Now Microsoft Office has a text editor (not Word!) that makes this kind of information management a lot easier: OneNote. The basic concept of OneNote is like a spreadsheet/loose-leaf notebook for text and some graphics. The top of the interface has Section tabs, and you can add a new one simply by right-clicking on an existing tab. They are also color-coded for even greater organization, if you need it (see Figure 6-40).

You can organize your notebook by project, client, subject area, or whatever makes sense in terms of creating Sections.

Then, within each Section, you can easily create new "Pages" by clicking in an empty side tab and filling in the Title (see Figure 6-41).

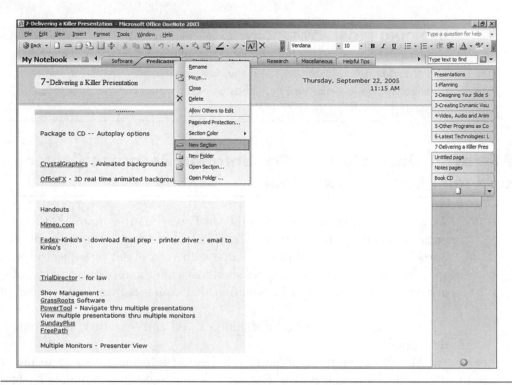

FIGURE 6-40 OneNote organizes your information in tabbed, color-coded Sections. You can add a new Section simply by right-clicking on a Section tab.

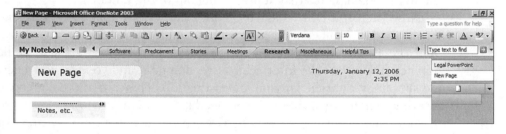

FIGURE 6-41 You create a new Page within a Section just by clicking an empty side tab, and you can name the Page by giving it a title.

OneNote Pages are free-form repositories of information. You can even record audio and capture or link video directly to a OneNote Page (see Figure 6-42).

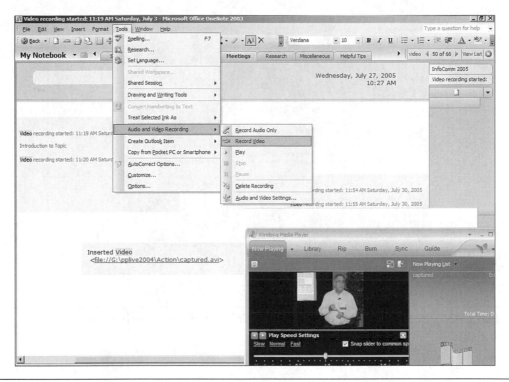

FIGURE 6-42   OneNote also supports multimedia like recorded audio and video.

Perhaps most useful is the ability to instantly copy and paste web pages into a OneNote Page; what is particularly helpful is the addition of the web link below the pasted object (see Figure 6-43). In addition, links within the copied text are also preserved, making it easy to reuse the source material from directly within OneNote.

The one truly remarkable feature of OneNote is the *Search capability*. Before using OneNote, I used Notepad *.txt documents scattered around my hard drive(s) and could never locate the correct text or Word document when I needed it. Within OneNote, you can type a search term and instantly locate all of your Notes for the entry by Section, Title, or Date (see Figure 6-44).

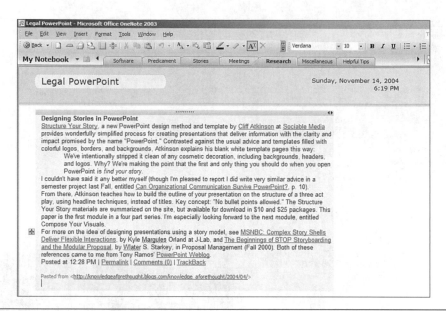

FIGURE 6-43 OneNote maintains links to material pasted from a web browser.

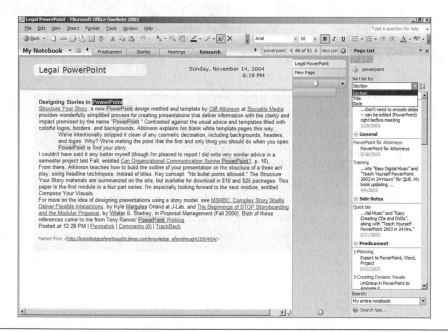

FIGURE 6-44 OneNote's Search feature almost instantly highlights all instances of a word or phrase throughout your notebook.

Another terrific organizational feature in OneNote is the use of *flags* to mark information for follow-up, tasks, or even to connect to Outlook. Suppose you had multiple presentations, all of which needed to go to Kinko's to meet certain deadlines—by assigning them each a flag in their own respective pages and sections, you could instantly see all of the flags together in the Note Flags Summary Task Pane and plan your trip to Kinko's accordingly (see Figure 6-45).

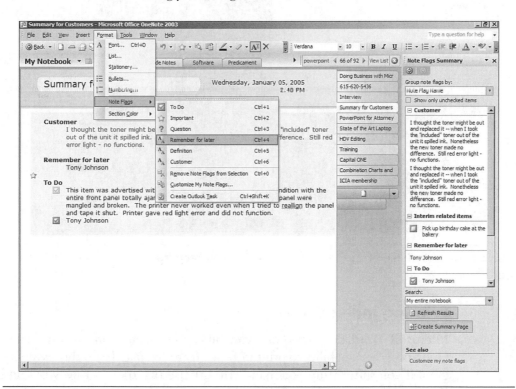

FIGURE 6-45   OneNote flags let you maintain accountability and further index your notes for quick review and recollection of important deadlines and facts.

Many presenters also prepare separate information on index cards to refer to during preparation or even during a talk. OneNote has an Index Card layout (see Figure 6-46) that simulates the actual physical cards, along with college-lined rulers (if you like). Set the Orientation to Landscape to make the cards available the way most people refer to them.

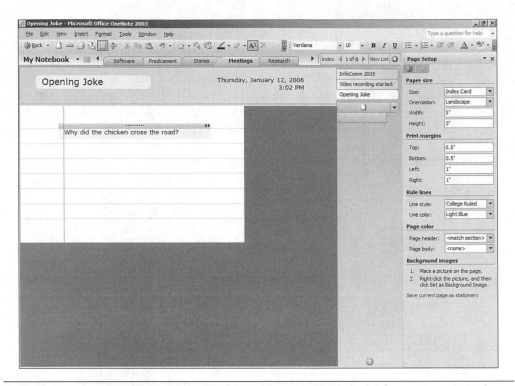

FIGURE 6-46   OneNote's Page Setup Task Pane lets you keep track of some notes in Index Card format.

Printing Index Cards

Microsoft Word does have one capability that is currently missing from OneNote: the capability to print in Index Card format. To do this (which is great if you suffer from poor handwriting), use the Tools > Envelopes and Labels feature (see Figure 6-47), which configures the Word document for three cards per page in the Avery 5388 format. The page is actually a Word Table, which you can modify and format using the Tables and Borders toolbar. When your labels are set up, use the Avery or similarly configured labels in your inkjet or laser printer.

Generally, the last thing a busy professional wants is yet another program to try to master. The great thing about OneNote is its intuitive nature—if you've gone to junior high and used a loose-leaf notebook, you "get" the metaphor instantly. And if you use OneNote to maintain your various pieces of information, you'll never lose a piece of research, a web link, a reference to a sound file or video, or even a username and password again.

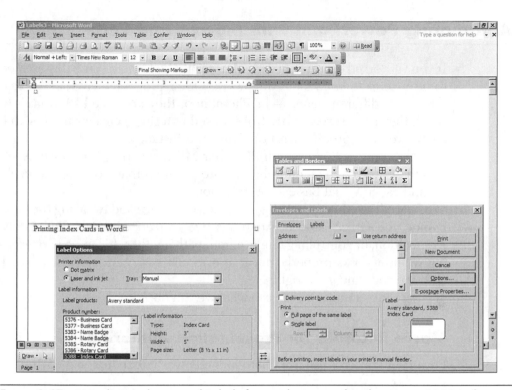

FIGURE 6-47 Word's Envelopes and Labels feature lets you select the Avery 5388 Index Cards and reformat them as a Word Table prior to printing.

BACKING UP YOUR NOTEBOOK If you use OneNote extensively, the information stored in your notebook will become very valuable. And, unless you fill it up with images, the files won't be large, so they will be easy to back up as long as you know where they are. Your OneNote tabs and files are stored in My Documents under *My Notebook*. If you back up this folder, you can restore your notebook or move it to another location.

SHARING ONENOTE INFORMATION You can also directly connect within OneNote to other users in a Shared Session. Starting a Shared Session lets you show the current or other OneNote pages to other users whom you invite, via email, to the session. These users can connect to your session through the IP address provided in the email along with the password for the shared session, which you will also need to give them.

Automating PowerPoint with Macros and Code

If you've worked extensively with Microsoft Word, you've probably created some macros to streamline your work. Other programs have similar features with different names—in PhotoShop, they are called "Actions." In short, they are a series of keystrokes saved as a single click or hot key that enable you to reproduce a set of commands instantly.

In PowerPoint, along with the other MS Office programs, macros are also the entrance to an entirely separate program that works in the background called Visual Basic for Applications.

As we'll see shortly by using the macro language and tweaking the code behind the Office suite of programs, we can do what is called Office Automation, or controlling one program with another. It can be very exciting when it works properly, but it also requires a lot of patience to work with the code and get it right.

Let's take a quick look to see what we can do.

Macro Recorder for Presentation Authoring

PowerPoint macros can work both in the PowerPoint editor and during the slide show.

In the editor, they are mainly used to accomplish repetitive tasks. For example, in Chapter 4, we created several drawing objects and gave them a Custom Animation. These are techniques that we are likely to reuse in the future.

So let's create a macro of the red circle that calls attention to an area of the slide by fading in.

To create a new macro, open the Macro Recorder by clicking Tools > Macro > Macro Recorder and naming the macro we're about to create (see Figure 6-48).

When the Macro Recorder begins, a small toolbar opens within the slide with only one button, which represents "stop." This means the recorder is *active*, and until the stop button is clicked, every keystroke you perform is recorded. So we can create our red circle, change the line thickness, make the Fill color No Fill, and add our Fade Entrance effect (see Figure 6-49).

Now move the selected red circle slightly before you run the macro.

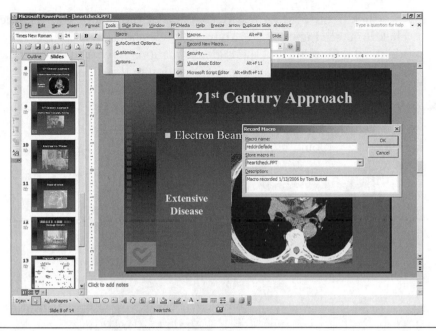

FIGURE 6-48 Opening the Macro Recorder lets us name the set of code we're about to create, which we can reuse over and over again in this presentation.

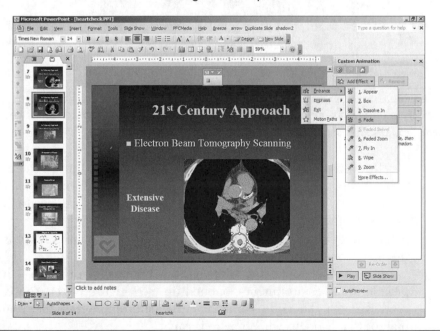

FIGURE 6-49 With the Macro Recorder active, everything you do in PowerPoint is recorded.

Click Tools > Macro > Macros, select the macro you recorded, and click Run (see Figure 6-50). Your red circle should be reproduced with the identical formatting and the Fade Animation effect. You can use the arrow keys to nudge it to the appropriate position in the slide.

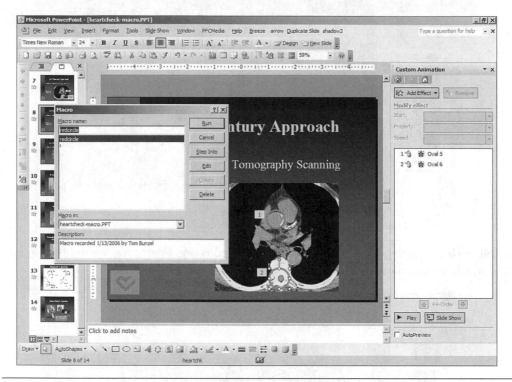

FIGURE 6-50   Running the macro you just created reproduces the identical set of keystrokes and gives you another shape with the same properties.

Now this is not exactly an earthshaking timesaver. But we can use it for two important illustrations: to show you how code (or subroutines) are created in VBA, and then to demonstrate some ways you can customize your PowerPoint workspace.

First, let's reopen the Macro list. Click Tools > Macro > Macros, select the macro you recorded, and click Edit.

Oh my God, what just happened? A brand new program—the VBA programming environment—opened up (see Figure 6-51). You can now read through the code controlling the subroutine (another name for macro) that happens when macro is run.

As we'll see in the following sections and case study, working with this code effectively can allow us to do some cool things.

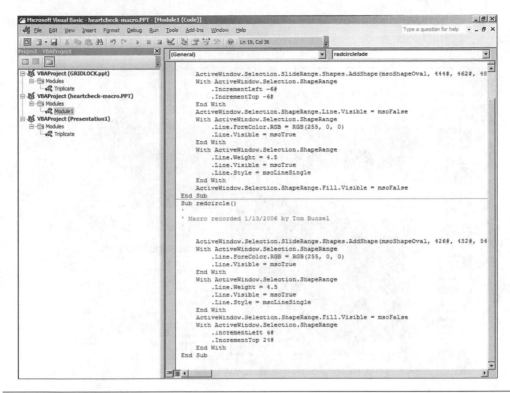

FIGURE 6-51 Editing the macro you just created opens the VBA editor for the PowerPoint file in which you've been working.

MACRO MVP The macro we created here is very simple, but if you want see examples of terrific timesaving macros in the form of Add-Ins for PowerPoint, visit the site of PowerPoint MVP Steve Rindsberg at www.rdpslides.com. He offers a free set of PPT Tools for those getting started with macros, and if you like those, there are more productivity tools you can try. Writing code and using macros is not for everyone, but if it's up your alley, these are eye-openers that can show you the way to creating your own small Office applications.

Customizing Your PowerPoint Environment

Before we continue in our examination of VBA code and some of the things it can do, let's use the macro we created to customize our Power-Point workspace.

Click Tools > Customize in PowerPoint, and in the Customize panel, click the Toolbars tab and press New (see Figure 6-52). In the New

Toolbar dialog box, name a new personal toolbar—perhaps it will be DrawingTools.

FIGURE 6-52 You can create a personal toolbar for yourself in the Customize panel by naming a new toolbar.

The menu is fine but useless without buttons, so let's click the Commands tab of the Customize dialog box, select Macros from the Categories list, and locate the macro we recorded for the red circle with animation (see Figure 6-53). Now drag the macro and drop it onto the toolbar.

Notice that you're not limited to macros; you can drag AutoShapes or any other command onto your custom toolbar to create an icon that will represent that command, allowing you to create toolbars that correspond to your own work flow (see Figure 6-54).

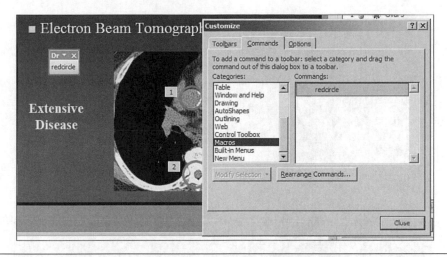

FIGURE 6-53   You can drag and drop commands including macros from the Categories in the Customize dialog box to create your own toolbars.

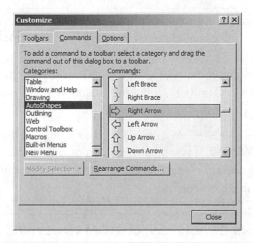

FIGURE 6-54   You can drag and drop commands representing your own frequent work flow choices to create your own task toolbars.

To have your macro represented by an icon of its own, select it within the toolbar and click Modify Selection in the Customize dialog box (see Figure 6-55). Select Default Style to make it an icon and then choose an icon from among the Change Button Image choices.

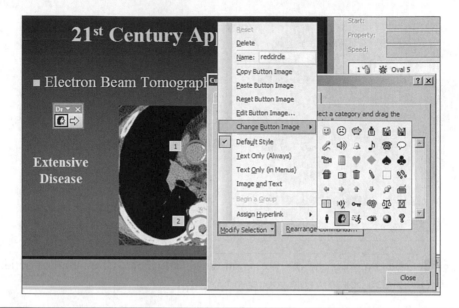

FIGURE 6-55 To use icons to represent your macros, select them in the toolbar and click Modify Selection to open the panel of button images or icons to apply.

Now, whenever this toolbar is open (and you can reopen it any time by clicking View > Toolbars), clicking this icon will re-create the empty circle with the Fade animation.

CUSTOM MENUS If you prefer, you can also customize your PowerPoint menus by dragging and dropping commands into the columns in the same way that you populated the custom toolbar.

LIMITATIONS OF MACROS, CUSTOM TOOLBARS, AND MENUS The macros you create with the recorder "live" inside the presentation or template in which they were created and saved. Unfortunately the toolbars don't reappear on other machines if you move the presentation or template and open it. Although the macros are still there, you will need to re-create any personal toolbars or menus on other machines on which you want to use these macros.

Live Buttons for Interactivity

In the section, "Macro Recorder for Presentation Authoring," we used a macro to make changes within our PowerPoint presentation while we were editing our slide show.

If you dig down into the VBA editor and begin to study it, you will find that the VBA programming language lets you control every object that you add to a presentation by changing its properties.

This is true of any Microsoft Office program that has VBA, which includes Excel, Word, and Visio. Back in Figure 6-8, it was the capability of VBA code to set the visible *property* of objects on a Visio *Layer* to false (invisible) that made the diagram interactive.

If we use the same concept within PowerPoint, we can use real-time interactivity while we are *presenting our slide show*.

This has special implications for training situations, but it really enhances any scenario where you want to engage an audience and get their reactions.

VBA OBJECT MODELS Each application that supports VBA uses what Microsoft programmers refer to as their respective Object Model. This means that within each application there is a hierarchy of importance and control from the greater scale (the application itself, like PowerPoint) to the individual object in an individual file down to an individual slide. Object models can be referred to as a chart or printed out. The Help system in each application's VBA environment can be useful in locating the part of an application's Object Model that you want to influence so that you can make appropriate changes to either its *properties* (how it displays or its inherent qualities like Fill color or visibility) or its *methods* (what it can do, like open or save a file, maximize a window, and so on).

Probably the easiest way to get a sense of the power of using VBA during a presentation is to return briefly to the concept we introduced in Chapter 4. If you recall, in Figure 4-33 we showed how the Action Settings of a selected object could make things happen (like a hyperlink or a sound) on a Click or Mouse Over event. One of the features of the Action Settings dialog box that was obscured in that figure is the ability to *run a macro*, in the same manner that we did it from our personal toolbar in the PowerPoint editor earlier in this chapter.

Using VBA and Vox Proxy for Entertainment and Training

So what does running a macro in the editor let us do?

Let's take a look at a simple slide for an education presentation called "Red Light, Green Light" (see Figure 6-56). The selected object here is the green light, and the Action Setting will play a macro called "makegreen." As you might guess, when the object is clicked, the macro runs, and the Fill color of the light turns from dark blue to green.

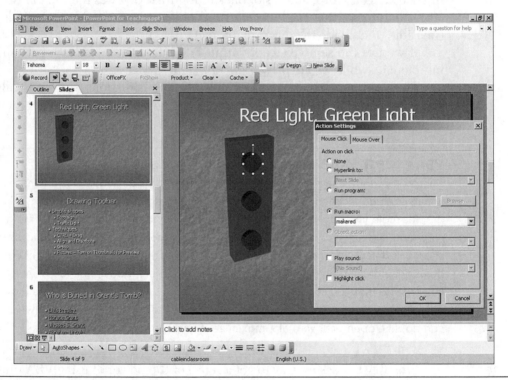

FIGURE 6-56 The Action Setting of a selected object in a slide can be set to run a macro when it is clicked or when the mouse goes over it during a presentation.

The macro itself can be revised for yellow and red as long as we know the RGB values of the actual colors so that we can refer to them by number. (If you recall, we worked with RGB values in Chapter 2 when our design called for us selecting a specific color value by RGB from a corporate logo to put into our branded slide or template.)

We can see the actual code in the VBA editor for the PowerPoint presentation, as shown in Figure 6-57.

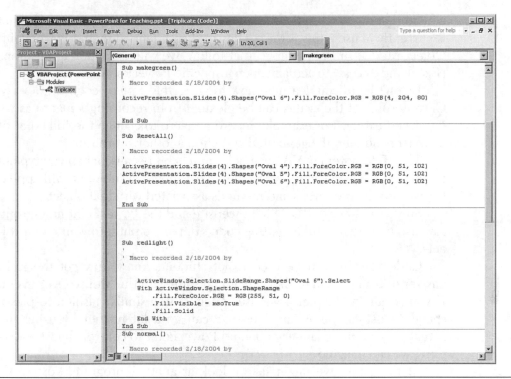

FIGURE 6-57   The macro code in the VBA editor can be constructed to change the Fill color of a specified object in the slide.

In this case, the VBA code to make the light turn green reads as follows:

```
Sub makegreen()
ActivePresentation.Slides(4).Shapes("Oval 6").Fill.ForeColor.
RGB = RGB(4, 204, 80)
End Sub
```

Similarly, another macro or subroutine can be written to reset all of the lights to their original color:

```
Sub ResetAll()
ActivePresentation.Slides(4).Shapes("Oval 4").Fill.ForeColor.
RGB = RGB(0, 51, 102)
ActivePresentation.Slides(4).Shapes("Oval 5").Fill.ForeColor.
RGB = RGB(0, 51, 102)
ActivePresentation.Slides(4).Shapes("Oval 6").Fill.ForeColor.
RGB = RGB(0, 51, 102)
End Sub
```

Notice that the term ActivePresentation refers to the PowerPoint file that is currently in use—this is the syntax used and defined by the PowerPoint Object Model. In the examples that follow, we will use other applications (Excel and Access) to actually open a specific PowerPoint file.

I won't lie to you: learning how to write this type of code is not easy. Getting some of the syntax can be gleaned from recording a macro as we described earlier. For example, record a macro to change the Fill color of an object and then the generated code into another subroutine.

The Help system in VBA can help quite a bit because when you type in the period following an object in the object model, a submenu will appear to give you the properties and methods associated with that object.

Steve Rindsberg's RDP Slides website and the PowerPoint newsgroup can also be very helpful in getting code samples to put into your own projects.

Code like this can be used to let students know they got the right answer or to cue them to "hot" areas of a slide with the Mouse Over event. If you recall, in Chapter 4 we used triggers in a similar fashion to play a specific Custom Animation. Here we can go a lot further by using the actual programming language behind PowerPoint to control almost everything we can imagine.

At this point, we might take a look at another program, Vox Proxy, which uses programming to make a set of animated characters move and actually talk onscreen. (www.voxproxy.com).

In Figure 6-58, the animated character Susan (one of the Microsoft Agent characters that Vox Proxy can control) enters the slide and gesticulates toward the traffic light.

Depending upon how you script the slide, Susan can make the light turn any color by simulating the click event and playing the same macros.

You can also get Vox Proxy characters to interact. Here Dave is asking Susan out, and he explodes (literally) when she says, "I hardly know you" (see Figure 6-59).

FIGURE 6-58   A Vox Proxy animated character can interact with the slide and with your audience to play macros and perform other kinds of tricks.

FIGURE 6-59   Vox Proxy animated characters can act out little skits with each other or with the speaker.

You can also have a character move around the slide and demonstrate things, like this Realtor application where Susan is showing a property and then a map (see Figure 6-60).

FIGURE 6-60 A Vox Proxy character can be used to gesture in different directions to physically point out objects in the slide.

All of this is accomplished through the Vox Proxy Add-In that puts VB Script (similar to VBA macros and code) into your presentation, and you can save and run it as a Vox Proxy file (*.PPV) (see Figure 6-61).

When this script plays in the slide, with each mouse "click" in the script, another custom animation entrance is triggered, showing the property and then the map of the area.

SYNTHETIC TEXT-TO-SPEECH Vox Proxy characters "speak" with synthesized speech that some audiences love (kids) while others may find annoying if overused. However, this technology is evolving, and you can also record actual sound files to put in the characters' mouths. In addition, they can talk in "speech bubbles" like cartoon characters that the audience or the user of a kiosk or CD can read.

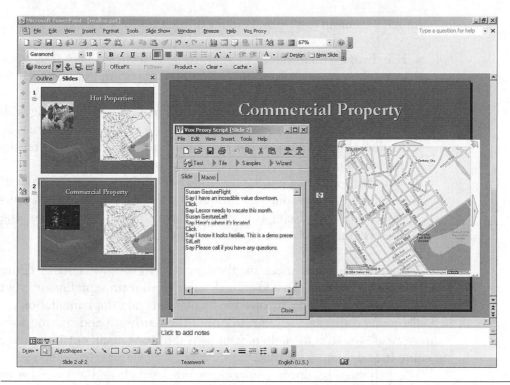

FIGURE 6-61   The Vox Proxy Script Editor controls the character's behavior and also simulates mouse click events in the slide.

Audience Response Systems (ARS)

Savvy presenters have long realized that competition energizes an audience and that the collection of instant polling data has at least two powerful benefits:

- Involving participants, particularly if they are broken up into teams, and giving them a stake in the presentation
- Providing the presenter with valuable and significant statistical data with which to plan future events and to grow his or her own user base and business

That's why there are entire companies dedicated to the task of handling user input during a conference and processing it in a manner that will be most useful to their client, the presenter. (Several of these companies are listed in the section, "Resources.")

An ARS scenario can be broken down into three main areas:

- **Hardware**—The devices used to physically collect the data instantly from attendees and the computer system that connects to these either physically or wirelessly
- **Software**—The programs used to display the questions along with the application that collects the answers and processes them—by sending them to another piece of hardware that displays the results and/or collects the underlying data in a database
- **Theatre**—Involves getting the audience excited about the process, delivering the questions and rewarding the winning team or otherwise framing and climaxing the event in a way that achieves the objects of the presenter (and if possible, the audience)

Generally, the third aspect, the theatre, is up to you. You need to figure out how an ARS system can add enough value to your presentation or event to justify the cost and time involved in its planning and implementation.

Then you can either attempt to install the hardware and run the software yourself (or with the help of your own staff) or hire an outside service to come in and do it all for you.

The two main hardware components are keypads and a computer or console that acquires their input and processes it into a database. Most modern keypads are wireless and run on a radio frequency. Usually the hardware that collects the data connects to a computer that runs the software for processing, and a hardware dongle may need to be connected to the computer to allow the software to run.

A presentation program (guess which one) is used to display the questions and multiple-choice answers.

In the case of TurningPoint, for example, an Add-In is loaded into PowerPoint, and when the program begins, a hardware wizard is used to make sure the keypads are set up properly to connect to the computer that will be running the show.

Then, within PowerPoint, the TurningPoint toolbar allows the user to insert various types of polling slides to construct multiple-choice questions, the results of which will be instantly collected by the keypads and transmitted to the control computer (see Figure 6-62).

For effect, a good system will have an audio timer with music to allow the participants enough time to answer each question.

Then, the answers can be immediately graphed and displayed (see Figure 6-63), or in some cases, the presentation may continue until a period when all of the questions and answers are shown and debriefed.

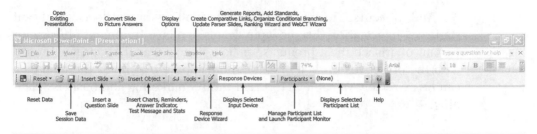

FIGURE 6-62   An ARS system like TurningPoint will have a way of using PowerPoint to present multiple-choice questions to the audience.

FIGURE 6-63   Using an ARS system like TurningPoint will let the keypad responses of users instantly be reflected in slides or other graphics or animation.

Some scenarios allow for gifts or prizes awarded with each answer. In some conferences, the ARS provider has a video of a horse or car race with special effects and plenty of pizzazz that keeps the audience in suspense as the results are shown with the cars or horses representing the competing teams.

A good presenter who can anticipate some of the results may also be able to use the results and how they differ from the audience's original expectations to make his or her point more dramatically.

6. POWERFUL PRESENTATION TOOLS

And, of course, to the extent that the polling data reflects significant statistical information (like how physicians perceive treatment efficacy for certain pharmaceutical products, or how financial analysts prefer to deal with the objectives of their clients), the database that holds the final data can be extremely valuable in terms of future marketing and business planning.

Using PowerPoint to Report Database Information

Audience response is a great way to get information *into* a database. But sometimes the information that is important is already in some kind of Structured Query Language (SQL) format residing somewhere inside a database table.

In some cases, this information is *dynamic*—it changes daily, hourly, or in the case of the stock market, every moment.

In a database like Access, the results are generally limited to a static written Report that is printed out or displayed in a PowerPoint slide.

Take-Off is a Belgian company that has created a set of tools that allow you to connect to such databases from within PowerPoint and report the up-to-the-moment results in a PowerPoint presentation or, in some cases, a screensaver. Here are the three different programs:

- DataPoint is a professional add-on that you can use to link your Microsoft PowerPoint presentations to other MS Office programs, and many more databases.
- MessagePoint will run a selected PowerPoint presentation as a screensaver.
- NewsPoint is a tool that will continuously monitor and download your specified RSS news feeds into a Microsoft Access database. RSS is a format used to communicate efficiently and automate the download of news articles from a given site over the Internet.

To get an idea of how Take-Off's various programs work, you can visit www.presentationpoint.com.

Training Scenarios: Keeping Score

What do kids in school and CEOs have in common?

Answer: They love competition, and they will do some amazing things for a free T-shirt.

As we finish this chapter, we'll go through a complete Office Automation Application that uses PowerPoint as a testing mechanism that asks questions in a presentation, and now that you've seen the ability to track clicks with macros, the answers will be collected in a *User Form* and sent to Microsoft Excel. Finally, the results will be graphically represented in a Visio diagram two ways—by the progress of race cars and race horses on a track.

The entire set of files and support for this scenario is available on this book's CD in a subfolder called "Quiz."

WATCH THE DEMO If you play the video quiz.wmv on this book's CD/DVD (in the "Quiz" subfolder), you can view a complete description of how the quiz application uses Office Automation to track student responses.

The Test Administrator has a User Form set up as an Answer Sheet in the VBA editor and creates a slide show of multiple-choice questions and answers (see Figure 6-64).

FIGURE 6-64   One PowerPoint presentation is set up as an administration file in which the questions and correct answers are logged into the system.

The audience is broken up into four teams, and as each student takes the text, he or she enters his or her name onto an Answer Sheet and joins a team (see Figure 6-65).

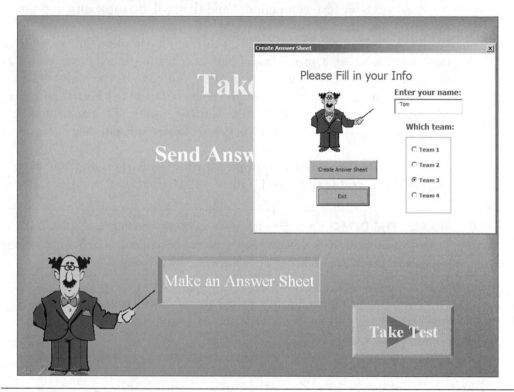

FIGURE 6-65   A macro opens a User Form in which each student enters a name and chooses a team before answering the questions.

As each Answer Sheet is completed, the results are sent to an Excel spreadsheet into a worksheet named for each student, and the results are graphed in a bar chart (see Figure 6-66).

PowerPoint opens Excel as an application and creates the results. Then after all the scores have been tabulated, a button in PowerPoint, pushed by administrator, sends the results to Visio (see Figure 6-67). For the horser-ace, the horn plays, and the horses are advanced according to each team's respective score.

The good news is that this is a cool idea. The bad news is that it's hard to give every participant a computer tied into the underlying database of answers and even harder to get this stuff to work reliably each time you change the test.

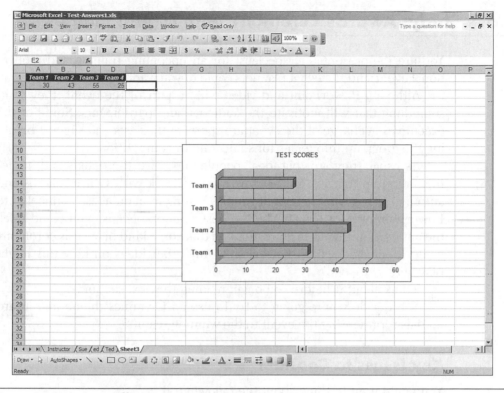

FIGURE 6-66   Using Office Automation, the results from the test taken by students are sent to Excel and graphed.

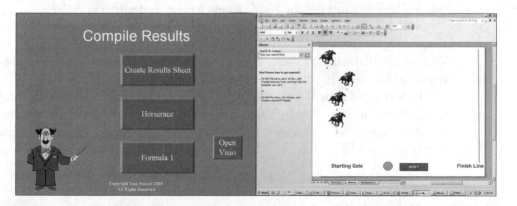

FIGURE 6-67   Using Office Automation, the results from the test taken by students are sent to Visio, where icons representing each team are moved in the proper relationship to their score.

Case Study: Awards Ceremony with Digital Images

You are the presentation specialist for an upcoming training and motivational event, and the event planners come to you wanting something special.

Although PowerPoint and video will be part of the event, they want something that will motivate the audience and participants. Some of the executives in charge of the event are sports enthusiasts and suggest breaking the group up into teams for some kind of competition.

As usual, they are "big idea" people and leave the details and implementation up to you. You've done a bit of work with Office macros and automation but want to keep it simple. You figure a database connected to PowerPoint would probably be the best solution because you could track the answers. And your instinct tells you that some kind of awards ceremony could be created within PowerPoint. Any other ideas on how this might play out?

Think about it before you begin reading the next section.

You decide you're going to try to use an Olympics theme and award medals representing the event to the winning team(s).

Key Issues to Consider

You might want to think about the following:

- How can you represent the winning team in PowerPoint?
- How can you get the right results to play instantly?
- What can you do to make the award slide as exciting as possible?

You decide that without going out of your mind, you can create such a scenario for four teams, which you originally call A, B, C, and D.

It turns out that if you calculate the amount of first-, second-, and third-place finishes (Gold, Silver, and Bronze) for these four teams, the number of possible outcomes is 24. (One team in each scenario finishes without a medal.)

ABC

ACB

ABD

And so on, as we can see in the Outline panel showing the "titles" of the 24 required slides in the resulting PowerPoint presentation (see Figure 6-68).

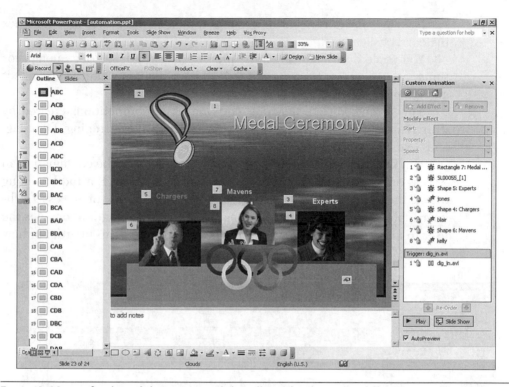

FIGURE 6-68   A final medal ceremony slide will need to have 24 different possible outcomes, represented by 24 different slides.

In order to refer to the correct slide that represents the outcome as determined by the event that the teams will compete in, you name the slides by the result titles and *hide the titles in each slide* (refer to Chapter 3). (This lets you identify the winning slide by its title, such as CAB.)

The winning order is determined by the Custom Animation in the slide—Bronze (3rd) appears first, Silver (2nd) appears next (of course now the audience realizes the winner, so music needs to play), and then the Gold medal winner is announced.

Because the teams are too large to show as groups, you use the digital pictures of the team leaders to represent each team and put a text box above each to name the team itself.

You use a digital camera to grab images of the team captains the night before the event, save them as TIF files, and insert them into the Power-Point medal slides.

Then you use the Insert > Duplicate Slide technique to create the 24 possible outcome slides.

6. POWERFUL PRESENTATION TOOLS

Now you need a trigger device that tabulates the scores and launches the correct slide.

You could do it manually if the presenter could delay long enough for someone to figure out the correct slide to play, but you want to automate it and keep track of the results of the various events.

The "events" are designed as corporate skill competitions created by your Human Resources department, with names like Listening, Planning, and Teamwork.

You finally decide that for each event, the scores can be contained in an Access database *table* and entered with an Access form. For the Listening event, the form would look like Figure 6-69. The form (or Access Dashboard, because it would open automatically with the program) enables the user to name the event and then assign values to the teams in order of how they finish—first = 3, second = 2, third = 1, and last = 0.

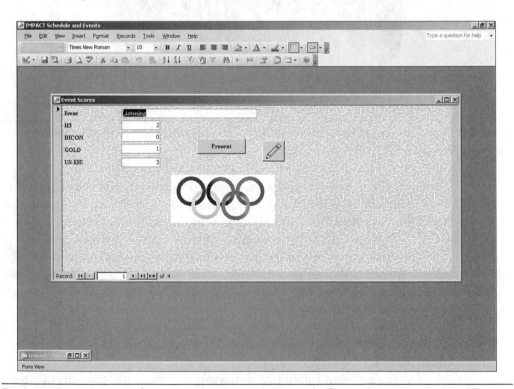

FIGURE 6-69 An Access form lets the user enter the results for each event, which will be stored in an Access table.

As the event scores are entered, a "Present" button runs a macro that runs the code in an Access module (see Figure 6-70).

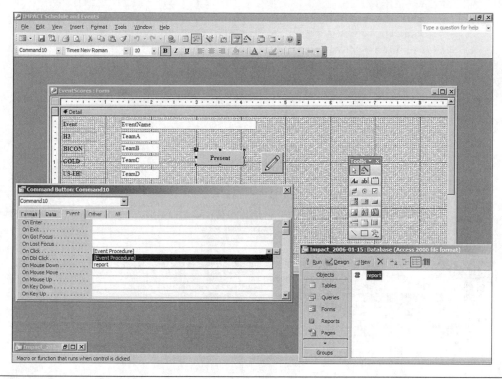

FIGURE 6-70   The button in the form launches a subroutine of code in Access.

Reviewing the code in the Module (see Figure 6-71), a *string variable* (text) is assigned for each medal (place finish), another for the Slide Number of the slide that will play in PowerPoint, and another for the Results (the winning combination, such as ABC, CAB, and so on). (The sample files and the entire module code is on this book's CD under this chapter as the text file Olympics.txt in the Olumpics folder.)

With the values assigned and winner determined, Access opens the PowerPoint file in presentation mode and displays the slides as follows:

```
If Results = "ABC" Then SlideNo = 1
If Results = "ACB" Then SlideNo = 2
If Results = "ABD" Then SlideNo = 3
If Results = "ADB" Then SlideNo = 4
If Results = "ACD" Then SlideNo = 5
If Results = "ADC" Then SlideNo = 6
If Results = "BCD" Then SlideNo = 7
If Results = "BDC" Then SlideNo = 8
If Results = "BAC" Then SlideNo = 9
If Results = "BCA" Then SlideNo = 10
```

```
If Results = "BAD" Then SlideNo = 11
If Results = "BDA" Then SlideNo = 12
If Results = "CAB" Then SlideNo = 13
If Results = "CBA" Then SlideNo = 14
If Results = "CAD" Then SlideNo = 15
If Results = "CDA" Then SlideNo = 16
If Results = "CBD" Then SlideNo = 17
If Results = "CDB" Then SlideNo = 18
If Results = "DCB" Then SlideNo = 19
If Results = "DCB" Then SlideNo = 20
If Results = "DAB" Then SlideNo = 21
If Results = "DBA" Then SlideNo = 22
If Results = "DAC" Then SlideNo = 23
If Results = "DCA" Then SlideNo = 24
```

FIGURE 6-71 The code behind the button (an Access macro) opens PowerPoint in presentation mode and shows only the appropriate slide with its animation.

In the example shown here, the Chargers finished third (Bronze), the Experts have just been announced as Silver, the music has begun to play, and the winning team captain is just about to be revealed as the Gold medal winner for the Listening event (see Figure 6-72).

FIGURE 6-72 Access opens PowerPoint and plays the correct slide with Custom Animation determining the order and music playing between the announcement of the Silver and Gold medal winners.

You test the application thoroughly on the presentation laptop and make sure you're there to run the event. As it happens, a glitch in one of the events results in a *tie*, which you have not anticipated and for which you have no provision.

You quickly open the PowerPoint presentation and change the winning slide to show two gold medals and a bronze as the speaker stalls to give you just enough time to make the changes. Then you play that slide manually and award the proper medals to the teams.

The audience is energized and cheers wildly with each event, and the event planner has actually gone out and purchased fake gold medals for the final overall winners. As a result, the motivational results are phenomenal, and the event is a huge success.

Summary

In this chapter, we went beyond PowerPoint to examine some presentation-enabling programs that in some cases can replace PowerPoint and in other cases complement our slide show.

Office cousins Excel and Visio each have their own capabilities to visually reorient data (the Excel pivot table) and dynamically represent information (Visio parametric shapes and Layers).

Beyond that, we introduced the capability to control PowerPoint and other Office programs with VBA (Visual Basic for Applications) and illustrated this feature with sample scenarios. The most basic code component is the macro, which can be quickly created with the Macro Recorder.

We also took an introductory look at other video programs that can capture PowerPoint presentations (Camtasia) and import PowerPoint slides for more complex productions (Communicator from Serious Magic).

Finally, we showed off a bit by controlling PowerPoint from Access and using PowerPoint as a quiz application to create training and motivational applications using Visual Basic for Applications.

Resources

VBA takes quite a bit of practice, and seeing how pros do it can streamline your learning curve. Here are some excellent resources for code and answers to questions to troubleshoot performance.

- Steve Rindsberg's RDP Slides site has an amazing FAQ that includes lots of info on programming PowerPoint—www.rdpslides. com/pptfaq/.
- You can access the PowerPoint newsgroup with a news reader at Microsoft.public.powerpoint or directly at one of many sites like http://snipurl.com/lkp4.
- Microsoft Developer Website for PowerPoint—http://snipurl.com/ lmip.
- Organize Online Content—www.onfolio.com.

Screen Capture Utilities for Training

Sometimes it's helpful to capture a series of computer screens quickly for training. Here are some good tools to consider:

- SnagIt—www.techsmith.com
- HyperSnap—www.hypersnap.com/

Audience Response Systems

Additional ARS tools include the following:

- For educators. EInstruction—http://einstruction.com
- IML—www.iml.co.uk
- Option Technologies—www.optiontechnologies.com
- Reply Systems—www.replysystems.com
- Service Provider: www.audience-response-rentals.com
- TurningPoint—www.turningtechnologies.com
- Ventuz—www.ventuz.com

PowerPoint Alternatives and Complementary Tools

Here are some other programs that can sometimes replace or empower your slide show production:

- TrialDirector (legal, courtroom)—www.indatacorp.com
- SundayPlus (faith-based)—www.sundayplus.com
- Photodex Producer; ProShow (photographic presentations and effects)—www.photodex.com
- Ontra Presenter (corporate kiosks and training multimedia)—www.ontrapresentations.com
- Apple Keynote—www.apple.com
- Quindi is a "meeting capture" tool that captures notes and video—http://www.quindi.com

CHAPTER 7

THE LATEST TECHNOLOGIES: BEYOND POWERPOINT TO THE FUTURE

As we've gone through working with PowerPoint and the related programs, you've probably gotten the idea that "presentation" in today's world has a new meaning. It is more about establishing a connection with your audience than just completing a single event, and in many situations, it will be an ongoing process.

Two converging technologies are responsible for this: broadcasting, including related new media such as DVDs and HD on the one hand, and broadband Internet and the ability to stay connected through the computer on the other.

For presenters, this means that creating a "slide show" is not enough. It is simply part of a continuous process that keeps the presenter connected to his or her audience, part of a greater communication strategy.

In this chapter, we explore some of the emerging technologies and concepts on the presentation horizon and discuss the important aspects of their successful implementation.

Online Presentations: The Fork in the Internet Road

One inevitable byproduct of the Internet revolution is that the web has become a distribution channel for presentations. In some cases, the presentations are a stand-in for when the presenter cannot make it in person; on other occasions, they are for follow-up or simply to supplement an ongoing dialog between the presenter and the client or audience.

Because PowerPoint has become a ubiquitous tool for presenting and the word itself is almost a synonym for the concept, the issue really becomes, how do you transfer your PowerPoint presentation to an online presence?

The answer, as always, depends upon a number of circumstances:

- Who is the audience, and what will they be using to view the material?
- What is the bandwidth available, and which operating systems are they likely to use and what type of browser?
- How complex is the material being presented? In terms of Power-Point, with its linked videos and other features, how do they translate to the web? (Only certain video formats will work online, and links can be problematic.)
- Which PowerPoint features must you absolutely have, and how do they work online?
- How much interactivity and contact must you have with the audience? (Will a simple show be sufficient, or do they need to see your face or have a way to ask questions?)

For each of these sets of criteria, there is a different solution or combination of strategies available for presenting online.

When to Save PowerPoint as a Web Page

Most users have seen that within PowerPoint, there is a Save as Web Page option under the File menu (see Figure 7-1).

This looks like a fairly straightforward way to create a version of your presentation that should play in all web browsers, right? Not quite.

When you choose this option, the Save As dialog box opens, but notice that the default File Format is not the standard HTML but rather the MHT (single web page) format that works *only in Internet Explorer* (see Figure 7-2).

So the promise of a web-friendly version is very appealing, but the reality is this—if you truly want a web-based version of PowerPoint, you will need to make some compromises. Some of the features like animation and transitions may not work in all environments—especially with users who do not use Internet Explorer or the Windows operating system.

If you want the widest possible playback capability, change the file type in the Save As dialog box to HTM, as highlighted in Figure 7-2.

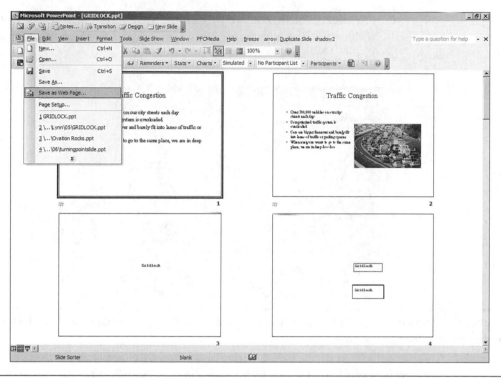

FIGURE 7-1   There is a Save as Web Page option directly available in PowerPoint.

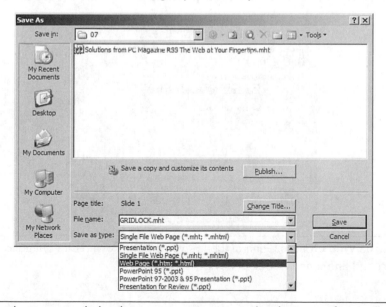

FIGURE 7-2   The Save As dialog box tries to steer you in the direction of a single web page (MHT) file, which works in Internet Explorer only but HTML is available.

When you click Publish, you are presented with more options (see Figure 7-3). Notice that the more browsers you decide to publish for, the larger the files will be.

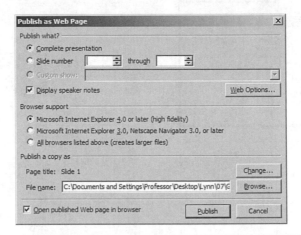

FIGURE 7-3 The Publish as Web Page option begins the conversion process to HTML format and provides other options for browser support.

Do you want to attempt to preserve your PowerPoint animations and make other modifications? Click Web Options (see Figure 7-4).

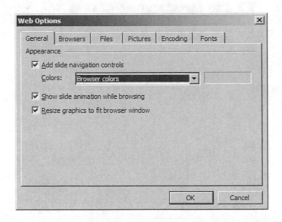

FIGURE 7-4 The Web Options General tab lets you enable PowerPoint animation (for Internet Explorer) and fine-tune the look of navigation buttons.

In the General tab, you can enable Show slide animation while browsing, but be aware that not all browsers will support it. You can also click to use the browser's native colors for the presentation's navigation controls.

In the Browsers tab, you can once again broaden the playback capability to browsers other than IE, but be aware that the lower you go in version number, the fewer PowerPoint features will be preserved (see Figure 7-5).

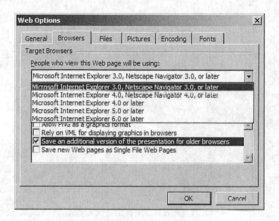

FIGURE 7-5 The Web Options Browsers tab lets you broaden the playback capability of the show, but you may still lose features on some platforms and in some browsers.

If you run into problems when you publish, the final three tabs may need to be investigated and changed. In most cases, the defaults will suffice. You can access the Picture tab to change the screen resolution of images (generally downward for smaller monitors in other countries), and if the fonts lead to surprises, you will want to visit the Fonts tab.

But now, you should be ready to publish. Unless you've changed the default setting for some reason, when the presentation is converted to HTML and "published" locally, it will open in Internet Explorer or your default web browser (see Figure 7-6). In this example, you can confirm that the file format is HTM by the filename in the web browser's address bar.

Notice another key issue: slides without titles look strange and awkward in the navigation panel on the left. In this instance, slide titles should be added to the presentation and the file republished.

But where is the file, and what do we do next?

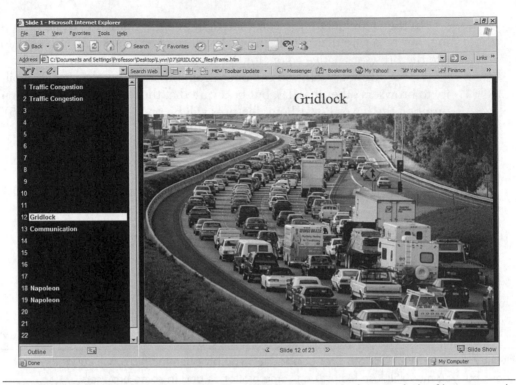

FIGURE 7-6   The converted PowerPoint file opens in Internet Explorer with the filename and format visible in the address bar.

This file was published locally to the folder for this chapter (07). Notice that there is an HTM(L) file with the name of the presentation (gridlock.htm) and a *folder of supporting files* (see Figure 7-7). This supporting folder contains many of the key image files (for navigation or pictures in the slides) that must be present for the presentation to play properly.

If we had kept the original file format (MHT), we would not need a supporting file folder on the server, but only later versions of Internet Explorer support this single-page file format. Browsers like Opera, AOL, and Netscape would not open it properly.

HTM OR HTML? Windows machines support only three letters for a file extension, so web pages saved by Office programs have only the three-letter *.HTM extension. This will work fine on most web servers except for so-called Index or home pages, which sometimes (on UNIX servers) need to be saved with four-character *.HTML extensions. The key point to remember is for the widest possible playback, save the files in .HTM and not .MHT format.

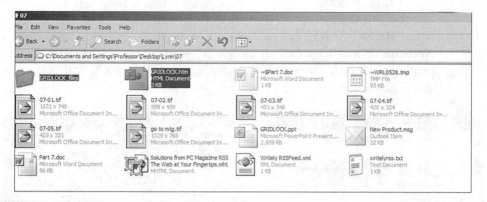

FIGURE 7-7   The web page file must also be accompanied by the folder of supporting files for the presentation to play properly.

Now you still need to move the *.HTM file and the supporting folder to a website by using either an FTP program or Internet Explorer's FTP capability. In Figure 7-8, we've accessed the FTP for a website through Internet Explorer (with a username and password for access). By opening the folder with the *.HTM file and supporting folder, we're ready to drag it into the site to be accessed on the Internet.

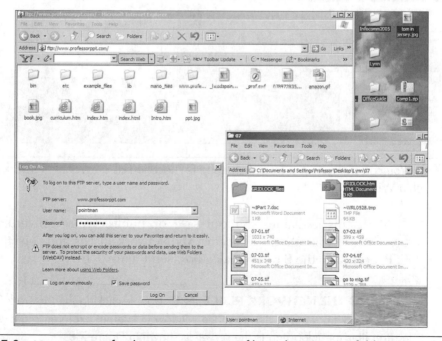

FIGURE 7-8   You can transfer the PowerPoint HTM file and supporting folder to a web server using Internet Explorer as long as you have access with a username and password.

You can also set up a "Network Place" as an FTP site to save to directly. Open My Network Places on the Start Menu in Windows XP and click Add Network Place. Figure 7-9 shows the next steps of the wizard, which prompts you with hints on how to set up an FTP location with a username and password.

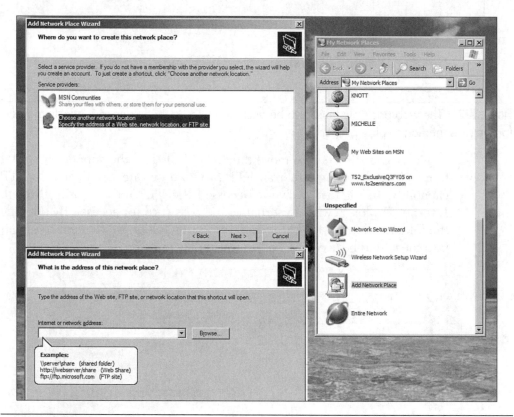

FIGURE 7-9   You can also set up a frequently used FTP location as a favorite Network Place directly within Windows.

With this available, you can save or publish your converted files directly to this location by clicking My Network Places and selecting the FTP location in the Save As dialog box (see Figure 7-10).

OPENING THE NETWORK PLACE IN IE   Double-clicking the Network Place directly in Windows will also open the window in Internet Explorer to allow you to drag files for uploading to the server as shown in Figure 7-8.

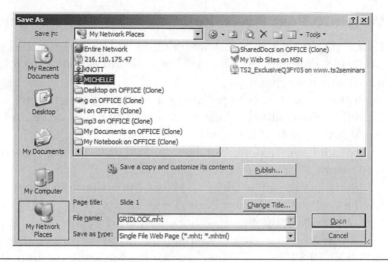

FIGURE 7-10   With a Network Place designated by name as an FTP site, you can (re)publish and save files there directly.

All these procedures result in the web page and supporting files residing on a website.

You should now be able to direct anyone to this location by copying the link from the address bar of the browser and then sending it via email: www.*yourwebsitename*.com/gridlock.htm.

Or you can create a link on your home page to the same web page on your website.

FOLDERS ON THE SERVER The relative position of the supporting file folder and the web page on the server is critical for the functionality of the PowerPoint presentation when saved as an HTM file. If there is a problem accessing the file, try moving the files up to the server directly using a third-party FTP program. It's also best to make all filenames and extensions lower case.

OFFICE ANIMATION RUNTIME Office Animation Runtime allows you to view PowerPoint 2002 (or later version) web presentations that contains animations in Microsoft Internet Explorer 5.0 or later if you do not have PowerPoint installed. For some reason, snipurl refused to shorten this download address, but you can find the runtime by searching on Windows Downloads under Office and PowerPoint 2003.

7. THE LATEST TECHNOLOGIES

When to Post PowerPoint as a PowerPoint File

If you take a look at the PowerPoint as HTM (or even the single-page MHT file, displayed in IE), it will have lost quite a bit of the flavor you put into it as a PowerPoint file.

Your transitions between slides and other timings won't work online even if you've enabled animation on publishing unless the user has a relatively new version of Internet Explorer.

In addition, hyperlinked files and Action Settings almost certainly won't work.

Some of this can be addressed if you know that your intended audience has PowerPoint or the new PowerPoint Viewer for PowerPoint 2003. (The link to download the Viewer is http://snipurl.com/jxzs.)

If you want to make the file play a bit faster and easier, save it as a PowerPoint *.PPS (Show) file by changing the Save as type drop-down option to *.PPS, as shown in Figure 7-11.

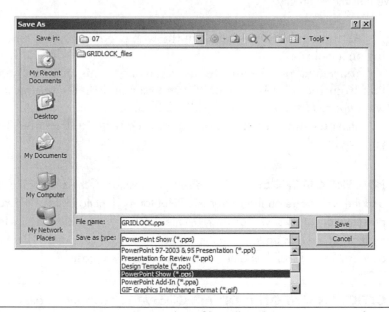

FIGURE 7-11   Saving a PowerPoint *.PPS show file will make it unnecessary for a user to open the PowerPoint editor to see the file. It will just play.

Now you can post the PowerPoint Show file on a website in the same manner as you did for the HTML version. The only difference is that the link will be www.*yourwebsitename*.com/gridlock.pps.

If the user has a Windows XP PC with PowerPoint installed, a dialog box will open asking the user whether to Open or Save the file.

SEE AN EXAMPLE You should be able to try both of these scenarios using my website.

http://www.professorppt.com/gridlock.htm for the saved web page.

http://www.professorppt.com/gridlock.pps for the posted PowerPoint show file.

Alternatively, you can instruct the user to right-click the link and save the target to a file locally. This will allow him or her to open the file in the PowerPoint Viewer or within PowerPoint on a Windows PC or the Mac and view the file in the same manner in which it was created.

WATCH OUT FOR LINKED FILES Remember that video and many audio files are linked to their PowerPoint "hosts." In addition, other hyperlinks to Excel graphs or other documents or files may be part of a PowerPoint presentation. The key point here is that these links are to local drives and folders in PowerPoint (like C:\User name\My Documents), and if these links are moved online, a web browser has no way to process them.

When using a PowerPoint presentation online, make sure that all linked files are in the same folder as the presentation itself and that they are moved up to the server together. Then test the links thoroughly.

Use the Package for CD feature (covered in detail in Chapter 8, "Delivering a Killer Presentation") to package the presentation(s) and linked files first to a local folder (before uploading them) to ensure that hyperlinks work properly.

Microsoft Producer for Video Presentations

Although it's easy enough to save a PowerPoint presentation as a web page or even post the PPT file itself on your website, this is generally not a viable solution for rich media presentations.

Presentations that include movies or Shockwave files, for example, have those files linked to the original PowerPoint presentation, so putting them online and having the links play correctly is a challenge.

Here is a slide with a media file: if we right-click the file and select Edit Movie Object, we can see that PowerPoint sees that this file is somewhere on the C:\ drive (see Figure 7-12).

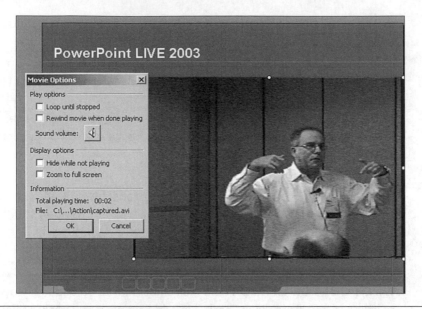

FIGURE 7-12   By right-clicking a video object in a PowerPoint slide, we can determine where the linked video file is supposed to be located.

Unfortunately, this embedded link will not translate to the web because C:\ is a Windows drive and will not be located on a web server, even if the video were a web-enabled file type like WMV, MPG, or MOV.

Although there are ways to make PowerPoint understand, for instance, that the movie is in the same folder as the presentation and upload them together, it's tough. One way to do it would be to use the Package for CD utility to put all of the files, including the PowerPoint file and the linked assets, into the same local folder and then upload them together to the same folder on the web server.

Another way would be to save the PowerPoint file as a web page, separately edit the web page to play an embedded Windows Media or other video file, and then upload the linked file. This requires some special HTML coding and is not always easy; Windows Movie Maker and Camtasia Studio can enable us to create individual web pages with embedded movies.

But there are some other scenarios. One of these is Microsoft Producer, a free download from Microsoft that enables you to combine slides from a presentation and other assets, specifically video, in a timeline. Then you can encode the video and publish the web-based presentation to play online.

NOTE To download Producer for PowerPoint 2003, go to http://snipurl.com/hr5j.

This presentation is a short training file about the Clip Organizer that we want to post online with the linked video in a web-friendly format.

Let's add a slide to the presentation with the video file that has some bullets about the subject of the actual video—in which the Clip Organizer is discussed (see Figure 7-13).

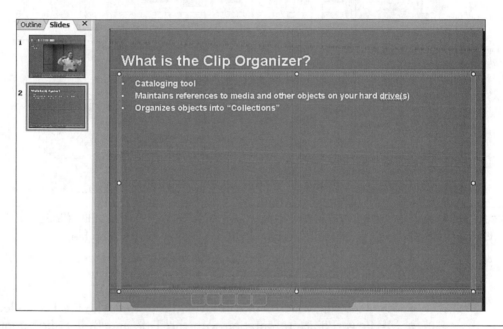

FIGURE 7-13   We can add a regular Title and Bullet PowerPoint slide to the file that will be imported into Microsoft Producer.

In a conventional PowerPoint presentation, we could combine these on the same slide, but in this case, we're getting ready to use Microsoft Producer.

Because this short sequence is about the Clip Organizer, I am going to open it from the PowerPoint Clip Art Task Pane and press PrtScr on my computer keyboard. In my image editing program, I will save it as a separate image file, called ORG.BMP, by pasting the Screen Capture in as a new image and saving it to a local folder (see Figure 7-14).

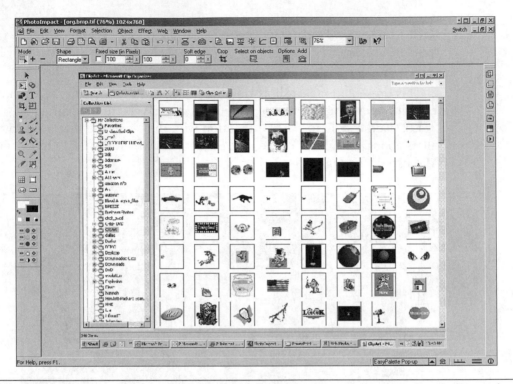

FIGURE 7-14   We can create an image file by using the Screen Capture utility (PrtScr on the keyboard), pasting a screen into an image editor, and saving the resulting file.

Now I've got three assets ready for Microsoft Producer:

- My video clip, which is in AVI format, captured with the DV codec
- My PowerPoint presentation with the Title and Bullet slide about the subject matter
- An image of what the Clip Organizer looks like

Now when I open Microsoft Producer, I can cancel out of the wizard because I want to learn how to import my own assets from different folders. Here's the interface—notice that it looks like a video editing program with a source area of folders for "clips" and a timeline in which to organize the content (see Figure 7-15).

If I double-click to open the Video folder, I can click Import and bring in the captured clip in which I describe the subject of the presentation, the Clip Organizer (see Figure 7-16).

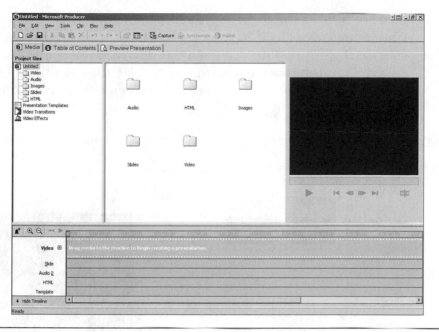

FIGURE 7-15   Microsoft Producer for PowerPoint is a timeline-based program with a clips area from which to drag assets into the production area.

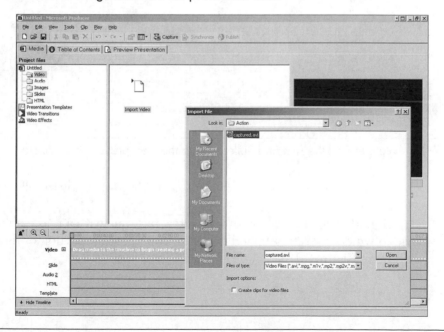

FIGURE 7-16   We import an AVI video clip into Producer that will be converted to a web-friendly format and linked to the slide.

Now the clip is ready to drag and drop into my timeline. Let's get the PowerPoint slide with the bullets—so I will need to import the entire presentation. I don't need the slide with the video clip referenced because it does me no real good—the video will be placed on the timeline separately—but that slide appears in my Slides folder with the one I want (see Figure 7-17).

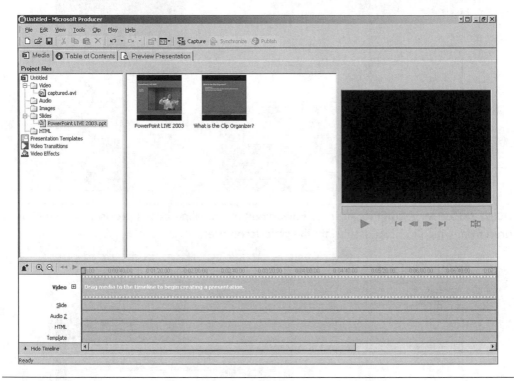

FIGURE 7-17 We can add the Title and Bullet slide to the web presentation clips area.

After I add ORG.BMP to my Images folder, I'm ready to roll (see Figure 7-18).

I go through the gallery of templates, pick one with a reasonably sized video window (320×240), and drag it to the template portion of the timeline (see Figure 7-19).

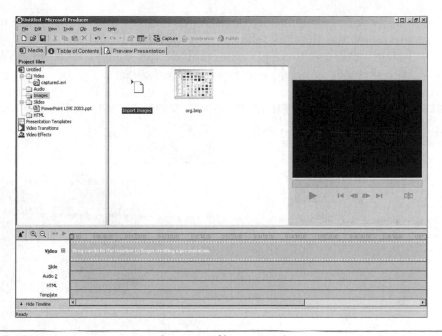

FIGURE 7-18 We can now import the image file into Producer.

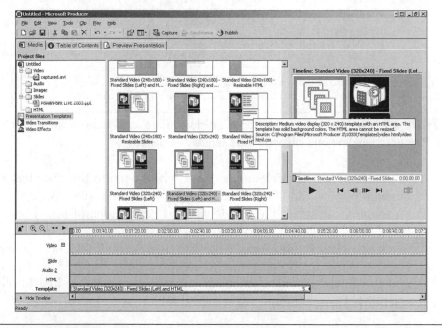

FIGURE 7-19 We select a web presentation template that will keep the video size relatively small for quick downloading.

Now, as I would in any similar video editor, I drag and organize my elements on the timeline, allowing my video to play over the slide or the image—because Producer will combine the smaller video in a Window with the slide or image assets (see Figure 7-20).

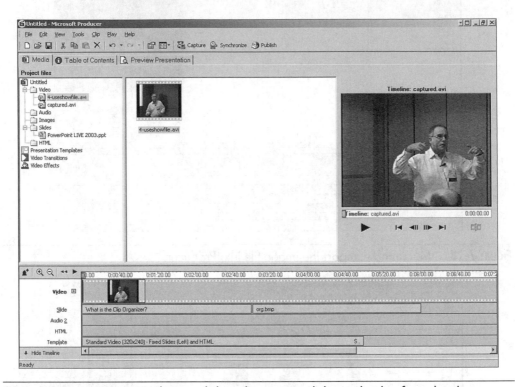

FIGURE 7-20   Now we can drag and drop the picture, slide, and video from the clip area into the Producer timeline and arrange their sequential display.

Notice that other elements that can be added to the Producer project are web pages or additional audio tracks—music or voiceovers.

Now I can select the Preview tab to get an idea of how my synchronized timeline will play and make any adjustments (see Figure 7-21).

I can click Publish under the File menu (or CTRL+U) to open the Publish Wizard and determine where I want the finished file (web pages and the linked encoded video) to go. I prefer to test it first locally, so I select My Computer and select a local folder (see Figure 7-22).

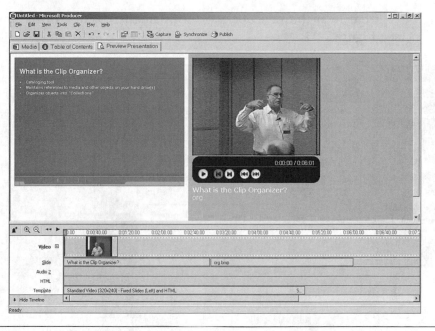

FIGURE 7-21   Producer will show us a preview of how the production will eventually look online.

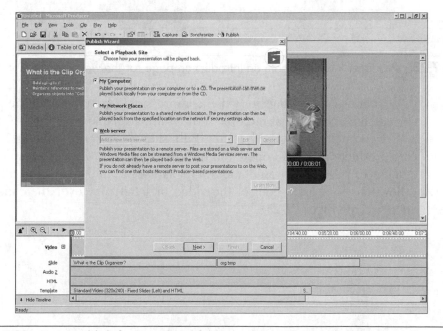

FIGURE 7-22   I can publish first to a local folder and then later upload the production to a web server.

I create an Introduction page with another picture of the presenter (see Figure 7-23).

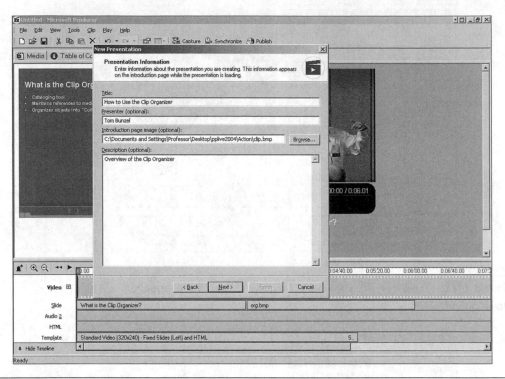

FIGURE 7-23   Producer lets you create an Introduction page for the web presentation.

I choose my settings for video compression—keeping them simple for broadband. Notice that multiple settings are available (see Figure 7-24).

I complete the wizard, letting Publisher encode my video and create my production. Then I open it in Internet Explorer to see the result. After the Intro page, the presentation plays as it will online, with the interface allowing the user to control the video or let it play over the slides and images (see Figure 7-25).

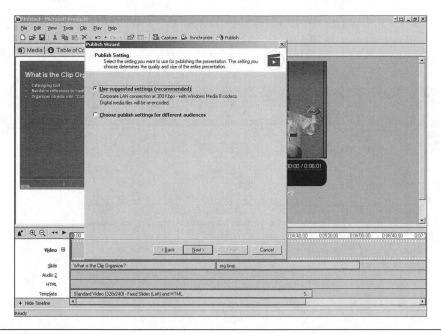

FIGURE 7-24   We choose some simple compression settings for the converted video file.

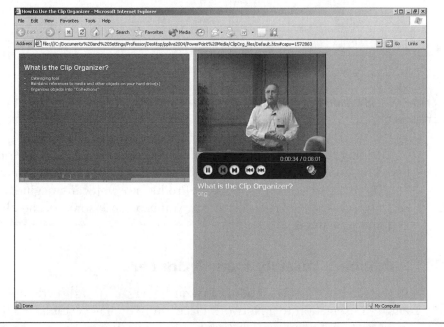

FIGURE 7-25   The final converted presentation will open and play the video in Internet Explorer.

If I check the underlying files in the folder where they were saved, I see a basic HTM page, along with a folder of supporting files (see Figure 7-26).

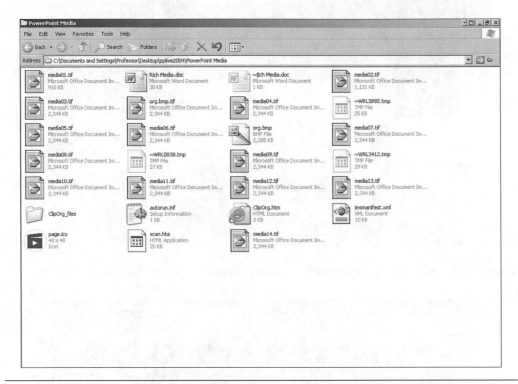

FIGURE 7-26   We can view the web page and supporting subfolder in the folder in which they were saved.

Posting the files to a website will result in a rich media presentation based on PowerPoint that will play the video content properly online.

There are some other aspects to Producer as you can imagine, but you can also save your project file so that you can reuse some of the elements and fine-tune the final result.

Publishing Directly from Producer

In the final step of the Producer Wizard, you can also directly upload the entire presentation to a Network Place after you have established it in the manner described previously (refer to Figure 7-10).

WMV MOVIE PLAYBACK Unfortunately, the WMV movies that have been saved by Producer and Movie Maker will play back best in Internet Explorer. To view the video on other platforms (UNIX, Mac), you may need a web browser that supports either QuickTime or Flash/Shockwave and the ability to convert PowerPoint to one of these formats.

Converting to Flash/Shockwave with Camtasia Studio 3.0

A number of programs are available to directly convert PowerPoint files into Shockwave format, and some of them will also create a web page to hold the file and provide you with tools to publish the files online.

Shockwave has a large advantage over the WMV movie format because more browsers and platforms will support playback.

In Chapter 6, "Powerful Presentation Tools," we used Camtasia Studio 3.0 to capture an entire presentation along with the speaker in a window. If we now return to that project and reopen it, we can use the Camtasia Editor to convert our project to Shockwave and create a web page to post online.

To begin the publishing process, we click Produce Video As in Camtasia Studio's main editor (see Figure 7-27). In the first part of the Publish Wizard, we select the SWF (Shockwave) format for output.

We can accept the defaults for the next few screens of the wizard (and make adjustments if necessary after we've created a few projects). In the final panel, we can see that four files will be generated in the target folder (see Figure 7-28):

- The Shockwave file itself (SWF)
- An XML file linking the video to the web page
- The controls that pop up in the Shockwave window
- The web page (HTML) that will hold the Shockwave file and support its playback

Keep in mind that all of these files need to reside in the same folder on the web server for the page to display properly and for the Shockwave file to play within a web browser.

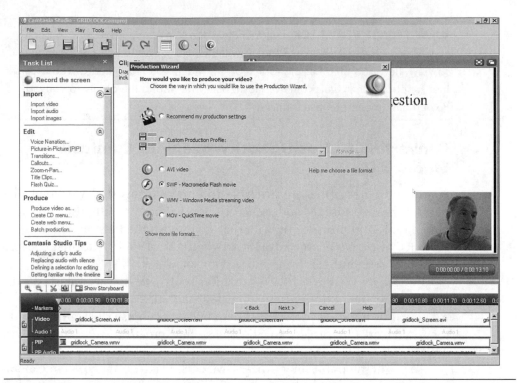

FIGURE 7-27 Camtasia Studio will enable us to publish a Shockwave file of our previously captured PowerPoint video file.

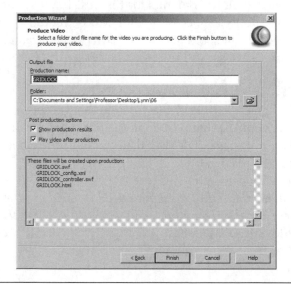

FIGURE 7-28 Camtasia Studio's Publish Wizard will create all four files necessary to play back the SWF file in a web page.

Figure 7-29 shows the production folder on the local hard drive with the four files. On the left, the SWF file is playing in Internet Explorer; however, this file will also play in any browser with the Flash/Shockwave player properly configured.

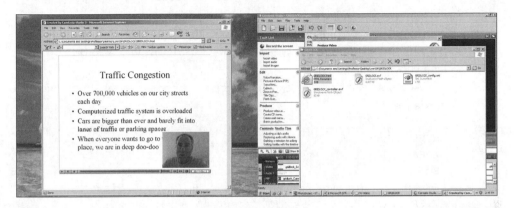

FIGURE 7-29 Double-clicking the HTM file will open it in a web browser that supports Shockwave (Internet Explorer or Netscape) and play the Shockwave file in the supporting folder.

ADDING OTHER ELEMENTS Camtasia Studio also has tools for adding a Web Menu, a Table of Contents, and a SCORM packaged e-learning lesson with the SWF file. The Publishing Wizard also lets you choose screen resolution and page background color for your web video.

VIDEO PLAYING WITHIN CAPTURED POWERPOINT VIDEO You can capture PowerPoint with a video file playing within a slide, but you would not use the Camtasia Add-In for PowerPoint (which captures the speaker in a window). Instead you could use the full Screen Capture utility included with Camtasia or the Screen Capture utility of Windows Media Encoder and capture the entire PowerPoint presentation full-screen, including the slides with the video playing.

You may have to fine-tune your settings for capture and screen size to get the video to play and be captured smoothly; however, a Pentium 4 with about 512MB of RAM will probably suffice with a decent graphics card.

This final full-screen video can then also be converted to a web-friendly (WMV, MOV, or SWF) format to post online.

7. THE LATEST TECHNOLOGIES

CREATING YOUR OWN WEB PAGE All the video formats have special coding requirements to get them to play within a web page, and some are specific to different browsers. The cool thing about Camtasia and some other Flash conversion programs is that they create the pages for you along with converting the video.

To get an idea of the complexity of coding HTML to use a video playback plug-in, open a page that is playing video or SWF files in a web browser and then click View > Source.

At a bare minimum, for example, here is the code for viewing a QuickTime movie file:

```
<HTML><HEAD>
</HEAD>
<BODY>
<EMBED SRC="pyramid.mov" WIDTH=320 HEIGHT=256 alt=""
AUTOPLAY="TRUE" CACHE="TRUE" controller="true">
</BODY></HTML>
```

Online Auditoriums: The Dynamics of a Successful Web Conference

Until recently, the web was essentially a broadcast medium for presentations. You could either post a PowerPoint file or convert it to Flash or HTML, and the user(s) could go online and view the slideshow.

At around the same time, wide area networks enabled distance presenting with various *video conferencing solutions*. These required a proprietary network (usually having extraordinarily high bandwidth for the time), which allowed the participants to see each other through two-way video equipment and share a computer screen or a *whiteboard* for brainstorming and collaboration.

Many of these types of systems still exist in larger corporations, but the expansion of the web has led to a proliferation of web conferencing tools that enable many of the same capabilities without a proprietary network by simply running a web browser.

Like many of the options that presenters have, determining which application to use is a matter of assessing one's needs and capabilities.

PREMIERE ONLINE COLLABORATION RESOURCE SITE Probably the very best source of information on this emerging technology and its ever-changing landscape is Robin Good's www.masternewmedia.org. More information on conferencing solutions, including reviews of various products, can be found at www.kolabora.com.

Many web conferencing solutions have the same basic idea—users can share a common view of a workspace through their web browsers, and generally they will connect to the audio portion of the presentation through a dedicated phone/conference line.

(Newer VoIP technology promises to eventually integrate the telephone portion with the onscreen video portion.)

In many such scenarios, the presenter will upload the PowerPoint slides for a presentation into the application, and they will need to be converted to images for the slide show that others will view and hear.

The application will typically also contain a virtual whiteboard (or area where brainstorming can take place) and a chat panel for instant messages between attendees and the presenter or others handling Q&A for the web conference.

With the proliferation of these applications into the online marketplace, different feature sets continue to emerge. Of the tools we have seen, the Citrix GoToMeeting program is representative of one that allows for the sharing of a computer screen and *keyboard and mouse controls*, making it a highly functional interactive presentation environment.

That is not to denigrate other solutions in this space. Microsoft's Live Meeting continues to integrate well with Microsoft Office in general and PowerPoint in particular; Macromedia Breeze offers a total web solution including its own video format (FLV) and publishing, polling, and conferencing components, but for the basic presenter, we are going to demonstrate the Citrix scenario in the next section, "Using a Dedicated Conference Solution."

Using a Dedicated Conference Solution: Citrix® GoToMeeting™

Citrix GoToMeeting is an excellent example of a web conferencing solution in which both the presenter and the attendees download components that enable online screen sharing directly from a desktop computer. With a flat-rate subscription payment, the presenter downloads the entire application and is able to host unlimited online meetings immediately.

The solution allows for a meeting to be scheduled for later or commenced immediately using the Meet Now function. At the start of a meeting, a control panel opens on the presenter's screen with easy-to-use options for screen sharing, attendee list viewing, and chat. Because a meeting requires participants, the presenter has various options for inviting others—including a telephone call with instructions, an email message generated directly from the console, and a copy and paste function for inviting others through instant-messaging applications (see Figure 7-30).

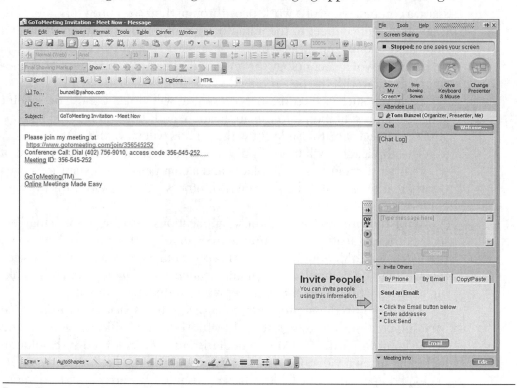

FIGURE 7-30 Like most web conferencing programs, GoToMeeting lets the presenter invite other participants via email programs such as Microsoft Outlook and IBM Lotus Notes.

As he or she gets ready for the meeting participants to arrive, the presenter in GoToMeeting can minimize the control panel and continue to work normally. PowerPoint slides do not have to be uploaded to an online application (see Figure 7-31)

Meeting participants receive an email or instant message with the link to the meeting, along with the telephone number and conference call ID code for the audio portion. Attendees can also go to the GoToMeeting website, click the Join Now button, and manually type in the meeting ID to enter a meeting (see Figure 7-32).

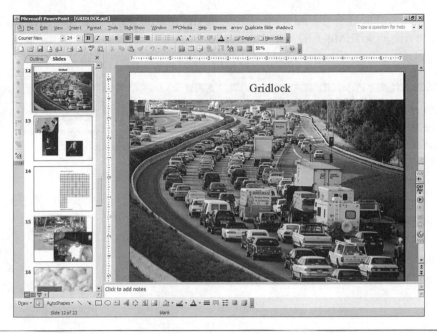

FIGURE 7-31 GoToMeeting lets the presenter continue to work as the meeting draws closer without the need to upload any slides.

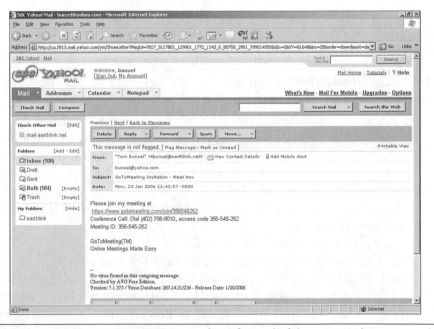

FIGURE 7-32 GoToMeeting participants can be informed of the meeting location and the appointed time via email.

Clicking the email link begins the automatic download process for the free GoToMeeting client that allows participants to attend the web conference (see Figure 7-33).

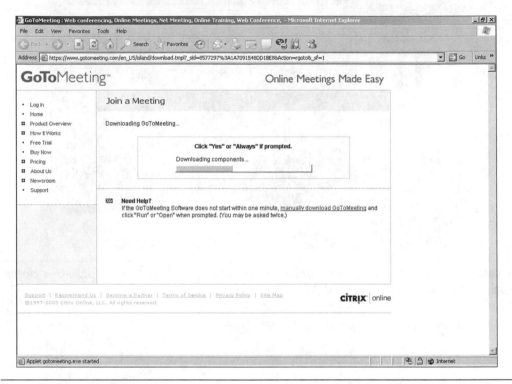

FIGURE 7-33   GoToMeeting participants automatically download the client application that enables them to join the meeting when it begins online.

Now the presenter can begin the meeting when he sees that his participants have "arrived" on the control panel. To show a presentation with PowerPoint for example, he simply opens the program and begins the presentation (see Figure 7-34). The presenter now clicks the Show My Screen option and decides to broadcast the screen with the presentation out to participants.

Among the options is to isolate a single application for broadcast (among the open programs), and to show the entire desktop or to broadcast "SCREEN CLEAN" with a simple blue background that hides irrelevant desktop icons from the participants. If you use the Meet Now function from within Microsoft Word, Excel, or PowerPoint, your meeting will open showing the screen you were on in that specific application.

FIGURE 7-34 GoToMeeting presenters can show a PowerPoint presentation normally and activate the screen sharing capability to broadcast the screen to participants.

The participants will by now have the presenter's screen up in their Viewer window (see Figure 7-35).

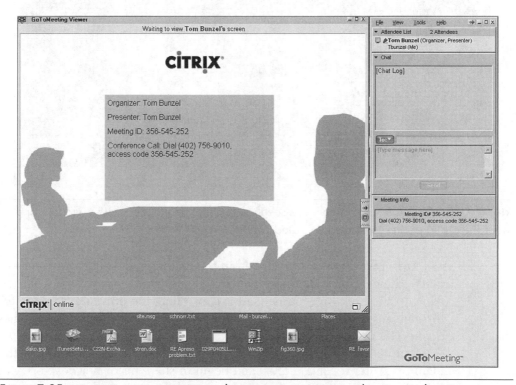

FIGURE 7-35 GoToMeeting participants have presenter's screen showing in the Viewer window.

With the screen shared, they see what the presenter chooses to show—the monitor with the PowerPoint presentation. In this case, it's the Gridlock presentation showing them what they are avoiding by not having to travel to the conference (see Figure 7-36).

FIGURE 7-36 GoToMeeting participants see the presentation in their Viewer window and hear the audio portion over the integrated conference call.

Any application can be shared in this manner, and even more importantly, the control of the mouse and keyboard can be given to any participant. In Figure 7-37, a participant is controlling the presenter's computer through his Viewer window, and highlighting a Word document he has opened for changes.

In addition, any participant can also be granted presenter status by the main presenter (or moderator) and begin to share his or her desktop with the other participants (see Figure 7-38).

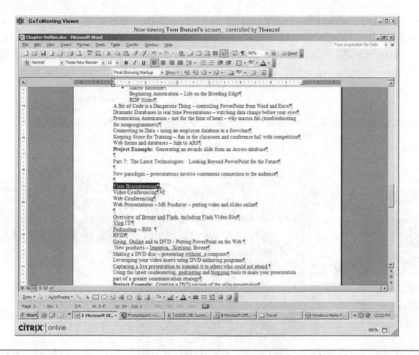

FIGURE 7-37 GoToMeeting participants can be granted keyboard and mouse control to collaborate on documents residing on the presenter's computer.

FIGURE 7-38 GoToMeeting participants can become presenters if they are granted the privilege by the main presenter (or moderator) and can show their own desktops.

7. THE LATEST TECHNOLOGIES

If enabled by the main presenter, all participants can use drawing and highlighting tools to make annotations that appear in everyone's Viewer window. The main presenter has the additional ability to use a spotlight tool and to erase all drawings (see Figure 7-39).

FIGURE 7-39   GoToMeeting participants have drawing and highlighting tools and their audio is heard through the same conference line.

In this way GoToMeeting becomes a fully collaborative web conferencing environment.

But there are trade-offs and limitations. Unlike the dedicated video conferencing systems, this scenario generally does not permit a separate video window showing the participants or the presenter.

And if the presenter attempts to show a slide with video, it generally won't be visible in "real time" to the audience—again due to user bandwidth constraints.

This brings up another point for presenters—it is important to know what the audience is actually seeing. Since your presentation system is performing normally, everything happens the way you expect. If you play a PowerPoint slide with builds or animation, you see no delay.

But the audience members are dependent upon the Internet for their connection, and some may even be on dial-up connections. (Though some solutions do not accommodate users with dial-up, GoToMeeting does.) In order to see what they're seeing, you might want to log on as a participant with a laptop and have its screen available to monitor what your audience is seeing.

The current telephone conference scenario for audio can also present some challenges. Sometimes the participants are asked to mute their phones, but bear in mind that this isolates the presenter and prevents him or her from hearing feedback like "slow down" or "speak up."

While chat is a good way to handle feedback and Q&A, chances are the presenter won't be able to do that and concentrate on the presentation since both require the keyboard and mouse. A good scenario has an associate or assistant filtering Q&A through the chat area and forwarding the most pertinent comments to the presenter.

Finally, there is also an option for recording the entire meeting including the audio portion, which you can then archive on your own network or website so that those who missed the meeting can review it—generally as a Windows Media file.

If you need it, you should also look for interactive polling capability which comes with many of these programs. While GoToMeeting has annotation features, other programs have a dedicated whiteboard. (Microsoft Live Meeting has these features but at this point seems to lack the ability to transfer remote control).

If video during the presentation or of the presenter is an essential part of your conference, you may need to investigate other solutions.

Online Video Solution 1: Broadcasting with Windows Media Encoder

In Chapter 6, when we used Camtasia Studio 3.0 for capturing a PowerPoint presentation with a speaker in the window, we mentioned Windows Media Encoder as a free downloadable alternative for doing almost the same thing.

Well, what if you wanted not only to capture a live presentation for review but also to broadcast it *live, real time*?

Windows Media Encoder is a low-cost solution to this problem, but it requires you to make a basic choice—capture either the camera feed (the presenter) or the screen (the PowerPoint show). You can download WME at http://www.microsoft.com/windows/windowsmedia/forpros/encoder/default.mspx.

(There are surely ways to switch between these two inputs, but they require additional hardware.)

7. THE LATEST TECHNOLOGIES

So let's go through the process of broadcasting a live presentation and *archiving it as a WMV Windows video file*.

Windows Media Encoder opens with a wizard that asks you to make this choice among others—either Broadcast a Live Event or Capture Screen (see Figure 7-40). (If you select Capture Screen and show a Power-Point slide show, that will be the event that is captured, archived, and potentially even broadcast.)

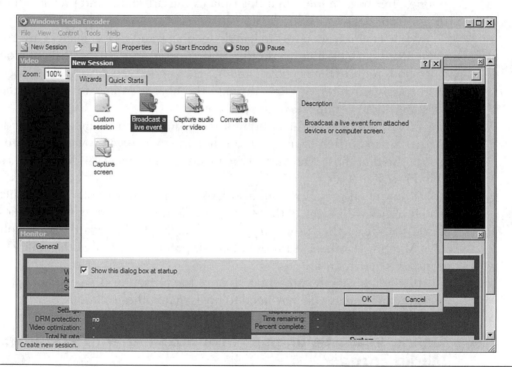

FIGURE 7-40   Windows Media Encoder's opening wizard lets you decide whether to capture and broadcast a screen event like PowerPoint or a live video input.

As you proceed through the wizard, you make choices as to the video quality of the transmission, which will depend on the bandwidth of your connection. You should select Pull from Encoder in the wizard's next screen unless you have access to a Windows Media Server.

You will need to note the URL or location of the broadcast on the network or Internet (see Figure 7-41). This will be the location to which viewers will need to go in Windows Media Player to view the event live.

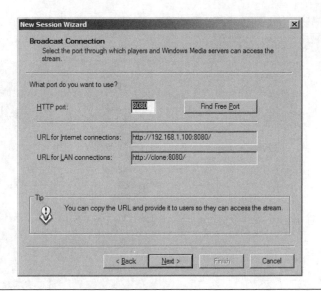

FIGURE 7-41 Windows Media Encoder's wizard tells you the URL to which to send viewers to watch the event through Windows Media Player.

You will see a screen to select the location for an archived WMV of the event.

If necessary, the broadcaster may need to configure the input devices—a camcorder or webcam to capture his or her image and a microphone as the default audio device (see Figure 7-42).

It's not too late to change back to a Screen Capture mode at this point, and you can return to this screen to begin or continue a broadcast alternating between live video and screen capture.

But now it's showtime. Click Start Encoding, and you are on the air (see Figure 7-43)!

NOTE If you were to select Screen Capture, you would continue talking into the microphone, but instead of looking into the camera, you would minimize the Windows Media Encoder and present material on the computer screen. Just like with Camtasia, a *hot key* would be available to end the screen capture and the encoding session.

At this point, your viewers should be alerted that you are on the air, and they should be tuned in to the broadcast. You should have scheduled this ahead of time and provided them with the URL for tuning in (refer to Figure 7-41).

FIGURE 7-42   Windows Media Encoder's options enable you to fine-tune the input settings and select the proper video device.

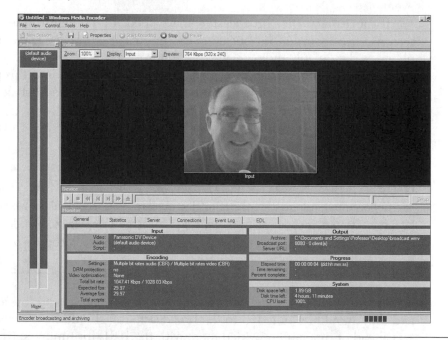

FIGURE 7-43   Windows Media Encoder shows your audio level and image as the camcorder captures and broadcasts your video live.

Each viewer needs to open Windows Media Player and click File > Open URL (see Figure 7-44). You might send them an email with this information so that they can copy and paste the URL directly into the dialog box.

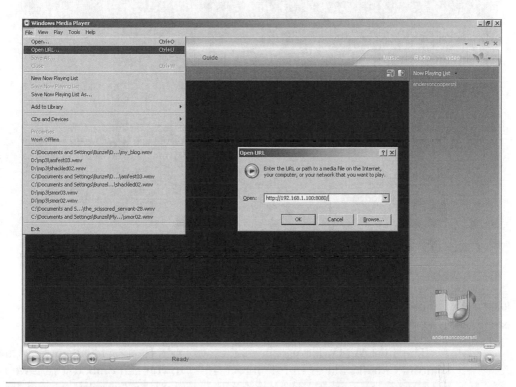

FIGURE 7-44 Those watching the broadcast will need to open the URL in Windows Media Player.

The viewers will see the live broadcast with a few seconds of delay as it streams over the network (Internet or LAN) (see Figure 7-45).

When the broadcast is complete, you close the encoder, but you're not quite done. You should have a file (broadcast.wmv) that you've archived in a safe location that you can now post online to have anyone watch who missed the broadcast.

In addition, Windows Media Encoder will allow you to *save the session*, which means that you can reopen the same options you just selected to begin another similar broadcast at a later date. You can save sessions for different configurations—screen capture or live broadcast—and for different screen resolutions.

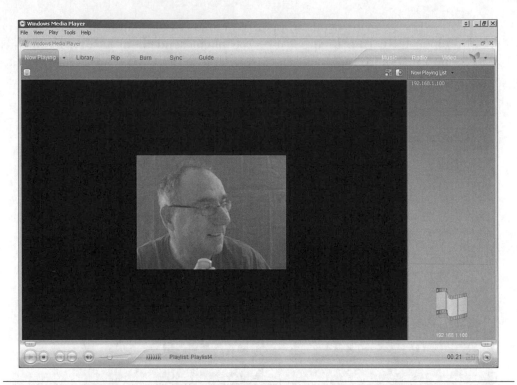

FIGURE 7-45   Those watching the broadcast on the Internet or over a LAN will see it a few seconds delayed.

The final WMV file can be made available for download to view in Windows Media Player (see Figure 7-46). Or, you can embed it in a web page using Microsoft Producer for PowerPoint or Camtasia Studio, as described earlier in this chapter.

Professional Alternatives

There are other hardware solutions that can enable the switching you need into Windows Media Player or replace it with a full Internet broadcast including polling and streaming studio:

- NewTek, the company that created the original video toaster, has a TriCaster, which enables the switching you would need to go out to a live media server or Media Encoder (www.newtek.com/tricaster/index.php).
- StageSync makes a product called Center Stage Producer to manage presentation inputs with two video channels (www.stagesyncsoftware.com).

■ The king of collaborative technology is probably Sonic Foundry's Mediasite conference capture and real-time streaming solution. It is not cheap, but it enables you to fully control the broadcast of a live event while you archive it and then make it available for streaming (www.sonicfoundry.com).

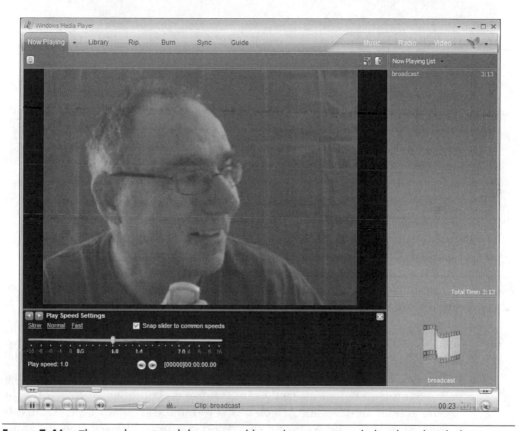

FIGURE 7-46 Those who missed the original broadcast can watch the downloaded WMV archive file on Windows Media Player (or in a web browser).

Online Video Solution 2: Skype, VoIP, or Instant Messenger

Right now, you may be saying, "Wait a minute, I've seen collaboration solutions with a video 'talking head' in a window, and they allow chat and perhaps even whiteboards."

Some of the products in the "Resources" section at the end of this chapter do allow for this—and then of course there are the Instant Messenger tools, including MSN, Yahoo!, and AOL.

PowerPoint 2002/XP had a broadcast component right inside the program that connected to "Netmeeting," an almost defunct messenger system that required a server and that is now presumably part of MSN.

Where this is all surely heading is Voice over Internet Protocol (VoIP), and the service to watch is probably Skype, which was just acquired by eBay (see Figure 7-47).

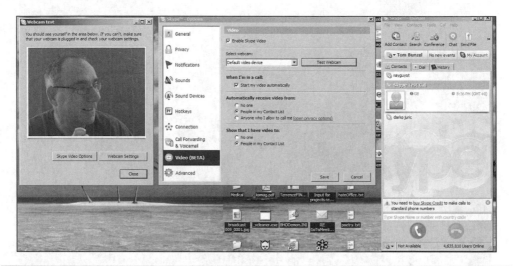

FIGURE 7-47   Instant Messaging systems that support a webcam or VoIP systems like Skype (shown here) will eventually support many conferencing features.

Eventually, many of the conferencing tools like shared applications and whiteboards will also come onto the telephony side, and services like this will also support PowerPoint and other multimedia presentation programs.

At this point, you could, for example, combine Skype with the OneNote Shared Session, which is covered in the section, "Using OneNote for a Simple Shared Notes Session," and you would have a free and quite functional collaboration solution.

Online Video Solution 3: Breeze

We mentioned Breeze briefly in Chapter 4, "Secrets of Animation and Navigation," when we began to talk about inserting Shockwave animation into PowerPoint. The Breeze plug-in for PowerPoint was described as a great little tool that facilitates using Flash in PowerPoint.

But it's part of the entire Macromedia Breeze publishing solution, which includes Breeze presentation, Breeze conferencing, and other components.

Breeze is always evolving along with its costs structure but is basically a per-user license subscription service that can be quite expensive and extensive.

The three main Breeze components and scenarios would probably be

- Rapid Training
- Marketing & Lead Generation
- Enterprise Web Conferencing

There is plenty of overlap among these components depending upon the specific needs of the company or institution implementing the Breeze platform.

In terms of presentations, the Breeze client in the Browser lets you upload a PowerPoint presentation and publish it as a Breeze presentation online (see Figure 7-48). Here, the presenter can be in a window and can show PowerPoint, Flash animation, and/or video.

FIGURE 7-48 Breeze provides a complete interactive platform for conferencing, training, and presenting.

The platform is growing in complexity as Macromedia has been acquired by Adobe, but it interfaces with other training applications like Captivate and of course accepts Flash video (FLV) and Shockwave (SWF) formats.

In addition, backend processing of information and publishing according to specified permissions is part of the platform, all according to optional packages that are available from Adobe/Macromedia (www.macromedia.com/software/breeze/).

WEBCAM VS. CAMCORDER FOR LIVE VIDEO CAPTURE Capturing video for a web conference application generally favors a webcam (USB) over a camcorder (Firewire and/or USB). Applications like Skype only recognize USB devices presently and may not work with USB camcorders, only the lower-end webcams. (USB camcorders have proprietary drivers that will work with some conference applications but may not work with others.) Windows Media Encoder has the advantage of working with both Firewire and USB devices; so does Serious Magic Communicator and Vlog It! (Refer to Figure 5-7 in Chapter 5, "Using Video and Audio Effectively," for more information on USB and Firewire connectors and cables for camcorders and webcams.)

Using OneNote for a Simple Shared Notes Session

If you're not quite ready for a full-blown conferencing solution and are a Microsoft Office user, you may not need Live Meeting or the MS Live Communications Server for simple collaboration sessions.

In our introduction to OneNote in Chapter 6, we mentioned that it was also a mini-conferencing tool. Let's see how this works. (Hint: It's a similar scenario as Windows Media Encoder, but instead of video, we're sharing OneNote pages.)

Our first step is to open the OneNote Task Pane (press CTRL+F1) and select Start Shared Session from the Task Pane drop-down menu (see Figure 7-49).

Select the page you're going to share, enter a password, and click Start Shared Session.

If you want to collaborate on a PowerPoint presentation, you can copy and paste the slides into OneNote.

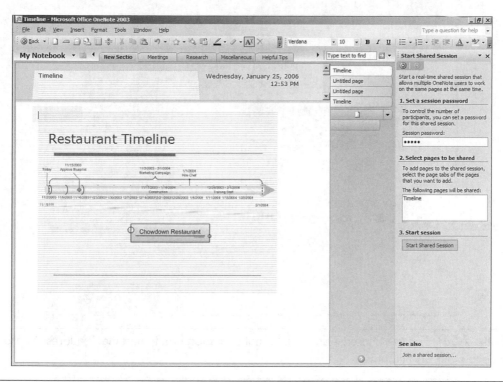

FIGURE 7-49 OneNote's Start Shared Session Task Pane lets you initiate a shared session.

When the Shared Session opens, you can click to enable Use the pen as a pointer and then click Shared Address Information (see Figure 7-50). The Shared Address Information dialog box gives you the IP address, which other participants will need to join the session. (You can click Invite Participants to generate an email to send to others automatically with the IP address and password information.)

Remote users follow the same basic steps. In OneNote's Task Pane, they can open a new section and then the Join Shared Session Task Pane (see Figure 7-51). The remote user needs the IP address (via email or some other way) along with the password to join the session—in order to enter it into the Join Shared Session dialog box.

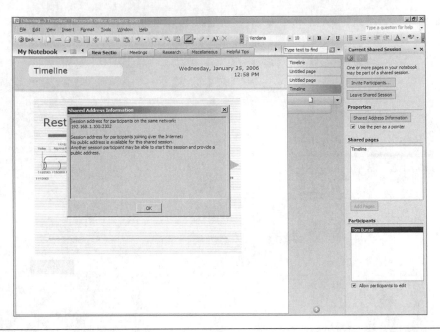

FIGURE 7-50 Use the Shared Address Information dialog box to find the IP address to provide to other participants.

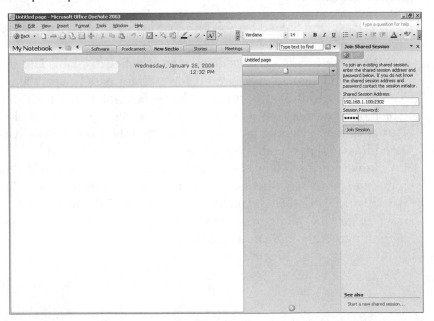

FIGURE 7-51 OneNote remote users can join the session with the IP address and password.

Then as you might hope and expect, the remote users can also mark up the diagram using OneNote's annotation features (see Figure 7-52).

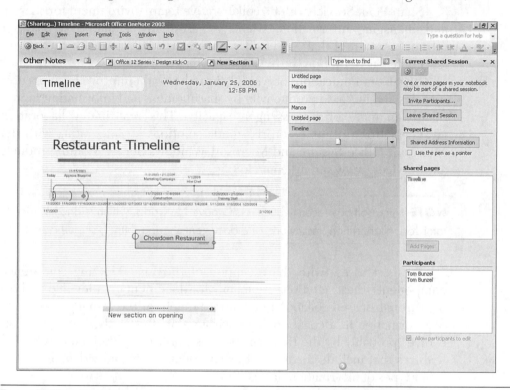

FIGURE 7-52 OneNote remote users can participate in editing the document.

When OneNote is closed, the resulting page is part of the Notebook of the various users; to make sure it's saved properly, you can use the Save As feature.

This becomes a great way to brainstorm documents including presentations. A simple telephone conference call or VoIP connection during the OneNote session is all you need to facilitate a discussion as collaboration takes place.

Microsoft SharePoint Services and Groove

As we've seen, the Windows Media Encoder solution is a broadcast feature for videos and screen captures.

OneNote has another specialty in sharing OneNote pages with the ability to support collaboration.

But Microsoft has other solutions for collaboration on a more structured level and involving routing documents.

SharePoint Services offer a collaborative team environment for sharing and managing information, which is essentially a shared website or intranet. As part of that "portal," Live Meeting would probably be the logical conference solution (http://snipurl.com/lxnz).

Live Communications Server 2005 can help you improve business efficiencies and increase productivity by sharing ideas and information immediately in more of a messenger capacity. This real-time collaboration (RTC) platform offers enterprise-grade solutions by integrating with the Microsoft Office System and Microsoft Windows Server System products and services (www.snipurl.com/alo8).

NOTE Microsoft has recently acquired Groove Networks, which is another facilitator for collaboration, teamwork, and document sharing (http://snipurl.com/lxnt).

In most cases (with the exception of the Live Meeting conference component), these solutions are mainly for document creation and authoring through shared collaboration—not so much for the actual presentation of information in a collaborative environment. But as these various tools evolve (probably by the time this book is published), they may well have features that include the ability to share documents and video, as well as other types of information, in real time.

This kind of real-time combination of collaboration, messaging, and communication would make them a powerful presentation tool as well as an authoring environment.

Continuing the Presentation Dialog: Podcasting and Video Blogging

Piggy-backed on the blog phenomenon, podcasting involves posting the MP3 files in just the right format with the proper web scripting so that pod readers and aggregators will find the content—sort of like newsgroup readers in the old text-only days.

What's cool about this is that it circumvents email and makes your content potentially available to those who seek it out on a regular subscription basis (known as RSS).

So how does this affect the use of presentations? Let's say you do a series of medical meetings or conferences, and a certain segment of your potential audience that would be interested in the content can't attend. You don't want to rely on them coming to your website to see the final video version. Or the content is such that it is always fresh or new.

If you put the (audio) content out as a podcast, you can allow the subscribers to get it through their podreaders and download it to portable audio devices (hence the name—although an iPod is not the only device that will work). Then they can listen to it in the car, while they jog or exercise, or whenever they want.

So how would this work with PowerPoint? If you recall, in Chapter 5, we discussed how to use the Record Narration feature.

In the Record Narration dialog box (see Figure 7-53), you need to check the Link Narrations in box, and also click to Browse in order to set up a subfolder for the narration files. (You should have already created an Audio folder in My Documents.)

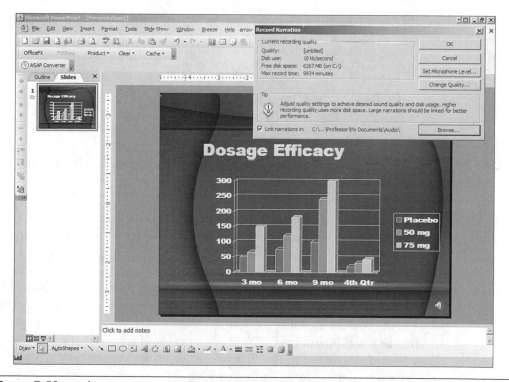

FIGURE 7-53   When you set up narration in PowerPoint, you can make sure that the linked files are saved to a specific folder.

Now when I click OK, I can record my narration for this slide into a microphone as the slide show plays, and the narration is saved as a standard Windows WAV audio file in the Audio folder (see Figure 7-54).

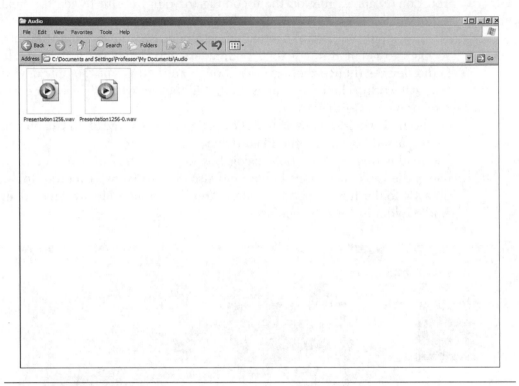

FIGURE 7-54   When the presentation is given and narrated, the final audio files are ready in the designated folder.

Now I could use any WAV-to-MP3 converter to encode the files into pod-friendly MP3 audio. Instead I am going to use the first podcast reading (and writing) tool I found on CNET downloads, BlogMatrix Sparks 2.0 (www.blogmatrix.com).

There are plenty of these tools out there already; what I like about this one is that it not only finds and subscribes to podcasts; it also makes the process of creating a podcast very simple.

Inside BlogMatrix Sparks 2.0, there is a sound recorder (like the Windows Sound Recorder) in the first panel, which lets you record a podcast and do some simple mixing and editing.

But you can also import a file (Import Music). Be careful, the default file is *.MP3, but if you select All Files under Files of Type, you will see your *.WAV files in the folder where you saved them out of PowerPoint (see Figure 7-55)!

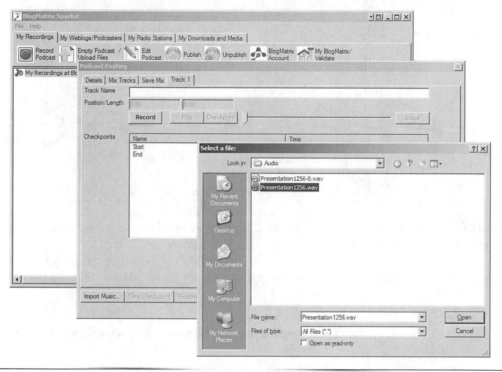

FIGURE 7-55   You need to convert the *.WAV audio to *.MP3 and select All Files to import the *.WAV audio files into BlogMatrix.

After you click Open, BlogMatrix will convert the file(s) to MP3 for you.

After you've named the "Mix" (Drug Efficacy), given it an Artist "tag" (Professor), and named the podcast in which it goes, you can Save the Mix (see Figure 7-56).

The final conversion of the files takes place.

Because I didn't want to get into scripting or creating my own RSS feed, I can take advantage of BlogMatrix's (temporarily) free hosting service to right-click and publish my podcast to its site (see Figure 7-57).

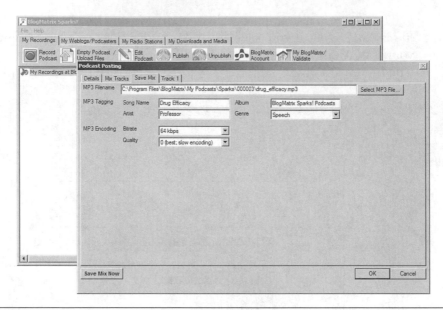

FIGURE 7-56 Before Saving the Mix for the podcast, you need to give it a name and a tag, which will help users locate the content during a web search.

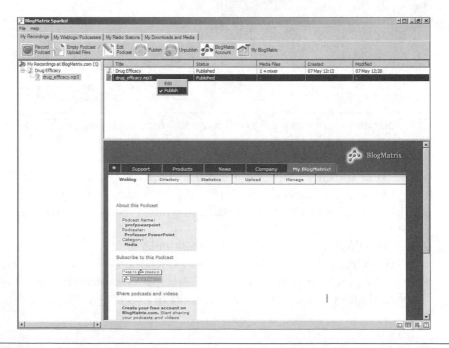

FIGURE 7-57 Publishing the podcast uploads it to the hosting site and establishes the viability of RSS connections for future downloads to users who have subscribed.

If I want to see the XML script, I can double-click it and open the Pod-casting options panel to add more media later on (after narrating a few more PowerPoint slides—see Figure 7-58.)

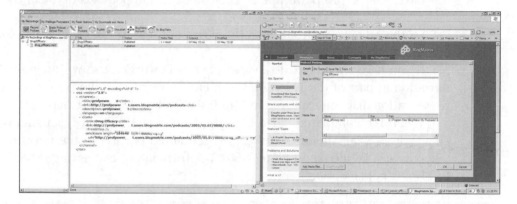

FIGURE 7-58   Using a podcast publisher, you will be able to add additional *.MP3 files to the subscription.

By making the RSS feed available through BlogMatrix's web page (My BlogMatrix on the right), I can access it in the podcast reader (on the left). Highlighting the URL lets me send this in an email to others who may want to enter it into their podcast readers to subscribe to it and eventually download my additional media files onto their portable devices (see Figure 7-59).

FIGURE 7-59   Using a podcast reader (left), users can subscribe to the podcasts (right), download the material, and eventually transfer the audio to portable devices.

7. THE LATEST TECHNOLOGIES

They would point to a URL like the following: (Don't subscribe to this—it was created for test purposes only.)

URL = http://profpowerppt.users.blogmatrix.com/podcasts/index.xml

So that's how you would use the narration feature of PowerPoint to create a Podcast.

If you have already made a video of your PowerPoint show (including narration as part of the video file), you can extract the audio from such a presentation that you captured in Camtasia Studio. (Refer to Chapter 6.)

When the completed video is in the Camtasia Editor, we can simply click File > Save Audio As and export the audio portion of the narrated video as a WAV file (see Figure 7-60). (Unfortunately, converting directly to MP3 is not an option here.)

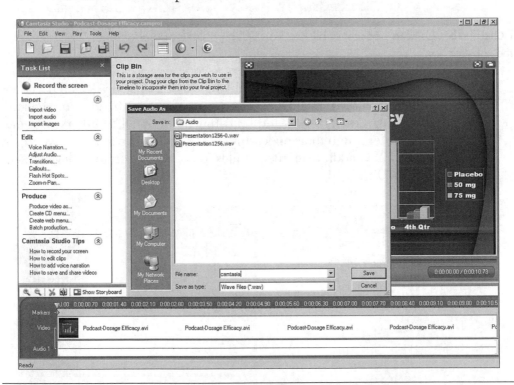

FIGURE 7-60 If you've captured an entire presentation with narration as a video file, you can extract the audio in a video editing program like Camtasia Studio.

But now we have another file to work with to create our podcast using BlogMatrix or any other tool of our choice.

Using this process, we can make the audio portion of our PowerPoint presentation available to listeners on a subscription basis through their podcast readers and enable them to hear our pearls of wisdom on an iPod, PDA, or any other device capable of storing and playing back MP3 (or WMA) files.

NOTE For more information on using RSS, check out Robin Good's collaboration site at www.kolabora.com.

Using Serious Magic Vlog It! for a Video Blog

Along with Ovation at the latest Consumer Electronics Show, Serious Magic also showed off its imminent new video blogging tool, Vlog It! With podcasts becoming so popular, the ability to add video is a natural evolution.

We already covered the power of Serious Magic Communicator, the main video tool that simulates a broadcasting studio. It's a great way to create video for PowerPoint or use PowerPoint slides in an online video.

Vlog It! is similar to Communicator in its interface, and it even has the same V-Screen feature that lets me appear as though I am anywhere in the world by using a virtual set.

I originally created my blog video in Communicator using the V-Screen and teleprompter and then dropped it into Vlog It! Amazingly, Vlog It! itself has these same features—the main difference from the Communicator product is that it doesn't output the same range of professional-quality higher-res video files (see Figure 7-61).

When the production is set, using the same basic concepts as Communicator in terms of dropping actions into the timeline and reading from the teleprompter, it's ready to record. Then use the Publish Wizard to post the entire video in an online blog.

The very cool feature is that as you "scrub" through the video, you can set a thumbnail image to link to the video in your blog simply by hitting CTRL+T (see Figure 7-62).

7. THE LATEST TECHNOLOGIES

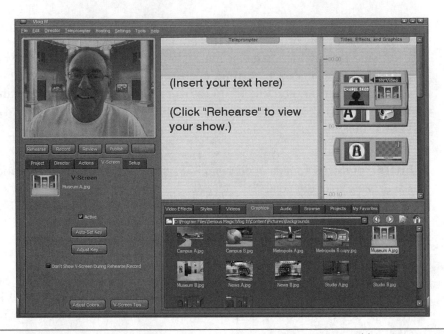

FIGURE 7-61 Vlog It! looks a lot like Serious Magic Communicator and lets you create a production using video and graphics.

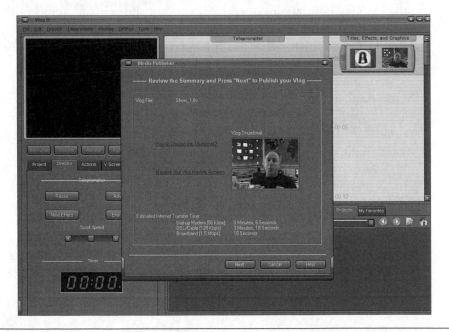

FIGURE 7-62 Select any part of your video or production as a thumbnail to link to the video in the blog.

Point to any online blog to which you have access. First you need to re-render or publish your file in FLV format (see Figure 7-63).

FIGURE 7-63 Publishing the blog locally first involves rendering the finished movie in a web-friendly (generally FLV) file format.

Then the file is going to be posted to your hosting server. The very coolest feature of Vlog It! is the ability to instantly drag and drop the thumbnail to generate the linked text to the video in your blog. (Although the blog text remains in the normal place, the video is linked to the hosting server from which it will play when the thumbnail link is clicked.) (See Figure 7-64.)

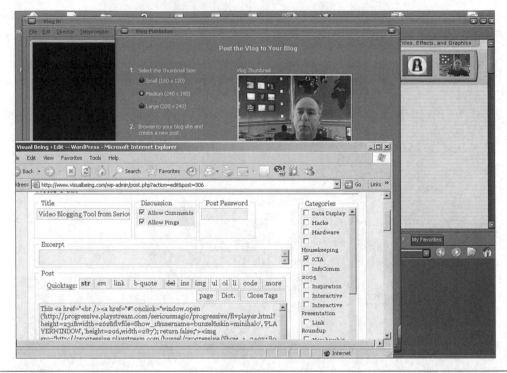

FIGURE 7-64 With a blog editor open, you can drag and drop the thumbnail directly into the interface to generate the linked text to enable the video to play within the blog from the host.

The Advanced Options of the Vlog It! Publishing panel also give you instant access to copy and paste the correct HTML into a web page or an email besides a blog (see Figure 7-65).

As a bonus of this product, the FLV file (which normally takes Flash to create and use) along with the thumbnail images from your blog are in My Documents\Vlog It!\My Output.

The advantage of a video blog is that the text in the teleprompter can potentially be searchable online, and with new video-enabled PDAs, it also takes podcasting to a new level.

As more and more portable devices play video, the subscription capabilities of text blogs will also be easier to incorporate into video downloads, making this a very cool rich media tool. In terms of PowerPoint and other presentation programs, I see the video blog as a significant value-add in terms of continuing the dialog with your audience and following up on the message in your presentation.

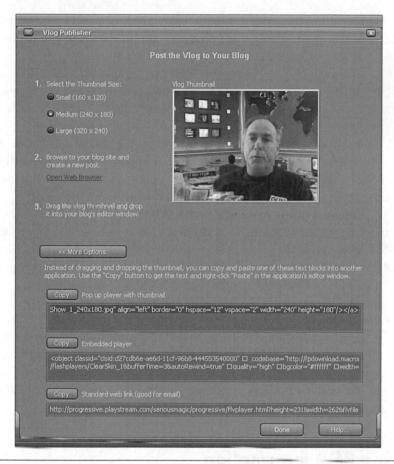

FIGURE 7-65 Advanced Options gives you more information for pasting HTML code into email or other locations to access the video blog.

Collecting Data with SMS

With the proliferation of cell phones, it is possible that they will soon replace the keypads in Audience Response Systems (ARS) and also will be used for many other meeting and presentation functions, including the collection of questions from the audience prior to or during a meeting.

The Q&A scenario is a huge improvement over the old "step to the microphone" method. A Q&A moderator can sort, select, and put the questions in order and context. Issues can be clarified before they are brought in front of the entire group and long, rambling questions edited. As questions are answered within the presentation itself, they can be dropped from the queue. Finally, with a real-time setup between the database and the projector, the questions can be shown to the entire audience as they are presented, making repetition unnecessary.

Companies like Pangolin (www.pangolinsms.com/) are now using Short Message Service (SMS) text messaging in this way to aggregate feedback and gather audience questions and user responses with telephone messages.

Another benefit is that the system stores phone numbers (which may not be a benefit if the users are later annoyed), and of course the range of the system is not limited to a convention area or even a city, but information can be distributed to and gathered from the entire world.

Pangolin offers a Windows-based control center called IMU (Interactive Messaging Unlimited). SMS text messages from cell phones come into the computer via a Multi-Tech MultiModem GPRS or MultiModem CDMA wireless modem allowing interactive viewer participation. Pangolin's IMU lets anyone with a mobile phone send messages that can be displayed over video, including large projection screens, on television, or even on web pages.

At this point, the interactive polling is generally done over a more protracted period of time, but the results are the same—graphical feedback and database collection. In addition, the ability to collect information in real-time during a live event or large trade show gives participants a greater sense of involvement.

Gathering RFID Information

In Chapter 6, we covered Audience Response Systems for retrieving opinions and other information from audience participants.

We also noted that some web conferencing applications include instant polling, and of course web forms can be used to acquire data from web users.

But what if the information that we need comes from uncooperative, mobile, or inanimate objects? How can such information be collected, processed, and presented?

RFID stands for Radio Frequency Identification. There are three parts to an RFID implementation:

- Tag (chip and antenna)
- Reader
- Database and software

Each tag holds unique data—a serial number and/or other unique attributes of the item in applications, including things like the following:

- Retail and Distribution
- Contactless Payment
- Keyless Entry
- Livestock Tagging
- Pharmaceuticals
- Logistics Assets (containers, trailers)
- Pet Identification

Because database information can be reported using PowerPoint, either by pasting the data or report into a slide or with more sophisticated tools (like the Take-Off software described in Chapter 6), the latest data acquisition tools become a significant part of the presentation process.

Lots of presentations involve inventory, catalogs, or other repositories of information that can be gleaned from emerging technology like RFID. For more information, visit these sites:

- RFID Journal—www.rfidjournal.com
- RFID Weblog—www.rfid-weblog.com

Authoring PowerPoint to DVD

In Chapter 5, we briefly discussed the differences between a DVD movie disc and a data DVD.

Let's quickly clarify the distinction between these two data formats.

A data DVD is just like a data CD, except that it holds a lot more data (4.7GB for standard-format DVDs compared to approximately 650MB for a CD).

You can use a data DVD to store any combination of computer files and formats, including PowerPoint presentations, movies, web pages, or images. As a disaster insurance backup, a data DVD would require a computer with PowerPoint (or the PowerPoint Player) to replace a corrupt or missing presentation. We will cover such disaster insurance scenarios in Chapter 8.

You can use a DVD movie disc to play a specially formatted set of video clips that are launched from an interactive DVD menu.

This is based on the emerging DVD standard for digital media, which is in the process of evolving toward high-definition formats with a competition between Blue Ray and HD-DVD, but right now, if you can author a simple DVD movie disc, you have the option of presenting without a computer, which is discussed next.

Presenting without a Computer

Imagine not having to load Windows or PowerPoint and having your presentation available in a nonlinear format where you can go to any series of slides or video whenever you want.

By having your presentation authored as a DVD movie disc, it can be played on a consumer DVD player connected to a large monitor or most projectors that take a *video input*.

The key to this process is understanding what it takes to burn an interactive movie DVD:

- An authoring program that converts video to MPEG2 format and can create the DVD menu structure
- Folder(s) of image files that you can organize into slide shows to be triggered by the DVD menu
- Folder(s) of video files that you can organize into Titles and possibly *Chapters* to be triggered by the DVD menu

DVD authoring programs can vary in price tremendously based upon the precision and complexity of the productions they can create and their ability to capture, edit, and *encode* (properly convert) video files. Higher-end programs may be able to accept higher-definition video formats, while more basic applications will be more limited in the menu structures they can create and in the video formats they can handle.

For example, in Chapter 5, we used Ulead DVD MovieFactory to *extract* DVD movies from a non-copy protected disc. The general use for this feature is to burn these files again to another disc—and it's a fairly advanced feature for a basic, budget-priced DVD authoring program.

MovieFactory's "big brother" in the Ulead product family is DVD Workshop. It has more sophisticated tools for authoring menus and editing and converting video, and at the higher-end of its product line, it even has device control for the highest level of HD-DVD video equipment (similar to Firewire/iLink but of significantly higher resolution).

Other software publishers like Adobe, Sonic Solutions, and Pinnacle have similar hierarchies of DVD authoring tools that are distinguished from ordinary video editing products.

As another example, Roxio's Easy Media Creator Suite has two programs that work with video—VideoWave for capture and video editing, and DVD Builder to create DVD discs with interactive menus.

The major difference, again, is that DVD Builder's final product is a DVD movie disc, which it burns after converting (encoding) the edited video into MPEG2 format but then converting it again to play on the special consumer technology that works on a commercial DVD player.

(Yes, these discs will also play on a PC—in Windows Media Player or a DVD Player like InterVideo's WinDVD.)

So how do we actually create such a disc? See the case study that follows.

Case Study: Turning PowerPoint into a DVD

As the presentation consultant to a medical facility, the principals come to your office with a problem and a question. They want to take a PowerPoint presentation out on the road, but they may not know if a facility has a boardroom, auditorium, or AV facilities up until the last minute and want to prepare for every eventuality. In addition, some of the presenters may not be comfortable with working a laptop and a projector.

"Can they use a DVD player?" you ask.

Sure, comes the reply—everyone has a DVD player these days.

The other idea the principals have is to produce some kind of disc to leave behind that attendees can review with a lot of the important information.

"Bingo," you say, "We can burn some copies of the DVD and put them into jewel cases."

"What about my slides?" the Director of Marketing says. "Isn't DVD just for the videos?"

"Well, we have a lot of cool video," the CEO says.

How can this project be produced and delivered?

Think about it before you begin reading the next section.

You already know that DVD has options for slide shows (or images sequences) as well as ways to break up video into titles and chapters.

Because you've read some of the other portions of this book, you know that you can export PowerPoint as a set of individual images in various formats (refer to Chapter 5).

You've also seen a bit of the DVD structure in Chapter 5, in which the product used was a simple authoring tool, Ulead MovieFactory 2.

But in this case, you figure you'd like to have a bit more professional look, so you open Ulead DVD Workshop.

Key Issues to Consider

You might want to think about the following:

- Making the PowerPoint content DVD-ready
- Assembling materials for the interface
- How the video should be presented

The interface of DVD Workshop after you open a DVD project resembles many video editors (see Figure 7-66). This is the capture step where you would acquire video from any number of sources, including a camcorder or VCR.

Fortunately for this project, the video has already been captured and used in various PowerPoint slides. As we did with Microsoft Producer (for web video, earlier), you can import the video files you intend to use into a Clip Library.

Notice the subsequent steps that you will need to perform to complete the DVD project:

1. **Edit** the video to get the segments just the way you want.
   This will include breaking up longer segments (Titles) into segments that will be navigable in a menu (Chapters).
2. Create an interface or **Menu** structure for the disc.
3. **Finish** the disc—that is, preview the links to make sure they work and then burn the final disc to a blank DVD disc.

In the Capture step, you make sure all of our video is available for our production.

In the Edit step, you drop entire video clips into the Title List—*if the disc were not further refined with menus, these titles would play consecutively like a long DVD movie disc.*

You add the video clips to the Title List in more or less the order you think they should play, and in the Preview window, you can play or scroll through our video and add new In and Out points to make sure that the segments begin and end with the precise frames you want (see Figure 7-67).

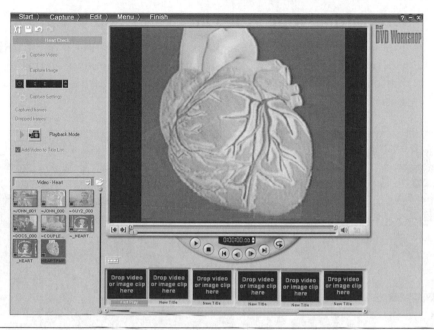

FIGURE 7-66 DVD Workshop opens in a Capture step that looks like most video editors.

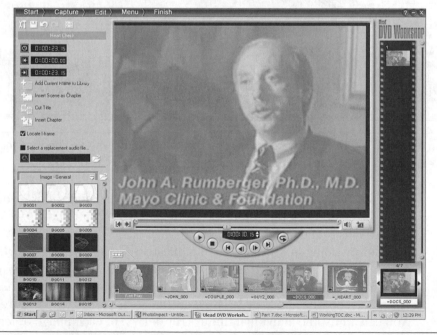

FIGURE 7-67 In DVD Workshop's Edit step, you can assemble the Title List and set new In and Out points for the video segments.

7. THE LATEST TECHNOLOGIES

Organizing Your Video into Titles and Chapters

For longer titles, you set Chapter markers, indicating a point within the video to which a user can navigate instantly from a menu. In this sequence, the chapter point indicates another speaker appearing in the video (see Figure 7-68).

FIGURE 7-68   In DVD Workshop's Edit step, you can add Chapter markers to the longer video segments to which users will be able to go instantly from a Chapter menu.

You still have to account for some of the PowerPoint slides—you open the Clip Library to the folder of exported PowerPoint slides (which you exported as sequential TIF images).

Before doing so, you used the Duplicate Slide feature of PowerPoint to break up the bullets so that a three-bullet slide became four sequential images (including the title). Now you drag and drop them into an empty Title placeholder, and they become an *Image Sequence* (see Figure 7-69). You can adjust the individual timings (or delays) of each image or leave the default of three seconds.

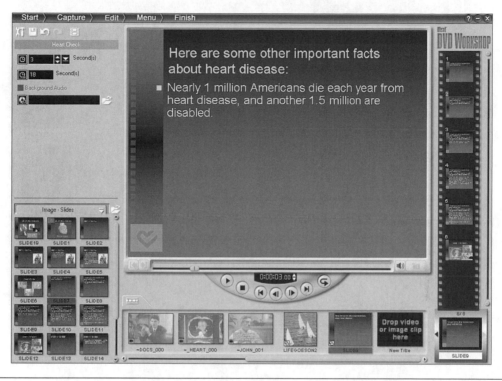

FIGURE 7-69 In DVD Workshop's Edit step, you can drag and drop images into a Title placeholder so that they become Image Sequences, or slide shows with automatic timings.

Creating Interactive Menus

Now we're ready for the interactive component of the DVD, the menu structure—we enter the Menu step. Here we find a graphics program for text, images, and objects that enable us to construct a "page" with links similar to a web page, only the links go either directly to Title videos, Chapters within a Title, or another Menu.

DVD Workshop comes with a number of Menu Templates that help you instantly organize a Title List, but we will create a custom menu using the corporate logo as a button (see Figure 7-70).

Notice that this simple opening menu has two kinds of links: thumbnail images and "bullets" comprised of a logo image and some formatted text.

The first two thumbnails link to the same Title, but by dragging and dropping the Chapter thumbnail into the second link, clicking it will go directly to the video of the second speaker in that Title.

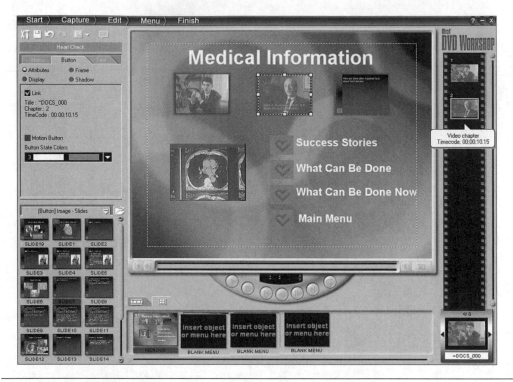

FIGURE 7-70   In DVD Workshop's Menu step, you use a sophisticated graphics program to build a page with links to various other elements, such as Titles, Chapters, or other Menus.

Creating a menu is a matter of using text, button, and graphical objects and placing them on a page in a manner similar to any graphics program. You select the objects to change their attributes or formatting and use the editing tools to align and modify the objects.

Then you drag the thumbnails of other Titles, Chapters, or Menus onto the objects to establish links.

Because we have three videos that comprise Success Stories about our product, we use a bullet ("Success Stories") to link to a secondary menu with these videos (see Figure 7-71).

Because you want to simulate PowerPoint as much as possible, for another slide sequence, we put the slides into successive Menus and use interactive buttons at the bottom of the screen to allow the user to move between the slides (see Figure 7-72). This gives the presenter or user the option to stay with a slide as long as he or she wants before moving on. You can also add other "hot" areas to various slides (as menus) that navigate to other videos or menus.

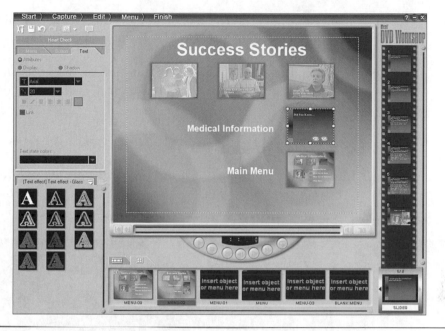

FIGURE 7-71   In DVD Workshop's Menu step, you use a secondary menu, linked to the first one, to allow the user to view any of a number of related videos or slide shows.

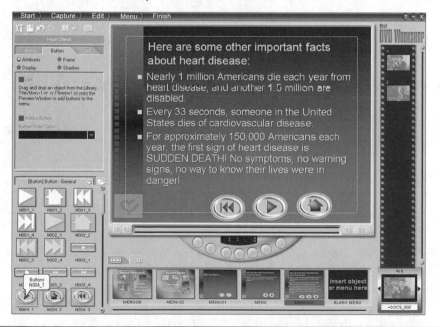

FIGURE 7-72   In DVD Workshop's Menu step, you can create other interactive menus with buttons to allow for navigation when the user wants to move to the next topic or jump elsewhere in the production.

(The ability to create more functional and visually exciting menus is what distinguishes a more sophisticated DVD authoring program from the more basic applications.)

You decide to drop another short title as a "teaser" into the First Play Title slot—it's about five seconds long, and then it leads to the opening menu.

Burning a True Movie DVD

Now it's time to click Finish and test the project (see Figure 7-73). The simulated remote control and links within the menus let you test the project completely.

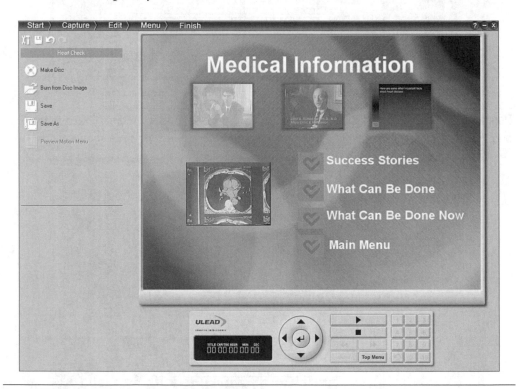

FIGURE 7-73   In DVD Workshop's Finish step, you can test the links and playback of your production.

When you are ready to burn the disc, you select a quality setting for compression of the final MPEG2 video that allows all of your content to fit on the disc (see Figure 7-74).

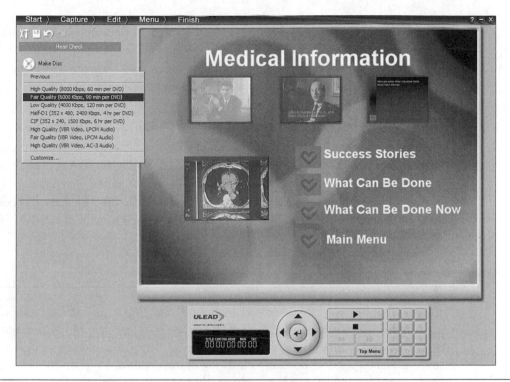

FIGURE 7-74   DVD Workshop's Finish step lets you set a quality setting for the final video.

The Burning Options under Make Disc let you save as a Disc Image (a virtual snapshot of the DVD project) that lets you burn copies in the future.

You can also save a DVD directory to maintain your working files and include a DVD player program on the disc (for those who may want to play it on a computer).

Finally, you will put a blank disc into a DVD recorder and burn the final project to a master. You give this to your colleagues as a presentation disc to take on the road, and you make copies to put into jewel cases for your clients.

The burning step can take a while because your video clips will need to be converted (encoded) to the properly compressed MPEG2 format. That's why saving a disc image for reuse of a project you may need again is a good idea.

7. THE LATEST TECHNOLOGIES

VIDEO CD AND SVCD Besides a standard DVD, authoring programs can also burn these other formats. VCD and SVCD are interactive movie formats that can be burned to and will play on ordinary CDs on a computer. In some cases they will also play on commercial DVD players (VCD more likely than SVCD).

CHECK YOUR MEDIA Blank DVD media have evolved greatly, but the best standard for playback on most commercial players is still the DVD-R format. If you want to take your disc to untested locations, this is probably the format of choice. If you travel with a DVD player or plan to use a consumer player with a remote control for presentations, thoroughly test your media and project on these devices before going in front of an audience.

Summary

In this chapter, we looked ahead to how PowerPoint and other types of presentations may take advantage of the ever-changing face of the technology universe. The first area we examined is the Internet, and we went over several strategies for posting our presentation online, either in HTML (web page) format or as a PowerPoint file to be downloaded.

We also discussed the problems and solutions for incorporating the video portions of our presentations in a web scenario. These involved using third-party programs like Camtasia Studio, Windows Media Encoder, and Producer for PowerPoint.

The web also enables conferencing, and here we went over a variety of techniques, including a shared OneNote session, a GoToMeeting web conference, Macromedia Breeze, and emerging messaging and VoIP technology.

Other technologies also have promise in terms of letting us continue the dialog with our clients. We looked at podcasting and video blogs, along with SMS and RFID for collecting and disseminating database information before, during, or after a presentation.

Finally, we discussed some of the issues involved with using our PowerPoint content on the emerging media of DVD. We took a look at Ulead DVD Workshop as an example of a high-end DVD authoring tool, and we saw how we could use PowerPoint slides and video in a DVD production that serves as a backup or substitute for a PowerPoint project.

Resources

Here are some additional resources to help you evaluate potential web conferencing solutions.

- Author's web conference about digital video using Genesys— http://videoserver.pstrat.com/mediasite/viewer/?peid=ceebb8c5- b13e-405e-9151-30cff6100850.
- Collaborative strategies—leading expert is Robin Good. www. masternewmedia.org. Purchase reports on latest products.
- Adobe/Macromedia's answer to this set of developer services is evolving under the name Macromedia Central 1.5—more information is at www.macromedia.com/software/central.
- WebCamDV—Orange Micro from OrangeWare Corp. www.orangeware. com/endusers/webcamdvfaq.html.

Web-Conferencing Programs

Here are some direct links to the conferencing solutions described in the chapter, along with others that have similar features:

- Microsoft OneNote—http://snipurl.com/fw7r
- Genesys—www.genesys.com
- GoToMeeting—www.gotomeeting.com
- Breeze—http://snipurl.com/hh8c
- Live Meeting—http://snipurl.com/cwpr
- WebEx—Video conferencing—www.webex.com
- Raindance—www.raindance.com
- Convoq—www.convoq.com
- Groove Virtual Office—http://snipurl.com/lxnt
- InstaColl—Simple setup between two systems; share documents; invite a friend; document-centric; no file conversion; save as Office file—www.instacoll.com
- Basecamp—Multiple people, multiple locations, multiple products; Web-based—everything happens online in Basecamp; Set milestones in Calendar; Personal version—"Backpack"—www.basecamphq.com
- Polyvision—www.polyvision.com
- Mind Manager—www.mindjet.com
- Glance—low cost; only screen sharing—www.glance.net

DVD Authoring

Here are some direct links to the DVD authoring solutions described in the chapter, along with others that have similar features:

- Ulead MovieFactory and DVD Workshop—www.ulead.com
- Sonic Solutions—DVDit and MyDVD Studio—www.sonic.com
- Adobe Encore DVD—www.adobe.com
- Video Capture Hardware and DVD Authoring—Pinnacle—www.pinnaclesys.com
- Video Capture Analog—Graphics Cards—ATI—www.atitech.com

Package Web Presentations

Here are some direct links to the other programs described in the chapter, along with additional applications that have similar features:

- Quindi Meeting Companion—Reasonable file sizes—QMD file format—www.quindi.com
- Apreso Classroom—www.apreso.com
- Tegrity Capture—www.tegrity.com
- Camtasia Studio 3.0 (Picture in Picture)—www.techsmith.com
- Collect, Organize, Share—Executive Summary—OnFolio—personal version $29.99—Integrate with Outlook—OnFolio panel in Internet Explorer—www.onfolio.com
- FlashPaper 2—PDF and Flash—www.macromedia.com/software/flashpaper/
- Articulate Presenter—SWF conversion—www.articulate.com
- PresentationPro—Convert PPT to SWF—www.presentationpro.com
- Impatica—www.impatica.com
- PointCast—online training—www.pointcast.com
- NXPowerLite—Compress and email presentations—www.nxpowerlite.com

CHAPTER 8

DELIVERING A KILLER PRESENTATION

In case you have a problem with the title of this chapter, keep in mind that when a stand-up comedian does particularly well, she says that she "killed." I am, in no way, advocating violence as a way of reaching your audience.

Having said that, after writing a couple of books devoted entirely to PowerPoint, I have come to the conclusion that way too much time is devoted to the *editing* portion; in fact, almost all of the preceding chapters deal with only the part of presenting that involves preparation and authoring of electronic materials.

You Are the Show

As a consultant, I have been privileged to work in the same room as several speaker coaches, which I mentioned in my section on preparation in Chapter 1, "Planning an Effective Presentation." This has made me acutely sensitive to an important fact: preparation and authoring is not enough; the success or failure of any presentation is solely dependent upon *results*—and that has to do with the event itself.

Although you might think that speakers are born, not made, I can tell you from experience that a bit of professional coaching can make a world of difference. Seeing yourself in front of a video camera can be painful, but it also leads to amazing results.

Coaches I have known often point out that the most coached athletes are also the most accomplished—that even Michael Jordan benefited from coaching at his nadir.

I suggest a video camera for any professional speaker, at a minimum for self-analysis. Using a tool like Camtasia Studio to videotape yourself giving the talk can help you immensely with your timing and confidence (refer to Chapter 6, "Powerful Presentation Tools").

Of particular interest to many speaker coaches are issues of *energy* and *positioning*.

Many professionals (physicians, educators, and accountants) depend upon visuals and use them as a crutch. Showing a cool video can only go so far—you still need to deliver valuable information in a way that interests your audience.

It's amazing what just a little bit of physical activity can do to stimulate your endorphins and provide some energy. I'm not talking about caffeine. I mean running up and down the hall, doing some jumping jacks, clapping your hands, and looking into the mirror in the bathroom and saying "You dah man!"

It may put a smile on your face, a bounce in your step, and make the all-important difference in your entrance and continued rapport.

Positioning works off energy. Speaker coaches watch their clients to see if they lean on the podium, slump against a chair, or otherwise drift away from the audience like a wallflower at a high school dance.

Successful coaches get their clients to free themselves of the podium entirely and make sure that they have an area in which to move freely up to and into the audience (à la Phil Donahue).

This subtly convinces the crowd that you are not afraid and are eager to engage them in dialogue. It makes you open to questions and also pumps you up with energy. Successful speakers don't ignore any part of the audience and make sure that everyone gets the benefit of eye contact.

Remember that you are the show, and your message is the focal point of the event. Letting an AV staff put a screen in the center of the stage or back wall is a no-no.

It will make you very limited in your ability to move around, lest you obscure the screen, and it will make your slide show take center stage—where you and your message rightly belong.

Experienced presenters put the screen off to the side, with the projector angled in its direction, and they put their laptops in a place where they can look at the laptop screen with a simple glance, without having to be tethered to a podium.

Checklist for Video Practice Sessions

One of the best articles I have ever read on using video was Speaker's Notes: "There's more than one way to use video" by Tim Zaun in *Presentations Magazine*, December 2003. It can be found online at http://snipurl.com/m0p5.

Tim suggests that you view and critique yourself presenting at least four times (ouch!):

- Regular video
- Muted (posture and positioning)
- Audio only (stuttering, uhs and ohs, too many buzzwords or clichés)
- In fast forward (static or erratic movement)

Preparing the Room

Perhaps as important as your own speaking skills, in terms of preparation, is setting up the room or venue itself and the equipment that will be needed to ensure the success of the presentation. If the speaker doesn't take enough time for a thorough setup and run-through, glitches may well delay the talk or make it impossible to play the role of a congenial host.

If you're testing microphones and laying down duct tape and wires while your audience is waiting to be dazzled, chances are you've already lost them.

Of course, there are many types of rooms you can work and different schedules that may prevent you from achieving the complete and thorough setup that you may need or want.

That's exactly why you need to anticipate and prepare for any eventuality.

First of all, take the time to think about what kind of room you'll be presenting in. Who is providing the audiovisual equipment?

If you are lucky, you have a professional team to rely upon to take care of these logistical details. In some cases, you may need to handle some or all of these matters yourself. We will go into what this may entail in more detail in the case study at the end of the chapter.

Which Computer?

Before you present, you must think about whether you will be connecting to a projector from your laptop or whether you need to load your presentation onto someone else's computer. If you're loading your presentation to another computer, are you prepared to move any linked files that may be impacted by such a move?

(Remember, all video files and many sound files in PowerPoint are linked and not part of the actual presentation file. Presentations and other hyperlinked documents must also be moved if you expect to use them.)

As you prepare for your presentation, you must also think about who is setting up the equipment and whether they know your preferences.

If you are in total control of the computer that will be presenting, it will prevent many potential glitches and give you a lot more time to prepare. If you are moving material to a conference computer, you will need to give some thought to the strategy you want to use in terms of how long you may have to accomplish this task, which file(s) you will need, and whether the hardware and software on the host machine will support all the media and features you intend to use.

For example, let's say you will be moving your presentation to a new computer, and the presentation is relatively simple and small, so you figure you can simply use a flash memory stick. Unfortunately the destination computer is still running Windows 98, which requires a driver for the flash memory stick(!). If you have anticipated this by asking the right question (Which operating system resides on the presentation computer?), you can provide such a driver on a CD or move the presentation on a CD instead.

Another issue would be bringing the data on a DVD only to discover that the destination computer has only a CD-ROM drive. These configurations are rare on high-end presentation equipment, but it could happen; Murphy's Law has a way of showing up when you are getting ready to present.

Using the "B" Key to (Re)connect with Your Audience

One of the most successful and high-impact techniques for focusing attention on the speaker and getting attention was demonstrated several years ago by my colleague Jim Endicott.

Like most speakers, as the room filled up, he had a PowerPoint slide show up on the screen, and I believe he even went into a few slides as he began.

Then he stepped to the keyboard at his presentation laptop and hit the "b" key—the image on the screen went dark. At the same time, he cued the lights to go up so that he was fully illuminated.

It woke the audience up to an important fact—he had important information, and he wasn't relying solely on the technology to connect with the audience.

He took that opportunity to get feedback about the audience's expectations, following up on the important aspects of preparation we covered in Chapter 1.

Then, with the audience convinced that he was committed to delivering value, he hit the "b" key again and used the visuals to supplement his message.

This connection to the audience is probably the best time to introduce the *value proposition* to the audience—to suggest what they will gain by paying close attention to you (and eventually to the slide show). Here are some examples:

- **Value Proposition—Sales**—Address the customer's needs; identify the pain—remember Jim Endicott's concepts in Chapter 1; differentiate your product or service
- **Value Proposition—Law**—Make the client's case; present the facts dramatically and effectively to support the closing argument
- **Value Proposition—Education**—Create a sense of wonder and inspire curiosity; get the audience to retain the information in a meaningful way
- **Value Proposition—Training**—Have attendees grasp and retain complex material; qualify and prepare them to proceed with competence and confidence
- **Value Proposition—Religion**—Inspire a sense of awe and commitment to something greater than oneself; move the audience to treat each other better and live a better life

The key to delivering on the value proposition may be in your *discovery activity*—like the legal profession, the better prepared you are through research and interviews, the more you will be able to connect with the audience with the projector *off*.

Dealing with AV Technology

When I coach or consult with presenters, one of the most commonly asked questions, and the source of the greatest anxiety, is the prospect of setting up prior to a presentation and making sure a projector, sound system, microphone, and other peripherals are working properly.

I think that's because even experienced computer users, who may very well master the software they use every day, still tend to fear hardware and rely on vendors or IT staff to "make the boxes work."

The good news is that projector technology has evolved to the point that three out of four times, at least just turning on the projector, connecting the laptop, and booting Windows results in a synchronized signal of your computer screen on the projector screen.

But just as we found with video, there are a few technical issues that you absolutely need to understand in gaining the confidence of setting up your presentation hardware, particularly in new and unfamiliar surroundings.

Why is this important? Because optimally, your projector should be the same screen resolution by default as your laptop for easy setup. (It can be of higher resolution but should not be lower if at all possible). So if you determine that you are running at a screen size of 1024×768 (XGA) and you are using a projector that is SVGA (800×600), it may not synch up with the laptop right away.

What should you do?

Go through the setup steps that follow anyway, but be prepared to make some adjustments.

You should know the screen resolution of your presentation laptop. There are two basic modes currently in wide use:

- **SVGA**—A screen size of 800×600
- **XGA**—A screen size of 1024×768

How do you determine the screen resolution at which you are currently set? Right-click on your Desktop and choose Properties. The Display Properties window opens (see Figure 8-1). Click the Settings tab (which is probably open by default).

FIGURE 8-1   When you right-click your Desktop and choose Properties, you can view the screen resolution or dimensions at which Windows is running.

Setting Up a Projector and Laptop

When you get to the venue, the last thing you need is stress, and yet getting a laptop to work with a projector you're not used to can be very taxing, particularly the first time.

See Figure 8-2 for the main connectors commonly found on most projectors.

The Sharp projector shown here has the following inputs:

1. VGA (monitor/projector) connector
2. S-VHS video input (from DVD player or VCR/camcorder) (Optional)
3. Composite yellow video input (from DVD player or VCR/camcorder) (Optional)
4. Audio input—Connect to headphone/speaker jack on laptop to route PC audio into projector speakers (see the section "Mastering Sound and Microphones") (Optional)
5. USB connector—Makes the Sharp remote control a portable mouse and requires software on the laptop (Optional)

8. DELIVERING A KILLER PRESENTATION

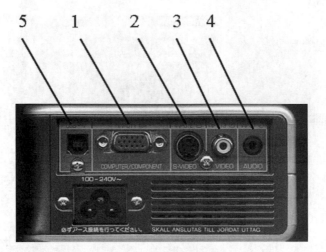

FIGURE 8-2   Most projectors have a main VGA (monitor/projector) plug along with inputs for composite and S-VHS video and mono or stereo audio (to its speakers).

Here are the main steps involved in connecting a projector to your computer:

1. Connect the VGA output from the laptop to the VGA input of the projector. The AV staff or the projector manufacturer (if you're on your own) should have such a cable available.
2. Turn on the projector. Sometimes you need to hit another button to leave "standby" and rev up the bulb. Use the controls on the projector or on the projector remote control (if available) (see Figure 8-3).
3. Turn on your laptop *(after connecting and turning on the projector—do these steps in order)*. If you're lucky you'll get a simultaneous display right away.
4. Whether you do or not, let Windows load on the laptop.
5. Look for the external display toggle FN key on your laptop. Typically, this is the F5 or F7 key, and it has three display settings:
   - Laptop only display
   - Projector (external only) display
   - Simultaneous display
6. Hit the FN toggle key once and see if the projector takes the image.
7. Hit the FN toggle key again, and you should get the simultaneous display you want.

FIGURE 8-3   Most projectors have a main button at the top and on the remote control that goes from Standby to Power On.

PROJECT SETUP RESOURCE For an excellent site with tips on setting up projectors, check out Epson Presenters Online (http://www.presentersonline.com) and their diagrams about projector setup and related issues.

If these steps do not result in a successful setup (and they generally will), do the following:

1. Make sure that the projector is looking for input from the laptop and not any other video input. On the Sharp remote (refer to Figure 8-3), there are three inputs—one for S-VHS, another for composite video, and the third for the laptop. The Sharp, like most projectors, finds the active inputs automatically, but if more than one is active, you need to select the laptop input.
2. If you still have a problem, make sure that the laptop is not running at a higher resolution than the projector. Determine if the projector is S-VGA, XGA, or higher in "native" (default) resolution. Try to set your laptop to the same resolution (screen size) using the previous steps (refer to Figure 8-1).
3. Finally, if you have a newer laptop and older projector, you've probably taken it down to 800×600 (SVGA) resolution—if that still doesn't work, you will need to lower the *refresh rate*—or the intensity of the signal coming from the laptop's graphics card.

4. Return to the Display Properties window shown in Figure 8-1. In the Settings tab, click Advanced. In the window that opens (see Figure 8-4), click the Monitor tab. Now lower the Refresh Rate from the drop-down list to 60Hz. This will hopefully allow the projector and the graphics card to communicate.

These steps will almost certainly enable you to set up a projector with your laptop running Windows and display your PowerPoint slide show onscreen. The default display setting here is for the projector to show the same image that is on your laptop's screen.

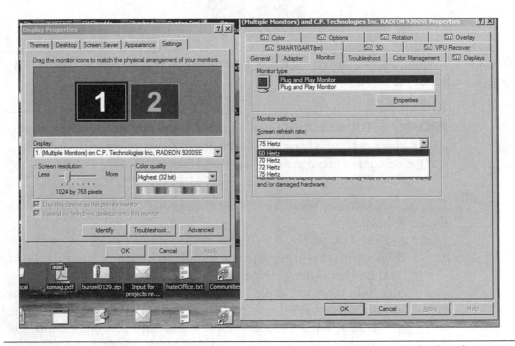

FIGURE 8-4 If necessary, enter the Advanced tab of Display Properties and select the Monitor tab to lower the Refresh Rate, probably to 60Hz.

GRAPHICS CARDS AND PROGRAMS There are several main manufacturers of graphics display cards, but the most common are ATI (shown in these steps; see Figure 8-8), nVidia, and Intel (laptops only). Depending upon your graphics card, the tab structure of the Display Properties window on your PC or laptop may differ from what is shown here, but you will have a screen size (resolution) slider in the main (Settings) tab and a refresh rate adjustment capability under the Advanced (Monitor) settings.

Using a Dual-Monitor Setup

As just noted, the standard laptop-projector setup has the projector showing a "cloned" image of the laptop—that is, the same monitor image is displayed on both screens.

In some cases (my Sony, for example), a laptop has the ability to change the settings in the Display Properties window and enable a second monitor or dual display (see Figure 8-5). The secondary monitor will appear (2), and you can click to activate it and then select Extend my Windows Desktop onto this monitor.

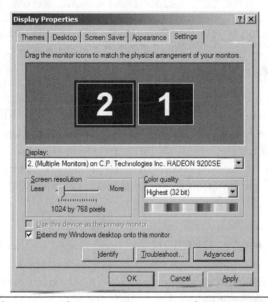

FIGURE 8-5   If available, a secondary monitor can provide an extension of your Desktop.

Now you can move your mouse or drag folders and files onto this new, fresh area of the Desktop and use it for the windows of open programs (see Figure 8-6). The secondary monitor will have a blank Desktop into which you can drag icons and files.

Now with the Extended Desktop set up, you're ready for the next section.

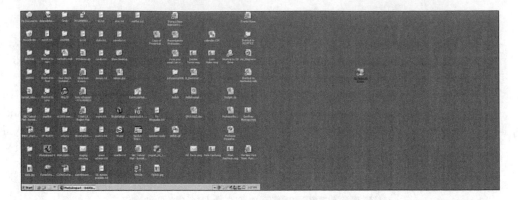

FIGURE 8-6 The extension of your Desktop provides extra blank space for files and folders.

Presenter View

If you have Extended Desktop available and invoke it, you can use Power-Point's Presenter view. What this does is send the full-screen presentation *only to the Extended Desktop (secondary monitor/projector)* while it loads the Presenter view console on your laptop monitor (see Figure 8-7). The Presenter view lets you control many aspects of your presentation and view notes and see hints on the next object to appear with an Entrance Animation effect.

SERIOUS MAGIC OVATION As we mentioned in Chapter 6, Serious Magic's new Ovation program takes advantage of the Extended Desktop dual-monitor setup to provide another set of presenter options as its player enhances the look of your PowerPoint slides.

IMATTE PROJECTOR UTILITY One technology you may also want to investigate is the iMatte projection system (www.imatte.com), which allows the presenter to "enter the projected image" and use his or her own body to manipulate portions of the slides or run a video. This serves to counteract the disconnect between speaker and slide show and combines the presenter and the electronic presentation into one entity.

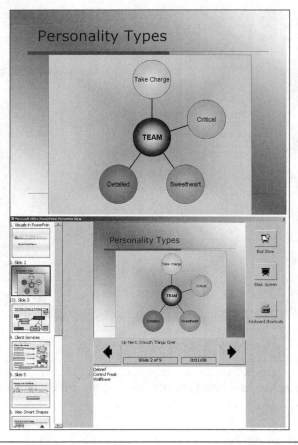

FIGURE 8-7 The Extended Desktop enables Presenter view, which lets you have a console with notes and hints on your laptop screen while projecting the presentation full-screen only to the secondary display (upper image–projector).

To enable Presenter view in PowerPoint (with the Extended Desktop already set up), click Slide Show > Set Up Show and then check the Show Presenter View option (see Figure 8-8). Use the drop-down menu to make sure that the secondary display gets the full-screen slide show.

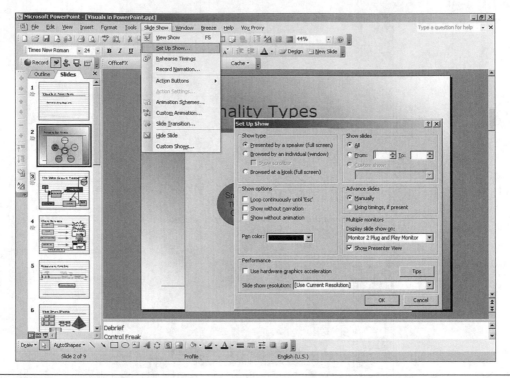

FIGURE 8-8 Set the option for Show Presenter View in the Set Up Show dialog box and make sure the show is sent to the secondary monitor.

Portable Mice

In a small venue, you may be perfectly comfortable using your laptop's onboard pointing device as you present and advancing the slides with the right arrow key and going back with the left arrow key (see the section "Running Your Slide Show").

But if you are in a larger setting, and particularly if you want to use professional speaker techniques like moving around your set and going out into the audience, you will need a remote wireless mouse (see Figure 8-9). Most units like this come with a small USB plug (transmitter) and the mouse itself (RF radio frequency receiver). There are generally the right and left mouse buttons and a laser pointer on simple devices; more complex portable mice may have scroll wheels and programmable buttons.

FIGURE 8-9   A remote mouse lets you advance the slide show from around your venue with a wireless connection.

HIGHER-END REMOTES More complex remote controllers are also available to run PowerPoint and to handle other programmable tasks. Check out the Gyro series from InfoGrip at http://snipurl.com/m0s8.

Mastering Sound and Microphones

Most presentations can handle a simple microphone setup if the room requires it. Generally, an AV tech will set up an amplifier and portable remote microphone like the unit in Figure 8-10.

You clip the microphone to your lapel and turn it on and off manually. (Make sure you turn it off when you take that last trip to the toilet.)

Other considerations arise if you are going to play audio and video as part of your presentation, as we covered in Chapter 5, "Using Video and Audio Effectively."

A small set of amplified speakers attached to your laptop may be sufficient in smaller venues.

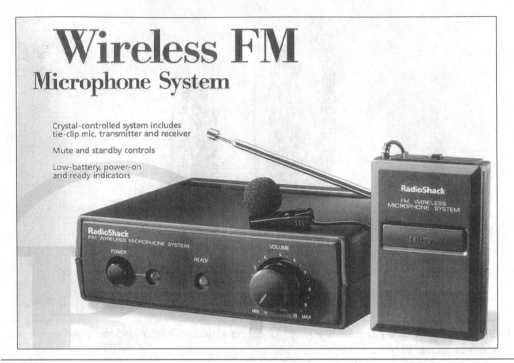

FIGURE 8-10   A simple remote amplified microphone will work adequately for most presentations.

In more sophisticated and grander settings, you will want a sound mixer, run by a professional or at least someone who knows your presentation needs, that can alternate between your voice (through the loudspeakers) and the video or audio content you are presenting. (See the section, "Case Study: Coordinating Presentations at a Large Conference.")

Running Your Slide Show

The actual PowerPoint show is a completely different animal from the safe world of the PowerPoint editor, where we confidently create slides and add effects.

When it's *showtime*, PowerPoint behaves very differently—it's actually a completely new and strange mode of the same program. And yet most presenters spend virtually no time practicing in Show mode.

Not only that, a vast majority of presenters actually open the Power-Point editor to begin their presentations, and a few of them actually present from the editor, advancing slides with views of the Notes panel, Outline, or Slide previews and even the Task Panes.

If you're not sure whether you're guilty of this faux pas or not clear about what I'm suggesting, go into PowerPoint and open a presentation. Press the F5 key. The screen is transformed, and your first slide, probably the Title slide, will appear *full screen*. This should be the image going out to the projector (see Figure 8-11).

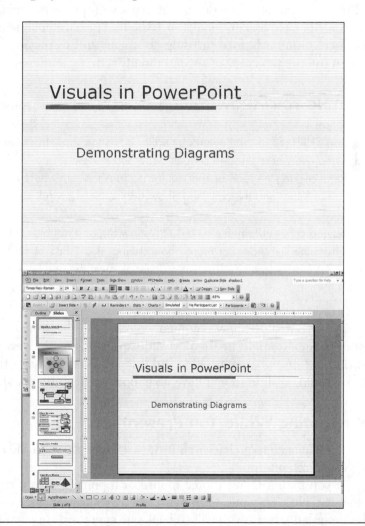

FIGURE 8-11   When you press F5 in the PowerPoint editor (bottom), the slide show appears full screen (top).

Figure 8-11 shows a dual-monitor setup; if you have a single monitor (or are practicing at your laptop without a second monitor or projector hooked up), the slide show replaces the editor full screen. Then you can toggle between the editor and the presentation by using the ALT+TAB key combination, which we discuss in the section, "Toggling with Other Programs as You Present."

If you're not confident beginning any other way than in the "real" PowerPoint (the editor), then do so, but blank your projector using the "b" key (as described earlier) and make sure the first or correct slide is showing on the local monitor before pressing "b" again and displaying the slide full screen (on the projector or second monitor) to the audience.

STARTING YOUR SHOW Pressing F5 in the PowerPoint editor starts the show from Slide 1.

Pressing SHIFT+F5 in the PowerPoint editor starts the show from the current slide in Normal view or a selected slide in Slide Sorter view.

Right-clicking the icon or shortcut for a slideshow anywhere on your Desktop or in a file folder and then clicking Show begins the show full screen from the first slide.

Saving a PowerPoint file as a *.PPS show file and double-clicking opens the show from the first slide. For more about saving as a *.PPS Show file, refer to Figure 7-11 in Chapter 7, "The Latest Technologies: Beyond PowerPoint to the Future."

With your slide show commenced, click on the screen, and the next event occurs. It might be the next slide appearing *or the next bullet or animation within the current slide*. Additional clicks advance the show—by event, build, or slide (if you have no animation in your slides).

Navigating While You Present

What if you need to go back a slide or two while you're in the middle of giving your presentation?

If you have a conventional mouse or a pointer with a *right-click key*, use it and click Previous. Otherwise, subtly return to your laptop and press the up or left arrow—you will go back one event at a time within an animation sequence or to the previous slide if there is no animation.

You can either right-click anywhere or click the Popup Toolbar in the full-screen slide show (see Figure 8-12).

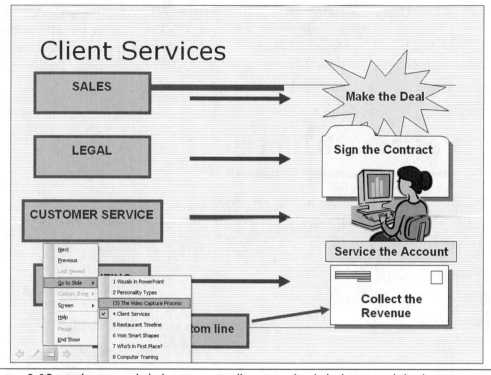

FIGURE 8-12 When you click the Popup Toolbar or right-click during a slide show, you get a contextual navigation menu.

One of your options is Go to Slide—and if you've been smart enough to put titles in your slides, you can locate any slide you want immediately and go there.

(To return to where you left off, repeat the process and select Last Viewed.)

Notice that the highlighted slide in Figure 8-12 is in parentheses. This is a *hidden slide*, which was omitted from the current slide show but is now going to be displayed, probably in response to a question from the audience. (For more about hidden slides, refer to Figure 1-14 in Chapter 1).

TURNING OFF THE POPUP TOOLBAR If you don't want the Popup Toolbar and are able to navigate with right-clicks, you can turn it off by choosing Tools > Options and unchecking the option to Show Popup Toolbar (during the slide show).

8. DELIVERING A KILLER PRESENTATION

Using the Popup Toolbar or the right-click technique provides other important options during the live show. Clicking Screen lets you select a Black or White Screen, Switch Programs, or access Speaker Notes. (I knew there was something I wanted to mention with this slide—see Figure 8-13.)

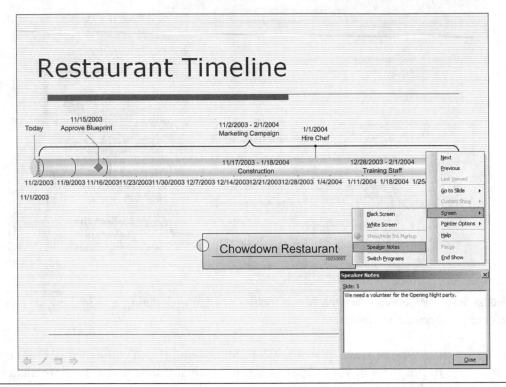

FIGURE 8-13   When you click the Popup Toolbar or right-click during a slide show, you can also switch programs, blank the screen, or access speaker notes.

At a recent training presentation that I gave for attorneys, I was amazed at the lengths some lawyers went to in order to highlight testimony during a presentation. Some of them would copy and paste portions of Word documents into PhotoShop and then try to use the Toolbox to call attention to the important phrases for the jury. The group was amazed when I used the Popup Toolbar or the right-click technique to access the Pointer Options. Besides changing a pen color for your annotations, there is also a very useful function for a *highlighter* (see Figure 8-14). This gives you the extra versatility of deciding exactly what to emphasize as you present.

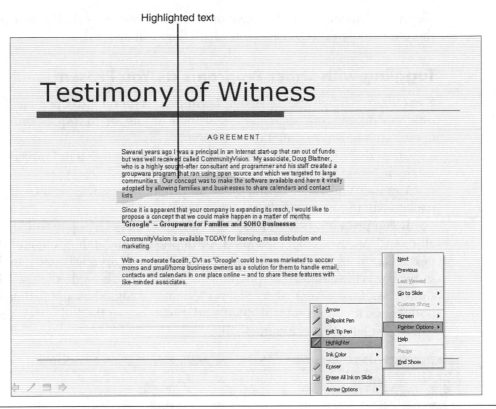

FIGURE 8-14 When you click the Popup Toolbar or right-click during a slide show, you can also use the Pointer Options to invoke a highlighter to point out important text or other information.

SAVING ANNOTATIONS If you use the Pointer Options and a pen tool or highlighter (or a tablet PC), when you close the presentation from show mode, you are given the choice to Save Your Annotations in the currently running presentation file. Doing so will preserve your real-time annotations but also changes the original slides, so save a backup file if you intend to do this during your show.

If you need to go to a specific slide frequently, you should note its slide number—then you can enter it on the keyboard at any time to display it onscreen. (We covered this technique as well as Custom Shows in Chapter 1.)

Remember that you also have the option to access other slide shows or programs using Action Settings and Hyperlinks (refer to Chapter 4,

"Secrets of Animation and Navigation"), but it is very important to practice these techniques on the laptop on which they will be used.

Toggling with Other Programs as You Present

Sometimes you will use an Action Setting or Hyperlink to open another program during your slide show, and then in answer to a question, you open a web browser or another document.

Or perhaps you have navigated to another presentation in PowerPoint using an Action Setting in order to show a particular slide.

You may find yourself with different programs open. How do you get back to where you were?

If you press but don't release Alt+Tab, you will get a popup window of all open Windows programs. Keep Alt depressed and Tab again, and the next icon among the open programs is highlighted. Directly below it in the status bar is the name of the program and open file. The slide show will be shown as: PowerPoint Slide Show—"Name of Slideshow.ppt." Release both keys with the icon highlighted, and it will reopen the full screen slide where you left off (see Figure 8-15).

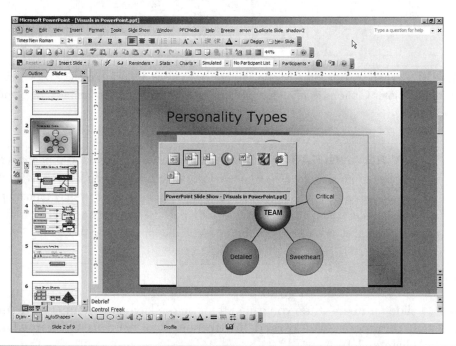

FIGURE 8-15   When you press ALT+TAB, you can toggle among several programs including the PowerPoint editor and then return to the slide show (full-screen) presentation.

If you are self-conscious about this technique, use a blank screen key *on the projector remote* to hide the process from the audience. Planning and practice can make you comfortable enough to set up a story or break at the point where you need to close some open programs and return to the flow of your presentation.

Action Items

Things come up during a presentation that may require immediate response or documentation. The ALT+TAB procedure enables you to keep other programs (Word, OneNote, Notepad, Outlook, etc.) available during a presentation in order to address these concerns.

PowerPoint 2002/XP had an Agenda and Meeting Minder feature that allowed for this within PowerPoint, but it wasn't used enough to keep it in the program for 2003.

You can handle this issue in a couple of ways. You can keep an Action Setting available in your slide show (refer to Chapter 1) that launches your favorite program (Word) or a Word document (Follow-up.doc) into which you enter the information that will require immediate response.

Or, you could simply launch the application that you know you will need to have available prior to the beginning the slide show and toggle to and from either program using the ALT+TAB keys during the presentation.

If you have a tablet PC, you can use your pen program to send annotations directly to OneNote and Outlook. On an ordinary laptop, you will need to go to your keyboard and type in the material you want to follow up on.

Preparing Effective Handouts and Notes

PowerPoint has a very specific understanding of and definition for handouts and notes.

When you select File > Print, you get an idea of that right away. First, under the Print What drop-down menu, you are asked to differentiate between Notes and Handouts (see Figure 8-16).

As Figure 8-16 also shows, the handouts have many different configuration options, including one (three per page) with blank lines for attendees to make comments during the presentation.

Printing notes really has only one option—the slide at the top and Notes panel with your inserted notations at the bottom.

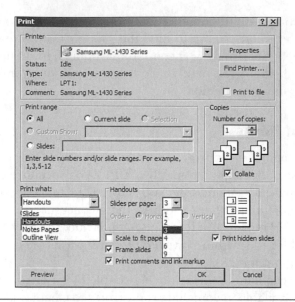

FIGURE 8-16 The Print What options in the Print dialog box ask you to choose between Slide, Notes, Handouts, and Outline.

But the big issue here is *how will you be using the printouts in the first place?*

Are the notes really your *handouts*? In other words, are the items you put into the Notes panel intended for your own preparation (which is what PowerPoint expects; for PowerPoint, Handouts are really just your slides), or is the information in the Notes panel intended to supplement your talk and be part of what you "hand out" to your audience?

Obviously this implies an important strategic decision because if you want to do both—use the Notes panel for your own preparation *and* put in items that you want for your audience—unless you are okay with the audience seeing your preparatory material, *you will need to differentiate between the two sets of information.*

This may involve maintaining two conformed sets of slides—one with preparatory Notes pages and the other with supplementary information Notes pages.

Or you can use this as an opportunity to get familiar with another program for your preparatory material (like OneNote; see Chapter 6).

But you should not leave this decision to the last minute, if for no other reason than it takes time to prepare properly printed materials, whether for your own use in rehearsal or in front of the audience or, more importantly, to represent you after you have left the stage.

Let's consider the alternatives discussed next.

Using Cliff's Notes

In Chapter 1, we mentioned Cliff Atkinson's excellent strategic book, *Beyond Bullet Points*. Cliff is a big proponent of using your Notes pages as supplementary material and even printing them as PDF files to make them into a booklet that contains the nuts and bolts of your presentation.

This frees the speaker up to use PowerPoint creatively and avoid the snags and pitfalls of putting too much information on the screen. If you take advantage of many of the scenarios we used in Chapter 3, "Creating Dynamic Visuals," you may have many slides that are used for specific effects and to communicate emotions. They won't have the information contained within them that would make them effective as Handouts without some notes to remind attendees of what was intended.

In some scenarios, the attendees will be held accountable for specific information within the presentation. This needs to be included in the handouts, but if you are using PowerPoint creatively, it may not all be present within the slides.

You should be aware that both handouts and notes pages have Master views that serve as blueprints, similar to the way we described Slide Master views in Chapter 2, "Implementing Professional Design Principles."

The Handout Master doesn't have all that much power. Clicking View > Master > Handout Master lets you determine which elements (slide no, date, etc.) from the Header and Footer are included in Handouts composed of various slide configurations.

On the other hand, the Notes Master view has some intriguing possibilities (see Figure 8-17).

Within the Notes panel you can change the font and its size to make it more legible if you are using Notes for your own preparation or to make the look of the page more appealing if you're using it for reference for your audience.

In addition, you have some flexibility in terms of resizing the relative placeholders for the slide and the Notes, and you can dress it up a bit with a corporate logo or other image.

Don't forget that placing the image on the Master will put it on every Notes page, but inserting images into the Notes panel for a specific slide will make it a reference to only that particular segment of the presentation.

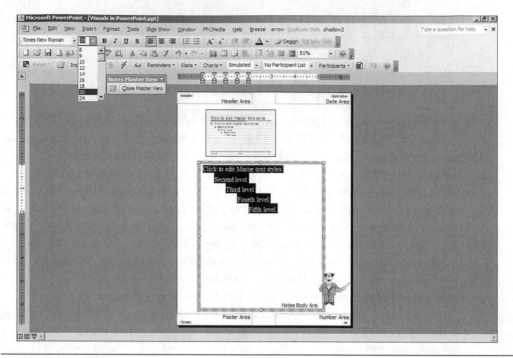

FIGURE 8-17   The Notes Master lets you reformat the contents of the Notes panel prior to printing.

Send to Word

Some further refinements in your supplementary material are available by using the File > Send to > Microsoft Office Word option in PowerPoint.

This brings up an option panel that provides six more page configurations mixing Notes and Handouts, including one additional two Notes panels per page option (see Figure 8-18).

After the configuration is chosen, the current version of the PowerPoint file is converted into an MS Word document that has all of the editing capability of any word processing file. This increases the print flexibility and allows you to further enhance its look with border, headers, footers, additional pages, and cover pages.

There is also the Paste link feature, which will continue to update the Word version as you make changes within PowerPoint.

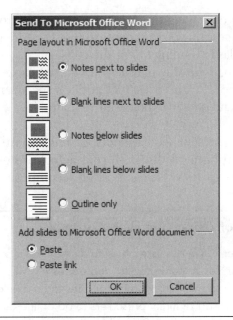

FIGURE 8-18   Using the Send to Microsoft Word option gives you more flexibility in terms of document handout material.

ONLINE PRINTING OPTIONS Time permitting—and always remember to leave enough project time for printing—you can take advantage of online printers that can deliver product anywhere. PowerPoint LIVE sponsor mimeo.com can provide very professional laminated copies of your handouts. VistaPrint (www.vistaprint.com) is another web printer that specializes in discounts with preset templates.

Notes, Tips, and Tricks

My colleagues in the presentation community, Julie Marie Irvin and Mary Waldera, made me aware of other ingenious solutions for using Notes. They use the Notes for their own preparation and place a premium on having them visible and available for clients during the presentation itself. Their suggestions include the following:

- When you are typing your Notes, double-space the information...it will be easier to read, similar to a teleprompter.
- When you are printing out your Notes, print them duplex, top-bottom. This way, when you turn your pages, you can see what is coming up next.

■ Insist on having the Notes bound at the top, not the sides…They will question you, but confirm that they are going to have to trim off the plastic binding or cut the coils.

The logic on this is that you will not have to turn the pages from right to left. This preserves podium space, and your eye contact with your audience will be easier to maintain.

Besides the usual paper handouts, a much more dramatic and effective option is distributing a disc with your actual presentation. In the next section we'll discuss how this can best be accomplished.

The Perils of Using Live Web Content

In Chapter 7, we discussed how to distribute our presentation online, either as PowerPoint files or converted to web pages (HTML).

Now, with so much information and research available online, there will be a desire on the part of many presenters to go online during a presentation and use external hyperlinks from PowerPoint or a live web browser during their presentations.

This is supported by the presence in many venues of wireless Internet access, along with the ability of many AV staffs to also make network cabling available for live web access.

Should you take advantage of this technology and make live web access part of your presentation?

I strongly suggest that you think twice about doing so. A non-loading or unresponsive web page can block the flow of your talk and shake your confidence. You're likely to stumble and apologize to the audience, and in most cases it's unnecessary.

Live web content should probably be used *only* if the most up-to-the-minute real-time data feed or information is vital to the impact of your message.

Otherwise, you are much better served by saving the web pages that you anticipate using during your presentation directly to a local hard drive on the presentation laptop and linking to them from within PowerPoint to their local folders. Make sure when you save these web pages in Internet Explorer or any web browser that you remember the destination folder and that all supporting images and linked files are also saved into supporting folders that will work locally.

Obviously, this is another aspect of your presentation that you should test thoroughly.

Moving a Presentation

Is your authoring computer your presentation machine? Maybe—maybe not. Do you need to share a presentation with other panelists? Have you brought a backup of your presentation on CD or DVD just in case? Do you want to distribute your presentation to others on CD or DVD? All these scenarios require that you move your presentation files—and this requires some thought and planning.

Moving your presentation can be as simple as transferring it to a flash drive and then loading it on a presentation computer that's shared with other speakers.

But as we've stressed throughout various chapters, when you use complex scenarios with Action Settings or linked files, including audio or video, they need to be moved together with the original presentation(s). And the links must be maintained with relative folders.

PowerPoint has long had a utility under the File menu called Pack to Disc; in 2003, it became Package for CD. Click File > Package for CD, and a set of options becomes available (see Figure 8-19).

Figure 8-19 shows a scenario where we have elected to create another folder directly on our root (C:) drive and name it Presentation. (That way no files will potentially be confused by being located in a folder under a different user name on another PC.)

Then we can still use the Add Files button to add additional presentation or supporting files (other programs or linked documents) just to be sure that they're included.

Options let us password-protect the production.

These files are then copied to the new folder, from which they can be burned to CD or DVD or transferred to a flash drive (space permitting).

Moving the PowerPoint package to a local folder first gives you a backup location from which to *test the package* before burning it. It also gives you a folder that you can burn repeatedly for backup or distribution, like the *disc image* of a DVD or CD compilation.

KEEP THE FILES IN THE SAME FOLDER As we have suggested throughout this book, keeping the PowerPoint files and their linked elements (especially video) in the same folder even prior to packaging them will further help protect playback integrity.

---

8. DELIVERING A KILLER PRESENTATION

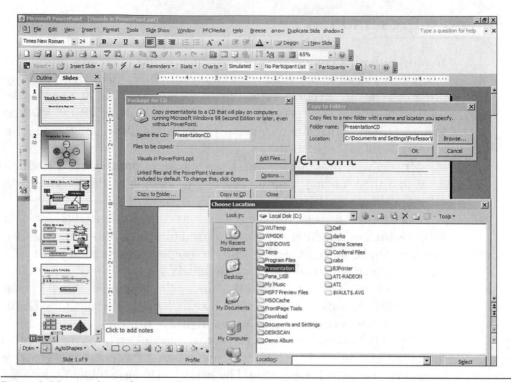

FIGURE 8-19 Package for CD allows you to copy the current presentation along with all of its linked files directly to a CD or DVD or to another folder.

This package, when burned to CD or DVD, gives you another way to distribute the presentation; it even includes a PowerPoint Viewer for users running Windows who don't have PowerPoint. It is also useful as a backup in the event of disaster (see the following) and a good way to move your files to another presentation machine.

Remember that if you use a DVD for this purpose, it is *completely different* from the movie DVD we created of our presentation in the previous chapter. This is a *data DVD*, which can only be opened on a Windows machine—but it is a completely faithful and perfect copy of the presentation you originally authored.

That being said, testing this package on the burned CD or DVD is highly advised before distributing it or relying on it as a backup.

Disaster Insurance

Stuff happens. Laptops get lost or stolen. Power fails. You know it's true.

If your machine freezes, do you have a story or anecdote to tell while you reboot that defuses the situation and makes it seamless? And while we're at it, disable all of your screensavers and virus protection programs—please.

Also, learn to present directly from the PowerPoint show—don't open the program and preview your slides. Unless you intend to edit your presentation as you speak (and that's a neat trick), right-click on your presentation file icon or shortcut and select Show from the drop-down menu. That will launch the first slide and not PowerPoint.

Thinking about and preparing for these issues will give you even more confidence when you take the stage, and even before that, it will give you the time you need to play the gracious host—greeting your attendees and making sure that they're ready to receive the very important message you've come to deliver with PowerPoint.

Backup

Throughout the previous chapters, we've identified key folders and files that need to be protected to make your presentation run correctly and to restore your important files in the event that your system fails.

Make sure that your key files, video and audio assets, images, templates, email, Office documents, and Internet shortcuts are protected, along with your PowerPoint files.

SAVING YOUR SETTINGS In Microsoft Office Tools under your Start Menu, there is a Save Your Settings Wizard that you can also use to safeguard many of the options you have set in your Office programs. In addition, try to protect the key document templates (Normal.dot for Word, Blank.dot for PowerPoint) along with templates you have created yourself that may contain key settings and macros.

At a minimum, you should have a flash drive, CD, or DVD with the packaged presentation that can be moved to a secondary machine in case yours malfunctions or disappears. (Don't keep this disc in your laptop or anywhere near it.)

In Chapter 7, we described procedures to create a movie DVD version of your presentation; this can be a great disaster-saver because all you need to run it is a consumer DVD player and a monitor or projector. You don't need your laptop.

Presenters at major events don't take any chances. They generally have a second laptop with a clone version of the final presentation(s) set up and ready to go in case of any glitch. A professional technician is working the control desk, and if anything happens, the audience may not even notice the switch from one PC to another.

Whatever the scale of your event, you should plan for the unthinkable. A set of overhead transparencies of your slides that you can use "just in case" can bail you out in a pinch.

Optimizing Performance and Preventing Freezes

If a program stalls or stops performing, pressing CTRL+ALT+DEL will open the Windows Task Manager in Windows XP (see Figure 8-20).

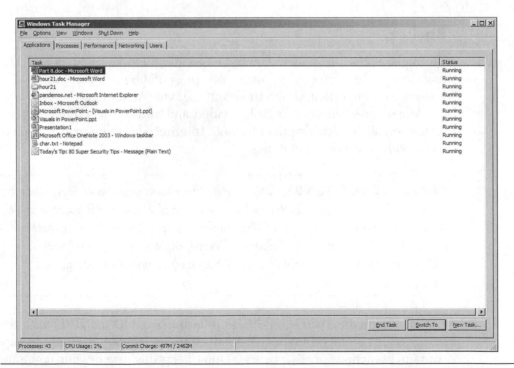

FIGURE 8-20 The Windows Task Manager can help you in a pinch to shut down unresponsive programs and regain system resources.

Click End Task for any programs that are Not Responding or to simply regain system resources. In a PowerPoint freeze, closing down PowerPoint and restarting the program can get you up and running. Remember the slide number of where you left off, type it in when the full-screen presentation is resumed, and hopefully you are back in business.

Before you present, do some housecleaning. Take a look at the System Tray, the area of preloaded programs on the lower right of your Windows XP Desktop.

If you don't recognize some of the icons and realize you don't need them, right-click them and try to turn off the automatic loading of these programs.

The more extraneous programs (or as Windows calls them, "services") that are running in the background of your presentation, the greater the chance for a screen freeze or disaster.

You can go even further by choosing Start > Run and typing in "MSCONFIG" (see Figure 8-21).

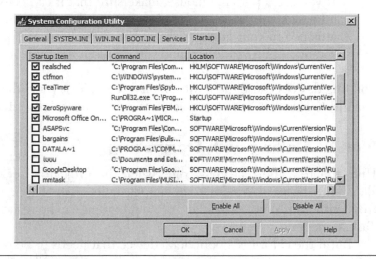

FIGURE 8-21 The Windows System Configuration Utility allows you to turn off extraneous startup programs and services.

Click the Startup tab. This shows you all the junk, er, programs that Windows loads on Startup.

Unchecking items that you don't recognize or that seem extraneous will disable them on the next reboot. Pay particular attention to the folder locations. Generally items in the Windows folders should be handled with care; items loading elsewhere can be disabled and the system tested without them.

If you really want to clean out the system resources, click the Services tab. Check the box to Hide all Windows Services. Now you can evaluate which other programs think they're so important that they need to run all the time.

The programs you want to keep are hardware *drivers* or enabling programs for your sound card, mouse, or other peripherals. Virus protection and anti-spyware needs to be evaluated on a case-by-case basis. Intrusive programs (Norton) may cause problems, and you may be able to disable them temporarily when you present and then resume them later on—when you go back online.

Notorious problem-causers include the following:

- Windows screensavers and "fun" special mouse icons or click effects—disable them.
- Power-saving utilities—sleep mode—turn it off.
- Extra mouse drivers—make sure only one mouse is active at a time. If you use a portable mouse, make sure that it can coexist with any others on your system, or make sure you don't have another mouse attached to your laptop. (The onboard trackpad or pointing device should not be a problem, and you should not disable it.)

Pointing devices cause the most screen freezes. Test yours thoroughly and don't just click-click-click too quickly. Windows doesn't like that.

Plan B: Stalling with Storytelling

Unfortunately, the time may come when the projector freezes during a slide show because Windows has simply stalled. This happens much less frequently with Windows XP, and often programs can be restarted with the Task Manager.

But if the culprit is a peripheral device that needs to be removed (like a remote mouse that is malfunctioning) or if a power failure has disrupted the presentation, you may need to *reboot*.

Depending upon the overall length of your presentation, this can be a minor inconvenience or a major disruption. But sometimes it is simply unavoidable.

There may also come a time at a major venue when AV professionals will come to your aid and help you restore the equipment.

In any case, the last thing you want to do is to stand there sheepishly and silently while your system comes back up and smile uncomfortable at the audience.

You should use this as an opportunity to show how well prepared and poised you are.

At a minimum, you should go out into the audience and ask for questions and get into an interactive dialog with participants about some of the key points you've been covering.

Or, you should come armed with a set of anecdotes or stories that illustrate your main points and spend the downtime telling them.

The result of such preparation is that you turn the disaster into a bonus. The audience appreciates your preparedness and ability to improvise, and everyone has empathy for someone who experiences misfortune but particularly one who rises to the occasion.

Avoiding PowerPoint: Using Facilitation Skills

The main point of this book has been providing skills for the use of electronic media, mainly PowerPoint and related programs, to enhance communications.

But it has been a theme of the preceding chapters that everything needs to have a purpose and that sometimes technology can get in the way.

There is an entire industry of presentation professionals who can work entirely without PowerPoint and do their communication by eliciting interaction from an audience.

Facilitators generally engage the audience in some kind of activity or learning exercise.

In fact, learning theory has shown that audiences come away with a greater sense of understanding material when they participate in the presentation process—and even more if they actually experience or teach the material to others.

Farmers Logic: Debriefing

Even if you are not a "trainer" or educator, the skills manifest in this presentation discipline have ramifications in all areas, including sales and marketing.

The reason is simple: unless the audience "gets it," your presentation was not a success.

A great example of this was a session I witnessed at a major pharmaceutical meeting. Several facilitators divided an audience composed of accomplished (and somewhat self-important) medical professionals into tables of small teams.

Each team member was given the pieces (in the way of partial clues) of a greater overall puzzle that had to do with a group of farmers. Each fictional farmer had a set of parameters—one farmer had a certain vehicle, raised certain animals, and lived in a certain part of the area.

Each team had to reassemble the clues from all of its members in order to solve the puzzle of which farmer drives the truck and which farmer grows the apples.

It was really amazing to watch each team's dynamics as a leader emerged and the participants tried to make sense of the clues and argued among themselves as to the best way to go about the solution.

The fly in the ointment was the unknown fact that each team had one member who had been specifically instructed as part of the rules *not to participate* unless he or she was specifically asked for information.

At the end of the game, the participants were invariably energized and enthusiastic—the winning team was jumping out of their chairs (they won a T-shirt).

But that wasn't the point.

The real payoff for the group was the debriefing of the event in which the teams analyzed their performance and figured out what went wrong and right.

The lesson learned was invariably that not just one learning or teaching style works—that audiences and participants behave and process information in different ways—and that to reach everyone, you need to appreciate the diversity of viewpoints. In fact you even need to reach out to those who are hanging back and not eager participants.

Anyone who has witnessed such a facilitation exercise will never show a boring, passive PowerPoint presentation again.

To learn more facilitation exercises, check out *Games Trainers Play* (McGraw-Hill Training Series) by Edward E. Scannell and John W. Newstrom in the training and management section of any business bookstore.

Flip Charts

The winners of the Farmers Logic exercise just described were invariably teams that not only elicited the information from their reluctant members but that also used visual aids strategically placed in the venue.

Organizers had put flip charts within easy reach of the teams.

As fast as computers are, there are few programs (see the section, "Using Visio for Real-Time Interactivity") that can keep up with the human brain. If you truly want to interact with an audience and accumulate feedback, learning to use a flip chart and recording the responses of the audience to important questions can be invaluable.

Again, this is not a training or educational tool. Let's say you are a sales or marketing pro. You may already ask the audience about their problems and "identify the pain," as described in Chapter 1. But writing their issues down in a tangible form convinces the audience that you truly care. And putting it out in bold strokes on an easel with thick markers has a convincing effect.

MORE STORYTELLING My colleague Terrence Gargiulo has made a career out of using stories as the vehicle for business communication (often avoiding PowerPoint in the process). He offers many specific suggestions for communications specialists on how to draw upon their own experiences and insights to communicate with narrative. His books include *Making Stories* and *The Strategic Use of Stories in Organizational Communication and Learning*. Find out more at www.makingstories.net.

Using Visio for Real-Time Interactivity

We've mentioned Visio at various junctures of this book as a great tool for keeping track of information and even presenting it as an alternative to PowerPoint.

Although very few computer programs can keep up with real-time audience interaction (maybe a table PC with the pen program can simulate a flip chart), there is one Visio template that can be of potential value in various situations that require drawing information from an audience in real time.

The Visio 2003 Brainstorming diagram template is a great way to quickly map out the ideas that you elicit from a group as they watch the diagram take shape (see Figure 8-22).

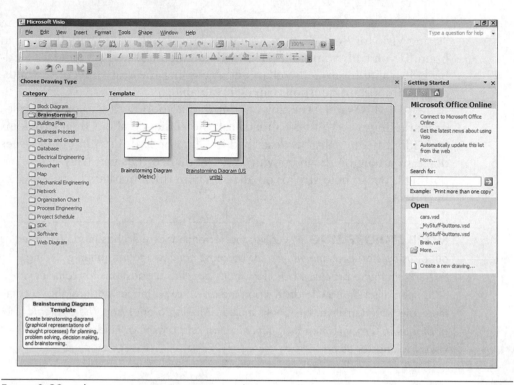

FIGURE 8-22 The Visio Brainstorming template can allow a presenter to map out the relationship of ideas visually quickly as they are developed.

The great attribute of this template is the Brainstorming menu at the top of the new diagram, which lets the user instantly add sub or peer topics to build a diagram with quick key strokes (see Figure 8-23).

Like the flip chart or the tablet PC, seeing their ideas taken seriously enough to become part of a serious diagram has the effect of energizing participants and fostering collaboration.

This information can be imported from or exported to an Excel spreadsheet or an Access database or copied into a PowerPoint slide.

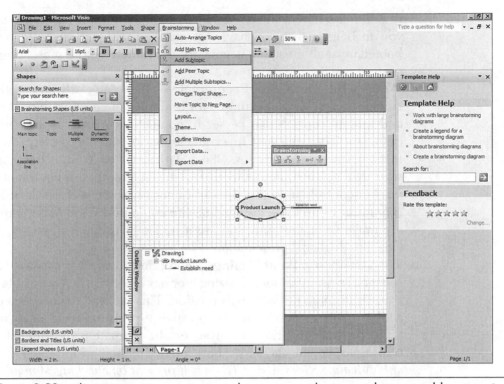

FIGURE 8-23 The Visio Brainstorming template comes with a menu that can add new topics in a map and name them with a few mouse clicks.

Gotchas to Avoid

In my experience, I have been stymied on several occasions just like you. Here are some common issues that can come up under pressure. If you know what causes them and how to get back on track, it can save you lots of stress.

- **Practice with the Remote**—Whether you use the projector remote control or a remote control mouse, make sure you understand the controls. Many have a button called "Freeze" that allows you to keep a frame on the projector screen indefinitely (or capture a video frame). If you press this button inadvertently and don't realize what you've done, you may not be able to continue and might think that either the laptop or projector has malfunctioned. Some remotes also have a "black" or "blank" screen button that may lead you to believe that you have not synched with the projector or booted up at all! Read the manual for the remote before presenting, or don't use it.

■ **Watch Out for Radio Frequencies**—In hotels with numerous conferences or large meetings with multiple venues, portable mice and remote controls can be set to conflicting or overlapping frequencies. This can lead to erratic behavior on the presentation machines or system freezes. Check with hotel or AV staff to make sure that if other presentations will be in progress, their remote mice or controls are set to other frequencies. Some wireless devices require software to be installed on the computer. Wireless remotes are available at Best Buy and are a minor investment to ensure a clean, professional presentation.

■ **Turn Off PowerPoint Timings**—Sometimes a speaker has saved a rehearsal session without realizing it or has otherwise activated automatic transitions or Custom Animation. This can lead to unexpected activity by PowerPoint when the speaker expects to be in control of his or her presentation. To avoid erratic animation or automatic transitions, go into the Slide Show > Set Up Show window and *disable Advance Slides, Using Timings if present by checking Manual.*

Presentation Checklist

You may not need all of the items listed here, and some may be part of the AV setup or someone else's responsibility, but it pays to consider these possible needs before you arrive on the scene and make sure you've taken them into account.

■ 1 LCD projector capable of accommodating your particular laptop computer (1024×768 resolution)
■ 1 6'-10' VGA-type cable to connect computer to projector
■ 1 12' Front projection screen at front of room
■ 1 Lectern on risers off to one side of the screen
■ 1 Lavaliere microphone w/ cables for *House* public addressing (PA) system
■ 1 Laser Pointer
■ 1 *Power strip* in the lectern extension cord

Before your arrival, make sure you have at least the following items available:

- Extension cord and surge protector (don't rely on batteries)
- Laptop power adapter (don't present on batteries)
- Packaged presentation on CD or DVD (Kept separate from laptop bag)
- Wireless mouse or remote (bring extra batteries)
- Extra audio and video plugs and cables (see Figure 8-24)
- Any adapters necessary for external monitor or CD/DVD devices
- All handouts and supplementary materials for your talk
- Recovery CDs and software for your laptop
- Laptop manual
- Projector bulbs

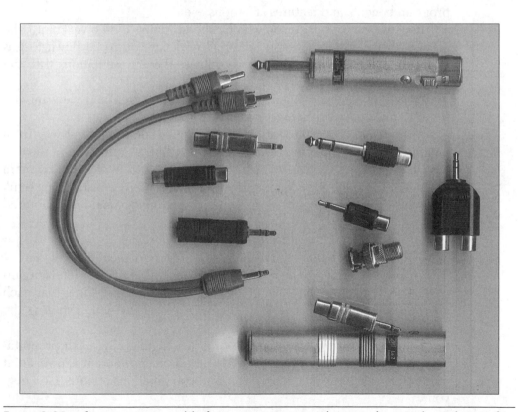

FIGURE 8-24 If you are responsible for managing a sound system, having the right set of audio adapters, plugs, and cables can save you a lot of grief.

8. DELIVERING A KILLER PRESENTATION

Here are some other suggested items that can help you avoid embarrassment:

- External USB hard drive or Zip drive with the presentation
- Overheads with the presentation to be used in a pinch
- Phone numbers of *local* laptop rental facilities that can provide a replacement

Case Study: Coordinating Presentations at a Large Conference

Your company has decided to be among the presenters at a large computer trade show where it wants to demonstrate its new software and present program benefits and features at various events.

Because you're the person who has been "doing the PowerPoint," the powers that be think it would be a real perk for you to be flown to Las Vegas for the event to help them coordinate their presentations with the local hotel and convention AV staffs.

"We think you're doing a great job," they tell you, "and we want you there to make sure everything goes off without a hitch."

Although you explain that authoring PowerPoint is a long way from handling major audiovisual hardware, they remind you that you're the one who has made them rehearse their presentations in front of a video camera and encouraged them to do more than show bullets. As a result, they think of you as the technical guru of presentation technology and have anointed you responsible for the results at the trade show.

Great, you think to yourself. What do I do next?

Think about it before you begin reading the next section.

You decide you're going to make this work by being completely organized. The one thing you have going for you is that you know that each speaker will either be using PowerPoint or physically demonstrating the software your company publishes.

You go through the conference program highlighting each presentation and dividing the list into those that are pure promotion (PowerPoint only), pure demo (using the product), and combinations of both (God help you).

Key Issues to Consider

You might want to think about the following:

- Have you created a suitable event template for consistency among presenters?
- How big are the venues where the presentations take place?
- Who is responsible for projection and sound?
- What other presentation requirements will there be? (DVD, VCR, flip charts, etc.)
- Can we get separate computers for the demos and the PowerPoint presentations?
- Can you establish a file naming convention to manage multiple presentations (Show_Name_Presenter_Name)?
- Can we use screenshots in PowerPoint in case the demos don't work? Should we have backup PowerPoint shows with screenshots just in case?
- Can one person (namely you) be physically present at all of the events?
- Who are the AV or catering professionals setting up the venue(s)?
- Can or should you outsource any responsibilities to others?
- When do handouts have to be ready, who is printing them, and how will they be delivered?
- Where can you get some aspirin or something a lot stronger?

Before You Leave

Prior to leaving for Las Vegas, you will want to create backups of every presentation and know whether each speaker will be presenting from his or her computer or will need to move his or her presentations to a master laptop either as part of a panel discussion or because conference staff requires it.

(If the conference staff insists that presentations be made available prior to each event, that means that they have a professional staff on site and will probably coordinate the event along with sound and projection. This can be either good or bad, depending upon how they perform.)

If presentations need to be provided, you need to determine when and in what format. You should tell your speakers to anticipate going over their materials on site in a *speaker ready room* for any final changes and to communicate with a control room to have their slides advanced.

If the conference is simply providing meeting rooms (at a hotel), you will need to check with hotel catering as to how and when these rooms are set up. You will also need to contract for local rental or service for AV—projectors and sound systems for the room(s).

You will need to let these folks know your expectations and parameters, including the quality of projection and accessories for sound (speakers, amplifiers, mixers, and/or switchers), along with remote controls and possibly extra laptops.

Unless you are a masochist, you will want to at least arrange for printing and delivery of all handouts prior to departure. Trying to find a Kinko's while you are coordinating presentations on site is not something you want to do.

It is also a good idea to check with the travel department as to when they have you arriving and how close to the venue(s) you will be staying. If there are multiple venues, you will want a map and information about transportation, distances, and parking, and you should try to arrange accommodations as close to the site(s) as possible. Arriving a day or two early might not please the accountants, but it will make your task a lot easier.

At the Venue

Major conferences can provide a forum for your speakers either in break-out panels or individual sessions, or they may be speaking as part of a larger *General Session.*

As an expert in Microsoft PowerPoint, you are expected to also be somewhat proficient in the effective use of presentation software tools, animation techniques, and audiovisual technology. Before a General Session, you will meet with the event organizers, speakers, and presenters, assemble presentation files, review and assess their slide decks with their various media files, make any necessary edits or updates, and confirm the desired show flow or agenda.

You will coordinate with the events staff and technical AV team in determining and confirming the speaker order, video/DVD/media file placement, Q&A/panel discussion staging, and quickly determine any unforeseen special requirements as well as potential event delivery trouble areas. You should put the event planners and presenters at ease by handling the technology and creative affairs, assessing the presenters' needs while addressing their concerns. Stress and anxiety levels are greatly reduced by the review process and your presence.

Either informally or at a predetermined speaker ready room, you will scrutinize all presenter slide decks for accuracy, spelling, and consistency. In many cases at larger venues, slide decks are then combined into one MASTER Show File, which is located on a secure, show-ready computer for uninterrupted viewing. In this case, your presenters will need to be prepared to give up final editing sometime before they normally would and also get used to giving up *direct* remote control of slide advancement—which will be handled by the conference AV staff. (They will signal the staff with another *cueing* device to advance their slides.)

You can assure your presenters that any changes to individual slides are not made without their (or your) consent. Their individual presentation template design on slide decks will be maintained unless a show template is supplied. If a show template is not supplied, you may be able to provide one if requested.

A pre-event presentation review allows presenters and clients to view the entire slide deck prior to a General Session and to meet with other presenters. A formal rehearsal may also be held after the General Session room setup is complete.

In most cases, a pre-event presentation review is held onsite the day or evening before the General Session. Or possibly the review can be held several days or weeks before the show at a pre-selected location.

A separate speaker ready meeting room may be reserved at the show hotel for the presentation review process. Presenters can gather at their convenience and comfort in a room away from the General Session room, allowing the conference technical AV team to set up the General Session room without interruption. You will need to coordinate your presenters' work in the speaker ready area in conjunction with the AV team and ensure that their slide decks are ready for the General Session and conform to the desired show flow or agenda.

Before the General Session, you can assist your presenters with their stage position, microphone placement, and remote control operation.

A backup laptop containing the final slide deck should be available and "show ready" in case of technical difficulty or last-minute changes requiring additional support.

To facilitate transfer of the materials, you should have multiple scenarios available—CDs and DVDs, portable USB hard drives, and flash drives. Just in case any speakers will be using older (Windows 98) laptops, you should be prepared with *driver software* for file transfer utilities and printers.

A speaker ready room will have a printer set up to output their last-minute notes or slide changes, but if their laptops don't connect easily to the printer(s), it could become stressful.

In the speaker ready room, you should be available to

- Revise PowerPoint slides on a tight deadline
- Create memorable slides with animation, diagrams, and graphs
- Tweak all timing and transitions to work flawlessly
- Check hyperlinks and video to make sure they function
- Check spelling, grammar, font size, and colors to maximize projection clarity
- Rehearse with a remote mouse and microphone and back up materials onto a secondary laptop

Last-Minute Details

You will probably want to make a project checklist, perhaps in an Excel spreadsheet with due dates or in OneNote of all the small details you will need to double- and triple-check.

Got sound? What kind? Who is setting up the lavaliere microphone? Is it properly connected to the house speakers? Who is switching the audio between your microphone and the laptop sound output if you play a video or want special effects during your slide show? Do they have a list of slides and a cue list?

Who is providing the remote mouse? Remember that wireless presentation mice use radio frequencies that can be interfered with by other peripherals, including the mouse next door. Have you tested yours recently?

Next, when was the last time you synched your video signal with the projector? Have you checked you MPG movies to see how they will project? (Sometimes MPG files behave weirdly with certain projectors—they don't like simultaneous displays and will only play either on the laptop or the screen.)

As previously described, most modern projectors are XGA—accepting a high enough refresh rate to accommodate a newer laptop. But if you have a cutting edge machine, and the venue provides an older projector, you should be familiar with your graphics adapter settings so that you can synch down to a lower screen resolution and refresh rate, if necessary.

Finally, locate a health club with a pool and Jacuzzi in your hotel or nearby. You will need it.

Summary

Delivering an effective presentation is a skill that is generally covered in business books and not mentioned much, if at all, in books about Power-Point. Still, the full-screen slide show portion of PowerPoint is probably as important to master, if not more so, than the editor because it will determine how the audience finally receives and responds to your message.

In this chapter we spent some time on preparation: laying out the room, dealing with AV issues, and connecting a projector to the laptop. Anticipating problems is the best way to avoid them, so we discussed the possible reasons why a projector might not accept a laptop signal (video and screen resolution issues) and dealt with some of the main glitches that can occur with presentation equipment.

In terms of disaster avoidance, we discussed the basics of moving a presentation for backup and ways in which to work around possible issues, such as having a set of transparencies, a DVD version of the presentation, or a good story to tell if you need to reboot.

PowerPoint has specific features to empower the presenter. We covered the highlighter tool for emphasizing portions of slides, as well as techniques for navigating around a slide show and the very helpful "b" key for blanking the screen.

Because handouts and notes are a big part of preparation and delivery, we went over the different ways to create effective handouts and how the Notes Master can help you reformat your notes pages effectively.

Finally, we went through the process of planning and running speaker ready services for a major professional conference with multiple presenters, along with checklists and agendas for dealing with all possible eventualities and issues.

Resources

For the past several years, I've been part of an amazing networking group of presentation professionals—the Presentations Council of InfoComm International (http://snipurl.com/m665). I've worked closely with three awesome chairmen, Bob Befus, Ray Guyot, and Todd Dunn, and I would recommend this organization to anyone wishing to broaden their educational and professional horizons in this field.

8. DELIVERING A KILLER PRESENTATION

My colleague Rick Altman produces one of the most intimate yet powerful programs for presentation professionals each year, PowerPoint LIVE (www.powerpointlive.com). Through my participation, I've been privileged to meet some of the most accomplished people in the industry and learn from them, including the corporations mentioned in the following sections.

Printing and Delivery

The most ubiquitous company for getting handouts ready on a tight deadline would have to be FedexKinko's (http://www.fedex.com/us/officeprint/main/?link=4.com).

Portable Mouse/Remote Controls

Some of the most popular and innovative presentation peripheral companies include the following:

- InfoGrip—www.infogrip.com
- iMatte—Projector utility to allow presenter into the image—www.imatte.com

PDF Writer

The PDF format is very popular and useful for handouts; here are the main programs that enable you to output in this file type:

- Adobe Acrobat—www.adobe.com
- Macromedia FlashPaper—www.macromedia.com
- Jaws PDFCreator—www.jawspdf.com

INDEX

THIS BOOK IS SAFARI ENABLED

INCLUDES FREE 45-DAY ACCESS TO THE ONLINE EDITION

The Safari® Enabled icon on the cover of your favorite technology book means the book is available through Safari Bookshelf. When you buy this book, you get free access to the online edition for 45 days.

Safari Bookshelf is an electronic reference library that lets you easily search thousands of technical books, find code samples, download chapters, and access technical information whenever and wherever you need it.

TO GAIN 45-DAY SAFARI ENABLED ACCESS TO THIS BOOK:

- Go to **http://www.quepublishing.com/safarienabled**
- Complete the brief registration form
- Enter the coupon code found in the front of this book on the "Copyright" page

If you have difficulty registering on Safari Bookshelf or accessing the online edition, please e-mail customer-service@safaribooksonline.com.

What's on the CD-ROM

The book companion CD-ROM contains numerous PowerPoint presentations and other examples from the book, two sample chapters from Cliff Atkinson's *Beyond Bullet Points: Using Microsoft PowerPoint to Create Presentations That Inform, Motivate, and Inspire*, and trial software from Instant Effects (OfficeFX), Serious Magic (Ovation and Vlog It!), and TechSmith (Camtasia and Snag It).

Installation Instructions

1. Insert the disc into your CD-ROM drive.
2. From the desktop, double-click on the My Computer icon.
3. Double-click on the icon representing your CD-ROM drive.
4. Double-click on the icon titled `start.exe` to run the installation program.
5. Follow the onscreen prompts to finish the installation.

NOTE If you have the AutoPlay feature enabled, the `start.exe` program starts automatically whenever you insert the disc into your CD-ROM drive.